Professional Housekeeping

Hutchinson Catering and Hotel Management Books

Series Editor: *John Fuller*

Professional Housekeeping

Doris Hatfield and Christine Winter

Hutchinson

London Melbourne Sydney Auckland Johannesburg

Hutchinson Education
An imprint of Century Hutchinson Limited
62–65 Chandos Place, Covent Garden, London WC2N 4NW

Century Hutchinson Group (Australia) Pty Ltd
16–22 Church Street, Hawthorn, Melbourne, Victoria 3122

Century Hutchinson Group (NZ) Ltd
32–34 View Road, PO Box 40–086, Glenfield, Auckland 10

Century Hutchinson Group (SA) (Pty) Ltd
PO Box 337, Bergvlei 2012, South Africa

First published 1986

Set in 10 on 12pt VIP Times by
D P Media Limited, Hitchin, Hertfordshire

Printed and bound in Great Britain by
Anchor Brendon Ltd, Tiptree, Essex

British Library Cataloguing in Publication Data

Hatfield, Doris
  Professional Housekeeping
  1. Building management
  I. Title   II. Winter, Christine
  647'.94   TX955

ISBN 0 09 159421 9

Contents

ORDER OF LIVERIES.

LIVERIES are given 1st April and 1st October of each year. Evening Liveries every Twelve Months. Tweed Jackets every Twelve Months (except the Hall Porter and Steward's Room Boy, they have a Tweed Suit). Hats, Gloves, and Stockings every Six Months, except on special occasions, such as Drawing Rooms, Weddings, etc. Orders for Gloves and Stockings for them will be issued from time to time as required. Macintoshes are given according to wear.

When Evening Liveries have been worn Six Months from date of entry into service, the wearer is entitled to a New Suit on the 1st of April prox. If within Six Months the wearer is not entitled to a New Suit until the following April. When Morning Liveries have been worn Three Months from date of entry, the wearer is entitled to a New Suit either in April or October, according to date of entry, but if not worn Three Months the wearer is not entitled to a Suit until the next term, or issue of Liveries.

Overcoats have to be worn Twelve Months before the wearer is entitled to another on the aforesaid date, 1st of April.

The same rule applies to giving up Liveries on leaving service. Within the above periods they are Lord Salisbury's property, over those periods they are the wearer's property.

Stable Liveries are given and retained on the same system.

Hatfield House,
    January, 1900.

AN EXTRACT FROM THE HOUSEHOLD REGULATIONS FOR HATFIELD HOUSE, 1900

From 'Life in the English Country House' Mark Girouard. Yale University Press, 1978.

Preface

This book has been written to meet the needs of those studying for degrees, BTEC diplomas and certificates, Open Tech and other professional examinations for the hospitality industry. It could also be used as a reference book for the use of managers, housekeepers, supervisors, and others involved in housekeeping.

For the purpose of the book the term housekeeper has been used, but in different establishments the job title may be different. Housekeeping in many establishments will be done by people with diverse titles such as 'manager', 'school matron', 'housemother', 'superintendent' or 'bursar'.

Part One of the book deals with the basic practical aspects of housekeeping. Building fabric and services have been briefly dealt with since they relate to the housekeeping function. Part Two covers management techniques, ideas, organization and control.

Our aim has been to include all the many and varied aspects of housekeeping and put them between one cover.

Although specialized topics have been researched, much of the material has been developed from our own working experience in the field. When writing a book of this nature it is pointless to try to 're-invent the wheel'; it is acknowledged that some of the contents have been researched before and are indeed available in other publications.

Some subjects have been treated in a general way, because the hospitality industry is so wide and varied, that there cannot be one set rule, only flexible guidelines.

The basic role of the housekeeper is to create and maintain a harmonious environment in which people can work, eat and sleep. It is a role frequently underrated and less has been written about it than other aspects of the hospitality industry.

Industrial disputes, break-downs in services and economic problems often force people to fall back on their resources and to return to some of the basic old materials and methods. Therefore, we have included some of the old as well as the new.

New methods and technology has to be accepted, but the old should not be discarded like antique furniture, old methods and materials have their uses and may even prove valuable!

Acknowledgements

The authors wish to thank the following manufacturers and organizations who have contributed information to make this book possible:

Belstead Brook Hotel & Restaurant, Ipswich
Desmond Band, MSAAT
Peter Bateman, Director, Rentokil
Simon Boosey, oriental carpet expert, Hitchin
County Fire Officer, Ipswich
Crown Electrics, Southwold
Susannah Collings
Anthea Beal
District Services, Ipswich Health Authority
Emmerson Hospital, Concord, Massachusetts, USA
Hilton Hotel, Jupiter, Florida, USA
International Wool Secretariat UK
Ted Jackson, Fabric Care Research Association
Peter Dickins
Mr U. Kläy, Chief Engineer, Basel Hilton, Switzerland
Miss K. Tobin, HCIMA
Mr L. Foord, Domestic Services Manager, Poole General Hospital, Dorset
The Residential Organization (Halls and Catering), Loughborough University of Technology
Mr R. Sheppard, General Manager, The Lygon Arms, Broadway, Worcs
Mr J. McSavage, Senior Lecturer, Dorset Institute of Higher Education
Mr A. Whittaker, Senior Lecturer, Dorset Institute of Higher Education

R. Jerman, decorator, Southwold
Mac Heath, Captain Morgan Antiques, Southwold
Mecanaids, Gloucester
Monthind Limited, Colchester
Murdoch Linens, Edinburgh
Norwich Hotel School
John Oliver Limited, London
Orchard Hotel, Perth, Western Australia
Portman Carpets, London
Primo Furniture Limited, London
Regent Hotel, Sydney, New South Wales, Australia
Roxburghe Hotel, Edinburgh
Servisystems Limited, Norwich
Shrubland Hall Health Clinic, Coddenham
Sleepeezee Limited London
Willis Faber and Dumas Limited, Ipswich

Mr J. Merricks, Merricks Sico Ltd, Ashford, Kent
Mr T. Jackson, Fabric Care Research Association, Harrogate, Yorks
Mr Cayley, Environmental Health Officer, Southampton
Mr Biggs, Christchurch Hospital Laundry, Christchurch, Dorset
Modeluxe Laundries
Dimex Ltd, Solihull, West Midlands
S.R.L. Sound Research Laboratories, Suffolk
The management and staff of the Basel Hilton

PART ONE
Operations

1 *The role of the housekeeper*

Housekeeping duties

All human beings need a comfortable environment in which to live, work and follow their leisure pursuits. The housekeeper will have different duties, depending on the priorities of the particular establishment. However, the following list gives most of the functions the housekeeper may have to fulfil.

1   To understand the function of the establishment and the needs of the occupants, and to create an environment to promote their welfare and comfort.
2   To look after the building and maintain the fabric, plant, equipment, furnishings and services on a cost effective basis.
3   To select, control and train staff to work effectively and in harmony.
4   To advise, when required, and work in co-operation with senior and other administrators, possibly architects and other specialists in related fields.
5   To control the financial, material and human resources within his/her scope, on a cost effective basis to the benefit of the organization.
6   To be aware of his/her position and status in the organization and to demonstrate his/her contribution and importance in the smooth running of the establishment and welfare of the people in it.
7   To organize the domestic services of the establishment and to be aware of the legal obligations and requirements imposed by central and local government legislation related to his/her field of operations.
8   To organize the daily, weekly and periodic cleaning of all rooms and areas used by staff and occupants of the building.
9   To select, control and store cleaning equipment and materials best suited to the use for which they are required, and to understand the scientific principles underlying their use and effectiveness.
10 In addition to creating a clean and comfortable environment, the housekeeper can help create a harmonious and aesthetically pleasing atmosphere by paying attention to colour, lighting and arrangement of furniture and artefacts.

Position and status of the housekeeper

The role of the housekeeper should never be undervalued and the status should be the same as that of any other departmental manager. In small establishments, the housekeeping may be done by the manager or in joint-management by his wife. In boarding schools, it is often the responsibility of the housemaster's wife or the matron. In small private nursing homes, it is often undertaken by the matron or a nursing sister. In small residential homes, it may be the responsibility of the warden.

Managers who will seek professionally qualified staff to produce food, will often leave the biggest capital asset to be cleaned and maintained with no professional housekeeper and minimal supervision. This often results in waste of money and human and material resources.

When economies have to be made, the housekeeping department often suffers. Therefore it is important that the housekeeper emphasizes the importance of his/her role and demonstrates it by efficient management of the department.

Cleaning

Organizing the efficient cleaning of a building is one of the most important functions of the housekeeper. If hotels are not well maintained, they will cease to attract customers. Public service establishments are supported by taxes and rates paid by the public and are vulnerable to public criticism. Dull and shabby offices are not conducive to good morale and the productivity of staff. Cleaning is dealt with in detail in Chapters 2, 3, 4 and 5. In order to choose good staff and train them effectively, the housekeeper must know exactly what their jobs entail, and the best way to fulfil these duties. We have, therefore, included detail on how cleaning, laundry, maintenance etc. should best be done, even though the housekeeper may not do these jobs her/himself. Details on managing staff and the legal obligations of employers and employees will be found in Chapters 21, 22 and 23.

Co-operation

All housekeepers must co-operate with senior administrators, and outside legislative bodies, such as the fire service, and the Department of the Environment.

It is desirable to demonstrate to those in authority, that the housekeeper can contribute and advise from his/her own knowledge and practical experience.

In working with architects and other specialists, she/he must have a general knowledge of the principles of plant, building methods and materials, how various sytems work.

Armed with this general knowledge, as well as detailed knowledge of the use of the areas under his/her control, and of the practical cleaning problems entailed, the housekeeper can contribute in planning. The housekeeper is in a unique position of being in close and more informal contact with the users of the establishment and its facilities and being aware of their needs and reactions.

She/he is in a position to assess consumer needs and the reaction to what is being offered.

Staff and customer welfare

In hotels and residential establishments, the housekeeper often has a very personal relationship with staff and customers and is often called upon to administer simple first aid, diagnose ailments, and call in medical services when necessary.

She/he can play an important role in the personnel and customer welfare and be a useful liaison between senior management, management and heads of other departments.

This role requires tact, discretion, understanding and interest in people.

General management

The housekeeper has control over and responsibility for considerable capital assets, materials and human resources, and must consider their most economical use. She/he should buy with care, appreciating the particular needs of the establishment, and ensure that materials are carefully stored and dispensed.

The housekeeper should also be aware of the importance of marketing and selling and what contribution she/he can make in this field. She/he should be able to forecast and budget for the needs of the department. These aspects are dealt with in Chapter 24.

Housekeeping in hotels

Hotels are commercially run operations for the customer who has a choice of where to stay, and pays for the accommodation and services received. The housekeeper has to bear in mind that the customers must be attracted to the establishment, so marketing and selling are important factors. Furthermore, the amenities and services must be geared to meet the demands of the market for which the hotel is catering.

Work organization is fairly easy in hotels because room use follows a regular pattern. Sleeping, eating and living areas are defined and the times when available for cleaning can be easily assessed. The use of bedroom accommodation can be anticipated, since occupants stay for a limited period of time.

Repairs and renovation can be carried out during periods of low occupancy and bedrooms cleaned during normal working hours. Airport hotels are an exception, since there is often day and night occupancy of bedrooms.

Many British hotels have developed from the early coaching inns, many of which can still be found as restaurants or country inns/hotels. However, there are many other types of hotel available to the modern traveller.

Types of hotel

Large luxury
These are of 5 star standard, for instance, the *London Hilton* and the many other hotels on Park Lane in London.

Commercial
These are business type hotels of varying standards, sizes and locations mainly in towns.

Franchise
These are hotels which are privately owned but operate under another trade name so taking advantage of mass marketing and purchasing policies, for example, some Holiday Inns.

Transient
These are short stay hotels, especially those at airports where a room may be sold more than once a day.

Seasonal/resort
These are hotels which operate mainly during one particular season a year, e.g. hotels at skiing resorts or the seaside. Some of the seasonal hotels close in the 'off season' period.

Motels
These are hotels based near motorways. They are often designed as chalet type accommodation, where the guest simply drives in, collects his or her room key at reception and there is ample car parking space near the accommodation. The rooms are usually quite basic and the main complex of the building with the restaurant etc. in a separate building.

Small private hotels and guest houses
These are privately owned and of varying sizes, standards and locations.

Speciality
These are hotels designed to cater for a special market, for example temperance hotels where no alcohol is served or Jewish Hotels where Kosher food is available.

Organization

In order to understand the role of the House-keeper, it is important to realize where he/she fits into the organization of the hotel. Figure 1 shows a typical organization in a large international hotel.

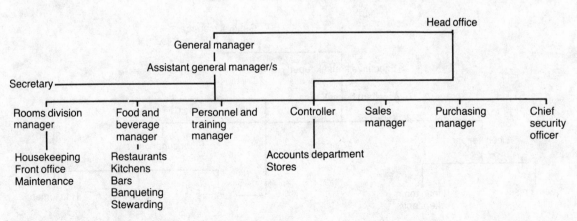

Figure 1   *An organization chart for a large international hotel*

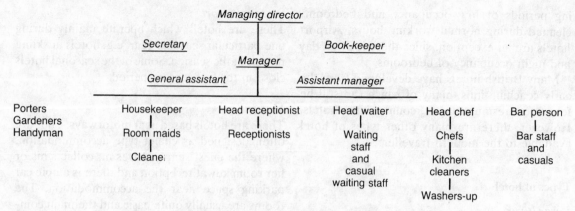

Figure 2   *An organization chart for a small hotel (25–50 bedrooms, restaurant and bar)*

Some hotels do not warrant a rooms division manager, so the executive housekeeper, chief engineer or maintenance manager and front office manager are all department heads, reporting directly to the general manager and his/her assistants. Figure 2 shows how a small hotel might be organized.

The housekeeper is responsible to the manager and is in contact with all other departments and with porters and the handyman. The general assistant will probably stand in for the house-keeper during his/her off-duty time.

Within the majority of hotels the housekeeper has his/her own department, which of course will vary according to the size and type of establishment. An example of how the department might be organized is shown in Figure 3.

Duties and responsibilities of housekeeping staff

The executive housekeeper
Figure 4 shows a typical job description of an executive housekeeper.

The assistant housekeeper
The assistant housekeeper aids the executive housekeeper in the smooth running of the hotel. She/he relieves the housekeeper on days off and also has specific responsibilities such as staff training, ordering of stores, responsibility for the housemen.

Floor supervisors
As the name implies, floor supervisors are normally in charge of one or more floors or areas of

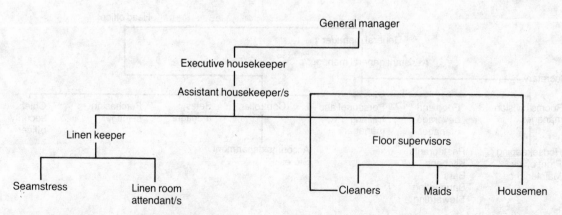

Figure 3   *An organization chart of the housekeeping department of a large hotel*

Responsible for the operation of all housekeeping functions in guest rooms, hotel offices and public spaces, including corridors and stairwells. With aid of assistant(s), supervises staff of floor housekeepers, maids, housemen, seamstresses, cleaners and clerks. Reports to the rooms division manager, executive assistant manager or manager.

● Establishes standards of cleanliness and room arrangement to be met by staff in accordance with management requirements. Institutes work rules to accomplish standards. Co-operates with personnel department in establishing training methods and procedures for development of employees. Balances staff working schedules to meet peak and slack periods and remain within union and labour law requirements. Maintains a close payroll control. Keeps a very close liaison with front office to ascertain and meet anticipated guest check-in and check-out.

● Makes periodic inspections of all areas to check on housekeeping standards. Issues necessary orders for correction. Meets regularly with engineering and laundry departments to ensure smooth flow of supplies and repair work. Responsible for the inventory of supplies, ordering replacement when necessary. Maintains linen room and repair services.

● Makes recommendations to management for modernization of equipment, methods or supplies. May work with engineering or management on rehabilitation or redecorating plans. May include night cleaning operations of kitchens, hotel offices and public space within administration.

Figure 4 *An example of a job description for an executive housekeeper*

rooms. They are responsible for the standard of cleanliness and appearance of the rooms in their area. They supervise the work of the maids and housemen under their control, and report damage.

Day maids

Day maids will be responsible for cleaning rooms within their sections (usually about fifteen rooms each) and they will sometimes clean corridors and service areas. In traditional hotels they will serve early morning teas. In some hotels without floor supervisors they will train new maids.

Evening maids

These are usually now only found in luxury hotels and some seasonal hotels. They are responsible for:

1 Turning down beds, closing curtains, switching on bedside lights and replenishing towels, as well as emptying waste paper bins etc.
2 Extra work that cannot be done in the day e.g. carpet 'spotting' (stain removal).
3 Answering guest requests for hot water bottles, bedboards, etc.

In airport hotels, evening maids would be expected to clean vacated rooms. If evening maids are employed, there will normally be an evening supervisor on duty with them.

Housemen

In some hotels, housemen are called house or linen porters.
House porters are involved in such work as moving furniture, shampooing carpets, wall washing, floor maintenance, high-level dusting etc.
Linen porters collect dirty linen and rubbish, and transport clean linen, stores, etc.

House cleaners

House cleaners are responsible for cleaning various areas of the hotel, such as public areas (toilets, foyers, and lounges, and sometimes restaurants and bars), back of house areas, locker and shower rooms for staff, back corridors, staff rooms and offices.

Linen keepers

Linen keepers are responsible for the control, supply and repair of linen.

Linen room attendants

Linen room attendants will aid the linen keepers with their responsibilities and relieve on days off.

Seamstresses

Seamstresses are responsible for any sewing work that needs to be done throughout the hotel. This includes repairs to linen, bedding, soft furnishings and uniforms. They will also do 'remakes', for example cutting up a damaged table cloth and making it into serviettes. They will also make special items, such as skirtings for a buffet table.

Conclusion

Until there are machines to make beds and clean toilets, do the dusting and polishing and any other cleaning, then there will always be a need for a housekeeping department. The type of guest may change and he or she may well have different needs or requirements, so, in order to keep in business, the housekeeper will be expected to provide the necessary housekeeping services.

New technology should make way for more efficient systems. which make life and work in the housekeeping department less physically demanding, but standards still need to be maintained.

Housekeeping in hospitals

The person in charge of housekeeping in National Health Service hospitals is known as the domestic services manager and he/she is paid according to a scale based on the size of the particular establishment/s for which he/she is responsible. Prior to 1974 a matron held overall responsibility for both medical and service areas of the hospitals which were measured by the number of beds that they housed.

Hospitals today, however, are measured in square metres – the greater floor area, the higher the salary scale will be for hospital management. The National Health Service is the responsibility of the Secretary of State for Health, whose authority is delegated into two main areas:

(a) The Department of Health and Social Security (DHSS)
(b) The Regional Health Authorities

From 1 April, 1983 hospital management is being re-organized. The Health Service had often

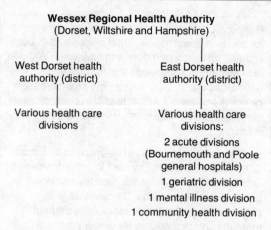

Wessex Regional Health Authority
(Dorset, Wiltshire and Hampshire)

West Dorset health authority (district)

East Dorset health authority (district)

Various health care divisions

Various health care divisions:

2 acute divisions (Bournemouth and Poole general hospitals)
1 geriatric division
1 mental illness division
1 community health division

Figure 5   *An example of Regional Health Authority Organization*

been criticized for being 'over manned, yet under managed'. The economic climate was such that savings had to be made in the National Health Service. This re-organization has affected the role of domestic services management.

Some authorities have regrouped their services, taking into account the needs of their respective districts. An example of this is the East Dorset Health Authority (see Figure 5) where there has been an immense growth in mental illness and the necessity for geriatric care.

The long-term advantage to the NHS of this re-organization is that money will be saved on management level salaries. In addition, because there is more unit responsibility, communication should be more effective and management more efficient.

Although some health authorities have 'contracted out' domestic services and others may have to in order to comply with Government policy, there are still many units which provide an 'in house' service.

Types of hospital, ward and medical institution

General and acute
This is normally the main hospital in a district and usually contains a casualty department, intensive care unit, medical and surgical wards besides many wards as listed below.

Orthopaedic
This is concerned with bones, ligaments, muscles and tendons.

Dental
A dental hospital or ward is mainly concerned with teeth.

ENT
This deals with ear, nose and throat problems.

Maternity
Maternity hospitals are concerned with childbirth and are often closely linked with gynaecology.

Childrens'
Sometimes called paediatric, these are concerned with childrens' illnesses.

Geriatric
These deal with the elderly.

Psychiatric
Mental illness is treated in a psychiatric hospital.

Long/short stay
This simply describes the length of time a patient is expected to remain in a particular ward or hospital. They are usually connected with geriatric and mental/physical handicapped units.

Rehabilitation centre
This is concerned with helping people to return to living a normal life again, for example after loss of limb.

Day centre
This is used by elderly and mentally or physically handicapped patients, where they may partake in activities and so relieve relatives at home.

Medical centre
This consists of doctors' surgeries and offices.

These are some of the hospitals and wards found within the National Health Service. The list of specialist units is endless but the responsibility of the domestic services manager is to select suitable staff, cleaning agents, cleaning equipment and methods of work to complement the particular area.

Duties and responsibilities
Figure 6 shows an organization chart for a domestic services department.

The domestic services manager
The domestic services manager is responsible for:

1 The smooth running of the domestic services department of a particular hospital or hospital units.
2 Advice on domestic services within the district.
3 Hygiene and cleanliness throughout the unit, with the exception of the catering department, the mortuary and often the operating theatres. These areas usually have their own specialist staff to deal with cleaning.
4 Health, safety and security.
5 Pest control.
6 Good co-ordination with other departments.
7 Control of any contract agencies such as window cleaners.
8 Staff recruitment, training and welfare.
9 Liaison with the unions.
10 Efficiency and cost effectiveness.
11 Cleanliness of staff residences.
12 Staff uniforms (sometimes).

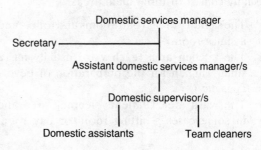

Figure 6 *An example of an organization chart of a domestic services department*

Assistant domestic services manager

The assistant domestic services manager aids the DSM in running the department. The assistant DSM will also have some specific responsibility such as staff training or being responsible for a particular unit, perhaps a small specialist chest hospital.

Domestic supervisor

The domestic supervisor is responsible for a certain number of wards and the domestic assistants who clean those wards. The main responsibility of the domestic supervisor is to ensure that the standard of cleanliness and hygiene within his/her area is maintained to the highest level and consequently, he/she is involved with the organization of work on those wards. Liaison with nursing staff is especially important.

Domestic assistant

Domestic assistants (Grade 1) are often employed on a part-time basis.

At the present time, all domestic staff in hospitals are governed by the Whitley Council's Handbook, which lays down all terms and conditions of employment. Domestics are paid a regular wage and receive weekend enhancements should they work on Saturday and Sunday. Saturday pay amounts to 'time and a half' and Sunday pay amounts to 'double time'. Many hospitals also operate a bonus scheme, negotiated between the trades unions and the management.

The job involves cleaning particular areas of the hospital, usually the wards. Hospital wards usually consist of three main areas:

1 The sanitary areas (bathrooms and toilets and a sluice room).
2 The kitchen area (each ward usually has a small kitchen for the preparation of beverages etc.).
3 The ward area (Patients sleeping area and in some cases a sitting room or day room area).

In the main, domestic staff are concerned with cleaning these three areas. They may also clear away food trays but do not normally serve food or beverages. Domestics also do not normally make beds – this is the task of the nurse.

In some hospitals, *housekeeping units* are in operation. They carry out the following duties:

1 Bed-making.
2 Service of food and beverages.
3 Clearing away of food trays and possibly washing up.
4 Arranging flowers and changing flower water.
5 Delivering and collection of the patient's mail.
6 Taking care of patient needs, e.g. shopping.
7 Care of patients' clothes and personal belongings.
8 Cleanliness and hygiene on the wards.

The reason for having a houskeeping unit is to reduce the domestic tasks of nurses and allow them to get on with the job of nursing.

Domestic assistant (Grade 2)

Domestic assistants (Grade 2) are also known as *team cleaners* because they work in a team. Team cleaners usually consist of a group of workers who get a higher rate of pay than that of a Grade 1 domestic. This is because their job involves the use of floor maintenance machinery. Consequently team cleaners must have a sound knowledge of all aspects of floor maintenance. They will normally also be involved with heavier cleaning work such as wall washing, curtain changing, cleaning the public areas including the toilets, and high dusting.

The future of domestic services management

A draft document on contracting out of hospital services (circular number DA(83)14) was presented to the health authorities in February 1983 by the DHSS, when the Government decided that all health authorities should seek to provide services by employing private contractors.

Domestic services managers were invited to comment on the document, but were also advised to obtain tenders from contract cleaners and to submit quotations for an 'in-house' service. Some District Health Authorities have decided to put domestic work out to contract, unless an in-house service could be provided at a lower cost.

The future trend in hospitals may be to change to a service which incorporates both the catering and housekeeping functions.

Private hospitals and nursing homes are also becoming more widespread. As more new hospitals are built the need for professional hospital housekeepers will certainly arise.

The present role of the domestic services manager may change. He/she may act as an advisor on hospital cleaning problems, and liaise with the contract cleaners. People will always need clean and hygienic conditions in hospitals and therefore the professional housekeeper will always be in demand.

A career in the health service

A graduate training scheme in domestic services is offered by some health authorities. The trainee is sponsored by the health service for a one year postgraduate training period. On successful completion of the training, a certificate is awarded and the participant is qualified to apply for a management post within the health service.

In most hospitals, training is very important. Apart from in-house training both domestic supervisors and domestic assistants are normally encouraged to attend day release or part-time college courses.

Housekeeping in educational establishments

Providing a housekeeping service for people in residential establishments such as hostels, boarding schools and halls of residence is of a different nature to providing similar services in hotels or hospitals. In hotels perhaps the emphasis is on aesthetics, in hospitals it is more important to be concerned with hygiene, but in institutional establishments thought has to be given to people who are living in a room, which is to be their

home for quite some considerable time. A further problem is usually a very tight budget.

All institutional establishments are managed in different ways but for the purpose of understanding a general view of housekeeping in such an establishment, examples of college/university halls of residence have been chosen.

In a relatively small college the person in charge of housekeeping is known as a domestic bursar. He or she is not only in charge of the housekeeping but also the complete residential management, such as the catering, maintenance and even sometimes the grounds or gardens.

Duties and responsibilities in a small college

The domestic bursar and his/her assistant will normally share the work of the department between them although the domestic bursar takes overall responsibility. One might be concerned with the catering side of the operation, while the other is involved with the housekeeping side. The domestic bursar will also be involved in forward planning operations for the smooth running of the establishment.

Domestic assistants

Domestic assistants are sometimes known as cleaners. As in the National Health Service, they are usually employed on a part-time basis, Monday to Friday. They are expected to perform the following duties:

1 Clean student communal kitchens (students are expected to do their own washing up).
2 Clean student communal toilets and bathrooms.
3 Clean corridors, stairways and utility rooms.
4 Service a section of bedrooms.

In halls of residence students are expected to make their own beds and to keep their bedrooms in a reasonable state of cleanliness and tidiness. The domestic assistant is normally responsible for approximately thirteen rooms and she/he will empty the waste paper bins and possibly clean the wash basin daily but each room will be thoroughly cleaned at least once a week or once a fortnight. This thorough clean will obviously be done on a rotation basis.

Porters
Porters are involved with the heavy work, such as moving furniture, clearing away rubbish and doing floor maintenance.

The linen maid
The linen maid is responsible for controlling the linen, bedding, curtains and any other soft furnishings which may be kept in the linen room.

The linen maid is responsible for despatching dirty linen to the laundry and checking the quantities of clean linen which are returned. She/he is also responsible for repairs.

Duties and responsibilities in a university hall of residence
Large universities are managed in several different ways. The accommodation manager may be in charge of the student accommodation on and off campus, but in other management setups, there will be an overall domestic manager sometimes known as a director of the residential organization. In this case, the director will be responsible for:

1   Catering.
2   Housekeeping of student halls.
3   Co-ordination of maintenance and repairs.
4   Organization of off campus student accommodation.

His/her most important responsibility is cost control and standards. In a university all administration comes under the responsibility of the registrar, but his/her prime concern is the academic side. The bursar on the other hand is in charge of services. In Figure 7, the department heads listed have the following responsibilities:

1   *The estates manager* is in charge of all building and maintenance including the grounds.
2   *The catering manager* is in charge of all the food and beverage outlets including the cleaning of those areas.
3   *The service manager or superintendent caretaker* is in charge of the cleaning of all public areas, classrooms, lecture theatres, laboratories and any other teaching areas as well as offices and toilets.
4   *The accommodation manager* is in charge of the cleanliness and organization of all student accommodation.

Although universities do get government grants, they are largely self-financing organizations and they must at least break even at the end of any one financial year. With this policy in mind, it is the job of the accommodation manager to play his/her part by marketing accommodation during vacations and keeping control over costs of the accommodation function.

One method of helping to bring in money to the university is by such functions as conferences, wedding receptions, summer schools, open university residential tuition and holiday lets. Not all universities are suitable to all of these functions, so other marketing plans must be put forward.

Apart from the financial side of the operation, the accommodation manager must be concerned

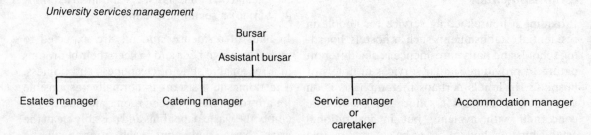

Figure 7   *An organization chart of accommodation management in university halls of residence*

with the well-being of the students and staff, the cleanliness and hygiene of the accommodation and of course the smooth running of the department. Figure 8 shows the organization chart for the accommodation management.

The assistant accommodation manager

He/she has responsibility for the conference bookings etc. A great deal of organization must go into this aspect of the job if it is to be performed successfully and gain repeat business. In a way the job of the assistant accommodation manager is similar to that of a banquet manager in a hotel.

The accommodation secretary

The accommodation secretary, apart from being a personal secretary to the accommodation manager, is also responsible for organizing student accommodation on campus. He/she deals with the UCCA forms and correspondence to students regarding accommodation.

The accommodation officer

The accommodation officer is responsible for placing students in accommodation off campus. He/she will visit various landlords wanting to let flats, digs, or bedsits to students and set rental terms and agreements with them. He/she must also set certain standards with external accommodation, for example ensuring that students have adequate washing, cooking and storage facilities as well as having a desk and lamp at which they can study.

The residential services supervisor

The residential services supervisor liaises between all the housekeepers of all the halls of residence, sorting out any major problems such as those connected with the laundry, maintenance, purchasing and staff wages.

The houskeeper

A housekeeper will normally be in charge of a hall of residence containing up to 500 beds. Students usually have single study bedrooms with shared toilet and shower facilities but in some colleges and universities there are also shared bedrooms. The halls may be single-sex or mixed but they are of two types:

1 *Fully catering halls* in which case the housekeeper is normally responsible for both catering and housekeeping services to the hall.
2 *Self-catering halls* in which case the housekeeper is simply in charge of housekeeping services as the students cook for themselves.

The housekeeper, who also is sometimes known as a domestic bursar, is responsible for the following in his/her particular hall.

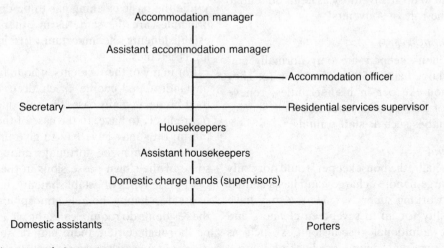

Figure 8 *Accommodation management*

1   Cleanliness and hygiene.
2   Pest control.
3   Keys and student mail.
4   His/her own staff welfare, work and supplies organization.
5   Linen.
6   Bed control – one person per bed so avoiding financial/ethical problems for the hall and study problems for the student. Sometimes there is a guest room in the hall and student friends are welcome to stay the night and pay a nominal charge for the accommodation.

It is common practice in many halls, for students to bring their own duvets – especially in self-catering halls. In this case, students would be expected to launder their own linen and also provide it. The advantage to the university would be a great saving in laundry costs.

The housekeeper in a hall of residence should always be on duty when the students, conference delegates or holiday makers check in. A rooming list will have been issued previously from the conference organizer or the accommodation secretary, so that he/she knows exactly who has been allocated to which room.

Room keys are handed out on arrival and often a small deposit is taken to cover the cost of the loss of the key or any damage to the study bedroom or breakages elswhere in the hall. When students check out, the housekeeper must always be on hand to do an inventory as items do tend to take on the role of souvenirs!

Assistant housekeeper

Assistant housekeepers are only normally employed in large halls of 500 rooms or more. They aid the housekeeper in his/her duties, relieve him/her for periods of absence and have specific responsibilities such as staff training.

Charge hand

In smaller halls, the housekeeper would normally have a charge hand. A charge hand has a similar role to a working supervisor. He/she may have responsibility for up to seventeen cleaners and may have additional responsibilities such as supervising spring cleaning, or checking that all conference delegates rooms have their beds made up and contain the appropriate literature.

Domestic assistants/cleaners

They work regularly from Monday to Friday but sometimes are expected to work at weekends, especially at the end of term when the students depart on the Friday and conference delegates arrive on the Saturday. On conference 'change over days' there is also a great deal of work to be done. Common hours of work would normally be 9.00 a.m.–1.00 p.m. or 10.00 a.m.–2.00 p.m.

Enhanced rates of pay are received for weekend work but some cleaners can be expected to be laid off during quiet vacation times. Pay and working conditions are laid down by the National Joint Council for Local Authorities in agreement with the relevant union, which may be the National Union of Public Employees (NUPE), the General and Municipal and Boilermakers and Allied Trades Union (GMBATU) or the Transport and General Workers Union (TGWU).

Porters

Porters are involved with the heavier jobs such as moving furniture, clearing away rubbish, high dusting and floor maintenance.

Housekeeping in residential homes

While the basic cleaning has to be done and the principles are the same as in other residential establishments, the important word in this heading is 'Homes'.

For many of the residents, who may be elderly or handicapped people, or children, it is indeed their home, in many cases the only one they have or are likely to have. In the case of the elderly or infirm, they may have had to give up their own home, and may be fortunate enough to have some of their own possessions in their rooms.

In these types of establishments, it is essential to create a happy, homely atmosphere, but since the residents do require care, the cleaning should be thorough. Often, there may be soiling which creates extra work and interrupts the regular flow of work and the people doing it require a certain dedication and temperament.

There should be a discipline and routine, as in other establishments, but co-operation with the residents is important, and according to their capabilities and with guidance from the medical professionals in charge, they can be allocated certain duties such as bedmaking or dusting to give assistance where practicable. However, the work must be supervised and inspected so the required standards are maintained.

Housekeeping in health farms or clinics

In these luxury establishments guests/patients/clients have sought quiet, rest and relaxation and relief from stress, as well as for the diet and treatments. There are similarities and differences between luxury hotels and hospitals.

Hotels and clinics

Similarities The furniture, furnishings and artefacts are in the luxury class and may be antiques, which require great care in cleaning (see Chapter 2). The cleaning should be meticulously carried out with the minimum disturbance to the guest.

Differences The guests may spend much time in their bedrooms, relaxing, so the availability of the rooms does not follow a regular pattern. There should be close co-operation with the person in charge of the treatments in order that bedrooms can be serviced while the guests are having treatments.

The temperature of the building should be higher than that maintained in hotels since the guests may be wearing bathrobes for much of the time and little else. Also some will be fasting and more sensitive to cold. Ancilliary heating should be available for individual use.

While quiet working is desirable in all establishments, it is even more important in clinics.

Facilities for hair washing and drying is also important for many treatments entail the wetting of hair.

Guests will also require more towels than hotel guests.

Since it is desirable that guests do not seek entertainment outside the clinic, games, music, reading matter should be available in the clinic.

More delicate furnishing materials may be used since they are not subject to the wear and tear from people coming and going in heavy outdoor clothes.

Since many of the treatments entail water therapy and showers available after treatments, there is not the need for so many private bathrooms. In fact, extra bathing is often discouraged. Hand basins, lavatories, and bidets will be adequate.

A shop where toileteries and swim and leisure wear can be purchased is useful. Many guests may not have brought all they need with them.

Clinics and hospitals

Similarities There must be consulting rooms and facilities for the medical staff as in hospitals.

Sanitizing of all treatment and bedrooms is as important in clinics as in hospitals.

Differences The décor, shower curtains etc. should not be as clinical in appearance as in hospitals – light pastel shades are less institutional in appearance.

The residents are in clinics voluntarily and the discipline and routines should be more flexible. On no account should the staff appear to be strained or hard pressed, but cheerful and helpful. While this is desirable in all establishments, it is even more important in these expensive establishments.

Further reading

Hurst, R., *Housekeeping Management for Hotel and Residential Establishments*, 2nd edition. (Heinemann 1980).

Lowbury, E., Geddes, A., Ayliff, G., and Williams, J., *Control of Hospital Infection* (Chapman and Hall 1981).

Maurer, I., *Hospital Hygiene*, 3rd edition (Edward Arnold 1985).

Miller, C. B., *Efficient Hospital Housekeeping* (American Hospital Association 1982).

Tucker, G., *The Science of Housekeeping* (Cahners 1982).

Tucker, G., and Schneider, M., *The Professional Housekeeper* (Cahners 1982).

Useful addresses

The Department of Health and Social Security,
Alexander Fleming House,
London SE1 6BY

2 Cleaning science

This chapter has been kindly written by J. McSavage, BSc.(Hons), MSc.(Physics), MSc.(Food science), MInst.P. Mr McSavage is currently senior lecturer at the Dorset Institute of Higher Education.

This chapter is concerned with understanding the cleaning process. The properties and composition of cleaning products are examined together with their application. Throughout the chapter reference is made to the important underlying scientific concepts.

It is necessary to consider two basic points first (a) why clean? and (b) what is the nature of dirt?

Why is it necessary to clean?

There are several important reasons why the removal of dirt from materials and surfaces is necessary:

1 *Appearance* Clean and well maintained surfaces and equipment create a favourable impression on the public and staff and give an indication of the operational efficiency of the staff.
2 *Hygiene* Several crucial areas, especially kitchens and washrooms must be kept clean to prevent cross-contamination and possible infection.
3 *Planned maintenance* A regular cleaning and maintenance programme will prolong the working life of furnishings and equipment.

The reasons are not listed in any particular order of importance, because this may vary according to the nature of the catering operation. In hospitals, for example, hygiene would be the most important reason for cleaning, while in prestige hotel and office areas, appearance would be the prime factor.

The nature of dirt

Dirt or soil can be described as any unwanted foreign material on a surface. Dirt can be classified into two main groups: (a) grease or oil-based dirt and (b) particulate dirt.

1 Grease or oil-based dirt consists of fatty organic material. Typical sources are food particles, machine grease and oil, sebum (a natural skin excretion).
2 Particulate dirt consists of inorganic material which is not water-soluble, for example, carbon, clay, rust, fabric debris. Typical sources are exhaust fumes, earthy and fabric materials.

Dirt is usually a mixture of fatty material and solid particulate matter. When this is the case the fatty material usually sticks to the surface, with particulate dirt bound to it. Most cleaning processes are designed to remove fatty material from surfaces and so cope with most types of soiling, whether fatty material alone, or mixed with particulate matter. Particulate matter alone is relatively easy to remove from surfaces.

Types of surfaces

The nature of the cleaning process depends on the type of surface to be cleaned. There are three main types of surfaces.

1 *Hard surfaces* Floors, walls, worktops, machine surfaces, crockery etc., with a wide range of possible materials – metals, plastics, ceramics, glass, wood etc. In this group of surfaces mechanical action can be used to support the cleaning action of any detergent.
2 *Soft surfaces* Fabrics used in upholstery, carpets and clothes. A wide range of materials are represented – cotton, wool, nylon, polyester etc. With this group of materials, the

amount of mechanical action to assist the cleaning action of the detergent is kept to a minimum.

3 *The human skin*   The nature of human skin is such that it can be sensitive to many cleaning agents. Therefore the range of cleaning materials is limited, but the cleaning process can be supported with considerable mechanical action.

The cleaning process

The cleaning process is one of the most fundamental processes in the catering industry. Most cleaning agents are used in the form of solutions and the following section outlines some of the important properties of solutions.

A solution is a mixture in which the dissolved substance (solute) is uniformly distributed in the liquid (solvent) and does not settle out. For example, common salt (solute) dissolves in water (solvent) to produce brine (solution). Water is sometimes called a *universal solvent* as it is able to dissolve a large proportion of known materials. However, water will not dissolve oil or grease-based materials. In the cleaning industry, the term *solvent* is usually reserved to describe liquids which can dissolve grease and oil. Methylated spirits and perchlorethylene are examples of solvents and are used in stain removal and dry cleaning processes. During the cleaning operation, cleaning solutions have to be made up. In order to produce the solution as effectively as possible, the following points should be noted:

1 *Temperature of the solvent*   A hot solvent, e.g. hot water, will increase the rate of solution. The quantity of solute dissolved usually increases with increasing temperature.
2 *Particle size*   The smaller the particle size, the greater the surface area in contact with the solvent. Therefore smaller particles will dissolve faster than larger particles. For example, castor sugar dissolves faster than granulated sugar.

It is best to ensure that your solute is in the smallest practical form. Note that many cleaning agents are available in liquid form, such as liquid detergents or ammonia solutions. In this case, the liquid concentrate is already in solution, so all you have to do is to dilute it to the correct working strength. It is therefore more efficient to use liquid concentrates when available, to make up cleaning solutions.

3 *Agitation*   A stirring action during dissolving helps to bring fresh solvent in contact with the solute and so speed up the process. Note that stirring should also be done when diluting a liquid concentrate in order to obtain a well mixed solution.

Rinsing and neutralizing

The large majority of cleaning agents are alkaline, ranging from pH7 to pH13. It is important that every cleaning operation includes a stage when all traces of the cleaning agent are removed.

Automatic washing machines and dishwashers include adequate rinsing cycles. The main problem area is in hard surface cleaning, such as floor cleaning or work top cleaning.

In this form of cleaning the final solution evaporates from the surface. If the final solution contains some cleaning solution, then alkaline residues can be left on the surface in the form of a white powder. This residue can cause severe damage to the surface finish and to the surface material. For example, an emulsion floor wax contains water which can activate the alkaline residue to form an alkaline solution. This solution can then react with the floor wax and break it down.

The rinsing operation is very important. The instructions regarding the use of each cleaning material must be closely followed. In most cases one or two rinses with clean water is adequate. However, when a strong alkaline cleaning solution is used it is advisable to add a little vinegar to the rinse solution. The vinegar, a weak acid, will react and neutralize the alkaline residue. This technique is used in floor stripping procedures. Conversely, when an acid is used in the cleaning process, for example, in stain removal, an alkaline rinse (dilute ammonia solution) is advisable. Sometimes adequate rinsing is difficult in practice. Certain materials, such as wool, can suffer chemical damage if left in contact with alkaline materials. This can cause problems in carpet cleaning. Therefore specialist cleaners and procedures should always be used in these situations.

The active ingredient in most cleaning materials is called the **surface active agent** or *surfactant*. Many types of surfactants exist but their action in the cleaning process is fundamental for all types of surfactants.

Let us assume that some oil-based dirt has to be cleaned from a surface. The cleaning process can be thought to occur in three stages (a) removal of the oil from the surface, (b) prevention of the oil from redepositing on to the surface and (c) dispersion of the oil in the cleaning solution leading to its removal during rinsing. Surfactants therefore have to be water-soluble materials and also act on oil-based materials. The structure of the typical surfactant molecule shows how this dual property can be possible (see Figure 9).

The structure can be described as tadpole-shaped with a *hydrophilic head* (water loving/water soluble) and a hydrophobic tail (water hating/fat soluble). The cleaning action of the surfactant can be explained in relation to its dual water soluble/fat soluble character.

The 3 cleaning stages as given above are now described in greater detail.

Reduction of surface tension
Water behaves as though it has an elastic skin. This skin is due to the existence of surface tension forces (see Figure 10). A water molecule in the bulk of the liquid experiences equal attraction forces in all directions. However, molecules at the surface experience a net force into the bulk of

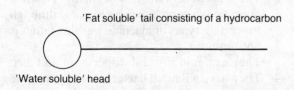

'Fat soluble' tail consisting of a hydrocarbon

'Water soluble' head

Figure 9   *Structure of a typical surfactant molecule*

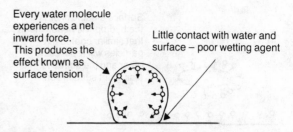

Every water molecule experiences a net inward force. This produces the effect known as surface tension

Little contact with water and surface – poor wetting agent

Figure 10   *Water droplet on a flat surface*

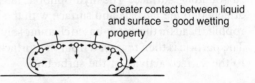

Surfactant molecules migrate to the surface lowering surface tension

Greater contact between liquid and surface – good wetting property

Figure 11   *Addition of surfactant to the water droplet*

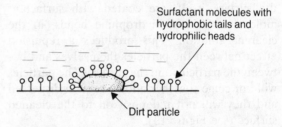

Surfactant molecules with hydrophobic tails and hydrophilic heads

Dirt particle

Figure 12   *Oil-based dirt particle in a detergent solution*

the liquid. A water droplet will tend to take on the shape with the least surface area for its volume – this shape is a sphere.

Water is a poor wetting agent, i.e. it will not wet a surface properly, and so dirt cannot be removed effectively. The addition of a surfactant reduces the surface tension. As can be seen from Figure 11 the surfactant molecules migrate to the surface of the water so that the hydrophobic section sticks out of the water. The result is a liquid with a lower surface tension capable of wetting a surface.

Removal of dirt from a surface
Surfactants are capable of removing dirt from a surface. As can be seen from Figure 12 the

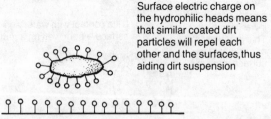

Surface electric charge on the hydrophilic heads means that similar coated dirt particles will repel each other and the surfaces, thus aiding dirt suspension

Figure 13   *Oil-based dirt particle suspended in a detergent solution*

surfactant molecules migrate to the dirt particle and surrounding surface. The hydrophobic tails are attached to the particle and surface with the hydrophilic heads in the water-based cleaning solution. The particle is then removed from the surface due to the surface activity of the surfactant.

Dispersion action

The soil particles removed from the surface, and the surface itself, are coated with surfactant molecules, all with hydrophilic heads, in the cleaning solution. This produces a repulsion effect between the particles themselves and between the particles and the surface. The particles will not come together and so remain dispersed and they will not redeposit on to the cleaned surface (see Figure 13).

Types of surfactants

The usual classification of types of surfactants is given in Figure 14.

Soap

Ordinary soaps are the *sodium salts* of *long chain*

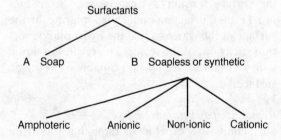

Figure 14   *Classification of surfactants*

fatty acids, such as *stearic acid*, $CH_3(CH_2)_{16}COOH$ (obtained from beef or mutton tallow) and *palmitic acid*, $CH_3(CH_2)_{14}COOH$ (obtained from palm oil). The fatty acids are present in the form of *triglycerides*.

In the soap-making process *sodium hydroxide* (caustic soda, NaOH) is added to animal fat or vegetable oil. The reaction can be summarized as follows:

$$\text{fat} + \text{sodium hydroxide} \longrightarrow \text{soap} + \text{glycerol}$$

This process is known as *saponification*. The soap produced from stearic acid and sodium hydroxide is *sodium stearate*, $CH_3(CH_2)_{16}COONa$.

A large variety of soaps can be produced from this basic reaction, the variations are as follows:

Fatty acid component	Base component
Saturated or unsaturated containing eight or more carbon atoms	*Inorganic bases* sodium, potassium, ammonia *Organic bases* monoethanolamine, triethanolamine

The property of the soap depends on its composition of the soap.

1   Sodium soaps tend to have a hard texture and a low solubility in cold or lukewarm water.
2   Potassium, ammonium and triethanolamine soaps tend to dissolve rapidly even in cold water and are softer in texture. Liquid or cream soaps are produced from these soaps.
3   Soaps produced from saturated fatty acids tend to be resistant to rancidity.

All soaps have the following properties.

1   They lower the surface tension. Soap solutions can wet surfaces readily.
2   They produce lather. For many cleaning operations a good lather is essential, although for certain types of machine washing lather is not required.
3   They can emulsify and disperse oil and dirt.
4   They have a limited bacteriostatic or in some cases germicidal activity – a useful property in most cleaning processes.

5 They *ionize* in solution to produce an active *anion*:

$$CH_3(CH_2)_{16}COONa \rightleftharpoons$$
$$CH_3(CH_2)_{16}COO^- + NA^+$$

Stearate	Sodium
Anion	Cation

The negative ion has the detergency properties, therefore all soaps are *anionic* surfactants.

6 They are incompatible with hard water. Hard water contains CA^{++} and Mg^{++} ions. These ions react with all soaps to produce insoluble calcium or magnesium soaps.

$$2(CH_3(CH_2)_{16}COO^-) + CA^{++} \rightarrow$$

stearate ion	calcium ion

$$(CH_3(CH_2)_{16}COO)_2 \, Ca$$

insoluble
calcium stearate

The insoluble material produced forms a scum which soils bath, sink and fabric surfaces.

7 They are incompatible with acid solutions. In acid solutions insoluble fatty acids are formed producing a scum which soils in the same manner as mentioned above.

Properties (6) and (7) can be considered disadvantageous, and limit the possible application of soap materials.

Soapless surfactants

Soapless surfactants, sometimes known as *synthetic surfactants* because they are produced by organic synthesis, use materials mainly from the petrochemical industry. As can be seen from Figure 14 they are subdivided into four main groups according to how the surfactant molecule ionizes in water.

1 *Anionic* The molecule ionizes so that the hydrophobic group carries a negative charge. The associated positive ion is usually sodium Na^+

2 *Cationic* The molecule ionizes so that the hydrophobic group carries a positive charge. The associated negative ion is usually chloride, Cl^- or bromide Br^-

3 *Non-ionic* In this group of surfactants the molecule does not produce ions.

4 *Amphoteric* The molecule possesses an anion and cation centre, the final charge being determined by the pH of the solution. For example, in acid solutions they behave as cationics and in alkaline solution they behave as anionics.

Anionics

There is a large variety of possible anionic surfactants. However, only a few of these are in common use and the most important groups are (a) the *alkyl aryl suphonates*, (b) the *alkyl sulphates*, and (c) the *alkyl sulphonates*.

The *alkyl aryl sulphonates* consist of three functional parts; the hydrophobic *alkyl group* linked to the *aryl group* (usually benzene) which in turn is linked to the hydrophilic sulphonate group.

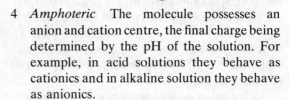

The figure above shows how sodium alkyl benzene sulphonate (ABS) ionizes to produce an active anion.

It is interesting to note that the first generation ABS detergents had branched alkyl chains. This produced 'hard' detergents which were not biodegradable, causing excessive foam problems in rivers and lakes. A second generation was produced with linear alkyl chains, LAS (linear alkyl benzene sulphonate) which was found to be 80 per cent biodegradable. It is possible to omit the aryl section and produces a straight chain alkyl sulphonate. It is ironic that the first generation

ABS was the most consumer acceptable and most economic to produce. It is still used in countries where the foam of waste water is not a serious problem.

The *alkyl sulphates* have the general formula on ionization

$$ROSO_3^- + NA^+$$

They can be produced by converting fatty acids to the corresponding alcohol and then producing the alcohol sulphate. It is claimed that the alcohol sulphates have detet ency properties similar to the corresponding fa ty acid soaps. However, the alkyl group can also be produced from petrochemical sources.

All the anionics have good detergency properties and of course have several advantages over soaps: they do not form a scum in hard water; they are compatible with alkaline, neutral and acidic solutions, and they tend to be neutral (pH7) in aqueous solution. However, most anionics have poorer soil suspension powers than soaps and so require 'builders' to improve their overall performance in detergents.

Cationics

Although Cationic surfactants display the normal detergency properties they are inferior to anionics and non-ionics. As they are also more expensive to produce, it can be seen that cationics are not in common use as surfactants. However, they do possess important germicidal properties and are used as disinfectants.

The typical cationic is a *quarternary ammonium compound* and can be thought of as a modified ammonium bromide or chloride.

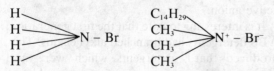

Ammonium bromide   Myristyl trimethyl bromide

Each hydrogen atom can be substituted by a hydrocarbon group. There are normally two to three methyl groups with one major hydrocarbon chain. This produces the characteristic 'tadpole' surfactant molecule shape.

The positive charge of the cation also means that it is strongly attracted to all types of surfaces. Many surfaces, especially fabrics, acquire a negative charge. This means that the cation will adhere to the fibres and keep them from matting. A cationic can therefore act as a fabric conditioner. It is important to note that anionics and cationics are incompatible, they react together to form inactive materials. Fabric conditioners are added only after rinsing. Cationics are compatible with non-ionics and so can be used to produce a cleaning agent with germicidal properties.

Non-ionics

Non-ionics exhibit the normal detergency properties except that in general they are poor lather producers. As the surfactant molecule does not ionize in solution it is relatively chemically inert. This implies that non-ionics will be compatible with most other ingredients in detergents, dissolved salts in hard water supplies, acidic and alkaline solutions. They have also two further advantages; they are very effective in removing grease/oil bound soil and being neutral they can be easily rinsed off surfaces. They are particularly suitable for crockery in machine dishwashing.

The main group of non-ionics are produced by a condensation reaction with ethylene oxide

$$\left[\begin{array}{c} CH_2 - CH_2 \\ \diagdown \quad \diagup \\ O \end{array} \right]$$

and fatty alcohols or alkyl phenols. The reaction is a type of polymerization where between eight and fourteen molecules of ehtylene oxide can be added to the alcohol or phenol group. The resulting molecule can be represented as

$$R - O (CH_2\ CH_2\ O)_n\ H$$

where *n* is the number of ethylene oxide molecules present, usually between eight and fourteen. They are known as fatty acid ethylene oxide condensates where the source material is a fatty acid, or they can be named according to the number of molecules of ethylene oxide present, e.g. nonyl phenol, 10 mol EO.

Another group of non-ionics in use are the *alkylolamides*. These are produced by the reaction between a fatty acid and monoethanol amine

$$\left[\begin{array}{c} H \\ \diagdown \\ \diagup \\ H \end{array} NCH_2CH_2OH \right]$$

The resulting compound can be represented as $R - CONHCH_2CH_2OH$. They are not used as surfactants on their own but they are important additives: they act as foam stabilizers; they enhance the detergency properties of other surfactants; they have an emollient effect and so protect the skin from the de-fatting action of most other synthetic surfactants.

Amphoterics
Amphoterics are able to display both anionic and cationic characteristics according to the pH. In acid solutions they are mainly cationic and in alkaline solutions they are mainly anionic. Amphoterics have been found to be non-irritating to the skin and eyes and so are used in shampoos and skin cleansers. Some amphoterics are excellent foam producers at neutral pH values and so can be used in carpet shampoos. They can also be used in acid cleaners because they are stable in acid conditions.

Cleaning products

The cleaning products available to the catering industry can be divided into four main groups.

1   Soft surface cleaners
2   Hard surface cleaners
3   Skin cleaners
4   Specialist cleaners

Each product contains a surfactant or a blend of surfactants together with a number of other ingredients. Each ingredient has a definite role to play. The final formulation of the product is designed to give optimum detergency performance for its intended use. Therefore the correct application of a cleaning product will mean an economic use of materials and labour.

The term *detergent* means 'anything that cleans' and is used for the final cleaning product available to the consumer. It is important to realize that if ready-to-use detergents were prepared from surfactants alone they would be so concentrated that it would be difficult to measure the small quantities required. Inert fillers are used to make the product easy to measure and easy to handle.

Soft surface cleaners
The most important cleaners in this group are the fabric cleaners, other soft surfaces such as carpets and upholstery covers require specialist cleaners. The cleaning of fabrics involves a limited mechanical action, because of possible damage to the fabric. This means that a large portion of the soil has to be removed by the chemical and surfact action of the detergent.

The main types of fabric cleaners are shown in Figure 15. Light-duty detergents are mainly used for cleaning delicate fabrics such as wool and silk. Heavy-duty detergents are used for cleaning mainly cotton fabrics, which can be heavily soiled. Table 2 gives the components of a heavy-duty detergent.

Surfactant system
For normal applications only one surfactant is used – this is usually soap (from tallow) or ABS for soapless detergents. However for a number of applications a blend of surfactants is used together with a foam control agent where necessary. A system containing two types of surfactants is called a binary blend.

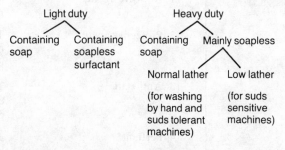

Figure 15   *Classification of fabric cleaners*

Filler

Sodium sulphate is used as an inert filler in powders. It produces a powder which is free-flowing and easy to handle. In liquid detergents water is used to dilute the products while urea, sodium sulphate and sodium chloride can be used to control the final density and viscosity of the product.

Builders

A builder is the term given to a material in a detergent which assists the action of the surfactant system. All heavy-duty detergents require builders. Their effect is usually synergistic (see page 37). Therefore the amount of expensive surfactant can be reduced without reducing the

Table 1   *Summary of additives used in cleaning products*

Type of additive	Function
1 Water softeners	To reduce the amount of detergent required
2 Filler	To give the powder free-flowing properties and to add bulk to the product
3 Foaming agents	To give a stable foam which can act as an indicator. When the foam disappears, then further detergent is required
4 Rust inhibitor	To protect metal parts in machines from rust and corrosion
5 Bleaching agents	To remove most of the stains from the wash
6 Optical brighteners	To give a fresh, clean appearance to the final washed product
7 Stabilizers	To keep the soil in solution and so prevent it re-entering the fabric
8 Bacteriostats	To reduce the number of bacteria present in the washed product
9 Enzymes	To digest insoluble protein stains
10 Drying agents	To help the final rinse solution to evaporate evenly so that the surface dries to a shine
11 Abrasive agents	To help remove stubborn stains and marks from hard surfaces
12 Protective agents	To protect the human skin against the drying out effect of some cleaning materials
13 Anti-static	To prevent fabrics collecting a static electric charge which can result in a poor finished product
14 Perfume	To impart a freshness to the final washed product

quality of the product. Although the term builder can be used to include almost every ingredient in a detergent it is used in the present context to include only inorganic alkaline materials.

The three main builders used in detergents are sodium tripolyphosphate, sodium silicate and sodium carbonate. They perform more than one function (see Table 4).

Table 2 *Components of a heavy duty detergent*

	Approximate percentages
Optical whiteners	0.2–0.8
Soil anti-redeposition agent	1.0–2.5
Bleach and/or enzyme preparation	20–35
Builders	40–50
Filler	25–10
Surfactant system	15–20

Table 3 *Surfactant system and its applications*

Surfactant system	Applications
Soap	Normal detergency uses
ABS (anionic)	Normal detergency uses
Non-ionic (low foaming)	Low lather uses
Anionic + non-ionic + lather control agent	Low lather uses
Anionic + soap	Low lather uses
Non-ionic + anionic	Heavy greasy soil

Bleach and/or enzyme preparation
These are considered together because they both perform a similar function – removing stains which the other ingredients would find difficult to deal with. The most commonly used bleaching agent is *sodium perborate*. It is an oxidizing bleach, removing stains such as tea, coffee and fruit juice. It acts at temperatures above 60°.

A number of detergents incorporate an enzyme preparation which digests protein. The proteolytic enzyme acts on stains such as milk, egg and blood. These are difficult to remove by any other means. The enzyme breaks down the protein to produce soluble compounds. However some enzyme preparations include an amylase enzyme which digests starch. Therefore starch-based stains such as sauce and gravy stains can be removed.

Enzymes are active between 10°C and 60°C and so are ideal for pre-wash soaking. At high temperatures the enzymes are inactivated. Therefore in a detergent containing both perborate and enzymes, the enzyme is active at low and medium temperatures and the perborate takes over at high temperatures. This means that for the low and medium temperature washes the perborate is not used and for high temperature washes the enzyme is not used.

A new development in detergent powders has recently taken place. It has been found that the addition of *tetra-acetyl ethylene diamine* (TAED) activates perborate at lower temperatures, at about 50°C. Therefore powders with TAED perform effectively at 50°C, with both the bleach and enzyme being effective. The advantages are

Table 4 *Functions of inorganic alkaline builders*

	Builder		
	Sodium tripolyphosphate	Sodium silicate	Sodium carbonate
Functions	Softens hard water	Softens hard water	Softens hard water
	Contributes alkalinity	Contributes alkalinity	Contributes alkalinity
	Aids soil suspension	Aids soil suspension	
	Good buffering action	Good buffering action	
		Corrosion inhibiter for stainless steel and aluminium	

that all types of fabrics can be washed together and the lower water temperature saves energy.

Anti-redepositing agent

Once dirt has been removed from a washed load then it is possible that some of the dirt suspended in the solution will redeposit on to the fabric. The result would be a greying of the surface. This effect will be greater for front loading washing machines where a smaller volume of water is used and so the concentration of dirt in suspension is high.

Most detergents use a material called *sodium carboxymethylcellulose* (CMC) as an anti-reagent. CMC has a great affinity for cellulosic fabrics and coats the fabric with a strong negative charge. This charge prevents the dirt in suspension from adhering to the surface. However, CMC was developed when the bulk of the wash was composed of cotton goods, and is not effective on other fabrics. Another material *polyvinyl oyrrolidone* (PVP) can be used as an anti-redeposition agent for synthetic fibres.

Optical brighteners

Optical brighteners are dyes which are absorbed on to textile fibres and are not removed by rinsing. They have the property of absorbing ultra-violet light and re-emitting this radiant energy in the form of visible light. The fabric will appear brighter than an untreated fabric. The spectrum of the emitted light has a high proportion of blue light, this balances any yellowness in the fabric. The fabric will appear brighter and whiter. The dye usually builds up to an optimum after ten washes. It is possible that a detergent powder can have a greater concentration of optical brightener. The brightening effect can then become apparent after the first wash, giving a favourable impression of the cleaning power of the product.

Liquid detergents

A full range of liquid detergents are available ranging from light-duty suitable for washing delicate fabrics, to heavy duty. The formulation of these products is similar to that of detergent powders. The manufacturer of liquid detergents has the added advantage of using simpler production equipment. The market for the range of liquid detergents is very competitive and it should be possible to obtain a suitable product at the 'right' price. Some manufacturers can produce a detergent to suit a particular cleaning application.

Solvent cleaning

The term *solvent* refers to the use of organic solvents in the cleaning of fabrics. Two situations exist where the use of solvents is necessary: (a) the degree of grease/oil soiling is excessive, (b) the use of an aqueous solution would harm the fabric finish.

For both these cases a detergent-solvent combination can be used. The function of the solvent is to dissolve the grease/oil. The surfactant acts as a wetting agent and emulsifier (a non-ionic is usually used). The detergent-solvent combination can be used as a pre-wash in commercial laundry work in situation (a) and as a dry cleaning aid in normal dry cleaning as in situation (b).

Typical dry-cleaning solvents are perchlorethylene, benzene petroleum ether and industrial methylated spirit.

Hard surface cleaners

Hard surfaces, incorporating such materials as wood, metal, ceramics etc. can withstand a reasonable amount of mechanical action. Therefore cleaning techniques make use of mechanical action and some cleaners contain abrasives to assist in this action.

It is important to realize that two distinct categories exist: (a) *dishwashing* where the objects to be cleaned can be placed in a cleaning bath or machine (this includes crockery, cutlery, glassware, cooking utensils) and (b) hard surface cleaning where the surfaces must be cleaned *in situ* (this includes worktops, floors, walls).

Multipurpose cleaners

There has been a trend to develop multi-purpose hard surface cleaners designed to cope with the job of cleaning grease, mud, etc. from hard flooring, doors and walls.

Most of the cleaners have (a) a surfactant system, (b) an alkaline system and (c) a water-softening system similar to fabric detergents. However, in addition to these standard ingredients certain hard surface cleaners contain (d) abrasives, (e) chlorine-based bleaches, (f) solvents.

The surfactant system This is usually a blend of anionics and non-ionics or anionic alone. This provides the wetting, emulsifying and suspension action.

The alkaline system A polyphosphate such as tetra sodium pyrophosphate together with ammonia and sodium carbonate (washing soda) can be used. This increases the grease removing property and acts synergistically (see page 37) with the surfactants. Sodium silicate acts as an alkali and a metal corrosion inhibiter.

Water softening action The polyphosphate also acts as a water-softening agent by sequestering calcium and magnesium ions from hard water. Washing soda also acts to soften water but by precipitation. EDTA (ethylenediamine tetra-acetic acid) can be used as a water softening agent.

Abrasives An abrasive cleaner, or scouring cleaner contains a high proportion of a finely ground mineral (over 75 per cent). Feldspar, calcite, dolomite are commonly used in abrasive products. The mineral powder assists in the physical removal of grease and other soiling from the surface. Abrasives are classified according to their hardness on a scale where diamond is 10 and talc is 1. This scale is called Moh's hardness scale, and is shown in Table 5. A material with hardness 7 will be able to scratch any surface with a value below 7 and can be scratched by any material on the scale above 7.

Chlorinated bleaches These have been found to improve the cleaning power of hard surface cleaners. This is because they have good oxidizing properties which can remove stains and react with all forms of organic matter, such as grease/oil films and food particles. They have also good disinfectant properties.

Table 5 *Moh's hardness scale*

Material	Hardness number	Comments
Diamond	10	
Corundum	9	
Topaz	8	
Quartz	7	Metals such as aluminium and copper are softer
Feldspar	6	Hardest mineral commonly used in cleaners
Apatite	5	
Fluorite	4	
Calcite	3	Mild abrasive in common use
Gypsum	2	
Talc	1	

The most commonly used chlorinated bleach in liquid form is sodium hypochlorite (NaOCl). It decomposes to produce oxygen and sodium chloride. The released oxygen is responsible for the bleaching and disinfectant properties. However, it also has some inherent disadvantages. First, sodium hypochlorite solutions are unstable and decompose, giving off oxygen. This means that the strength of the solution gradually diminishes as it is stored, and storage containers are fitted with vents to allow for the escape of the released oxygen. Second, it cannot be used with most other cleaning materials: it will oxidize most other surfactants; it reacts with acids to produce free chlorine gas, which is toxic; it reacts with ammonia to produce chloramines, which produce acrid fumes which cause respiratory distress. However, new surfactants are being developed which can be mixed with sodium byprochlorite to produce a relatively stable solution.

Another group of chlorinated bleaches are the chlorinated organic compounds. The main advantage of these compounds is that they can be produced in a dry powder form and are more stable in storage. They are easier to handle and can safely be brushed off when spilled on the skin or clothes.

Potassium and sodium salts of dichloroisocyanuric acid are the most widely used compounds of this group. They become active when dissolved in water – reacting with water to produce hypochlorous acid ($HOCl$). The hypochlorous acid decomposes to liberate oxygen – the basis of the bleaching process.

Solvents Although the alkaline surfactant system, with some aid from abrasive and bleach components, should be capable of removing all oil and grease stains, it is found that for excessive soiling, solvent action can increase the cleaning power of the product. The group of solvents used are the *glycol ethers*, which are water soluble and non-toxic. The most commonly used compound from this group is etaylene glycol monobutyl ether.

Skin cleansers

Using solvents and surfactants removes a proportion of the natural oils of the skin. Excessive exposure to these chemicals can, therefore, lead to excessive moisture loss. The skin becomes dry and hard or 'chapped'. Skin emollients, such as lanolin, can be used to protect the skin against further loss and allow moisture to penetrate the dry skin.

Barrier creams can be used to protect the skin when working with chemicals, such as degreasant, which can dry and defat the skin. The sensitivity of the skin to various chemicals varies from person to person and it is a wise precaution always to wear rubber gloves when using cleaning solutions.

Specialist cleansers

Foam cleansers
Most carpets and upholstery fabrics have to be cleaned *in situ*. The main difficulty is that the material cannot be rinsed and excessive dampness may cause damage to the object being cleaned.

Fabric foam cleansers are formulated to produce large amounts of foam. The cleanser lifts and holds the dirt in the foam. The foam is formulated so that it dries quickly and becomes brittle. The dried foam and dirt can then be vacuum cleaned or brushed away. The surfactant used in this type of cleanser must therefore be a good lather producer and tend to crystallize on drying. Anionics and amphoterics are used in this application.

Lavatory cleansers
An acid-based cleanser is usually used to remove staining in toilets. This staining is produced by scale from hard water salts and iron and copper stains from the water supply and/or corroded pipework. The main ingredient is an acid salt, sodium bisulphate ($NaHSO_4$) together with 1 per cent pine oil and 1 per cent ABS to improve the wetting power of the cleanser. It should be noted that a cleanser of this type has little disinfectant action. The cleanser must be used in conjunction with a disinfectant or disinfectant-based cleanser. It is important that the two products are used at different times because of the dangers of mixing chlorinated compounds with acidic solutions (see page 35).

Pollution

Biodegradability
In the late 1950s and early 1960s there was great public concern about the quantities of foam produced in rivers and lakes. This was found to be due to the presence of the synthetic surfactants used at that time, mainly sodium tetrapropylene benzene sulphonate (an anionic). This compound was not completely degraded by the bacteria naturally present in sewage treatment plants. Compounds with very slow biological breakdown were termed 'hard'. The cause was found to be the branching of the alkyl chain which is not commonly found in natural organic materials. Straight chain alkyl groups were developed and these proved to be 'soft'. It has been agreed in the UK that only 'soft' surfactants are used.

Enzymes
It has been claimed that use of an enzyme-based detergent can produce dermatitis when handling the solution, and skin irritation and dermatitic effects from clothes washed in these products. However, it should be realized that the quantity

of enzyme preparation in the product is low, around 0.5 per cent w/w. Therefore it is unlikely to be the cause of these complaints. It is a wise precaution to wear rubber gloves for all washing activities especially when using heavy-duty cleaning products, as many of the chemical ingredients can produce skin complaints.

Compatibility

Many cleaning products are a complex mixture of chemical compounds. The manufacturer must ensure that the materials do not react with one another, i.e. they should be *compatible*. If two compounds are known to react with one another and so alter the properties of both, they are said to be *incompatible*. For the same reason it is important that the user should be aware of the dangers involved and therefore not mix cleaning agents.

Many examples of incompatibility have been mentioned in this chapter. One of the most serious is the reaction of soap with hard water salts – calcium and magnesium salts – to produce insoluble calcium and magnesium soaps, known as scum. Soap is also incompatible with acidic solution, the fatty acid is precipitated.

Another example of incompatibility is the reaction between anionic and cationic surfactants. This means that they cannot be used together. When they are used in the same operation, for example, when a anionic detergent is used followed by a cationic fabric conditioner, then the fabric must be well rinsed after washing before the conditioner is added.

Chlorine-based compounds are incompatible with acids and ammonia solutions as mentioned on page 35. Where they are being used as disinfectants, then chlorine-based compounds are incompatible with any form of organic matter. The working strength of the solution is reduced as the organic matter is oxidized. It is therefore good practise to remove excessive organic soiling before applying a chlorine-based disinfectant cleanser.

Synergism

Many commercial detergents contain a mixture

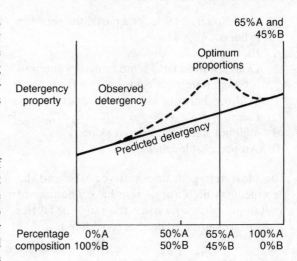

Figure 16 *Synergism produced by two surfactants A and B*

of surfactants. When two surfactants are added together it is observed that the detergency produced is greater than the predicted detergency, i.e. the sum of the two. This effect is known as synergism or mutual reinforcement. It seems that one surfactant can enhance the properties of the other, as illustrated in Figure 16.

This effect is not just restricted to surfactants, other chemicals can enhance the detergency properties of a surfactant. For example phosphates and silicates are known to do this.

The ideal detergent

The various chemicals used in the formation of detergents have been discussed in this chapter. The skill of the manufacturers is to blend the ingredients together to produce a product which will perform the cleaning task as efficiently as possible. The list given below highlights the properties of an ideal detergent.

1 Dissolves readily in water.
2 Good wetting properties.
3 Good emulsifying properties.
4 Removes dirt effectively and keeps it in suspension.
5 Good foam control – produces an adequate

stable foam suitable for a particular washing process.

6   Biodegradable.
7   Does not produce a scum in hard water and is compatible with acids.
8   Will not harm or discolour fabrics or surfaces.
9   Will not harm the human skin.
10 An acceptable smell.

The ideal detergent does not yet exist and the detergents available at present have a number of limitations, especially when the range of fabrics and surfaces to be treated is considered.

Disinfectants

Although disinfectants are not cleaning agents, they are used in the cleaning process. Disinfectants are used to remove or destruct harmful bacteria and not to clear away dirt. The problem is that disinfectants do not even kill all germs but they are acceptable to industry if they kill 99.99 per cent of known bacteria. In such a situation, 100 germs in every 1,000,000 will survive. In a ten-hour period, under favourable conditions, these 100 germs may multiply and produce 1,000,000,000 bacteria! In order that a disinfectant may kill bacteria there are several important points which must be borne in mind.

1   Using a suitable cleaning agent, a specific area must first be cleaned in order to remove the dirt. The disinfectant may then be used. A fluid disinfectant can only kill germs when it has been absorbed by them. If the area has been cleaned, the bacteria are now more accessible to the disinfectant.
2   Bacteria and fungi can increase their resistance to disinfectants. As with drugs in the human body or use of pesticides in farming, gradually stronger solutions have to be used to combat harmful situations. The trend in many hospital wards at present is not to use disinfectants for daily use but merely if there is an infection.
3   In order to be destroyed, bacteria need to absorb disinfectant. For this reason they should be suspended in a disinfectant solution. It is therefore wise to follow dilution directions carefully.
4   Bacteria have been known to survive in disinfection solutions – yet another reason to follow instructions precisely. If the solution is too weak, the disinfectant will have less killing power.
5   Disinfectant solutions are usually more effective if hot water is used.
6   In order to be effective, disinfectants need time to be absorbed by bacteria cells.
7   The effectiveness of disinfectants is also reduced by inactivating agents such as, vomit, urine, cotton floor cloths and mop heads, hard water, blood and even certain types of plastics and sponges.

Sterilization

Sterilization is the only successful way to destroy all living microbes. This is why the correct washing procedures are essential in laundries or such machines as Autoclaves are used in hospitals. It should be remembered however, that as soon as a sterilized item comes into contact with the human skin or even the air that we breath, it can become contaminated.

Note   At the time of writing, certain plastics containing biostats are being developed. Items produced from such a material will inhibit the growth of bacteria. In the future it is feasible that all items such as toilet seats will indeed be made of such material.

Conclusion

Developments are constantly taking place regarding new products and new cleaning methods. It is important to evaluate these properly before changing any system. Manufacturers and suppliers can be used effectively for information and advice regarding the use of their products.

Further reading

Allen, D., *Accommodation and Cleaning Services*, Vol. 1 (Hutchinson 1983).

Chalmers, L., *Chemical Specialities* (Godwin 1978).

Davidson, A., and Milwidsky, B. M., *Synthetic detergents*, 6th Ed. (Godwin 1978).

Kirk, D., and Milson A., *Services, Heating and Equipment for Home Economists* (Horwood 1982).

Useful addresses

Lever Brothers Ltd,
3 St James Road,
Kingston-upon-Thames,
Surrey KT1 2BA

The Proctor and Gamble Educational Service,
PO Box 1EE,
Gosforth,
Newcastle-upon-Tyne NE99 1EE

Unilever Education Section,
Unilever House,
Blackfriars
London EC4

Useful films

What is Soap?, *Outline of Detergency*, *Chemistry of Soapless Detergents*, *Hard Water*, *Physics and Chemistry of Water*, *Flourescers*, available from

The Scottish Council for Educational Technology,
Dowanhill,
74 Victoria Crescent Road,
Glasgow

Contract Cleaning & Maintenance Association,
Suite 75/76 Central Buildings,
24 Southwark Street,
London SE1 1TY

3 Cleaning routines

Public areas

These are found in all types of establishment. The cleaning routine adopted will depend upon the function of the establishment, and the type of person using it.

Lobbies and foyers

These are large circulatory areas, from which customers and clients receive their first impression of the establishment. Ideally, these areas should be cleaned between midnight and 7 a.m. or during a low period. In some establishments it is necessary for cleaning to be carried out constantly. In any case, tables must be wiped frequently, ashtrays emptied and cleaned, newspapers and magazines tidied and pieces removed from the carpet by the discreet use of a carpet sweeper or long-handled brush and dustpan. It is likely that in large establishments this area may be cleaned by contract cleaners. The cleaning of these areas may be the responsibility of the head porter or, in smaller establishments, the housekeeper. Whichever it is, he/she must make a point of meeting the cleaners responsible for the cleaning at least once a week.

Glass is usually very much in evidence in these areas – glass doors, screens, mirrors etc. and it may need daily attention over and above the periodic window cleaning services.

Steps and entrances should be clean – apart from appearance if these are not clean, dirt will be brought into the building. A brush should be kept at hand for swift sweeping during the day. A large doormat will also prevent dirt being carried in.

The warmth (or coolness) in contrast to the outside atmosphere is the most welcoming feature, but lighting is important to create the desired atmosphere. These are also waiting areas, so there should be comfortable chairs and tables, with adequate task lighting for reading. The whole area must be kept looking fresh and attractive, and light bulbs and fittings kept in working order. Clocks showing the correct time are essential. Since these areas receive a great deal of use and wear and tear, carpets and furniture will have a much shorter life than in other areas.

Residents' lounges

Most hotel bedrooms now have television and comfortable chairs, so residents' lounges are not used as much as in the past. Generally they should be as luxurious as the standard of the hotel warrants. Small tasteful objets d'art can create a luxurious atmosphere, and an interesting old clock, flowers or attractive furniture will add to the atmosphere. Standard lamps give good lighting for reading.

The carpet and furnishings can be of a more delicate colour than in the circulating area. Magazines (up to date) should be arranged on a side table. Sometimes a writing desk with notepaper is provided. This room (or rooms) will usually come under the control of the housekeeping department and be the responsibility of a regular maid or maids who will be familiar with what it contains and report any damage or missing items. Lights should be switched on by the staff at dusk, curtains drawn. During the day cushions should be 'plumped up', magazines tidied and ashtrays emptied.

Clinics, where the air of luxury and relaxation is important, are similar to hotel lounges. Day rooms in hostels, and hospitals should also be cheerful and attractive, although the furniture and furnishings will be of a more durable nature.

Lifts

These should be cleaned as part of a working schedule during the period of minimum use.

They should be put 'out of action' by using a special key, changing the control from automatic to manual. Floor, walls and ceiling should be cleaned appropriately depending upon the materials, and sprayed with a sanitizing liquid. There should be a 'No Smoking' sign both inside and outside and wall mounted or floorstanding ashtrays outside the lift.

Self-operating lifts should be inspected frequently during the day to see that they are in good condition. Airfreshener should be used several times during operational hours, but not have too pungent a smell. Lifts should be serviced regularly, usually by the makers or installers.

Restaurants, butteries and bars

Housekeeping is often thought to be concerned only with bedroom accommodation, but an equally important function is to ensure the smooth running and maintenance of standards in restaurants, canteens and all food and beverage service areas.

In small establishments the cleaning of these areas is frequently left to those involved with the service of food and drinks. Whoever does the cleaning of a food and beverage area, each person should be responsible for a defined area. The items within that area should be listed, and the order and frequency of cleaning set down.

Because of the nature of the soiling and the use of food service areas, they should be considered separately from the accommodation departments. Soiling occurs as a result of dust, nicotine staining, smoke from candles and flambé lamps, wine stains, grease, food crumbs, sugary deposits and odour absorption. In restaurants, often directly accessible from outside the building, there will be more street dust. There will be heavy concentration of staining from spillages from buffet tables, service hatches and counters and around and under tables and chairs.

The availability of restaurants and bars will determine when daily and weekly and periodic cleaning can be done.

Daily cleaning

Tables, chairs, dumb waiters, trolleys, window sills, skirting boards, doors and doorframes should be cleaned daily.

- Wipe any stickiness or grease with a cloth wrung out of a solution of detergent and water or vinegar and water. Dust and polish, paying attention to table and chair legs, and stretcher bars.
- Service counters should be washed and sanitized, soiled glass cloths removed.
- Wash or wipe and polish tablemats.
- Dust any artefacts.
- Vacuum carpets, spot clean any recent soiling, or attend to floor depending on the nature of it.
- Attend to flowers, candles, lamps, and replace on tables.
- Wash trays and ashtrays.
- Report any unusual soiling or evidence of pests.
- After each session, see tables and floors are free of crumbs (carpet sweeper may be adequate for this), spot clean any recent soiling.

Weekly cleaning

- Clean mirrors, glass shelves, wash all vases.
- Dust pictures, frames and glass.
- Clean silver and any metals not lacquered, cutlery and plate.*
- Use cobweb brush on high ledges, cornices, lamp brackets.
- Wash and polish trays.*
- Remove stains from tea and coffee pots.*
- Dust high shelves, picture rails, door frames, light brackets and bulbs.
- Remove darkened bulbs.

Periodic cleaning

- Clean windows, paintwork and walls, picture glass.

---

* In large hotels these jobs would normally be done by the stewarding department (wash-up).

- Vacuum upholstery and curtains.
- Wash and clean light shades.
- Clean carpets, curtains.
- Wash drapes.
- Clean grills and extractor fans/vents.*

To each daily cleaning list one or two of the weekly duties should be added. The periodic cleaning can be done at off-peak periods in the week, or season or at night.

Function rooms

A plan of the function room should be made to help the customer, banqueting organizer and housekeeping staff. It can be done using cardboard cut-outs.

The housekeeper should also be given details of the function, including name of customer, date, room used, type of function, time, numbers, whether a mixed group, menu, whether flowers are required, any special requests, whether a cloakroom attendant is required, number of waiting staff.

With this information the housekeeper can organize the things for which the department is responsible.

- The furniture, tables and chairs should be dusted and cleaned as required.
- The room should be cleaned and the carpet vacuumed.
- Tablecloths should be made available for the waiting staff.
- Linen napkins (if requested) and waiter cloths should be counted out.
- Flowers should be left in water for a few hours before being arranged, and the oasis should be soaked. The flowers should be arranged and left ready to go on the tables shortly before the guests arrive.
- Check all lights and that heating/hotplate points are functioning. (In large hotels this may be done by a banquet porter, responsible to the food and beverage department.)
- Curtains should be drawn for an evening function even if it is not dark when the guests

arrive. It may be difficult to draw curtains when there are guests in the room. The room should be well aired, and warm for the arrival of the guests, and if possible the heating reduced during the time it is in use. (In large hotels this will be the responsibility of the duty engineer or banquet head waiter.)

- Attend to any special requests.
- Cloakrooms should be clean and fresh. Toilet paper, soap and sanitary pad dispensers should be full. Check ashtrays and waste paper bins. Coathangers, cloak room tickets must be available. A pincushion with pins and safety pins, a clothes brush and tissues are all useful things to have available and show thought and care on behalf of the establishment. The cloakroom attendant might also have a sewing kit. A function unit should have its own first aid box.

Discussion with the person responsible for functions, the Banquetting Manager if there is one, is very important and have established what preparation, and in particular, what clearing up the waiting staff will do.

The waiting staff may be provided with uniform, if so it will be the responsibility of the housekeeper to see that it is ready for use.

In establishments where rooms have dual purpose, there may be much movement of furniture, and it is advisable to supervise the furniture removal and storage of it. Corridors should not be cluttered and no heavy or sharp edged items placed on top of upholstered furniture. Tables and large pieces of furniture should be handled carefully and eased round doorways sideways to avoid damaging paintwork and the furniture itself. All the profit from the function can be lost if there are repairs to be made on valuable items of furniture, and redecoration is required.

After a function the room and furniture should be looked at for soiling and cigarette burns. The linen should be unfolded in case items have been wrapped up, (coloured paper napkins, for example, will stain) and for wet patches which may cause mildew stains while awaiting laundry collection.

Air the room thoroughly and use airfresheners,

so it is fresh for inspection by potential customers. A function room 'after the ball' is not a cheerful sight and should be made clean and fresh as soon as possible. If functions are not regular business, it may be necessary to have a team of cleaners to call upon for the occasions, in the same way that the extra waiting staff come in for functions.

Check that fire extinguishers have not been tampered with and are in their correct place.

Service areas

Sluices in hospitals and service areas in hotels need cleaning as much as other areas. They may not be available at the time adjacent areas are being cleaned, but at a convenient time they should be cleaned. To facilitate hygienic conditions the surfaces, walls and floor should be of an easy-clean finish. Shelves should be at a convenient height and width for easy cleaning. A dado at trolley height will prevent the walls from being damaged.

In the bedroom service rooms there should be a sink/sluice with hot and cold water, for washing mops and buckets. Waste bins should be designated for different types of waste. There should be lockable cupboards for cleaning agents and equipment, and separate cupboards for bedroom supplies, such as tea and coffee. The cleaning of the service room should be a designated job.

Offices

In establishments, offices are in use around the clock, so it is sometimes very difficult to maintain a high standard of cleanliness. The housekeeper should discuss the most convenient time to clean such areas with the people who work there. In some cases it might be better to have a gang of cleaners to 'have a blitz clean' from time to time.

The majority of office workers, however, use their offices during the day. This facilitates cleaning services early in the morning or in the evening. Such cleaning jobs are often ideal for part-time staff or contract cleaners.

The standard to which an office is kept clean and tidy often has a psychological effect on both the user and visitors to the office. It is of utmost importance that guidelines are laid down as to the cleaner's responsibilities.

It sometimes may be necessary to encourage the users of the offices to be more tidy themselves, to prevent mishaps such as vital papers being thrown away.

Consulting, waiting and interview rooms

These should be light, cheerful and comfortable in order to put the occupants at ease. Ascertain from the consultants what is required by them, and make a check list of their requirements, to which the member of staff attending to the rooms can refer.

Waiting rooms should have comfortable chairs, a coat rack and umbrella stand. People in waiting rooms are often under pressure. Pictures, flowers and/or plants, magazines and newspapers will add interest and help those waiting to relax. Consider the people using the rooms, and imagine how they will be feeling, and what will help to put them at ease.

If children are likely to be clients, a low table and a few indestructible toys and some picture books will keep them interested.

If smoking is allowed, there should be ashtrays which are emptied frequently.

The lighting should be adequate for reading and the room warm.

In an interview room, the interviewer will require a desk or table, which should be arranged so that he/she is not facing the light. Arrange the furniture so that both interviewer and interviewee are seated at an angle to the window. The interviewee may need a small table near his/her chair. These rooms should be ventilated and aired after use.

Medical consulting rooms and laboratories

These should be clinically clean to the same standards as hospital cleaning to prevent cross-contamination and to ensure the success of experiments in laboratories.

Computer installations

These must be absolutely dust free. Dust control mats should be used both outside and inside the main door to the computer room. The floor should be vacuumed with machines that are adequately equipped with filters.

Hard floors can be dry-mopped with the 'forsaga type mop' which uses disposable mop heads which collect dust through the static electricity in the atmosphere. The temperature and humidity levels should be checked daily to ensure the atmosphere is constant.

Libraries

The main purpose of a library is to house books, and these attract dust like any other item in a room. The books should be removed periodically and the shelves dusted and polished. The books should not be pulled out by the top of the spine – nor packed so tightly that it is impossible to get one's fingers round the spine. To remove dust from the top of the book, gently bang two books together and use a soft clean hand brush to brush round the edges of the pages, or use the soft brush attachment of a vacuum cleaner.

Task lighting is obviously very important in any library.

Libraries also house visual display equipment, audio and video cassettes, microfiche and microfilm. Equipment for viewing needs to be dusted, kept covered and protected, since it collects a lot of static dust.

Communal toilet areas

These should be clean and hygienic. Ideally there should be an attendant present, but if this is not possible they should be inspected frequently.

Generally in hotels, restaurants, cafeterias canteens, the cloakrooms and toilet areas should be checked in the morning after the daily cleaning, and after lunch, before dinner and last thing at night. The person responsible should ensure that no noxious matter is left, no taps dripping and and that the plugholes are free. There should be an aerosol spray available for the removal of graffiti. Ashtrays should be emptied and cleaned and soiled paper towels removed. Fresh supplies of soap, towels and toilet rolls should be delivered. Hand basins and toilet seats should be rubbed down (with different cloths) and lost

property collected and handed over to the correct authority.

Swimming pools, saunas and gymnasia

These should be spotlessly clean because of the risk of bacteria flourishing.

Outdoor pools need special attention. They should be kept covered when not in use to prevent leaves clogging the filters. The walled surfaces need to be vacuumed daily to prevent the build-up of algea. The chlorine content of the water and the functioning of the filter need to be checked.

The pool surround should be clean and safe, and the foot bath (if there is one) should have the water and disinfectant changed regularly and frequently depending on the amount of use.

Neglected swimming pools, saunas and sitz baths, Turkish bath areas and patio slabs or tiles can have a build up of mould and outside there may be moss. This can be removed by scrubbing with a deck brush or a nylon scouring pad and water to which bleach is added. The strength of the solution depends upon the severity of the growth. On patio concrete slabs or bricks a red brick can be used like a scrubbing brush as an abrasive medium to remove stubborn growth. When bleach has been used, the area should be thoroughly rinsed with clean cold water.

Examples of work routines for public areas

Routine or daily tasks
1   Dust all surfaces from high to low areas. This will include all pictures, ledges, tables and chairs.
2   All ashtrays to be emptied and washed out.
3   All waste paper bins to be emptied.
4   All flower arrangements checked and water changed.
5   Lifts dusted and vacuumed.
6   All carpets vacuumed – any spots to be removed.
7   All hard floors to be dry mopped and then spray buffed.
8   Finger marks to be removed from all doorways and other glass panels.

9 Toilet areas to be cleaned. Toilets to be checked constantly throughout the day.

10 Lounge area to be checked constantly throughout the day.

Periodic work – weekly or monthly

1 All ventilation ducts to be cleaned. Vacuum with a soft brush attachment and then wash grilles with a neutral detergent solution.

2 Wash and polish all wood work.

3 Dust or vacuum walls.

4 Clean all directional signs.

5 Clean all light fittings.

6 Send cushion covers to be laundered.

Occasional work – yearly or as necessary

1 Shampoo carpets.

2 Scrub and reseal floors.

3 Wash down washable walls.

4 Wash down all doors and doorframes.

5 Vacuum ceiling tiles.

Bedrooms

Although the cleaning or servicing of bedrooms varies from establishment to establishment, the basic tasks are always the same. This section will concentrate on the servicing of hotel bedrooms.

In many hotels, the rooms provide the greatest income. In order to help to maintain standards and sales, the Housekeeper's product (the rooms) must be sold in perfect condition.

The business function of the housekeeping side of the operation has to be managed professionally. Only by thorough training and good work procedures and policies can the housekeeping function be run efficiently.

Duties of a day maid

1 *Appearance check*

When the day maid comes on duty, he/she reports to the housekeeper's office and the appearance is checked by the supervisor. The uniform should be in a good state of repair. A good general appearance sets standards and gives confidence to the maid and the guests. The supervisor can also use the occasion to notice if the maid is ill or unhappy.

2 *Issued with key*

For security reasons, master keys should be signed out at the beginning of a shift and signed in again at the end of a shift. The maid's key should be kept about the person at all times in order to prevent theft or loss. It may be secured round the waist by a chain or leather thong or be attached to an expandable key ring and clipped to the uniform.

3 *Issued with work sheet*

The work sheet should be prepared beforehand by the supervisor, who receives all the necessary information from reception or the front office as it is sometimes known. It includes details of arrivals, VIPs, special requests (e.g. cots, rollaway beds, bedboards, flowers etc.), expected departures, tour or group movements, in order that the maid knows what lies in store. Special details may also be given at this time by the supervisor, for example, 'Please clean all the departure rooms first as there is a tour checking in at 1.00 p.m.'

4 *Issued with cleaning supplies, equipment and linen*

The issue and control of these 'tools of the trade' varies from establishment to establishment.

In some hotels there is a large maid service area on each floor which contains

Linen cupboard
Stores cupboard for guest supplies, e.g. writing paper and soap
Equipment cupboard for dusters, cleaning supplies, vacuum cleaner etc.
Wash basin and sluice sink
Toilet
Area to park the trolley
Telephone
Computer terminal displaying rooms status on that particular floor
Table/desk and a chair
Hatch to linen chute, where dirty linen may fall directly down to the laundry

If a properly equipped service as described above is on the premises, then there is no need for supplies to be issued in the housekeeper's office. The advantage of issuing them in the office, however, is that a very tight control may be kept on the amount of stock issued and used by staff.

5   *Packs trolley*

This holds the supplies and equipment ready for the day's work. In some cases it is preferable to have the trolley stacked for the next day, before the maid goes off duty, so ensuring an early start the following morning.

6   *Checks rooms status*

The maid either does a physical check to see whether the rooms are vacant, occupied or departures, or uses the computer terminal. With this information he/she can then proceed to clean the rooms without disturbing guests. In some hotels an early status check enables reception and housekeeping to do a comparison report on the exact occupancy level of the hotel for accountancy and record purposes.

7   *Cleans rooms*

The order of cleaning is directed by the floor supervisor.

As the maid cleans each room, he/she marks the work sheet with the appropriate information, ticking the rooms off when each has been finished. Under the remarks column, he/she may indicate repairs and maintenance or that a guest is 'not packed' if he or she is supposed to check-out. Under 'beds slept in' column, he/she indicates the number of guests using the room so that a tally can be made with reception at the end of the afternoon, for accountancy purposes.

Room cleaning procedure

Different housekeepers and companies prefer the guest bedrooms to be cleaned in different ways. The procedure given is therefore simply an example.

1   Knock on door. If room vacant proceed to clean. Wedge door open. Place trolley across doorway.

2   Open curtains. Open window if possible.
3   Collect used magazines and newspapers. Empty ashtrays and waste paper bin.
4   Make bed.
5   Dust/damp dust/polish. Clean mirror. *Dust from high to low surfaces*.
6   Replenish guest supplies such as laundry bags and laundry lists, writing paper.
7   Vacuum clean carpet. *Work from far side of room towards entrance*.
8   Inspect for neatness. Check for lost property; maintenance repairs; tidy curtains, cushions, bedspreads, etc.
9   Turn off lights

Bed making procedure

There are many ways of making a bed and the procedure given is just one example. Many American hotel companies use the method known as 'The Correct Maid', whereby the maid need only walk around the bed once to do the job rather than be tired moving backwards and forwards. In European countries, where duvets are used, a different method is required.

A   *Stripping*
1   In occupied rooms, remove the guests night clothes. Fold neatly/hang behind bathroom door.
2   Remove bedspreads, blankets and pillows. Place on chair – never on floor!
3   Remove dirty linen.
4   Check if underblankets, pillow underslips, blankets and bedspreads need cleaning.
5   Allow bed to air if possible.

B   *Making up*
1   Smooth out underblanket.
2   Open out and place bottom sheet into position.
3   Make secure – mitre corners.
4   Open out and place top sheet into position.
5   Put blanket in position.
6   Turn back top sheet at head end and secure.
7   Secure bed clothes at foot of bed. Mitre corners.

8 Put on bedspread. Check that it hangs evenly. Fold back head end.
9 Renew pillow cases.
10 Put pillow in position. Open end of pillow case facing away from room entrance.
11 Turn back bedspread to cover pillow.
12 Inspect for neatness.

Key points to be observed when servicing bedrooms

The maid should work as quietly as possible, so as not to disturb guests. Banging equipment about also causes unnecessary damage. Cleaning must be thorough – in, under, on top and behind everything. Final appearance is of utmost importance – this makes the first impression on the guest on entering the room. If a picture is crooked, it may spoil the look of the room and reflect on the attitude of the maid. Courtesy toward the guest is important.

- Check for a 'Do not Disturb' or 'Please make up my room now' card.
- Always knock on the door before entering the room.
- Always greet the guest in the corridor.
- Do not touch any of the guest's belongings.
- Be willing to help the guest – this is usually simply a case of providing relevant information.

Economy is important.

- Check air conditioning or heating system.
- Switch off lights and taps.
- Distribute only the prescribed amount of 'give aways'.
- Take care not to damage fixtures, fittings and furnishings.
- Report any damage or repairs as soon as possible.

Security should always be observed.

- Close windows and doors properly.
- Take care with keys.
- Report suspicious occurrences.
- Hand in lost property immediately.
- Work with trolley parked across the open door or as otherwise instructed.

The following equipment is used for cleaning bedrooms

- Vacuum cleaner and attachments
- Trolley
- Dusters and polishing cloths
- Chamois or imitation leather
- Door stop or wedge
- Recepticle for rubbish
- Deck scrubber or squeegee mop ⎫ for hard
- Bucket and floor cloth ⎬ bathroom
- Cleaning cloths ⎭ floors
- Glass cloth
- Bottle brush in a jar for plug holes
- Cobweb brush (not feathers)

Cleaning agents used for cleaning bedroom areas

With modern surfaces such as melamine or formica the only cleaning agent that is required is water with perhaps a little neutral detergent. However, other items would normally be issued to the maid or cleaner.

Furniture polish – aerosol, liquid or wax paste according to the type of furniture.

Carpet shampoo and other stain removal agents (to be used only after special training and supervision).

Floor cleaning agents, such as detergents and polishes, if there is no carpet.

Detergent for general cleaning.

Deodorants/air fresheners (to be used only when really necessary).

Fly and insect sprays.

Glass cleaner for windows, pictures and mirrors (some establishments simply use water plus vinegar or methylated spirit).

Cleaning routines

There are basically three types of cleaning routine and it is the housekeeper's responsibility to set and control the tasks to be completed in each routine as well as to stipulate the standard to which the tasks are to be done.

Routine work – daily tasks This is basic work done on a regular daily basis.

Periodic work – weekly or monthly tasks This is work which does not need doing every day but must be done from time to time in order to avoid build up of dirt and to keep up appearances.

Occasional work – yearly tasks This work is often termed 'spring cleaning', when an area is given a thorough clean. As the cleaning is very detailed, the work needs to be well planned and carried out at an appropriate time.

Examples of each category are given below.

Daily or routine work

1 Check room, wardrobe and drawers (if a departure), take any 'lost property' to house-keeper and report any apparent new damage in order to try and catch the guest before departure.
2 Remove any trays, soiled crockery, dead flowers, etc. Empty waste bins and wipe interior. Empty ashtrays and wipe.
3 Strip bed(s), fold soiled linen and place on trolley. Remove towels, face flannels from bathroom, fold and put on trolley. Change bedcover if necessary.
4 Brush or hand vacuum upholstered furniture, feel down sides of the cushions for stray objects.
5 Dust all surfaces including television screen, telephone and light bulbs.
6 Dust interior of wardrobe, clothes rail, draw-ers, shelves, etc. Replace any missing coat-hangers.
7 Spray polish all hardwood surfaces.
8 Spot clean carpet if necessary and vacuum.
9 Replenish amenities tray and replace plants/flowers, etc.

Bathroom

1 Clean handbasin, bath, bidet and lavatory and adjacent walls.
2 Wipe towel rail and shower curtain rail.
3 Check shower curtain, change if necessary.
4 Wipe shelves, skirting boards, doors and door frames, polish mirrors.
5 Replenish soap and dispensers.
6 Replace clean towels.
7 Sanitize sensitive areas; overflows, outlets, lavatory seat, door handles.

8 Check lights and electric sockets.
9 Flush toilet.
10 Clean the floor.

Note: Never allow clean linen to be left on the floor outside the bedroom door, nor soiled linen piled in corridors. Trolleys provided should be used, or collapsible shelves or window-sills in the corridors will eliminate this common but unde-sirable habit.

Periodic work (weekly or monthly tasks)

1 Bedroom doors and door frames to be washed and polished. Brass strip to be scrubbed and polished (if at the carpet join).
2 Walls to be washed, marks attended.
3 Furniture to be washed down using one-third part vinegar to one part water.
4 All lamps to be wiped and shades cleaned.
5 All mirrors and pictures to be cleaned including television screen and fire precau-tion notices.
6 Curtains to be washed or cleaned if neces-sary, curtain rail and hooks to be checked.
7 Bed bases checked, vinyl areas washed, upholstery vacuum cleaned, bed legs and castors tightened.
8 Mattress checked, vacuum cleaned and turned. All bedding to be cleaned.
9 Upholstered furniture vacuumed and sham-pooed.
10 Telephone to be cleaned.
11 Windows, window-frames and window-sills washed and polished.
12 Skirting board to be cleaned.
13 All waste and san-bins to be washed out.
14 Mini-bar to be cleaned and defrosted, kettle to be de-scaled.
15 Wardrobes to be cleaned internally, drawers wiped out and re-lined where necessary.
16 Light switch and wall socket plates to be wiped.
17 Carpet to be vacuumed, paying attention to carpet edges, using suction attachment; shampoo if necessary.
18 Stationery folder and notices to be replaced as necessary.

Occasional work – yearly tasks

A *Prepare the room*

1 Remove all linen and bedding. All these items must be cleaned.
2 Remove all soft furnishings – cushion covers and curtains. Send for cleaning.
3 Take down pictures and mirrors and table lamps. (Flex should be tidily rolled up.) These items should be stored away to prevent breakages. (They may be put in the wardrobe.) Other loose articles e.g. ashtrays, waste bin etc, should also be stored away.
4 Move furniture into storage areas. (French polishing and re-upholstering etc. may take place at this time.)
5 Should redecoration be necessary, the decorators may now move in.

Note Should no storage space be available, furniture may be placed in the centre of the room and covered over with dust sheets.

B *Cleaning*

1 Start from high to low surfaces. Ceilings may be washed or vacuumed. Walls and wall coverings may be washed or vacuumed. Paintwork to be washed down. (Wall washing to be done from bottom, upwards.)
2 Shampoo carpet, allow to dry and then vacuum.
3 Furniture to be washed down, polished and put back into position. Upholstery to be shampooed.
4 Beds should be vacuumed and mattresses turned. They may then be put back into position.
5 Pictures and mirrors to be cleaned and re-hung.
6 Lamps should be cleaned. Lamp shades may be vacuumed or washed, according to material. Place into original position.

C *Making ready*

1 Hang clean curtains.
2 Put on clean cushion covers.
3 Make up beds with clean bedding.
4 Dust all furniture and fittings.
5 Replenish guest supplies.

6 Vacuum carpet.
7 Check that everything has been cleaned to standard required and that everything is in good working order.
8 Return room to reception.
9 Complete room history report/record.

Bathroom and toilet areas

Dirt in these areas comes from a variety of sources.

1 Mineral deposits from hard water.
2 Human organic matter, grease, dead skin, hair and excreta.
3 Toilet preparations, talcum powder, nail varnish, hair spray, oils, creams and toothpaste.
4 Moulds produced by moisture (steam and condensation), organic and mineral matter.
5 Dust from towels and carpets.
6 Dirt brought in from outside on shoes and clothing.

Some of these can be avoided by using preventive measures.

1 Deposit from hard water can be reduced by installing a water softener.
2 Frequent and regular cleaning will reduce build-up of deposits.
3 The judicious use of germicides will reduce the risk of infection.
4 Immediate attention given to dripping taps will prevent the blue or rust stain, from a copper or iron deposit.
5 Avoidance of the use of cleaning agents containing an abrasive agent which produce their own deposits.
6 Good ventilation.

Baths, hand basins and showers

A squirt of liquid detergent and a rub down with a warm, wet, lintless cloth or plastic foam or J-cloth should remove normal scum without damaging the surface. It is also harmless to the skin. Persistent soiling can be removed by the use of a nylon scouring pad. Special attention should be paid to the area round the taps, and the edges of the basin and shower trays. Overflow outlets should be cleaned with a bottle brush. If this is kept in a small jar of germicide, the risk of spreading bacteria will be reduced and if done daily, a build-up of slime will be avoided. Plug holes should also be cleaned with the bottle brush and hairs removed with a hair pin or skewer. Dripping taps can cause stains, which can be removed using a proprietary brand of bath stain remover.

Sanitary fittings should be dried off with a clean cloth or disposable towel, not a soiled guest towel! Grab rails, soap dishes, taps and plugs should be cleaned, dried and finally buffed up. When a descaler has been used, it should be thoroughly rinsed off, since it will 'lift' the plating on chromium fittings. Rubber gloves should be worn when using descaler and care taken so that it does not come in contact with the eyes.

Lavatory pans

The toilet should be flushed and then the prescribed cleaning agent squirted round the inside of the toilet pan while scrubbing well with the toilet brush. The bend should be cleaned below the water level and underneath the rim at the top of the pan. The toilet should be flushed, rinsing the lavatory brush, and the cistern and outside surface of the lavatory pan and seat cleaned. All the surfaces should be dried with a cloth. The seat and upper and lower surfaces of the lid should be polished, and toilet paper and sanitary bag supply replenished. The underside of the rim of the pan should be checked with a mirror: it is surprising what grime it may reveal!

The sani-bin should be emptied by the cleaner or, if it is the sealed type, it should be emptied regularly by the contractors. Any faults in the toilet mechanics should be reported.

Shower heads

These should be removable and the type which is self-draining will prevent warm water being retained and offering the ideal environment for bacterial growth. Shower heads should be regularly soaked in a descaling agent (kettle descaler or white vinegar) and holes cleared with a stiff brush or a pin.

Shower screens

The more complicated the screen or shower door, the more difficult it is to keep in good condition. They should be washed with a mild alkaline detergent, using a brush to get into crevices, thoroughly dried, and polished with a spray furniture polish.

Shower curtains

Glass fibre, cotton and polyester curtains should be washed gently avoiding wringing and twisting and after rinsing hung up to drip dry. Plastic shower curtains should be brushed with a soft scrubbing brush and alkaline detergent. They should be dried off with a cloth, paying attention to hems where dirt will accumulate. Moulds can be removed with a weak solution of bleach, but it should be tested first as there is the risk of removing the colour. The curtain rail should be dusted and polished with spray polish, or simply wiped and buffed up.

Danger spots

In areas where cross infection is a hazard (see Figure 17), the use of an iodine-based germicide spray is effective.

A specialist service can be employed to carry out regular inspections. They will examine all fittings and fitments and pin-point trouble spots. They can scale down build-up of dirt and examine the drains and plumbing. They can also carry out a regular disinfection of the whole sanitary area.

Alternatively, this can be done by an in-house maintenance team. Housekeeping staff should know how to deal with simple emergencies like blocked drains, using a suction bell, or washing soda. A piece of curtain wire is also sometimes effective.

Cleaning agents

The cleaning agents chosen will depend on budget restrictions, company policy, surfaces to be cleaned, personal preferences and hygiene restrictions. Discount price is perhaps the least good reason for selection, and it should not be the only reason.

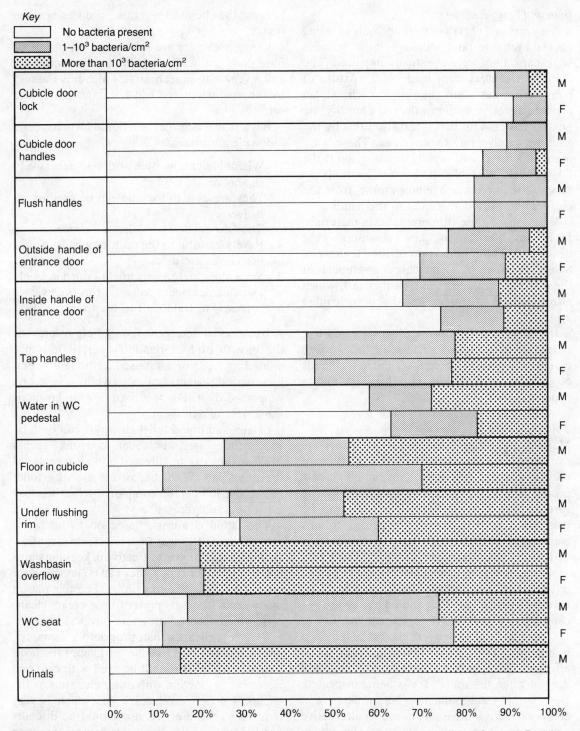

Figure 17 *Total colony counts. Courtesy of M. F. Mendes and D. J. Lynch, Research and Development Division, Rentokil Ltd, East Grinstead.*

Bath and basin cleansers

Some years ago abrasives were the only cleaning agents available, and although most surfaces were hard, they were eventually impaired. The abrasive cleansers were made of a mixture of pumice powder and chlorine bleach or an alkaline agent (a soap powder) to emulsify the grease. Pastes were developed from this by the addition of glycerine or soft soap. These were more expensive, and rapidly deteriorated if the lid was not firmly replaced after use. These cleansers also required much 'elbow grease' from the cleaner and were detrimental to the hands.

With growing use of more delicate materials, for baths and basins, new cleansers were developed. The introduction of the Health and Safety at Work Act, increased awareness of the effect of cleaning agents on the staff, which also encouraged the develoment of new cleaning agents.

If and where an abrasive cleanser is used it should be with caution because of the damage that may be done to the surface, and to the hands of cleaning staff. It can also leave behind a deposit.

Toilet cleansers

Many of the proprietory brands of cleaner are overrated and the extravagant use of them is unnecessary and expensive. They can also create problems by building up their own deposit. The careless use of these harsh chemicals can be dangerous. It is extremely dangerous to mix chemical cleaners: bleach used in conjunction with other cleansers, for example, can cause asphyxia. Sanitizing channel blocks can be placed in the rim of the lavatory, but these should be used with discretion. They should not be used to camouflage a permanent unpleasant smell.

Crystalline toilet cleansers should be left for a minimum period of two hours in order to be effective. They could be left by the cleaner and flushed when the toilet area is being inspected. However, in establishments where toilets are in continual use it is advisable to use an alternative agent. Crystalline agents should never be used in conjunction with any other cleaning agent,

because the chemical reaction produces noxious fumes.

Cream cleansers are safe to use on plastic or fibre glass baths. These have an ammonia base and a very soft, fine abrasive which it is claimed by the manufacturers, will not damage delicate sur.aces.

Bactericidal detergents in liquid form have the following advantages:

1 When bought in bulk are not excessively expensive.
2 They are easy to use and can be used on all surfaces.
3 They do not scratch delicate surfaces.
4 Rarely harmful to the user, especially if rubber gloves are used.
5 Since these detergents are 'all purpose' only one cleanser needs to be on the trolley.
6 It is easy to train staff to use them.

A bactericidal detergent should help to prevent the growth of bacteria. However, if it is not diluted correctly or if it is used continually over a long period, bacteria can survive in or even be supported by it. For this reason some hospitals use a neutral detergent.

Cream and liquid toilet cleansers can both be successfully used as toilet cleaning agents because they can be directed into all recesses of the toilet pan. With the correct use of a toilet brush, the job can be completed to satisfactory cleaning standards.

The liquid cleansers, based on hydrochloric acid are much stronger than the cream cleansers. Although they are very effective in keeping stains and water marks at bay, they can be dangerous if not used with care and caution. For this reason many establishments prefer to use cream cleansers, which need a little more physical effort.

Bleach is cheaper than proprietory cleansers, and it acts as a bacteriacide, and keeps the lavatory pan white. It should be used with care and never in conjunction with other cleansers as the chemical action produces a gas which is very harmful to the user. Its use should be discouraged, since it can do irreparable damage if spilt on carpets, clothing or linen.

Floor cleansers

There are many floor cleansers available, and the choice will depend upon the type of floor. A neutral or bactericidal detergent is suitable for most hard floors, which should be washed by hand or with a 'squeegee' mop. The floor should be swept first or vacuumed to remove fluff, dust, broken glass etc. The floor should be cleaned last, with the cleaner starting at the farthest point from the door, and continuing backwards to the door.

Sanitizers

This word has not yet found its way into the *Shorter Oxford Dictionary*, but comes from the word 'sanitary' 'pertaining to or concerned with the promotion of health'. By sanitizing one is reducing the microbes and bacteria to an acceptable level, but not destroying them. A disinfectant, however will destroy bacteria. Toilets and bathroom fittings can be sanitized, but where there is a danger of harmful infection, a disinfectant should be used. Because of the 'clean smell' of a disinfectant, it is often confused with a cleanser. However, it does not clean, and should not be used as a cleanser.

Deodorants and air fresheners

A deodorant can be used to remove a temporary unpleasant smell. It does this by ionization of the offending particles or by having a stronger odour than the smell.

Equipment

The following items of equipment will be used in bathroom and toilet areas.

1 Vacuum cleaner for carpeted areas.
2 Floor cloth and bucket.
3 Wet mop.
4 Deck scrubber.
5 Sponge/scourer.
6 Tea towel/glass cloth.
7 Toilet cloth.
8 Cleaning cloth for applying agent when required. Damp duster.
9 Rubber gloves.
10 Toilet brush and container.

Glass cloth

If tooth glasses are washed by hand they should be dried on a clean glass cloth or sent down to the 'wash-up' for sterilization. A separate glass cloth may be used to shine up bathroom mirrors. Glass cloths or tea towels used in the housekeeping department should be colour-coded for exclusive use in it. They should be laundered daily, or clean ones issued daily.

Sponge/scourers

A sponge/scourer, colour-coded disposable cloth or another type of cloth used to clean baths and basins, should be washed out after use each day and allowed to dry.

Toilet cloth

A separate cloth should be used exclusively for cleaning the external surfaces of toilets and bidets.

Floor cloth and deck scrubber

Hard floors should be vacuumed or swept, then washed by hand using a floor cloth, wet mopped or cleaned with a deck scrubber. After use, the floor cloth and mop should be washed and left to dry. The deck scrubber should be left to dry with the bristles hanging down to prevent them rotting.

Toilet brushes

They should be carried in a container, and after use washed and rinsed in a disinfectant solution, and left to dry. They should not be left in disinfectant in a plastic container since plastic deactivates disinfectant.

Rubber gloves

Staff should be issued with and encouraged to wear rubber gloves to avoid any skin reaction to the cleaning agents or contamination from sensitive areas. After use gloves should be washed and hung up to dry by the fingers.

Work routines

As in other areas, a routine of daily, weekly and occasional cleaning should be worked out. The following is an example.

Daily cleaning

- Remove all soiled linen, used tooth glasses and soaps.
- Empty waste and sani-bins and ashtrays.
- Sweep floor.
- Clean wash basin, shelf and mirror.
- Clean bath and shower tray including tiles and all fittings.
- Clean bidet and toilet.
- Damp dust any shelves, ledges, shower rail.
- Change shower curtain if necessary.
- Remove any marks from walls or door.
- Replace clean ashtrays.
- Clean the floor by whatever method is required for its surface.
- Note any necessary repairs.
- Replace sani- and waste bins after cleaning them.
- Replenish towels, soaps, tooth glasses, toilet rolls and guest supplies.
- Check the room to ensure that everything is clean and in good order.
- Take any lost property to the housekeeper or supervisor.

Weekly or monthly cleaning

- Change shower curtain.
- Wash down all tiles and walls. Pay special attention to grouting which may need scrubbing.
- Clean round all taps and plug holes.
- Clean overflows.
- Clean and polish bath panel.
- Wash all exposed pipes, or the casings.
- Wash behind and under toilet pans, hand basins and pedestals.
- Remove any hard water or other stains from baths and basins.
- Scrub plastic seal round the bath, basins and shower trays.
- Descale shower heads.
- Polish mirrors.
- Wash windows.

Many of these tasks are done daily, and if the daily cleaning is thorough, many should not be necessary.

Occasional cleaning

- Wash ceiling and walls, doors and door frames.
- Clean air vents.
- Wash light grilles or covers.
- Wash shower curtain rings.
- Wash carpet, if present, or reseal floor if necessary.

Inspection of bathrooms and toilets

Since bathrooms and toilet areas are very sensitive, scrupulous cleanliness is essential. When inspecting these areas the following check list should be used:

1   Plug holes and plugs.
2   Overflows.
3   Waste and sani-bins.
4   Air vents.
5   All corners and ledges where fluff or dust may accumulate.
6   Water marks or build-up of scale on any sanitary fittings.
7   No residue of any cleaning agent on sanitary fittings.
8   Shower curtain and rail.
9   Full complement of towels, new soap and any other toilet accessories that may be supplied by the establishment.
10 Tooth glasses in place or dispensers filled up.

Staff areas

It is desirable that the Staff Areas should be cleaned and well maintained as a designated job, allocated to one of the housekeeping staff or someone responsible to the head waiter, depending upon the area being serviced. A badly organized and neglected staff area will create the wrong attitude and cause breakages, damage and possibly pilfering. There should be the same supervision of the cleaning of the staff areas as there is in the public areas. Staff areas include: All back corridors; locker rooms and changing rooms; staff toilets and showers; offices; service areas and staff accommodation. The staff canteen and food and beverage services are normally cleaned by food and beverage staff.

Back corridors

Ideally these should be regularly decorated in bright or light colours as they rarely contain any natural light. The floors should have a non-slip finish and should be very hard-wearing and easy to clean. Modern rubber floor coverings are ideal. Lighting should be good to compensate for internal situations. All wall corners should be protected either by heavy duty plastic corners or metal edging. A stout wooden 'bumber bar' should be fitted to protect walls from trolleys and other equipment. The height of this bar is a critical feature.

Back corridors should be cleaned at least once a day, during a quiet period. Any ledges should be damp dusted, finger marks or spillage marks removed from the walls, and floors should be scrubbed and buffed up (if the surface requires such treatment). Lifts should also be thoroughly cleaned at least once a day.

Locker rooms

Locker rooms should be adequate in size and should be well ventilated. Lockers should be positioned off the floor and at a suitable height, to enable cleaning underneath. They are usually made from metal, so if they are positioned on the floor, they get damaged by cleaning machinery and the bottoms rust through when the floor is scrubbed. Locker rooms should also have benches or other seating arrangements.

It is desirable that the locks and locker keys are provided by the personnel office, so that, if a key is lost, stolen or forgotten, then the member of staff may still gain access to his or her uniform. If the personnel manager also holds a duplicate key, locker checks may be carried out if and when necessary.

Locker rooms should be thoroughly cleaned on a daily basis with special floor treatments taking place periodically. When an employee leaves, then the locker should be emptied and thoroughly cleaned out. From time to time lockers should be washed down and tops should be dusted on a regular basis. Ashtrays and bins should be emptied daily.

Staff accommodation

In hotels provision for staff accommodation can be expensive. It is becoming less common in the UK and Europe. However, in some hotels in isolated areas, or where transport is difficult, a house in the grounds may be used for staff accommodation and under the control of the housekeeper. Hospitals, boarding schools, and halls of residence in campuses provide staff accommodation, usually purpose built, and they are looked after as hostels.

In all establishments there is a statutory obligation to provide staff toilets and washing facilities. By law a minimum number of toilet units is required to be supplied for use of staff and guests.

It is essential that all toilet areas are kept scrupulously clean, but this is even more important for toilets being used by food handlers.

They should be cleaned at least once a day and checked during the day in a similar way to guests' facilities.

The policy on the care and cleaning of staff accommodation may be the responsibility of the directors or board of governors, and carrying out this policy is the responsibility of the housekeeper or domestic supervisor. Much time can be spent in tidying rooms before they can be cleaned, so guidelines should be drawn up on the responsibilities of the occupant. The occupant will usually have to make the bed daily, remove all dirty crockery, empty the waste bin, clean the ashtray, and tidy personal belongings.

Weekly or bi-weekly cleaning can then be done by cleaning staff. The occupants should be told on which days rooms will be cleaned, so that they can be left tidy. Cleaning staff should be instructed to note the state of the room, and if not acceptable to report it to the housekeeper. It is advisable for the staff maid to make the bed on bed-changing day, in order to see the state of the bed and bedding.

There should be adequate shelf and drawer space for staff to keep their personal belongings and to encourage tidiness. The housekeeper is at liberty to inspect drawers, cupboards and wardrobes. Dirty linen, stale food and dirty crockery secreted in cupboards are a health hazard.

There should be a drawer with a lock in the room for the occupant's private papers or possessions, but the rest should be available for inspection.

Any damage or unsavoury condition found in the bedroom should be reported and dealt with by the housekeeper, manager or personnel manager, who is responsible for staff accommodation.

Staff sitting rooms are an area which may give the housekeeper more headaches than the guests and public rooms. Staff rooms should be cleaned daily, with perhaps a rota of staff using the rooms responsible for seeing that they are left tidy before the cleaner comes in. Involve the staff in selecting a colour scheme for their room and select a finish that is easily refreshed and the colours changed. The furniture should be sturdy, with simple lines, removable cushions and with covers that can be easily laundered. It is not advisable to have the staff room furnished with broken and worn out furniture.

Fibre tiles for the floor look cheerful and are washable and replaceable. A natural leader comes up in every group of five or seven people in any community – allow him/her to take responsibility for compiling a tidying up rota. No room can have any semblance of tidiness unless there are places to put things, so storage space is vital.

If possible resident and daily staff should have separate sitting rooms.

Windows and mirrors

The exterior of windows and glass is usually cleaned by professional window cleaners, or by specialized maintenance staff. When asking for estimates from window cleaners, stipulate which windows will require cleaning monthly and which bi-monthly as some need cleaning more often than others. If interiors are to be included, state clearly which are to be done – some smaller windows can be cleaned by the establishment's own staff. Since security is of great importance when someone has access to premises, always ask for references and check the insurance cover.

The National Federation of Window Cleaners will supply the name of a local member and deal with complaints against its members.

Window cleaning aids and materials

There are a number of window cleaning tools and materials. Scrim (a woven jute material used with water) has a natural gum which helps to clean and it leaves no linters.

Chamois leather is also used with water. It is expensive and should be thick with no thin patches. It should be squeezed, not wrung out, to remove excess water, and after use rinsed and squeezed out and kept in a polythene bag. If allowed to dry out they become brittle. They should be used with plain water or vinegar and water, but not detergents which remove the natural oils. They are not very effective for removing grease.

Man-made leather substitute is a non-woven cloth which looks and feels like chamois but is cheaper than the real thing. It can be used with detergents.

Squeegees consist of a rubber blade set in a plastic or metal holder with a long telescopic handle. They are used with water or water and detergent. Long sweeping strokes from top to bottom apply the water, then strokes from side to side remove it. They are suitable only for large windows and outside use. The blades are replaceable. For exceptionally high and large windows, the water can be applied by a hose or a special water applicator.

Sponge squeegees have a sponge and blade incorporated in the same head. The surface dirt is removed by the sponge and water and detergent, then excess water removed by the blade.

Window brushes effectively remove heavy soiling, but leave the windows very wet. The excess water should be removed by using a sponge squeegee.

There are magnetic cleaners which clean the exterior of the window, while the inside is being cleaned, using a magnet inside the sponge. This is good in theory but in practice they rarely work, and they are useless where there is double glazing.

In addition to vinegar and water, plain water, water and detergents and methylated spirits, there are proprietary cleaners available as aerosols, liquid sprays or creams, which are most suitable for interior glazing and mirrors.

The fluid is a grease solvent, and creams contain a mild abrasive such as precipitate of whiting or jewellers rouge. When the fluid evaporates, there is often a dust left from the abrasive which can collect in crevices. Sprays should be used sparingly, and creams are not suitable for ridged or deeply patterned glass.

The cleaning of exterior glazing should never be attempted unless safety precautions are taken, and would generally never be undertaken by housekeeping staff. The exterior of some windows can be cleaned from the interior, for example, those which open on the inside of the build-ing or swivel windows. However, staff should never be allowed to sit on the window sill to perform this task.

Mirrors should be cleaned carefully, ensuring that no fluid penetrates at the edges to the back of the glass, where it will damage the silver backing. Use a tightly squeezed chamois or imitation leather, using water and vinegar, or a cream cleanser. The latter is not so suitable for framed mirrors since the fine powder precipitate can build up between the frame and the glass.

Aerosol polish should never be used on mirrors, as it tends to build up and smear.

4 Cleaning methods

Manual cleaning methods

Sweeping
A brush with either a short or long handle can be used. Use short smooth strokes, and sweep directly into a dust pan, avoiding spreading the dust. When using a long-handled brush, use smooth strokes and sweep away from yourself. Slightly damp tea leaves or a special dust control preparation sprinkled over a very dusty area will help to lay the dust.

Scrubbing
Very little hard scrubbing is required for modern surfaces. Scrub gently, in straight lines away from yourself. Rinse well to remove soap or detergent.

Polishing
Apply polish sparingly. Use one cloth for applying it and one for rubbing up or buffing. Use a soft brush for carved or engraved items, to get the polish into the crevices, and another for its removal.

Dry mopping
This is done with a cotton mop head, which may or may not be impregnated. Impregnation stops the dust rising. Use smooth figure-of-eight strokes. Carry the mop, head uppermost, very carefully where it may be shaken into a bag (not out of an open door or window) and cleaned.

Wet mopping
This should always be done with a bucket at hand, so the mop may be rinsed and squeezed after every few strokes. Rinse thoroughly and squeeze after use and hang up to dry. Always start either wet or dry mopping at the farther end of room or corridor and work backwards. When wet mopping is in progress, signs or notices should be placed indicating that the floor is dangerous to walk on. If signs are not available, some sort of barrier should be placed to prevent people walking on the wet area.

Dusting
A soft lintless cloth should be used. Avoid using any old rag which will leave its own dust as it disintegrates. Fold the corners into the centre of the duster and bunch into the hand so that loose corners are not left dangling. Do not open the duster out in the room being dusted, nor shake it from the window. Carry it carefully to where it can be washed when finished with. Start dusting an object at the top. Impregnated dusters will reduce the spreading of dust.

Damp dusting
This is preferred in many establishments, because airborne bacteria and dust are not so easily spread. Surfaces can be wiped as well as dusted, removing any dirty or sticky marks at the same time. A suitable cloth at the correct level of dampness should be used, so as not to leave smear marks. Unless the cloth is rinsed out after use it will become smelly and respread the already collected dirt.

Cleaning equipment

Good workmen always look after their tools, the aids which make their work easier.

A 'tool' is an aid that is used by hand, whereas a 'machine' is a tool that works with mechanical help. The only machine which is issued to room maids, is a vacuum cleaner and ideally each maid should be issued with her own.

Vacuum cleaners

Upright
There are three main drawbacks. The traditional vacuum cleaner is the faithful 'Hoover'. The older design of upright vacuum cleaners have several disadvantages. First, the bag is positioned on the outside of the machine, where it can easily be knocked when full, so tearing the inside bag and respreading the dust. Second, most upright cleaners are designed with a stout rubber bumper band round the base, preventing the head from banging into furniture and skirting boards and causing damage. However, it does prevent the user vacuuming right to the carpet edge, thus leaving a thick pile of fluff round the edge of the room. Third, many upright cleaners have a very deep head which does not always fit under furniture, especially beds. The handle is also sometimes a problem in that it is not adjustable enough to be lowered so allowing the head to penetrate under low furniture.

When purchasing a modern upright vacuum cleaner, the following points should be looked for.

1 Quiet motor.
2 Dust bag which can easily be emptied.
3 Dust bag fitted on the inside of the machine (in a plastic casing).
4 Thin head and an adjusting handle to enable the machine to reach under low furniture.
5 Brush adjustment to suit various depths of carpet pile.
6 Top entry for the dust bag, so that dust fills the bag in a natural manner rather than having to force its way past the hot motor and through accumulated dust in the bottom of the bag.
7 Practical access to the motor so that repairs, clearing blockages and replacement of rubber drive belt can take place.
8 Set of attachments suitable for carpet edges, furniture and soft furnishings etc.

Upright vacuum cleaners are not suitable for modern floor coverings or carpets that are stuck down to the floor or have a thick rubber backing. This is because of the design of this particular type of cleaner. Air is sucked into the head through the carpet and the beater bars dislodge the dust so that it can be sucked up into the bag. If the carpet is stuck down to the floor, then this princple cannot be applied, the carpet is not successfully cleaned and the vacuum cleaner wears out or is constantly in need of attention.

Cylinder
Cylinder style vacuum cleaners are also not without their problems. First, industrial designs must be bought as the domestic variety are not made for the purpose of constant use. Second, the dust bags need frequent changing and this can prove to be expensive if they are not the reusable type. Third, they topple over easily, which can be very annoying for the operator. Fourth, some hoses break very easily or are damaged by maids or room service trolleys running over them. Maids should therefore be taught to keep cylinder vacuums especially tidy while in a corridor area. Fifth, NHS regulations specify that vacuum cleaners need three filters and not all designs are able to meet this requirement. Cylinder style cleaners do however have their advantages. They are very flexible and clean under any piece of furniture. They can be used on hard as well as soft floors, because they have adjustable heads. They always come supplied with a set of attachments so that they can be used to clean furniture, beds and soft furnishings. Back pack models are also available for high dusting and the removal of cob webs.

Constellation
Constellation designs are usually round in shape. They are built to run on a cushion of air, rather like a hovercraft. A thick rubber bumper is fitted to the broadest part of the machine to prevent any damage by accidental bumping into furniture. Constellation models have similar advantages to cylinder styles and because of the fact that they are light and easy to use are ideal for the small older type of establishment where they need to be carried up and down steps.

Operation and care of vacuum cleaners

Dust and debris is collected in bags or canisters suitable for the type of machine.

1   Textile filter bag suitable for general cleaning of light fibrous dusts.
2   Metal canisters for the collection of sharp-edged debris, warm dust and liquids.
3   Disposable paper sacks used for the hygienic disposal of dust which may be of a toxic nature, used in conjunction with exhaust filters which clean the air before it is passed back into the atmosphere.
4   Plastic sacks used for immediate disposal of all types of dirt.

Some machines are fitted with two container bags. The dust-carrying air passes through a disposable filter bag, then through a textile filter bag, then through an exhaust filter cartridge. This is important in environments where there is risk of cross infection.

There are various attachments for both upright and cylinder cleaners for cleaning: hard floors, carpets, upholstery, radiators, cornices and pipes, light fittings, walls, crevices.

Machines will only work as efficiently as the care and maintenance allow them. Attention is required if the vacuum cleaner develops any of the following faults.

1   There is any change in the sound of the motor.
2   The debris circulating round the brushes and agitators is rattling.
3   The machine is failing to pick up.
4   There is dust collecting outside the canister or collection sack.
5   Any smell coming from the motor.
6   The motor and casing is getting hot.
7   Any apparent leakage.

Vacuum cleaners should be stored tidily after use, with the flex coiled up properly and kept in a place where they will not be damaged or tampered with. The dust bag or canister should be emptied regularly and accumulated dust and fluff removed from the blades, brushes, wheels and hose. The wheels should be oiled to prevent squeaking, but never touch the motor. The flex should be in good condition, with no bare wires. The plug should not be loose, cracked or damaged in any other way. As with any other piece of mechanical equipment, vacuum cleaners should be serviced regularly so that perfect performance may be maintained. Servicing may be done under contract with the supplier or by the establishment's own maintenance staff. Spare parts are often more easily replaced when a service contract or service agreement is in operation.

Central vacuuming system

This is built in the fabric of the building like a plumbing or central heating system. Usually in the basement there is a large motor and collection canister from which there are pipes leading to points all over the building to which different machines are connected. The dirt is carried along the pipes to the collection canister. The advantages of this system are that it is quiet in operation and a lighter appliance is used by the operator. The disposal of the dirt is made in one operation, instead of from individual machines, and the spread of bacteria is reduced. The apparatus used by the cleaner is simple and requires little maintenance.

The system does, however, have its disadvantages. It can only be installed during building, and this is expensive. If new wings are added at a later stage, and the system is not fitted exactly, efficiency may deteriorate. Long lengths of hose are required to reach from the outlet points. This can be dangerous, as people may trip or trolleys run over them.

This central vacuum system is not common in the UK, but it is found in some hospitals.

Carpet sweepers

These are hand-operated, requiring no electric power. They have one or two revolving brushes which throw the dirt and dust into the box containing the brushes, the base of which is hinged for emptying. Some models have additional brushes which loosen the dirt which a central brush sweeps up. Others have circular brushes at the front corners which sweep corners and edges of the carpet. They can be used on hard floors and have adjustable brushes which can be raised or lowered according to the floor surface.

They should be emptied frequently to prevent dust being respread. They are very useful for quickly removing crumbs or debris from floors between the cleaning schedules, for example, in a restaurant or foyer.

Dry mops

These are made of cotton yarn and fitted on to a metal or plastic stock, with either a long or short handle. They are used with or without impregnation of a cleaning and sanitizing fluid. There are four main types: horizontal dry mops, scissor dry mops, duster dry mops, and duster dry glove mitts/mops.

The National Health Service uses several types of disposable mop for the purpose of check cleaning. Check cleaning is done after the main cleaning of the day is complete, when the cleaner checks to see that the level of dust and fluff on the floor is minimal. A disposable mop head is used so that the dust collected is simply disposed of, reducing the problem of airborne bacteria in the ward. The two main types of disposable mop heads are heavy tissue paper, which is torn off a roll and clipped on to the mop head, and fine polythene with a fleecy backing, which attracts the dust by static. This 'forsaga' type of disposable mop head is torn by perforations from a roll, and attached to the mop head.

Dry mop heads can be used instead of damp dusting high ledges and radiators. Dry mopping is also used instead of sweeping, because it reduces the amount of dust rising and then resettling. It is used in conjunction with a vacuum cleaner or on its own, before hard floor maintenance. When floors are buffed or spray cleaned it is advisable to pass a dry mop over the floor to collect any particles of dust or residual spray. Dry mops with regular cotton heads should have the facility whereby they can be removed from the mop itself, for cleaning or sterilizing.

Wet mops

Wet mops are made from long cotton yarn. This yarn de-activates disinfectant, so they are not effective for use with disinfectant. Wet mops are available either with round heads, known as 'dolly mops', or flat heads known as 'fan tail mops'. Fan tail mops with cotton yarns, which have been stitched together, are the better type of mop, as the yarn will not break away from the mop head so easily. Trailing pieces of mop will not then be left on the floor, resembling dead rats' tails. Fan tail mops are also more hygienic, as they can be removed from the mop for washing and sterilization.

Dolly mop heads cannot be removed for cleaning, so they are less effective as a cleaning tool. The dirt is pushed deeper and deeper into the head and can then be re-distributed over the floor.

Wet mop buckets

In order to mop a floor efficiently, the buckets of water must be changed as frequently as possible to prevent dirt from being re-applied. The dolly mop is usually supplied with a colander-type wringer. After mopping the floor, the mop is dipped into the bucket and then wrung out by pressing it down and round. This action squeezes all the dirt back into the head, so that the water is immediately dirty.There is a compartment type of bucket which divides the clean water from the dirty, but this type does not solve the problem of dirt remaining in the mop head.

If mops and buckets have to be used, then a double bucket is the best type to have. One bucket contains the clean water, while the other is fitted with a roller wringer or press wringer. This system forces the operator to change the water regularly, because the bucket containing clean water becomes empty, as the level of dirty water rises in the neighbouring bucket. Double buckets are usually supplied on trolleys, thus making the operator's work easier.

'Step on' buckets are also available, but these have the same disadvantage as the dolly mop type of bucket. The operator wrings the mop out by using a 'roller wringer' which is attached to the bucket. Consequently, dirt is being returned to clean water. If an establishment has a supply of this type of bucket, a solution would be to purchase additional ordinary buckets and use them in conjunction with the mop buckets, or simply use two single buckets each with a wringer attachment.

Squeegee mops
Squeegee mops are generally used more on the domestic market than in large industrial establishments. A squeegee mop consists of a plastic foam head attached to a metal plate which is hinged in the middle. When the lever on the handle is depressed, the hinge operates a squeezing action, forcing the water out of the sponge. When using this type of mop, especially in a hospital situation, care must be taken over selection of the sponge. Some plastic foam sponges have been found to be an ideal breeding place for bacteria, while others are known to de-activate disinfectants. Squeegee mops can also be used for washing down certain types of wall, including tiles.

After use, mops and buckets should be thoroughly washed out and left to dry. If possible, buckets should be turned upside down, especially if they are not plastic. Mops should be hung with their heads uppermost, to prevent the head from rotting or becoming smelly. Detachable heads should be removed and laundered.

Brushes and brooms
Brushes have bristles of hair, fibre, nylon or wire secured into a wooden, polypropylene or metal stock. They can be secured by wire, glue or by a combination of both. Brushes have long or short handles according to their purpose.

It is advisable to buy a brush of good quality, which is indicated by the way the bristles are secured in the stock or head. This is difficult to

Table 6   *Types of brush*

Brushes	Description	Use

Sweeping brushes
(a) Soft
(b) Short or long handles
	Plastic or wood stock.
	Nylon or hair bristles.
		Sweeping hard surfaces.
		  Skirtings, hearths,
		  corners or edges where
		  vacuum cannot reach.

Sweeping brushes
Hard (a) and (b)
Short or long handles.
	As above, stiff plastic or
	  fibre bristles.
		Carpets, fibre or carpet
		  tiles, edges where vacuum
		  cannot reach.
		Upholstered surfaces using a
		  spotlessly clean brush.

Cobweb brushes	Feathers, teased synthetic
	  fibres, hair, at the end of
	  a long bamboo rod or
	  telescopic extending pole.
		Dusting cornices, picture
		  rails, chandeliers.

Bannister brushes	Made of the same materials as
	  soft hand brushes, but
	  bristles all round stock.
		For dusting between bannister
		  rails, wrought iron
		  filligree.

Scrubbing brushes
(a) Winged – hard or soft
	Nylon or wooden stock hard
	  bristles.
	Winged brushes allow cleaning
	  of corners.
		Scrubbing smooth surfaces,
		  wood or melamine.

(b) Butcher's scrub	Plastic or wooden stock. Nylon and stainless steel bristles or fill.	Used on butchers' blocks

Table 6 *Types of brush – cont.*

Brushes	Description	Use
(c) Churn scrubber	Like winged but with a longer handle.	Used in cooking boilers, sinks (small, difficult tiled areas).
(d) Deck scrubber	Similar to winged with a long handle, with or without water channel.	Tiles, floors.
(e) Tank brushes	Similar to winged with bristles all round the stock.	
Brooms	Similar to hard sweeping brush with stiffer bristles, set in wooden stock.	Used with or without water for stone floors, patios, etc.
Bottle brush or tube brush Valve brush	Bristles set in twisted wire.	For cleaning spouts, bottles and narrow necked vessels.
Nail brushes	Wood or nylon stock. Nylon or fibre or rubber bristles.	
Shoe brushes	Hard and soft. Wood or plastic stock.	Hard for removing mud. Soft for applying polish. Soft for polishing. Shape or coiler should differentiate for different colour polishes.
Clothes brushes Hat brushes	Hard, medium, soft.	Brushing clothes. Softer bristles for fine or delicate fabrics.
Silver brushes	Soft bristles set in wooden stock with long handle.	Removing polish from engraved or embossed silver or metal articles.
Crumb brushes	Soft bristles set in a curved stock frequently ornamental, matching the crumb tray used with it.	For removing crumbs from the table cloth.
Stove brushes	Hair or fibre bristles in wooden stock.	Applying polish and burnishing metal fire stoves and grates which are not already lacquered.
Lavatory brushes	Plastic stock with handle and small head of nylon bristles.	For cleaning lavatory basins. Must be rinsed and returned to holder which in turn should be sanitized.
Hearth brushes	Hair or fibre bristles set in a wood or metal stock.	For sweeping hearths where there is a live fire.

see, if the bristles are separated it is possible to check whether they are secured by a wire going through them or by glue filling the whole of the socket. The stock of a long-handled sweeping brush or broom should be secured to the shank by a screw, not a nail, which will work loose. Some brushes such as cobweb brushes, have telescopic handles.

Care of brushes
When not in use they should be kept in a broom cupboard. They should never be left standing on the bristles, but should be hung, or have the heads resting on a rack. After use, fluff and fibres should be removed. They should be washed frequently and allowed to dry with the heads down so that the moisture does not soak into the stock. Scrubbing brushes should be hung up or left on the side to dry, not left wet in the bottom of a bucket. Nylon and polypropylene brushes should not be exposed to excessive heat. Nylon has a temperature tolerance of 40–130 °C and polypropylene 20–95 °C.

Cleaning cloths
Every type of cleaning cloth presently in use consists of either textile or wood fibre. In many establishments rags such as written-off sheets or towels are used for cleaning. They are suitable for some jobs, but if they begin to disintegrate they leave behind linters on cleaned surfaces. Holes are dangerous as they can catch on knobs or handles, and if a large item is being cut up for dusters, it is wise to have the edges roughly hemmed. Man-made fibres are non-absorbent and less suitable. Immitation leather cloths such as vileda cloths are ideal for damp dusting. They must be thoroughly washed and left to dry after use. They can also be used in place of real chamois leather.

Dusters
Dusters may be purchased in a variety of colours, which is useful for identifying dusters for use in different areas or for different purposes. The most traditional colour is yellow which is a very loose dye. Checked dusters are also available, but the soft lint type duster is more suitable for pol-

ishing. A duster of good quality should be purchased. Edges should be well finished off and it should be a good size. It should be rubbed to see that it is lintless, so particles are not left on the surfaces being dusted. They should be absorbent, and the texture such that will hold dust particles.

After use, the dusters should be washed and hung up to dry ready for use the next day.

Disposable cloths
There are many makes of these, and they are used for damp dusting, especially in hospitals. A non-woven cloth with ionically blended bactericides and indicator stripes is available for specific use in hospitals and food preparation or food service areas. It is designed to be used as a damp duster, the bactericides killing bacteria at the same time as the removal of dust. The indicator stripes fade as the effectiveness wears off indicating to the user that it should be disposed of. Such cloths are effective if properly used, but they are expensive.

The non-impregnated disposable cloths are widely used for many purposes, and have the advantage of being easily washed and rinsed and lintless. They should be disposed of at the first signs of disintegration.

Buckets and floor cloths
These are as traditional and old-fashioned as Mrs Mop, but are still required in some situations, and every maid should be provided with a good quality plastic bucket and floor cloth. They are often required effectively to clean areas too small for a mechanical machine, such as bathroom and balcony floors. A hard scrubbing or deck brush may also be necessary.

For any job the water should be changed frequently and the appropriate cleaning agent used. After use the buckets should be washed out and left to dry upside down. Floor cloths should be washed or sent to be laundered and left to dry. Brushes should be thoroughly rinsed, shaken and left to dry either hanging or left on their side.

Dust pans
These are usually of plastic or metal, the former not being suitable for use where anything hot may

be swept into it. They can have either short or long handles, and have a hood or cover to prevent the dust escaping. They too should be washed out and dried after use. A shovel is made of metal, has no hood and is used for shovelling coal or for removing ash from a hearth. It is sometimes mistaken for a dust pan and vice versa.

Rubber gloves

Many establishments supply cleaning staff with rubber gloves. They are easily marked with a name, and should be exchanged on an old for new basis. It is advisable to have in stock a variety of sizes as the cleaner will be discouraged from using them if the wrong size is issued. In the long run it is advantageous to purchase gloves of good quality. After use they should be washed and hung from the fingers to dry. They must be dried inside out. The inside is more important than the outside.

Cleaning trolleys

Cleaners usually have to carry around a variety of cleaning agents, equipment and supplies, which are awkward to transport. By reducing the variety of items and standardizing cleaning agents, methods and guest supplies, the maid or cleaner will have less problems in carrying his or her equipment around and remembering which item to use on what surface.

A variety of cleaner's trolleys are available but they should be chosen with the following points in mind.

1 Swivel wheels, for easy running.
2 Light and easily manoeuvrable.
3 Not too high, so that when fully loaded, the operator can still see over the top.
4 Easily cleaned and no risks of rust marks.
5 Suitably sized compartments for storage of supplies.
6 Well balanced to take heavier equipment such as buckets and vacuum cleaners.
7 Facilities for carriage of dirty rubbish and linen.
8 Lockable lid or secure container for items such as lost property or keys left behind by guests.

Safety steps

These are essential in any department where employees are expected to clean any area beyond their reach. Safety steps are made with a solid frame, large rubber feet at the bottom of the ladder, and there should be a handrail. They should be stable enough to remain upright even if the user is slightly unsteady. For situations where only a little extra height is required, the stool type is suitable. When stood upon this remains fixed but when weight is taken off it can be moved easily on its casters.

Heavy-duty cleaning equipment

Large public areas such as hotel foyers, airport lounges, hospital ambulatory areas and open plan offices need special cleaning equipment.

Heavy-duty vacuum cleaners

These are essential when dealing with industrial situations. In non-clinical areas such as banquet rooms, it is sometimes advantageous to buy the type of vacuum cleaner that simply has a large metal or plastic tank in which to collect the dust. No fiddly bags are required and the machine is just as suitable for the sucking up of water – provided that the tank has first been emptied of dust!

Wet vacuums

These can be purchased in various sizes according to the requirements of the establishment. They can be used throughout the establishment, except of course where cross-contamination controls are in operation. Their main use is where there are floods or spillages, but they are useful in floor maintenance or even carpet cleaning, where they help to speed up the drying process.

Scrubbing machines

These are a basic requirement when hard floors are installed in reasonably large areas. Most machines may be fitted with a variety of brush or pad which are coloured or graded according to the type of job for which they are intended. Pads are by far the cheapest method of this type of floor maintenance, but some people argue that brushes do a better job and last longer. If both are used with care and thoroughly washed out and dried after use, results can be perfect.

High-speed polishing machines

These are only worth buying if there is a large area of floor that needs regular buffing or polishing, as this is their only purpose. They are not as versatile as regular scrubbing machines but they are far quicker at doing the job for which they are intended. Apart from buffing a floor up or polishing it, high speed machines are most useful for spray cleaning. This method of cleaning a hard floor is both quick, easy and efficient, provided that the operator is well trained and a suitable product used.

Wet floor signs

These are essential in these days of safety-conscious staff and management. They may be purchased in numerous sizes, colours and styles but whatever the design, it must do its job of accident prevention, be easy to use and easy to carry around. Thick ropes and stands are useful for cordoning off areas. People in public places usually recognize that a roped area is out of bounds, but additional signs are more helpful and reinforcing.

Back pack vacuums

These are most useful in older buildings where ceilings, curtains and ledges are high. Back pack vacuums, when used properly, are an efficient way of keeping dust levels at bay, as well as for such things as the removal of cobwebs. They are of course an additional expense when often an ordinary vacuum cleaner might suffice, but in very large areas where constant high cleaning work is carried out, they are an asset.

Pile brush machines

These are an aid to the shampooing of carpets, whichever method of carpet cleaning is used. Pile brush machines are used to brush the pile back up to its original position in height but more important, to remove any deep set fluff, grit or dust so ensuring that the carpet enjoys a longer life.

In heavy traffic areas, such as lobbies or foyers, the pile brush machine should be used from time to time not only to remove this deep set dirt but also to enhance the appearance of the carpeted areas.

Scrubber/drier machines

These can be large, expensive and rather cumbersome, and they should be bought only for large areas of hard floor. They do the job of a scrubbing machine and a wet vacuum both at the same time. The machine needs to be filled with a solution of detergent and then as it is driven the brushes in the front are fed with the detergent and the scrubbing begins. The squeegee attachment is fitted directly behind the brushes, so that as the machine moves forward, dirty water expelled by the brushes is sucked up into a container in the machine by means of a vacuum. Such machines have limited use as they cannot be used for high speed polishing work.

Litter-clearing machines

These are worth investing in if there is a large area that needs to be cleaned outside. There is nothing more unattractive than an entrance drive, car park, patio or pathway which is scattered with litter. Rubbish and leaves are particularly a problem in cities especially if the establishment is situated on a windy corner.

Spray and pump dispensers

These are used for polish, detergents and disinfectants. They reduce wastage and spillage and help the user to apply or spread the contents in controlled quantities evenly. They are available from 600 cc capacity to 5 litres. Dispensers should be clearly labelled showing their contents and/or with a colour code marking.

The colour code system

This is used in all aspects of cleaning in hospitals to prevent cross infection. The hospital ward is classified into three main areas: sanitary areas, ward areas and kitchen areas. Any equipment, including rubber gloves and plastic aprons, is colour-coded. For example, in sanitary areas all items are colour-coded red or pink, so rubber gloves, aprons, disposable cloths, and larger equipment, such as mops have a red tag on the handle. In ward areas, all items are colour-coded blue. In kitchen areas, all items are colour-coded green. The principle of the system is that items of equipment should only be used in the area for which they are colour-coded. Ideally they should be stored within those areas, so that bacteria will be confined to that area. This principle must be strictly adhered to in operating theatres where cleaning equipment should remain in the zone of the theatre.

The cleaner's cupboard

It is of utmost importance that the person who has the responsibility of cleaning the public and staff areas also has a cupboard or service area in which to keep his or her cleaning equipment and materials. So often the phrase 'just a cleaner' is heard but if we are really going to keep up stan-dards of housekeeping in these areas, then clean-ers must be encouraged to take pride in their work. One way to try to motivate cleaning staff is to give them responsibility. They need their own small tools, dusters and polishes which they can look after and somewhere secure to keep them – such as a cupboard or store. This cupboard should be large enough to keep all the necessary cleaning agents, equipment and trolley. It should be supplied with shelves, racks, hooks etc., so that items may be stored tidily at the end of the day. A sluice is also ideal, enabling the cleaner to wash out such things as floor cleaning pads and brushes. To avoid wastage and to control usage, the cleaner's cupboard should only contain ade-quate amounts of supplies for daily cleaning programmes.

A separate cleaning material store room should be under the direct supervision of the housekeeper or his/her assistant. Such a store should be under lock and key to prevent theft or vandalism.

Table 7 *Common, non-proprietary materials used in cleaning and stain removal processes*

Washing soda	A cheap alkaline grease solvent.
Caustic soda	A strong corrosive poison which breaks down heavy grease deposits.
Vinegar	With water and a chamois leather will remove soiling from polished wood surfaces, and neutralize strong alkaline detergents.
Ammonia	Highly volatile, alkaline, used for neutralizing strong acids, and in metal polishes.
Carbon tetrachloride	A grease solvent for removing grease stains, beach oil. Highly inflammable.
Salt	In solution will stiffen up cane or basket, soften stains (blood) as a mild abrasive.
Whiting	A mild abrasive mixed with water or grease solvent and used in metal and glass polish.
Jewellers' rouge	Similar to whiting, but finer.
Turpentine	Highly inflammable, a grease and paint solvent.
Bicarbonate of soda	A mild alkali used in solution for the removal of acid stains and as a neutralizer. It is non-toxic.

Table 7 *Common, non-proprietary materials used in cleaning and stain removal processes – cont.*

Methylated spirit	Highly inflammable and toxic, used for the removal of grass stains, and as a medium for mild abrasives. A grease solvent. It should never be used on acetate or triacetate fabrics or on French polished surfaces.
Glycerine	Used diluted, equal parts with warm water, will soften stains. Used on windows will prevent condensation.
Hydrogen peroxide	A slow acting oxidizing bleach. 20 vol strength dilute 1 part to 6 parts cold water. Not to be used on nylon or flame resistant fabrics. It is non-toxic so suitable for removing stains from china.
Borax	A non-toxic powder, alkaline, will act on acid stains, diluted with warm water.
Amyl-acetate (non-oily nail varnish remover)	A volatile solvent, will remove nail polish stains, and it is equally effective in removing varnishes and the surface of French polished surfaces so should be used with care. It should not be used on acetate or triacetate fabrics.
Lighter fuel	A volatile solvent similar to turpentine and carbon tetrachloride.
Salts of lemon	A toxic substance but effective in removing rust, ink and set blood stains.
Chlorine bleach	Bleaches fabrics, porcelain surfaces, it should never be used in conjunction with other chemicals. It has germicidal properties, but should be used with care, as it will rot vegetable and animal fibres.
Potassium permanganate	Bought in crystal form and when dissolved in water can be used as a wood stain.
Sawdust	Can be used as an absorbent for spillages difficult to remove, e.g. vomit, oil, paint. Damp sawdust spread on a floor with excessive dust will facilitate the sweeping up without dispersing the dust.
Aluminium	A sheet of aluminium or an old aluminium saucepan used with washing soda and boiling water will remove by electrolysis tarnish from silver. If the silver is exposed for too long the silver plating will also be removed.
Lemon juice	Has the same properties as vinegar (acetic acid). Used for delicate fabrics. When used with salt will remove tarnish from brass and copper.

5 Standards and control: the role of the housekeeping supervisor

The main responsibility of the housekeeping supervisor is to control the standards of work within his/her particular area. Most of his/her working day will therefore be taken up with checking and controlling the cleaning duties of maids or cleaners. A supervisor rarely has the authority to decide when spring cleaning, redecoration or refurbishment should take place, but he/she should report diminishing standards caused by age or general wear and tear.

The supervisor is responsible for work performance and productivity of staff by checking that cleaning tasks are being performed to the highest possible standards in the shortest time. It is his/her duty to report problems to the housekeeper or to take action. It may be that he/she is able to identify a training need if a maid is slow in completing her quota of rooms.

Any area which is used by people not only needs to be clean but also properly supplied. For example, a hospital patient should be supplied with a clean rubbish bag on the side of the bedside cabinet, the public toilets properly supplied with sufficient quantities of soap, towels and toilet paper, or the hotel guest with writing paper or a note pad and pen by the side of the telephone.

In order that the business administration side of an accommodation operation runs smoothly, there need to be various systems to keep control over room occupancy. For this reason communication between housekeeping and reception departments is essential.

Example of a method of room control

As with cleaning, checking an area must be done in a methodical manner to maintain speed and efficiency.

1 Walk in one direction around the room.
2 Check from high to low surfaces in order that no area is missed.
3 Look in, under and behind all fixtures and fittings.
4 Use a check-off list as a means of control.
5 Check that the room has been prepared to the standard required.
6 Note anything which needs to be repaired or brought up to the required standard.
7 Follow up notes by taking appropriate corrective action.
8 When satisfied that the room or area has been prepared to the prescribed standard, then it may be returned to reception (this only applies in a hotel).

Room inspection

The main purpose of room inspection is to ensure that the required standards of appearance and cleanliness are being met. First impressions count and those impressions can then be transmitted *ad infinitum* during conversations to friends, family and colleagues. Word of mouth advertising can be an accommodation establishment's best or worst media.

The supervisor should also check the standard of repair and maintenance. This is important for the health and safety of employees and guests, as well as to ensure that everything is in good working order. No hotel room should be returned to reception unless it can be sold in perfect order.

If a supervisor is doing his/her work job correctly he/she will notice any deterioration in the

Floor Supervisors Room Inspection Report

Date: ....   Room: ....

	OK	Remarks
1 **Closet/wardrobe**		
(a) hangers (6)		
(b) shelf		
(c) rail		
(d) coat hooks		
(e) folding luggage bench		
(f) cleanliness		
(g) spare blanket		
(h) spare pillow		
2 **Minibar/teasmaid**		
(a) general condition		
(b) cups, glasses		
3 **Luggage bench**		
(a) general condition		
(b) dusting & drawers		
4 **Desk**		
(a) stationery folder contents:		
6 bond paper		
4 bond envelopes		
1 pen		
(b) dusting & drawers		
5 **Wall mirror**		
(a) dusting & cleanliness		
6 **Wall picture**		
(a) dusting & cleanliness		
7 **Telephone directories**		
(a) general conditions		
8 **Chairs**		
(a) spots & dusting		
9 **Windows**		
(a) cleanliness		
(b) window safety catch		
(c) curtains & blackouts		
10 **Television**		
(a) turned off		
(b) working order		

	OK	Remarks
11 **Night table**		
(a) general condition		
(b) dusting & drawer		
12 **Radio cabinet**		
(a) general condition		
(b) working order		
(c) shelf		
13 **Lamps**		
(a) operation		
(b) dusting		
14 **Carpets**		
(a) vacuum & under bed		
(b) spotting		
(c) general condition		
15 **Walls**		
(a) general condition		
(b) cleanliness		
16 **Upholstered sofas and beds**		
(a) spotting		
(b) condition		
17 **Bedspreads**		
(a) spotting		
(b) condition		
18 **Telephone**		
(a) cleanliness		
19 **Bathroom**		
(a) bathtub		
(b) sink cracked		
(c) towel shelf		
(d) toilet bowl		
(e) toilet flush & handle		
(f) bath mat & supplies		
(g) floor		
(h) towels		

Inspected By ....

Figure 18   *The housekeeper's checklist*

state of the décor or fixtures and fittings in the rooms and report these to the housekeeper.

An aeroplane never proceeds to move along a runway unless the pilot has covered the cockpit check-off list, ensuring that everything is in correct and functioning order. The same type of procedure should be followed by the housekeeping supervisor when checking a room (see Figure 18). Although it is not common practice to use such a list for every room every day, the report can be used as a basis for a supervisor's training. The details and standards will soon become set in his/her mind and he/she will therefore have no need of a list, only a note pad to jot down any observations that need attention.

Quality control in hospitals

In order to maintain high standards of cleanliness in hospitals, a similar type of check-off list is normally used. The *USE* system of control is a popular one. This system provides for a systematic assessment and recording of all standards achieved by domestic staff. The assessment of work is normally carried out fortnightly or monthly, often depending on when the domestic staff bonus payment is made. The control is carried out by the domestic supervisor in charge of the particular ward and cleaning staff, but it should also be carried out in the presence of the ward sister or head of department. The ward sister may then point out any domestic matters which she considers a problem. This system is designed not only to maintain standards of cleanliness but also to help interdepartmental relations between nursing and domestic departments.

It is usually laid down by hospital management policy that 70 per cent of items in wards and 40 per cent of items in offices are checked and recorded on the special form (see Figure 19). When the control is complete, the form should be signed by the supervisor and also the user (ward sister). It then goes to the domestic services manager, who takes appropriate action, if necessary.

In addition to the assessments made by the supervisors, random checks are also made by domestic services managers and also by bacteriologists who take swab counts of levels of bacteria on various surfaces throughout each ward. If the count is too high then an infection is declared and the domestic services manager is expected to put a 'scrub-out' into action immediately. A 'scrub-out' means that the ward must be thoroughly cleaned from top to bottom, so reducing the level of infectious bacteria and safeguarding the health of the patients. A scrub-out needs careful organization to ensure that the work is done as quickly, quietly and efficiently as possible, without unnecessary discomfort to the patients or upset of nursing and ward procedures. If domestic staff are adequately trained then if and when such an occasion arises, the work will be done with the minimal amount of fuss.

Hospital: ___	Ward: ___	Date: ___	
Item	**Grade**	**Comments**	**Action**
Sanitary fittings	1	Toilet seats	Remove urine stains
Kitchen fixtures and fittings	1	Exterior of fridge dirty	Thorough clean – use multisolve
Floors	1	Slippery	Strip and re-seal
Doors	1	Sister's office	Remove old sellotape
Electrical equipment	1	TV screen smeary	Use crystal

Overall impression: Standards are continuing to improve but attention to detail still required.

Overal rating for this area: ___ Signed: ....
Domestic supervisor
Signed: ....
Ward sister

Figure 19 *Example of a quality assessment form*

Note: An actual form would obviously list many other items. On completion of the assessment exercise, the grades would be totalled and the higher the figure, the cleaner the ward.

Job knowledge

In order for the housekeeping supervisor to be able to plan and organize his/her work, it is important that he/she has sufficient knowledge of the following details.

Staff

How many staff are there? Are they all on duty (none off sick or on holiday)? Are there any staff problems, such as personality clashes or staff with personal problems which may affect their work? Where are they all working?

Maids and cleaners are usually assigned to their own particular section but the vacant areas have to be covered. Work is sometimes split up and shared out but more commonly relief staff do it. Some cleaners are better than others, even though they may have all received exactly the same training, and the supervisor should have the flexibility to allocate the good person to an important area, for example, cleaning a VIP suite or scrubbing out a ward.

Cleaning aids

Is there sufficient cleaning equipment, cleaning agents or materials and are there enough supplies, such as linen?

The supervisor should know how to get around problems of shortages and when to inform the executive housekeeper if they persist.

Special functions

Is anything special happening today/this week? For example, at the end of term in a university all student rooms must be thoroughly cleaned, and, perhaps, prepared for conference delegates. Spring cleaning might start in a particular ward. A third example could be that the Presidential Suite is to be used as a meeting room, so ashrays must be emptied and the room tidied at the designated coffee break times.

Room status

There are many ways to communicate the status of a hotel room.

In the present context, however, it is necessary for the floor supervisor to be familiar with the various classifications of room status and how to organize the appropriate cleaning and preparation.

Expected departure

The guest should check out today. Wait till he or she has actually moved out of the hotel before cleaning the room, in order that it may be cleaned thoroughly and time is not wasted.

Check-out or departure

The guest has paid his or her bill. Check whether he or she has actually physically moved out, before cleaning the room. (The guest may be having breakfast or buying a newspaper before returning to the room to pack or use the bathroom.) If there is any damage or lost property, the guest may still be around in the hotel, perhaps having a coffee or waiting for a taxi.

A check-out room must be thoroughly cleaned, checked to ensure that everything is in perfect order and returned to reception as quickly as possible, in order that it may be re-let.

Occupied or stay-on

The guest will be staying in the hotel again tonight. The hotel staff may or may not know the date of departure. In luxury hotels, occupied rooms are cleaned in a similar way to check-outs. In other hotels, the cleaning procedure is different.

If possible the room should be cleaned as early in the morning as possible, so that if the guest wants to return to the room to work or relax, it will be clean and he or she will not be disturbed.

In some hotels, check-out rooms take priority in cleaning order. They may be needed for airline crews or tours arriving early in the day.

In an occupied room, it is important that none of the guest's personal belongings are moved, except when necessary for cleaning.

Arrivals

These are the rooms required the same day for arriving guests. Sometimes the arrival times, guest names and number of guests per room are also given by reception.

If an arrival time is given, it is imperative that the rooms are ready by that time – the guests will be waiting to check in.

In the smaller, better class hotel, where the guest's name is known, the room is prepared especially for him or her. A regular guest often prefers to have a certain type of room, facing a certain aspect and with a certain coloured décor. He or she may wish to have a particular colour of flowers put in the room, or have other special requests such as a bedboard, hot water bottle or a non-allergic pillow.

In this type of hotel, it is advisable for the housekeeper to keep a book or register, listing the requirements of regular visitors.

VIP

'Very Important Persons' are usually received on a special list from Reception.

VIPs receive special service. They are often given a complimentary basket of fruit, an arrangement of flowers and sometimes a complete bar set-up in their rooms. They may be allocated a suite, or the room itself may even be complimentary. They usually receive extra giveaways from housekeeping, in the form of perfume, after-shave, special soap etc.

VIP status varies from establishment to establishment. They may be employees from the hotel's own company, for example, visiting general manager or vice-president. Alternatively, a VIP could be a member of the Royal Family, Head of State, Member of Parliament, Film Star, Pop star, TV Personality or the head of an important company which brings a lot of business to the hotel.

Whoever the VIP is, he or she should be treated as such by housekeeping staff and the room must be cleaned and prepared to the highest standards possible.

Crew room

Many airport and city hotels have contracts to supply a certain number of rooms per day to a particular airline, for the use of the crew. Usually, housekeeping are informed of the exact check-in and check-out times per crew, as it is important that the rooms are ready on time.

In some hotels crew always have the same rooms, which can sometimes be a problem because they are always cleaned quickly and there is a risk that the standards in those special crew rooms will begin to fall, causing complaints

from the airline and possibly the loss of an important contract. Alternatively, air crew may be given rooms at random throughout the hotel, as long as they are situated in a quiet location.

It is the floor supervisor's task to ensure that noise is kept to a minimum on the corridors, especially near crew rooms where airline staff may be sleeping throughout the day.

Group or tour rooms

Tours or groups are taken at virtually all hotels these days, due to the increased popularity of package tour holidays and travel. Tour rooms are usually let at reduced rates but for housekeeping, this does not mean that they should be given less service or cleaned less. Tour members are still guests, bringing money into the hotel!

It is important that tour rooms are all clean and ready for the arrival time. They are normally allocated on a particular floor or floors, making life easier for the tour leader, but sometimes more difficult for the housekeeper. With tour rooms, the supervisor should check with the housekeeper for any special orders, for example sheets may not need to be changed every day, or no evening 'turn down'. He/she should also ensure that the maids are informed of tour arrival and check-out times as there is likely to be an influx or exodus of people and luggage around those times and therefore maids are advised to keep well out of the way, to avoid what often appears to be a stampede!

Conference rooms

Conference rooms are usually, of course, the rooms where the conference is held and this part of the operation is often prepared and cleaned by the banquet or food and beverage department.

Conference bookings, however, sometimes also involve the use of *syndicate rooms* which are often the bedrooms. Delegates break away from the main conference and work together in small syndicates. Sometimes the bedroom is left as it is except for the supervisor being asked to put a few extra chairs inside. Alternatively, preparation of a syndicate room can be a mammoth feat of organization, with the removal of beds, and banquet tables being put up in their place. Syndicate rooms are easy to clean once they have been prepared. The supervisor should ensure that at the designated break times, the room is tidied, bathroom checked, ashtrays and waste bin emptied.

Day let

A room is referred to as a day let when it is let for part of a day. It may be used as an interview room or some other business nature but it may also be used by a guest who wants to just sleep or rest for a few hours after or before a long journey, for example at an airport hotel. The supervisor must ensure that the room is ready on time in the morning but even more important, that it is cleaned as quickly as possible when the guest checks out in the afternoon or early evening. This means that the room may be re-let again that night.

Family plan

This term means that a room is let at a special rate, usually for parents sharing a room with one child who sleeps on a roll-away bed. The roll-away bed, of course, must be placed in the room under the direction of the supervisor, who must also ensure that extra supplies, for example extra tooth glass, face flannel or towels, are placed in the room.

Long-stay

Long-stay guests are those guests who stay in the hotel longer than average. In some hotels a long-stay guest may even become resident.

Long-stay guests need special treatment as they usually become well known and can become part of the hotel, as it becomes their home. The supervisor will usually be aware of the particular guest's idiosyncracies, likes, dislikes and preferences. As the guest is likely to stay for a long time, it is of utmost importance that the room is kept as clean as possible, despite the fact that there might be an unusual amount of luggage or other personal belongings.

A long-stay room need not be cleaned in such depth as a normal overnight, occupied room, however it must be thoroughly cleaned once a week.

Reporting systems

Whether computers are installed into a hotel or not, the floor supervisor will have to complete various reports, if the housekeeping department is to remain a smooth-running one. Listed below are some of the reporting systems which are used in hotels today.

Housekeeping daily report

This is the floor supervisor's working report during the day (see Figure 20). In the morning he/she acquires the basic information from reception, either in the form of a list or from the computer or room status indicator. He/she can then fill in the form ticking in the appropriate boxes. During the course of the day, he/she will follow through the status of the room. For example, rooms 125 and 126 checked out unexpectedly. They were cleaned and returned to reception in the state of ready to sell. Room 129 remains occupied, room 128 needs to have stains removed from the carpet at some appropriate time and room 130 needs to have its black-out curtains repaired. Although room 127 was a check-out, it has not yet been returned, because the toilet is blocked and the plumber has not yet had the time to mend it.

The houskeeping daily report usually has four copies, which are distributed as follows: top copy – supervisor's working copy; second copy – sent to reception (or information could be fed into the computer terminal); third copy – sent to the accounts department (or again information could simply be fed into the computer); fourth copy – kept as a housekeeping record.

Comparison report

A comparison report (see Figure 21) is used to compare the status of rooms records held by reception (or in the computer) against the housekeeping physical record. In some hotels a com-

Floor .....1..   Date:...12 July (a.m)

Room Number	Vacant	Expected departure	Occupied	Number of guests	Remarks
120			✓	1	
121	✓				Vacant
122		✓	Check-out	2	Ready
123		✓	Check-out	2	Ready
124		✓	Check-out	2	Ready
125			Check-out	2	Ready
126			Check-out	2	Ready
127		✓	Check-out	3	Out of order, Toilet blocked
128				3	Carpet needs spotting
129				1	
130				2	Black-out Curtain torn

Floor supervisor....E. Bamkin.

Figure 20   *The floor supervisor's working report*

parison report takes place both in the morning and the afternoon but this is only common where no computer exists. In other hotels this particular report is done in the afternoon, just before the floor supervisor goes off duty. The comparison report is similar to the daily report and shows the rooms status at a set time.

A comparison is particularly helpful to reception especially if they are short of rooms, but its prime function is for accounting purposes. By comparing the status of rooms on a daily basis control may be kept over rooms earnings.

Trouble report (Figure 22)

During the course of the day, the supervisor is likely to come across several items that need to be repaired. He/she must therefore decide whether the repair is an emergency or urgent, or whether it may just be added to the list of repairs. If a repair is an emergency immediate action should be taken. For example, if all the ladies public toilets are blocked, then the supervisor should contact the plumber, who should tackle the job immediately. An example of an urgent job might be to repair a bathroom grab rail, which has come away from the wall and is therefore dangerous. The room would probably have to be put out of order until the job is done, to guarantee the safety of the guest. An example of a normal repair job would be a loose lamp head. The supervisor could

Floor ...1...   Date:..12 July.. (P.M)

Room Number	Vacant	Expected departure	Occupied	Number of guests	Remarks
120			✓	1	
121			✓		
122	✓				
123			✓		
124	✓				
125			✓		
126	✓				
127	✓				Out of order Toilet blocked
128			✓	3	
129			✓	1	
130			✓	2	
				Supervisor...E. Bamkin.	

Figure 21   *Comparison report*

simply exchange the lamps in the guest room, putting in a lamp of good working order and taking the damaged lamp to the workshop for the electrician to repair.

When items are removed from a location and taken to the workshops, they should have trouble reports attached, so that the article does not get lost, and when it has been repaired, it may be returned to its permanent place. Trouble reports usually have three copies and are distributed as follows: top copy – given to the tradesman concerned (e.g. plumber or carpenter); second copy – held by chief engineer as a record of the work so that planning, control and costing may be carried out; third copy – kept by floor supervisor as a record and a method of follow-up.

Maintenance tag
A maintenance tag is attached to the article concerned by the supervisor, but only the top portion *A* is completed by him/her (see Figure 22). He/she also completes a trouble report, which simply reads 'see Maintenance Tag No. 146897', and delivers the trouble report to the chief engineer's office, and the labelled article to a collection point in the workshop.

It is then the chief engineer's responsibility to assign the job, giving part *B* to the tradesman, and holding part *C* in the office, attached to the related trouble report.

Housekeeping evening report
When an evening turn-down service is in opera-

| Maintenance | ◯ | Tag |

Date..

Article...

Location..

Repair _____

_____

_____

_____

Signed...
Job no. 146897

A

Job no. 146897   Date...

Name...

Repair...

Time allocated..

Materials used
_____

Returned to... **B**

Job no. 146897   Date.............................

Name...

Repair...

Article...

Location..
C

Figure 22   *Trouble report*

tion, there are usually a number of evening maids as well as an evening housekeeper on duty. During the course of the evening, various problems may crop up, many of which the evening supervisor will be able to cope with. Naturally, there may also be problems from time to time for which he/she cannot take responsibility. Any problems that do crop up during the course of the evening should be written in a special log book, in the form of an evening report. It is most useful if the evening supervisor also writes down that all pass keys are correctly counted and safely locked away at the end of the shift. This is just another form of security control.

The following morning, the housekeeper or his/her assistant will review the evening report and take any necessary follow-up action.

Training report

In the larger hotels there will be a training policy set up by management. Each department head is responsible for the training within that department and the job of the personnel and training manager is to co-ordinate the training function within the establishment, offering advice where applicable.

In some hotels the housekeeper prepares a training report, advising the personnel and training department and the general manager, of training carried out during the past month.

Other reports

The size and type of establishment will decide the amount and type of various reports to be completed. Other reports the housekeeper may have to complete include

Crime reports
Health and safety or accident reports
Reports in connection with discipline
Reports in connection with staff evaluation in
    preparation for a pay rise, promotion or
    transfer

Returning rooms to reception

One of the floor supervisor's main responsibilities is to return clean and ready rooms to reception as quickly as possible to ensure that guests will not be kept waiting.

The following are some of the systems used.

Rooms ready lists

In smaller hotels where face-to-face communication is easy, the housekeeper may simply go round to the reception desk and tell the receptionist which rooms are ready and/or give him/her a list of confirmation.

Telephone

The housekeeper phones down the ready rooms as soon as they have been checked. One of the main problems with this method is that it is time consuming, especially if the phones in reception are busy.

Rooms status indicator

The rooms status indicator uses a system of lights. A light board is situated : the housekeeper's office, in the floor services and in reception, where it will be connected to the room racks which contain details of guests occupying rooms. When the guest pays his/her bill and checks out, the cashier flicks a switch, which sets a flashing light in motion, indicating to both reception and housekeeping that the room is now a check-out room. By seeing the flashing light, both the maid and the floor supervisor know that this particular room can now be cleaned. Once the check-out rooms have been cleaned, they can be inspected and are returned to reception by the floor house-keeper, by operating a key or by pressing the appropriate room buttons. This changes the room status from a check-out room with a flash-ing green light, to a vacant, clean and ready room with a plain green light.

The receptionist then re-sells the room. When it is re-occupied, he/she presses a small button on the room rack, changing the status of the room to occupied by turning the light completely out. When the guest checks-out, the whole process begins again. Before computerized systems were introduced, this method of rooms management control was excellent but in many large hotels it has been replaced by updated computer systems.

Computer

There are many computerized rooms manage-ment systems available some incorporating a light indicator system as described above. The light systems have proved to be very successful and have been taken a step further with the intro-duction of jacks or plugs.

Stage 1

The guest checks out and this information is fed into the computer by the front office cashier. The flashing light indicator by the side of the room begins to operate. (In some cases the computer cuts out mini-bar and telephone services at this stage, so preventing staff from using guest facilities.)

Stage 2

From the light indicator (sometimes known as a 'bud box') in the floor service area, the maid knows which room are check-outs and can pro-ceed to clean them. Some sophisticated rooms management systems issue the maids with jacks or plugs, which they insert into small connections in each room that they clean. The connection is usually situated near the message light near the bedboard or the mini-bar. When the jack is inserted the computer is advised that this particu-lar room is currently being cleaned. It has two advantages. Reception can begin to prepare rooming lists, as they can observe from the light indicator which rooms will be returned next. In addition, the housekeeper may locate where the maids are working and in some cases calculate how long it takes them to clean each room.

Unfortunately this system is uncommon and stage 2 is usually bypassed.

Stage 3

Once the room has been cleaned, the supervisor will check it and if it is indeed ready to return to reception, he/she will jack the room in a similar way to the method described above. By jacking the connection, the computer is advised that the room is clean and ready to sell, and the light indicator will stop flashing.

Stage 4

Once the room is re-let, the receptionist will feed the relevant information into the computer, and the light will go out, advising the housekeeping department that the room is now occupied.

Some of the most modern computerized sys-tems have abandoned the light indicator system. They simply throw out printed lists of rooms status for the housekeeper, or throw up lists on a visual display unit. When the supervisor is returning rooms on a computerized system such as this, he/she has to phone clean and ready rooms down to the housekeeping office, where the information is keyed into the terminal. In a superior method the supervisor simply dials a code from the telephone in the guest room, which advises the computer that this room is now clean and ready to sell. The room status in the computer is therefore automatically changed.

When the room is on vacant status, some computers have the power to cut out all services to that room, saving energy and preventing pilferage. Care must be taken with such cut-off systems, however, as the room may take a long time to heat up again and the fridge part of the mini-bar may defrost, and electricity may be needed for extra work by the housekeeping or maintenance staff.

Further reading

Braham, B., *Hotel Front Office* (Hutchinson 1985).
Miller, C. B., *How to Organize and Maintain an Efficient Hospital Housekeeping Department* (American Hospital Association 1980).

6 Fabrics

Housekeepers should have an understanding of the constitution of fabrics in order to clean them effectively. The fibres that are most commonly used today can be divided into two main categories – natural fibres (animals or vegetable) and man-made fibres (regenerated or reconstituted or synthetic). There are also mineral fibres, such as asbestos (calcium, magnesium silicate). Table 8 shows the uses of the vegetable and man-made fibres.

Animal fibres

Wool
The most commonly used wool comes from sheep. Although expensive, wool is extensively used in the hotel and catering industry for carpets and upholstery and to a lesser extent uniforms. Because of its natural crimp, wool does not flatten or crease easily. For this reason, it always maintains a good appearance. It is hard-wearing and reasonably easy to clean, as it has a good resistance to soiling and is fire resistant. It is also warm and takes colours well. Owing to the high price of wool, it is often used mixed together with nylon or other man-made fibres commonly in an 80/20 ratio.

Other wools include mohair and cashmere (wool from two different types of goat); camel (the soft undercoat from a camel); and angora (the soft fur from a type of rabbit). All these wools are very warm, soft and expensive. They are not commonly used in catering and are mainly used in the clothing industry.

Silk
Silk is produced from the cocoon of silk worms. Most of the silk on the market today is produced from cultivated worms in silk farms, such as the Lullingstone Silk Farm in Dorset where fabric for Princess Diana's wedding dress was made.

Silk is not often used in industry because it is difficult to iron, easily water marked, damaged by strong acids, rotted by sunlight and very expensive. It is however used in some luxury suites and apartments as a wall covering or cushion covers and can even be used as sheets.

Vegetable fibres

Cotton
This comes from the cotton plant seed and is grown extensively in India, the USA, Egypt, the West Indies and China. Although expensive it is still used for bed linen, table linen and uniforms. Owing to the high cost, many companies are gradually replacing cotton items with polyester and cotton mix fabrics.

Cotton is strong, absorbent, and easily laundered, and more resistant to bleaches and alkalines. It is more flammable than linen, especially the brushed type such as flanelette. The labelling should clearly indicate whether the fabric has been treated to make it less flammable.

Mercerized cotton – is cotton of which the fibres have been smoothed, giving it a sheen. Before the invention of man-made fibres, it was widely used to simulate silk, and used for sateen and in cotton damasks. The process for producing this shiny cotton fabric was discovered by a Lancashire man, John Mercer in 1850. He was

Table 8 *Fabrics/fibres and their uses*

VEGETABLE FIBRES

Cotton fabrics

Calico	Used in upholstery
Corduroy	Furnishings and upholstery
Denim	Upholstery
Drill	Overalls
Flannelette	Bed linen
Lawn	A very fine cotton
Muslin	Used in the kitchen for straining
Towelling	Towels examination couch sheets
Winceyette	Sheets
Poplin	Trade name given to the weave curtain linings
Velvet	Curtains

Linen fabrics

Damask	Table linen
Huckaback	Hand towels
Tea towelling	Tea and glass cloths
Sheeting	Bed linen
Turkish/Terry towelling	Towels and curtains

Other vegetable fibres

Jute	Sacking hessian wall coverings
Hemp	Ropes
Sisal	Carpet backing, underlays, doormats
Kapok	Cushion filling and padding

MAN-MADE FIBRES

Regenerated fibres (rayon)

Viscose rayons

Acetate rayon	Clothing and in place of silk
Triacetate, e.g. Tricel	In clothing and furnishing fabrics

Modified viscose

Vincel	Clothing
Evlan	Cheaper carpets and upholstery
Sarille	Candlewick bedspreads
Durofil	Upholstery
Fibrolane	Blended with wool or cotton towels and blankets

SYNTHETIC FIBRES

Polyamide	Nylon	Bed linen, clothing
	Celon	Curtains, blankets
	Perlon	Upholstery, bristles
	Enkalon	Carpets
Polyester	Terylene	Clothing, furnishings
	Dacron	Bedlinen
	Crimplene	Paddings/ fillings
		Net curtains
Acrylic	Acrilan	Blankets
	Courtelle	Carpets
	Orlon	Clothing
Polypropylene	Ulstron	Blankets
Polythene	Courlene	Deck chair material

involved with the dyeing of cottons, and discovered, by accident, that cotton fibres immersed in a strong solution of caustic soda had their structure altered, and when kept at tension, took on the characteristic sheen. Curtain lining has the threads of mercerized cotton for the warp, giving a sheen on the right side. Because of the stretching of the thread during the mercerizing process, poor quality lining material may shrink. It is interesting that Mercer, involved in the textile industry, should have the same name as the Guild founded in 1127, for vendors of small articles and silks and velvets.

Flannelette is a cotton fabric with brushed fibres giving a fluffy surface resembling flannel. The teased cotton entraps air and makes the material warmer to the touch than smooth cotton.

Percale cotton is a high quality cotton which has been treated with chemicals. It is softer, lighter, faster drying and more crease-resistant than plain cotton. Percale goods require little or no ironing, and are therefore suitable for home or on-site laundering.

All cottons tend to shrink during the first few washings unless they have been pre-shrunk. Shrinkage does not detract from the quality, but means that the weave has closed up and the material will appear thicker after laundering.

Union linen is a mixture of linen and cotton with more linen than cotton, while union cotton is a mixture of cotton and linen with more cotton than linen. Both unions are tough and hard-wearing, combining the qualities of each fibre.

Damask

Damask is a term which refers to the weave and not to the fibre. This weave is used for linen, cotton, wool and silk and man-made fibres, and is frequently found in table linen. Normal weaving has weft threads stretched the length of the loom, and the warp threads going over and under the weft threads alternately. Damask patterns are produced by carrying the warp over two, three or up to nine weft threads. These 'floats' produce the characteristic sheen of the patterns in damask, which show in reverse on the wrong side of the fabric. Double damask has extra threads in the weft making a stronger and more durable fabric.

Although damask is often woven in two or more colours and with different fibres, for table linen it is usual for the fibres to be of one colour, and of all cotton or linen or a mixture of these two. Some cheaper damask table linen may have the warp thread of rayon or the other man-made fibre. Cotton damask does not have the crisp shiny finish of linen. It requires a stiffening agent (such as starch) in the final rinsing or a stiffening agent sprayed on during the ironing process.

To distinguish cotton from linen damask, apply a drop of oil to the sample. Linen will appear transparent, but cotton will not. Applied dressing may make cotton damask shiny and resemble linen. When selecting damask it is important to see that the fabric is closely woven and the warp threads not too long or loose. Both cotton and linen damask articles wash well but do need careful ironing. Linen ironed damp will have a natural lustre and stiffness.

Linen

Linen is an umbrella term used for any other fabrics used for bedding ('bed linen') or table cloths, napkins, etc. ('table linen'). Pure linen is the most expensive fibre used for table and bed linen, and is not now often used alone. Most 'bed linen' or 'table linen' will today be made from cotton, or poly/cotton.

The linen fibre is produced from flax, one of the oldest textile fibres known. It was introduced to Ireland by the Phoenicians and Britain gets most of its supplies from Ireland. The flax plant has long stems which after cutting are allowed to rot in water. During this process all but the strongest fibres deteriorate.

The best linen has long smooth fibres about 60 mm in length. The ends which are inferior to the rest are removed and used as tow. Good quality linen has a smooth lustrous appearance, it is cool to the touch and absorbent, but less absorbent than cotton. If tow is incorporated, a less smooth fabric with irregularities results, recognized by the 'slub' effect. Frequently particles of

wood matter known as shrives are found adhering to the tow flax.

For good quality table linen special looms are set up for weaving the fabric to the width required for tablecloths and table napkins. Such articles will have two selvedge edges and two hems. The weave can incorporate, for large quantities, monograms, names or logos of the establishments.

Linen is hard-wearing and easily washed, but requires careful finishing, and it should not be subjected to strong alkaline solutions.

Animal fibres are much softer than vegetable fibres and have more natural elasticity. Wool especially has to be cleaned carefully as the fabric is absorbent and will stretch or shrink if washed incorrectly. Wool is weaker when wet, can be damaged by heat and alkaline agents. It can also be attacked by moths and beetles.

Vegetable fibres are strong and absorbent and launder well as they are actually stronger when they are wet. Although linen and cotton can withstand high temperatures, they are weakened by acids and crease easily. They must be stored in warm, dry and well-ventilated areas to prevent mildew. Vegetable fibres are generally cooler than animal fibres. This is due to the fact that pockets of air are trapped in the short fibres of wool, whereas vegetable fibres are longer.

Man-made fibres

How man-made fibres are made

Man-made fibres are made from raw materials as diverse as wood pulp and oil derivatives. These materials are converted chemically and/or physically into fibre-forming substances which ultimately are in the form of a viscous liquid. This liquid is forced under pressure through spinnerets (jets consisting of many very fine holes) to form a continuous bundle of filaments. This latter process is known as extrusion. Additions at this stage usually ensure that the property imparted is permanent and not removed at a later stage of processing or during use. Typical additives can be dye-stuffs, anti-static agents, or flame retardant agents. The spinning process, by which the prepared chemicals are converted into fibres, is performed in three main ways.

1 Wet spinning   The filaments from the spinneret emerge directly into chemical baths which cause the viscous liquid to solidify.
2 Dry spinning   The fibre-forming chemical is dissolved in a volatile solvent which evaporates in warm air after the filaments leave the spinneret.
3 Melt spinning   The hard polymer is melted, extruded through the spinneret and cooled in air to solidify into filaments.

The filaments are spun in different ways to produce yarns with different characteristics. For example

1 Continuous monofilament: a single continuous filament.
2 Filament yarn: several monofilaments are spun to produce a filament yarn.
3 Staple: filaments are cut into short lengths and spun to produce a staple yarn.

The filaments can be reshaped so that the fibres no longer lie parallel, and produce a yarn which is bulkier and textured. Air incorporated in the fibres produces a yarn which has greater thermal insulation and absorbency.

Various finishes can be applied to the fabrics to improve their performance. The fabric can be impregnated with water soluble resin, then heated to cure the resin. This improves crease resistance. The fibres can be given a silicone coating and a wax finish to give a shower-proofing effect. Some manufacturers have produced fabrics with in-built, permanent, anti-static properties. Static electricity produced by some man-made fibres is one of the disadvantages. Spraying non-treated textiles with an anti-static spray or using an anti-static conditioner in the rinsing water will eliminate the static.

In general man-made fibres melt when under great heat, unlike untreated cotton which burns with a flame. Fabrics used in public buildings should be treated to render them flame retardent.

Man-made fabrics should be cleaned or laundered according to the coding on the label. Hard spin drying will give some fabrics permanent creasing.

Regenerated fibres

Viscose rayon

This is one of the most important man-made fibres. It consists of wood pulp and cotton waste mixed with caustic soda (which strangely enough is also used to unblock toilets and drains). Viscose rayon is colour-fast because the colour is added while it is in liquid form. It is cheap, pleats well and can be made with an easy care finish. As it drapes well and is not affected by sunlight, it can be used in the manufacture of curtains. It must be washed carefully in cool temperatures. Like wool it loses its strength when wet.

Cellulose esters

These are commonly known as acetate and triacitate. They are made by soaking cotton waste in acetic acid, so care must be taken not to spill nail varnish remover (acetone) on these fibres. Cellulose esters also lose their strength when wet, so care must be taken when washing. When ironed too hot, they will also acquire a shine.

Triacetate has quick drying properties similar to nylon and is particularly suitable for garments with pleats. It is also used in hand-knitting yarns, furnishings, woven and knitted dresswear and linings. As it drapes well, is crease resistant and is not affected by sunlight, it may be used quite adequately for curtains.

Modified viscose

Viscose, made from cellulose, is absorbent and has been widely used in most textile applications. Modified forms include high strength yarns in tyre cords, crimped fibres in carpets, and clothing. Viloft, a new tubular viscose fibre has extra absorbency and loft.

For the housekeeper, evlan is probably the most important of these fibres, as it is used a great deal in the carpet industry. It is chemically treated so that is has a crimp which resembles wool. Evlan has a good resistance to abrasion and the crimp helps it to be more resilient (it springs back up instead of lying flat after it has been walked on). The cheaper carpets can be made from 100 per cent evlan, but often it is mixed with either wool or courtelle in a 50 per cent ratio. Modified viscoses have good strength when wet and are used in the manufacture of clothing. Sarille, in particular, is used for dresses and suits.

Synthetic fibres

Synthetic fibres are produced totally from chemicals. Nylon was the first of these fibres to be produced in America but new types of synthetic fibres are constantly appearing and the many different trade names often make their identity very confusing.

Polyamide
Nylon is an example of this group of fibres and it is produced from the benzene in coal, hydrogen, oxygen and nitrogen. Polyamide fibres are long, smooth and durable with high tensile strength, and resistant to abrasion, rot and mildew. They are cheap to buy, can easily be blended with other fibres and are fire resistant – they melt rather than burst into flames.

Nylon is light, easy to launder and very quick drying. It is resilient to most chemicals but tests should always be carried out on an unseen part of the fabric before total immersion.

Nylon has a low heat resistance, melting at quite low temperatures. The exception to this is one type made from polymer adipic and hexamethylene diamine.

Brushed nylon has one surface brushed to produce a soft fluffy finish. It is warmer and more absorbent than smooth nylon.

Other polyamides are perlon and enkalon.

Polyester
Terylene was the first polyester fibre to be made and it is produced from the by products of petroleum (ethylene glycol and teraphthalic acid). Polyester will not shrink or stretch but it has the advantage of being very elastic. It is very strong,

crease resistant and blends well with other fibres, especially wool and cotton.

Cotton and polyester has similar qualities to percale cotton, being light, soft and easily laundered. If folded when still warm from the dryer will require little or no ironing. This mixture will not withstand heat over 80 °C and should not be mixed for laundering with linen, cotton or union. It is not suitable for articles that need to be sterilized. The ratio of polyester to cotton is 67/33 or 50/50.

With constant washing, the colour fades and it is common to find that the sheets will not be matched according to their varying degrees of shades of colour. In time the cotton will wear out far in advance of the polyester, leaving the fabric limp and because of the non-absorbent properties, useless for the purpose of rags.

Other polyesters include dacron and trevira.

Polyacrylonitrile (acrylics)
Such fibres are produced from acrylonite, from the refining of oil and coal. Acrylic fibres combine durability and an inherent softness and warmth and produce easy care fabrics with a wool-like handle and appearance. They are used extensively in long pile fabrics, furnishings, carpets and hand-knitting yarns. Common trade names are acrilan, courtelle and orlon.

It is common to find acrylic blankets in hotels today because they are cheaper than wool, do not shrink or stretch, are not affected by sunlight and are hard-wearing. Acrylic fibres however must be washed carefully as they are very absorbent. They can support 'static' and are not very resilient to abrasion – little balls of matted fluff cling to the fabric.

Modacrylic fibres such as acrilan SEF and teklan have similar textile properties to acrylics but they are also flame retardant. They are used in furnishings, carpets, sleepwear and toys.

Polyolefines
This generic term is not recognized in the EEC Directive but is used in the UK collectively to describe polyethylene and polypropylene which are official generic names. These fibres, being

non-absorbent and relatively inert, have not been used in normal apparel but have important industrial uses – in fishing gear, ropes and cordage, packing and sacks and in carpet backing. They include courlene and polysoft. The housekeeper would probably deal with two main sub-groups of this product.

Polypropylene (for example, ulstron) is used in the textile industry, but in catering establishments it is common to find moulded seating made from polypropylene and the white chopping boards found in kitchens.

Polythene (for example, courlene) is used for deck chair material and also in car upholstery. The housekeeper would most commonly use polythene as a means of protection and as rubbish sacks.

Polyvinyls
PVC is found in catering establishments in the form of flooring and seat covers.

Polyurethane
Elastane fibres, such as lycra and spanzelle, are based on polyurethane. Their main characteristics are high stretch and recovery and good resistance to many chemicals and perspiration which degrade ordinary rubber. Elastane yarns are used for stretch fabrics (such as stretch covers).

Fabrics and their uses

When choosing fabrics, consideration must be given to their properties, advantages and disadvantages.

For example when thinking of how the fabric will wash, the housekeeper must consider whether the fibres are *hydrophile* or *hydrophobic*. Hydrophile means that they absorb liquids easily and therefore care must be taken in laundering (e.g. the natural fibres and rayon). Hydrophobic means that they are less absorbent and are therefore easy to launder (e.g. synthetic fibres and triacetate).

Uses for man-made fibres

Workwear
Polyester blends with cotton or modal have to some extent replaced the traditional heavy cotton drills used for overalls, because they are lighter, cooler, retain a crisp appearance and have a longer life. Nylon, woven or knitted and often brightly coloured is used for lightweight fashion-type overalls.

Bed linen
Large quantities of man-made fibre are used for sheets and pillow cases instead of the traditional cotton or pure linen, and man-made fibres now account for almost 40 per cent of bed linen. The market is now moving steadily towards blends of polyester/cotton or polyester/modal as an alternative to fitted nylon sheets. This change is in part due to the easy care of polyester/cotton sheets.

Continental quilts (duvets)
Easy care fabrics such as nylon or polyester/cotton are used for the removable outer cover of continental quilts, and the use of synthetic fibres, mainly polyester, as a filling for quilts makes them washable as well as providing a good warmth to weight ratio.

Blankets
The most widely used man-made fibres are acrylic and viscose in blends with wool. The acrylics provide a combination of softness and warmth with easy washability and attractive colour possibilities. They can also be used in electric blankets.

Curtains
Cotton prints and similar fabrics made from modal/cotton are largely used for curtain fabrics. Other fabrics used include stitch-bonded fabrics in viscose/nylon; brocades in viscose/cotton or viscose/acetate, and colour-woven fabrics with a polyester warp and acrylic weft. Knitted fabrics have been tried from time to time and there is a renewed interest in this possibility. Where flame retardent properties are required for example, in public buildings, modacrylic is suitable.

Upholstery
Acrylic velvets, printed, plain or sculptured, are

important in primary upholstery because of their appearance retention and soil resistance. Also used are polypropylene, viscose with nylon, and cotton/modal/flax blends.

Carpets
Man-made fibres are very suitable for carpet printing making patterned carpets available at very competitive prices. Some of the special qualities of man-made fibres, like cleanability, colour fastness, resistance to mildew and rotting, have enabled carpets to be laid in areas considered unsuitable for natural fibres, like kitchens, bathrooms, playrooms, food halls, restaurants and public houses. The cheapness of man-made fibres is also encouraging the rapidly growing use of carpets in areas like schools, libraries, and hospitals where the sound-deadening and cushioning effect are valuable benefits for the occupants.

Nylon staple is also being used, normally in 20 per cent blends with other fibres, to improve their wear characteristics, hence the expression '80–20 blends' used in the carpet trade.

Furnishing fabrics

Bedford cord
A strong cotton fabric with a heavy rib running lengthwise. It tends to soil and wear at areas of concentrated use more dramatically than some other materials. It is used for upholstery and bed covers, and should be cleaned by brushing, vacuuming and light sponging.

Bonded fabrics
Felt is a bonded fabric where the wool fibres are closely linked. It shrinks and puckers if wetted. Man-made fibres, not having the inherent felting properties of wool, are bonded with a chemical agent. They have a matt finish and a wide range of colours. They are used for wall coverings and sometimes for furnishing. Dry cleaning is probably the safest method of cleaning, but follow the instructions if given.

Brocade and brocatelle
Brocades were originally all silk. Now a mixture of cotton and silk or man-made fibres are known as brocatelle. They are made in traditional patterns woven and with slight relief, and are used for curtains, bed covers and the heavier qualities for upholstery. Dry clean according to instructions where they are given.

Brocarts
This is a loosely woven coarse cotton brushed to increase its insulation property. It is used as interlining for heavy curtains.

Brushed cotton
It is a loosely woven coarse cotton brushed to increase its insulation property. It is used as interlining for heavy curtains.

Calico
This is woven cotton material, usually from raw cotton. It is comparatively inexpensive in its rough state. It is used in the final stage of upholstering furniture before the final cover is fitted or loose covers. It is amenable to dyeing and stencilling and can be used for curtains and other furnishings. It washes well, but will shrink and be bleached in the washing processes.

Cambric
A lightweight cotton fabric, this is used in lining. Down-proof cambric is used for duvets and cushions. It is not feather-proof. Wash as for cotton, but when used for cushion or duvet covers the cleaning will depend upon the filling.

Chenille
'Chenille' is the French word for caterpillar and the yarn from which chenille is woven resembles a hairy caterpillar. It was widely used in Victorian times (and still is) for curtains, table cloths and upholstered furniture covers. It has a deeper pile than velvet, but this does flatten. Modern chenille is made from cotton, viscose or synthetic fibres. Polypropylene chenille is hard-wearing. It should be cared for in the same way as other pile fabrics.

Chintz and cretonne
These are closely woven printed cottons. Cre-

tonne is woven from a coarser fibre than chintz. Chintz can be glazed. They are used for curtains, bed covers and loose covers. Dry clean or wash according to instructions (if given). Chintz can be reglazed by dry cleaners. Spray starch or finish will refresh house-washed chintz articles but is not practical for large items.

Corduroy

This is usually made from cotton, but is sometimes a mixture of cotton and man-made fibres. It has a short-cut pile ribbing with a one-way nap and must be cut to allow for this. Dressweight corduroy is not suitable for furnishings. It is used in light upholstery, curtains, cushions and bed covers. Corduroy can be washed and if dried in a tumble dryer, most of the creases will be removed. Careful pressing on the wrong side will remove more stubborn creases. To avoid crushing the pile, the right side should be on a soft resilient blanket surface. It may shrink, so follow any given instructions.

Damask

This is produced in silk, linen, cotton, wool and man-made fibres or mixtures of these. The heavier qualities are used for upholstery and lighter weights for soft furnishings. Linen and cotton are used for table linen. It should be washed in the same way as other fabrics made from the same fibres. Curtains containing rayon should be lined since the sun's rays will rot the rayon.

Denim

This is a hard-wearing and fairly inexpensive coarse cotton twill. It is woven in different weights, the heavier type being suitable for loose covers. It is used for loose covers, cushions and simple bed covers where low cost and hard usage are factors. It is washable, but may shrink.

Dupion

This is a fine fabric originally woven from raw silk, with a slub effect. Now it is usually made from a mixture of man-made fibres such as viscose and acetate. It comes in a wide range of plain colours. There is also a wide range of qualities so attention should be paid to the wrong side of the fabric which will show the closeness of the weave; the closer, the better the quality. It is used for curtains, cushions and bed covers. The curtains should be lined. Only the best quality should be used for loose covers and it should never be used where there may be heavy soiling. It should be dry cleaned.

Draylon

Draylon is the most common material used for upholstered furniture. It has similar properties to velvet, but a coarser fibre and, being of man-made fibres, is spongeable and tougher. The closeness of the weave of the ground material indicates the quality of the cloth. It should be vacuumed to remove dust and sponged with an upholstery shampoo to remove slight soiling. Heavy soiling should be cleaned only by professional cleaners.

Glass fibre

This fabric is translucent, flame retardant, crease-resistant, shrink- and moth-proof. The fibres break easily if subjected to excessive handling or constant rubbing against a curtain pelmet or window-sill. They are inclined to become charged with static electricity and consequently attract dust. It is used for unlined curtains and shower curtains, and should be hand washed in the bath to avoid twisting or crushing which will break the fibres. Wear rubber gloves to prevent skin irritation. Drip dry, do not use clothes pegs and fold as little as possible.

Leather or hide

This is expensive and should not be used where there is any likelihood of vandalism. The skin should be even and without blemishes. It is hard-wearing, but without proper care it will perish and crack. It is used for covering upholstered and padded furniture. The fine thin leather, skiver, is used for panels, desk and table tops. Wash with a cloth squeezed out of warm soapy water, rinse with warm water. Do not use detergent. Apply hide polish if it has a wax finish or hide food if it has a resin or cellulose finish. These polishes can be purchased at saddlers or leather shops. Do not apply too much moisture to buttoned upholstered furniture.

Simulated leather

There is a wide range of simulated leather which is much less expensive than the real thing. It has a cotton backing which stretches and is more resilient than vinyl. Simulated suede and leather are difficult to identify without close examination so try to see the back of the material. A reliable manufacturer will indicate on the label if it is leather or simulated leather, although the price would also indicate this. It is important to know whether it is leather or imitation because the care is different.

It has similar uses to real hide, but simulated suede can also be used for curtains and bed covers. Wash with warm water and detergent, rinse and dry off with a soft cloth. Never use a wax polish on any vinyl or plastic coated material.

Linen

This is strong and hard-wearing but creases easily and is expensive. Linen-union, a mixture of cotton and linen fibres, is cheaper and more crease resistant. A number of 'linen-look' or 'linen-type' materials with a slub weave are made from man-made fibres and mixtures with cotton, and these are usually crease-resistant. Linen is used for loose covers, upholstery, curtains and bed covers. It is washable but large items should be dry cleaned.

Matelasse

This is a fairly heavy and hard-wearing fabric, made of two pieces of material bound by the weave, which gives it a quilted effect. It is usually made with cotton or viscose or a combination. It is crease-resistant, and does not flatten. Its wearing qualities depend upon the fibre used on the upper surface. It is used for upholstery and bed and divan covers. It can be used for curtains, but would only be suitable for large windows since it does not readily drape. It must be dry cleaned.

Moquette

This is a heavy pile material. Better qualities are made of wool pile with a strong cotton base. The less expensive moquettes are made from cotton. It is crease-resistant and the pile does not flatten. The pile can be cut or uncut and the pattern is often outlined by differences in the pile. It is very hard-wearing, and is used mainly for covering upholstered furniture. It can be cleaned by brushing and gentle vacuuming.

Rayon

This is the generic term for man-made fibres from cellulose, derived from wood pulp and cotton. Superficially it resembles silk and has good draping qualities and lustre and is soft to the touch. It is frequently used with cotton to produce a simulated brocade or damask. It is adversely affected by sunlight and strong heat. It can be used alone or in combination with other fibres, for curtains or bedspreads. Alone it is not suitable for upholstery. It will wash but requires careful ironing with a cool iron. Large articles are best dry cleaned.

Repp

This is a hard-wearing medium-priced fabric with a horizontal rib. Better qualities are made from wool, but it is produced in cotton, silk and viscose. Wool repp and better qualities are used for upholstery, while others are suitable for loose covers, curtains and bed covers. It should be dry cleaned – only wash if labelled pre-shrunk.

Satin

A lustrous fabric made from silk, rayon or mad-made fibres. It is woven so that most of the warp (lengthwise) threads show on the surface producing a smooth glossy surface. It is suitable for curtains, bed covers and cushions. Dry cleaning is advisable since ironing may show water and pressure marks.

Sateen

This material resembles satin, but is made from cotton and mercerized cotton. The weft threads give the surface sheen. It is produced in a wide range of colours. It is not suitable for hard wear on its own, but is used for lining curtains and bed covers. Alone it is washable, but since it is usually a lining fabric it should be treated as the accompanying fabric. It may shrink if not of a good quality, so only a good quality should be used with superior furnishing fabrics.

Sheers

These are light-weight, open-weave fabrics made from man-made or cotton or wool yarns. They are produced in a wide range of weaves, colours and designs. They are used for see-through curtains, for use at windows or as room dividers. Their care depends on the fibre from which they are made. Because of the open weave they should be treated with care to avoid stretching or snagging.

Tapestry

This is made from cotton or wool yarns, fairly coarse, and woven on a jacquard loom, producing a figured fabric incorporating a variety of colours. The closely-woven good qualities are expensive but hard-wearing. The heavy variety made from wool is suitable for upholstery but cotton tapestry tends to shine and wear at pressure areas. The ligher tapestries are suitable for bed covers and curtains. They should be dry cleaned.

Ticking

This is a strong twill-weave, feather-proof, cotton fabric. It is relatively inexpensive and used primarily for covers for feather-filled pillows and cushions. It can be used for loose covers for trendy décor effects. It can be washed but it may shrink.

Tweeds and boucles

These are usually a mixture of wool and man-made fibres. They are largely fashion fabrics and should be looked at carefully. They are produced in a variety of weaves and fibres and fillers. If loosely woven they lose their shape and snag. They tend to shrink and collect dust. They are used for covering upholstered furniture, curtains and bed covers. They should usually be dry cleaned, but treat according to instructions. If possible ascertain from which fibres they are made.

Terry cloth

This material is similar to bath towelling, but that used for furnishings does not have such a high terry ratio and the pile is on one side only. It is available in a variety of colours and widths. It is suitable for bathroom curtains, cushion and couch covers in treatment and consulting rooms. Wash as for bed linen. It may shrink more than towels because of its looser weave.

Velour

This is a heavy pile fabric made of cotton, but sometimes with a mixture of viscose. It is used for curtains but the pile should run downwards. Heavier qualities can be used for upholstery. It should be dry cleaned.

Velvet

This fine pile fabric can be made of silk, cotton or nylon fibres. Acrylic velvet has a cotton backing or a mixture of nylon and cotton. It comes in a wide range of colours and is widely used for curtains and cushions. Only better quality should be used for upholstery, but dralon has largely superceded velvet for this. The pile should run downwards on curtains and chairbacks and from back to front on chair seats. It should be brushed or vacuumed with the pile. Most velvets are machine washable, but must be tumble dried to remove creases.

Velveteen

This is a cotton velvet, and lacks the lustre of velvet made from silk or viscose. It should be dry cleaned.

Genoese velvet

This is a figured velvet, usually with an acrylic pile, which can be cut or uncut on a satin background. Its use and care are similar to those of velvet.

Further reading

Rees, A., *The Science of Home Economics and Institutional Management*, 3rd edition. (Blackwell Scientific Publications 1983).

Useful addresses

The British Man-Made Fibres Federation,
24 Buckingham Gate,
London SW1E 6LB

Courtaulds Ltd,
Celanese House,
22 Hanover Square,
London W1

The Fabric Care Research Association,
Forest House Laboratories,
Knaresborough Road,
Harrogate,
Yorkshire HG2 7LZ

The International Wool Secretariat,
Wool House,
Carlton Gardens,
London SW1Y 5AE

The Silk Centre,
Dorland House,
18–20 Regent Street,
London SW1

7 Furniture

Materials

The housekeeper has to select suitable furniture and to care for it, and must have a knowledge of the materials and the methods of construction used in the manufacture of furniture.

Hardwood

These include walnut, oak, beech, rose, sapele, afromosa, mahogany, ash, plane, elm, birch, ebony and sycamore. Good quality furniture may be made from solid wood, or softwood with a veneer of hardwood.

Furniture should be inspected at the joints for signs of veneer applied to an inferior wood or plywood. The bottom and back of an item should be looked at, for rough softwood and plywood are more susceptible to woodworm.

Modern hardwood furniture is often treated with a polyurethene finish to render it ring-proof and heat resistant. This can be treated with a silicone spray polish. Untreated wood should be fed with a wax polish.

Softwood

These include pine, fir and larch yew. Deal is the name given to pine and fir of which there are three types; white, yellow and red. Red is considered superior to the others. Soft woods are used for furniture on their own or for the unseen parts of hardwood furniture. Most fitted furniture units and beds have deal frames. Where legs or castors are attached there should be a block of hardwood which will not split. Pine furniture is often treated with a polyurethene lacquer and can be wiped with a damp cloth and will accept a silicone polish. Softwoods are rich in resin and if not com-pletely seasoned may 'weep'. Being soft they are more readily attacked by the furniture beetle.

White wood or bass wood

This is soft, easily worked and straight in the grain and uniform in texture. It also takes glue very well and is used for white wood furniture which is painted or enamelled.

Plywood

As the name implies, this is made of three or more layers of wood glued together at right angles or diagonally, then placed under pressure.

Plywood affords greater strength to a thin board. It is estimated that a piece of plywood is four times stronger than solid wood of similar thickness. The method of manufacture prevents splitting and renders the material free from the risk of warping or shrinkage. It will, however, absorb moisture and, if left wet, layers will bubble and separate. If the edges are left raw and rough, the furniture beetle can have easy access. It is suitable for backing cabinets and wardrobes and for linings and bottoms of drawers. Because of the large sheets in which it can be made, it is used for screens and partitions.

Cane

This is the stem of one of the small palms (calamus or rattan) or the larger grasses (bamboo). It is light, strong and resilient. The thick canes are used as stays, legs and frames. The split and thin canes are used for weaving. These are soaked in water and woven in basket weave or into a mesh, as in bergere furniture. Cane furniture, although it collects dust, is easily cleaned. It does not hold its shape unless very well made.

Dehydration will cause the cane to flake and split, so it should not be placed near radiators unless they have humidifiers.

Cane can be attacked by woodworm, especially if used in conjunction with plywood. Bamboo is used in conjunction with chipboard, plywood and softwoods.

When buying cane furniture, check that the item is firm, not too springy and a good shape. Special attention should be paid to the finish around the legs and arms of chairs. Sharp ends should be woven in and not protruding.

Applied split canes should be firmly secure. Look for any signs of splitting where the small pins secure it to the frame.

Look at the quality of drawers and the back of an item.

Cane furniture collects dust and should be vacuumed using the smallbrush attachment first, then the fine nozzle and polished with a spray polish. Basket chairs and tables can be washed, preferably out of doors using a garden hose. (Do not use water if there is plywood in the structure.) Scrub with a solution of salt or borax (1 teaspoon to 1 pint water). Use a small brush to get into recesses. Rinse thoroughly with cold water. Leave to dry out of doors or in a current of cool air – not near a radiator. Polish with a spray polish. Bamboo should be kept in good condition by polishing occasionally with linseed oil. Cane seats which have sagged can be washed (allowing the solution to soak in) with a hot solution of water and bicarbonate of soda. Press the seat up so the seat is above the level of the frame. Wipe off the moisture and leave out of doors to dry. Reseating of cane chairs should be done by a professional.

Rush

This is usually used for the seats of chairs and stools and should be treated as for cane seats.

Bentwood

This is usually made of ash, birch, willow, oak or beech. Instead of being sawn to a curve, the wood is bent by being subjected to moisture and heat (see Figure 23). It is used for making small tables

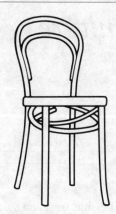

Figure 23 *Bentwood chair*

and upright chairs. It is very light and strong since there are few joints in the construction. The seats of bentwood chairs are of cane or plywood.

Attention should be paid to the joints when purchasing – they should be screwed. If the chair becomes unstable, it may be the screws need tightening.

Tubular

This is metal framed furniture, with a chrome or plastic-coated finish (see Figure 24). The gauge of the tubing varies and cheap tubular frames give way at stress points, especially when the tube has been flattened at bends. The frames hold chair seats and backs and table tops of fibre glass, polypropylene or laminated chipboard. Some chromium plated chair frames are supplied with

Figure 24 *Hammock/sling-style chair*

thick foam filled cushions which are easily replaced and therefore more economical than upholstered furniture. Treat with a spray polish.

Propathene structured foam
This has produced a new concept in furniture, as well as in many other products. It is tough, will not rust or splinter, is light and easy to handle. It will not shrink and has a low reject rate since leg and arm members are moulded in one piece. The mouldings can be drilled, screwed, nailed or stapled by normal production methods, but many of these operations can be eliminated as many conventional joints can be designed out. Many items can be moulded in adaptable modules and linked together. There are some units which combine tables and chairs, but they are not adaptable and are uncomfortable. They are easily cleaned, and resistant to stains, but not to cigarette burns which melt the material.

Coupled glass
This is propathene structured foam in which glass fibres are chemically bonded to the polymer, offering increased tensile strength and rigidity. Wash with warm water and a detergent.

Hardboard
This is used in the manufacture of cheap furniture. It is thin, but in some ways preferable to plywood since it will not harbour woodworm. It will buckle and deteriorate if allowed to get wet.

Polypropylene
This moulded plastic is used for chairs and tables in conjunction with a tubular metal frame of heavy guage mild steel. It is light, flame resistant and tough. It is suitable for stacking chairs, cinema seating and bathroom chairs. Wash with warm water and a detergent.

Antiques

Anything over 100 years old is classified as an antique. Because of its age and destructability an antique is not often in everyday use, or where it will get hard and careless usage. This is a vast field, and the housekeeper should have on his/her book shelf a reference book on the identification of styles and care of antiques.

Identification
This is all important, for a valuable item can be used, mistreated, and even destroyed because of lack of knowledge. It is necessary not to be misguided by the apparent shabbiness of a piece of furniture – an immaculate item may well be a reproduction. Frequently an antique can be found in a lumber cupboard or in use in a staff room, having been discarded because of its shabby appearance. When in doubt call in an expert.

Structure
Antique furniture has been built by traditional methods, wood joined with wood, dove tailing, mortice and tenon dowels etc. Badly repaired furniture may have nails, screws and glue evident.

Care of antiques
Old furniture, cupboards, chests and drawers frequently have a musty smell. This can be removed by rubbing the surfaces with a cloth wrung out in vinegar. The wood should not be made so wet that moisture seeps through into the joints, softening the glue and swelling the wood. Keep the drawers and doors open and leave in the open air if possible.

A piece of old furniture should never be placed near a radiator or a heating duct. Place humidifiers on radiators in rooms where there are antiques. Do not move pieces unnecessarily.

The wood should be fed with wax polish. Silicone spray polish should be used sparingly because it will eventually leave an unsightly film. This should be kept for melamine and plastic coated surfaces.

Light surface grease or build-up of old polish can be removed with vinegar and water: 1 pint vinegar to 1 pint water. Wipe over with a chamois leather wrung out in this solution, dry off with a dry cloth and polish. To remove a heavy build-up without damaging the patina, use half a pint of boiled linseed oil mixed with half a pint of turpentine or white spirit. Add a dash of vinegar, shake well, and apply with very fine steel wool, grade 000. Remove oil and dirt with a soft cloth dampened with a little white spirit to remove remaining grime, then polish with beeswax polish.

Antiques should be inspected periodically for woodworm, especially in spring time when they become active, paying attention to backs and bottoms of chests, drawers and drawer recesses. Soak such areas liberally with woodworm killer using a paint brush or with a proprietory woodworm killer using the nozzle supplied.

Small articles can be wrapped in a cloth soaked with paraffin and enclosed in a plastic bag, and left in an outside shed or garage for a week or two. This will kill all woodworm. Regular dusting with a cloth impregnated with paraffin is a deterrent to woodworm.

The flat surfaces of antique pieces such as dumb waiters can be protected by a piece of plate glass cut to size and shape. Where this is not practicable, avoid using polyurethene lacquers, but use a heat and water resistant acetone-based french polish. This is much more acceptable for antique and good quality furniture.

Glass ring marks can be removed by rubbing along the grain with metal polish, or linseed oil and cigarette ash made into a paste. Bad ring marks should be treated by an expert. Scratches can be rubbed with the cut side of half a brazil or walnut, or rubbed with wax boot polish of a suitable shade.

Antique upholstered furniture is made with hessian, horsehair and flock with metal springs and canvas webbing in a hard or soft wood frame. When treating covers, it is necessary to remember that the dye from the flock and dirt which will have accummulated can come up and stain the cover, therefore inspection should be made before any moisture is applied to the cover.

Reproduction furniture
This is available for all periods. It is usually of good quality wood and workmanship, so it should be treated with care. It is usually less expensive than antique furniture and is readily available, so any number of matching pieces can be purchased. It stands up to hard use and central heating, and table tops are usually treated to be heat resistant and water repellant.

It is unwise to fill a room with a large number of identical pieces, because they will look mass-produced. Pieces should be varied and chosen with discretion.

Lacquered furniture
This is usually old and of Oriental design. The base is of either wood or papier mâché on which a filling of whiting, plaster of Paris and glue mixture is placed to give a relief design. This is rubbed down and then a lacquer is applied. Sometimes mother-of-pearl is incorporated. The design is varnished and rubbed down and varnished again. Because all the design is applied, lacquered articles should be treated gently and washed with warm soapy water and polished with a dry chamois leather. Lacquered furniture is fragile and should be treated as a delicate antique.

Choice of furniture

Before choosing furniture, assess the environment in which it will be used – furniture in hotels will be different from that in schools or hostels. Whatever the environment, furniture should be strong, pleasing to the eye and contribute to the atmosphere required. It should be practical and the best quality the budget will allow. It should comply with the fire prevention legislation of 1980 and 1981: upholstered furniture must be able to resist ignition by cigarettes and matches. It is illegal to sell furniture which does not comply with the 1980 regulation. Foam fillings are cheap and effective but bring severe fire risks as they burn readily and give off toxic fumes. Figure 25 shows warning labels that should be looked out for. Furniture manufactured for the domestic market is not suitable for establishments.

Always 'shop around' to two or three reputable manufacturers. They should be members of the British Contract Furnishing Association (BCFA). Do not select merely from a catalogue.

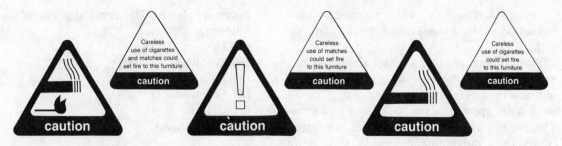

Figure 25 *Warning labels. Furniture which would not satisfy the match or cigarette tests will have to carry two labels: a display label and a permanent label*

Assess the reaction of the manufacturer to a request for testing by the Furniture Industry Research Association. If it has not already been done for the company, this association will undertake testing for non-members for a fee. This is costly but if several thousands of pounds are being spent, the cost of testing is small in comparison.

Have measurements of the area and a plan to draw in (to scale) the area covered by a piece of furniture. High backed chairs and bulky upholstered furniture will crowd a small area while giving no extra seating. Furniture can be used as room dividers, for example. Bookcases back-to-back, placed at right angles to a wall will break up a large area. Similarly settees will enclose a small seating area, making it more intimate.

The furniture should stand steadily with weight on any part of it. A chest of drawers may not be balanced if a full top drawer is drawn out. Hinges should be recessed into the wood, and drawer pulls and door knobs should go right through the wood and be secured at the back. Knobs merely screwed in, especially in softwoods, will quickly loosen. There should be no rough edges and all wood should be smooth and not heavily knotted.

Hardwood furniture is most suited to up-market establishments. It should be stained first and then polished and too high a gloss may indicate that it has been stained and polished in one process, so that the polish will either chip or wear off.

The edges of wood veneered chipboard should be protected by a solid wood lipping. Laminated finished chipboard should have the edges finished with a laminate strip applied with hot melted glue. Since they are likely to chip, a better quality will have a fibre glass moulded edging. This is known as GRP (Glass Reinforced Plastic).

Joints should be inspected closely since they are very important and an indication of how well a piece of furniture is made. Where two pieces of wood are merely abutting and held in place with a staple or nail, the result is a weak and insecure joint.

Fibre glass furniture should be checked to ensure that the colour goes right through the material.

Upholstered furniture

Frames
These can be made from wood (hard or soft), metal, plastic, fibre board or hardboard.

When the frame is totally covered it is usually of soft wood, but can be of fibre board or hardboard. Traditional hardwood frames are joined by dowels and glue with corner supports and stays where necessary. Frames of modern furniture are usually jointed by screws, staples and glue. Staples can provide a stronger and cheaper means than screws, but they must be evenly spaced, firmly inserted and used in conjunction with glue.

There are two types of metal frame.

1 The metal is a design feature of the article itself.
2 A totally covered frame.

Metal frames may appear to be stronger than wooden frames but they can bend and suffer from metal fatigue at the joints.

Hammock type chairs, which are made of canvas supported by a metal frame, do not stand up to hard usage.

Plastic frames produce a lighter article but they are sometimes artificially weighted to give an impression of durability. Moulded plastic frames have foam applied to the back, seat and arms. The plastics used can be glass fibre reinforced resin; rigid polyurethane foams; and, more expensive but stronger than these, expanded polystyrene (EPS).

Suspension

This is the part of the chair or settee which bridges the frame to support the padded seat or cushion. The types of suspension are

1 Webbing with spiral metal springs.
2 Zig-zag metal springs.
3 Rubber webbing.
4 Diaphragms or woven elastic.

Types 1 and 2 can be felt through the canvas tacked over the base, while types 3 and 4 are usually exposed to view.

Upholstery

The padding placed over the frame or suspension or a plastic or plywood base is called upholstery. Upholstering is done in three ways.

1 By padding with blocks of latex or plastic foam on a base of wood, slatted wood or slightly resilient straps attached to the frame.
2 Sprung upholstery. This is composed of one of the following
   (a) Hessian on the bottom covering the materials above.
   (b) Criss-crossed webbing to which are sewn the springs.
   (c) A series of spiral springs.
   (d) A cover of hessian.
   (e) Coarse horse hair stuffing.
   (f) Hessian.
   (g) Hair stuffing.
   (h) Calico.
   (i) Soft wadding, kapoc or flock (in old furniture).
   (j) Furnishing fabric cover.

3 Foam upholstery. This is made of one of the following
   (a) Hessian.
   (b) Webbing.
   (c) Foam.
   (d) Soft wadding.
   (e) Calico.
   (f) Fabric cover.

Covers

The cover of upholstered furniture can be very misleading and the quality of the chair should not be judged by the cover alone. The type of cover chosen will depend upon the use to which the furniture will be subjected. See Chapter 6 for a discussion of furnishing fabrics.

If the covers are going to be custom made, it is useful to have extra pieces cut and made up to cover the arms and the backs of the articles to protect them from body contact. Loose cushions should be reversible and they should have zip fastenings. Heavy buttoning does tend to collect the dust and is not advisable.

Loose covers should be considered, as they are easy to clean and to renew.

Care of upholstery materials

Emergencies
Deal with accidental spillages immediately to avoid staining. Liquids should be mopped up quickly so as not to allow seepage into the interior of the furniture. Stains should be identified and removed with an appropriate cleaner but often a carpet shampoo – the dry foam variety – will clean away general stains.

Daily
When the piece of furniture is being dusted, it may be brushed down with a small clean hand brush or vacuumed, preferably using a small dustette type of vacuum cleaner. A powerful vacuum cleaner may dislodge the filling and loosen any buttons.

Weekly
A thorough clean using crevice tools of a vacuum cleaner making sure that there are no food parti-

cles or other foreign bodies that may have become lodged down the sides.

Spring cleaning

Avoid letting any upholstery covering get too dirty. It is advisable to put upholstery cleaning out to a professional.

Record keeping

As with all items, it is essential that the housekeeper should keep a file on all furniture for reference purposes. Details from the manufacturer should include date of and where purchased, the make up and method of cleaning the item of furniture.

Common problems

In hotels and catering establishments the following dangers should be guarded against.

Pets Hairs, claws and grease from their coats can cause smells and dirt. They may carry infection and fleas.

Condensation If upholstery or soft furnishings are pressed hard against a window or wall where there is condensation, then the fabric may become stained or water marked. Such stains are difficult to remove.

Dry heat This will dry out furniture, causing the wood to shrink, joints may become unstable and the wood may crack and warp. Avoid placing wooden furniture near radiators.

Sunlight This can fade fabric and wood. Care should be taken to place furniture out of strong sunlight or to use suitable blinds.

Cigarettes Even with the new laws, cigarettes and matches can still cause fires, especially if they roll down the sides of sofas and chairs. Unsightly holes can be caused by hot ash or a cigarette butt being dropped especially on a plastic type fabric. Smoke and nicotine stains fabrics and causes stale smells.

Food and beverage Wherever food and drink is served, there is the risk that someone will knock something over and stain furniture.

Guests sitting on the edges of cushions or arms This can damage the interior of the chair or sofa, spoil the appearance and perhaps loosen joints. Rather like a mattress, seat cushions can be turned to help even wear.

Choosing upholstered furniture

The cover can hide a multitude of sins, so check more than the softness of the piece of furniture. Look at the base of the article, feel through the canvas or calico base cover to see whether there are cross pieces of wood into which the legs or castors are fitted. The seat or cushion should be slightly domed, to allow for drop after being sat upon. Feel the back of the chair to see if it is sprung. Feel the edge of the seat for gaps, rough edges and raw edges of material.

Piped corner edgings will receive constant wear: the material itself should be brought over these edges and the piping placed lower down.

If buttoned, the depth into which the button is sunk will give one an idea of the thickness of the padding. Look at the edges where they have been machined. There should be no sign of tension in the material and the stitching should appear to be close.

Sit in the chair, and see that an armchair lives up to its name and gives support to the arms. There should be support for the back and the seat not too deep so the edge comes beyond the knees. The feet should be able to touch the floor when sitting in a relaxed comfortable position.

Chairs being chosen for the elderly, disabled or infirm should be of such a height that the body does not have to be lowered into the seat, and the arms placed so that the occupant can get support to lift the body from the chair. The back of the chair should be of such a height to give support to the shoulders if real relaxation to the head is required, but this may not always be desirable because considerable soiling can result where the head rests.

When sitting in the chair, one should not be aware of any hard edges where the padding is not adequately covering the frame. Where there is exposed wood frame, see that it is smooth and not highly varnished. There should be no signs of deeply knotted wood or splitting, nor of nails or screws. There should be no sag in the cover.

It is inadvisable to select vinyl covering with superfluous stitching or buttoning. Moisture can penetrate the holes made by stitching and can rot the cotton backing.

Avoid any upholstered furniture of a design that has sharp edges; curved and padded edges will wear longer. Braid and fringes should be avoided for furniture being used by the public. It can quickly deteriorate with absent-minded plucking. If possible, select armchairs and settees on which the upholstery has a 10 cm clearance of the floor to avoid soiling and scuffing by feet.

Bedroom fixtures and fittings

Wardrobes

When selecting wardrobes or hanging cupboards, consider the likely duration of the stay of the guest. For 'in-transit' guests, a small hanging cupboard is adequate, with or without a door. A height of 180 cm, depth of 55 cm and width of 500 cm is adequate. Beside the full-length hanging space, there can be a series of drawers or shelves with a hanging space of 150 cm for men's suits above them. For short-stay guests, shelves are more practical than drawers. Large free-standing wardrobes should be in sections and assembled when *in situ*.

Hanging rails should be of metal because plastic or wooden rails will sag. There should be no length more than 50 cm without support.

Plastic clip closure gadgets do break. Magnetic catches are preferable, but a lock with key gives the guest security. Some wardrobes have an interior light which is controlled when opening and shutting the door. It should be placed high up, where it is unable to touch any clothes.

Hinges should be recessed, with a stop so that the door cannot swing back too far. It is essential that the wardrobe is well balanced and not likely to topple when the door is opened.

In modern hotels, wardrobes are usually built in, saving space and money. Doors are usually of the sliding variety to save space. Besides shelves

for clothing, there is usually a large shelf at the top of the wardrobe, where the housekeeper may store spare blankets and pillows. Keeping spare items in the guest room also saves time and energy on the part of the maid – should the guest be uncomfortable he or she need only look around the room and find what he/she wants.

Many guests take coat hangers as souvenirs, so it is now common practice to install fixed hangers. In halls of residence, the wardrobe may also be extended to house a wash basin, vanity unit and additional shelving so that the studio room may look as comfortable as possible.

Luggage rack

Hotel bedrooms should have luggage racks to prevent damage to chairs and wear and tear on bed covers. There are folding racks with metal legs and canvas straps which are the cheapest. There are also wooden racks, like a table with slats across the top. The advantage of these two types is that they can be used in the bedroom, often placed at the foot of the bed. They can also be used as rests for service trays. Fitted bedroom furniture usually has a luggage rack as part of the standard fitting.

The wall at the back of the luggage rack should be protected. The height of the rack is important; it should be lower than the desk or dressing table so that suitcases do not have to be lifted too high.

Luggage racks may also be used as a spare bench if they are appropriately covered. They may be built down to the ground offering the guest additional drawer space, but if they are of standard design, space must be left to enable the floor beneath to be cleaned.

Chests of drawers, dressing tables, desks and televisions

The general points on selection of furniture apply to these items. Drawers should be smooth, and rest on continuous runners. Plastic laminate-lined drawers with a ski front are easy to clean and do not require lining. Plastic drawers should be of a strong gauge, with sides as deep as the front of the drawer. A depth of 15 cm is a useful size in residential establishments. One large, deep drawer of some 30 cm will accommodate woollen jumpers and uniform overalls etc.

A television will often be placed on top of the chest of drawers although it is preferable to leave them free standing on legs of correct height.

Ideally televisions should be switched off at the mains after use, to prevent fire. As a precaution, nothing should be placed on top of the TV.

In both studio rooms and regular guest rooms, the desk usually doubles up as a dressing table. A mirror should be placed above the desk and a lamp that is strong enough for applying make up and for doing close work should be provided. Depending on the positioning of the desk, it could also suffice as a bedside table.

Bedside tables

The general points of structure should be looked for. The height should relate to the bed – the top should be at the same level as the top of the bed for easy reach of the bed occupant. Consider what it will have to hold (for example early morning tea tray, bedside lamp, ash tray, book, spectacles) and choose an appropriate size. Sometimes it will be shared by the occupants of two beds, so it might be placed between the beds. A lower shelf will give extra space if the area is limited. Where there is a door the way it opens should be noted, and the door should open away from the bed, but sliding doors may be more convenient.

Many fitted units have bed head and bedside cabinet or table incorporated. These have the disadvantage that they tend to enclose the bed which has to be pulled out for making. The table is *in situ* permanently, whereas a free-standing table can be used elsewhere and moved if a double bed is exchanged for a single, for example.

Coffee tables

A coffee table is normally situated next to the arm chair in a bedroom. It must be exceptionally well built as it is likely to be mistreated, and the surface can often be damaged by hot cups and alcohol. A nest of tables has the advantage of containing three or four tables in one unit, saving space but providing occasional tables when required.

Lamps

In modern hotel bedrooms it is unusual to find the old-fashioned central light. Instead there are small pools of light around the room, making the light much softer. There is usually a standard lamp positioned near the armchair for reading purposes, plus bedside lighting and a light in the hallway of the room. Each of the bulbs should be at least 60 watt. The desk lamp, should be 100 watts. Some hoteliers attempt to save money by reducing the wattage in all lamps, but the complaints received often outweigh the savings made.

Pictures and mirrors

There should be a mirror over the desk so that it may be used as a dressing table. A long mirror should also be found in a hotel bedroom. This is usually placed on the wardrobe door, on the back of the bathroom door, or on the back of the door leading out of the room. Pictures give a room life and interest. In luxury hotels an artist is sometimes commissioned to complete a special set.

Fitted furniture

Fitted furniture is usually constructed in veneered soft woods, plywood or chipboard, or laminated plastic. Special custom-built fittings will be made in hard wood to fit in with the existing woodwork or furniture. Fitted furniture limits the versatility of the room but can be fitted to the customer's requirements. Bedrooms so furnished have a uniformity since to be cost-effective the units should be produced in quantity, although minor adjustments can be made. However, fitted furniture provides a practical and economical way of furnishing studio bedrooms and hotel bedrooms.

Check that the exposed sides of the furniture match the front or can be papered to blend in with the rest of the room. Dressing table, bed head units or desk and luggage rack pieces are best cantilevered so the carpet can be laid and cleaned without interruption. The back of the top of the luggage rack area should be built up to prevent damage to the wall. If the budget will allow it,

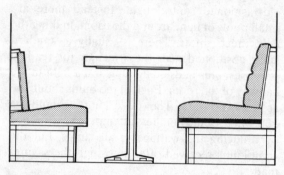

Figure 26 *Banquette seating*

fitted furniture should be backed. Using the wall as the back of the unit is cheaper, but there is a danger of damp or condensation unless there is adequate ventilation.

If dampness occurs in a fitted wardrobe, fit a plywood back, 6 mm thick. Leave a space of 12 mm between the ply and the brick wall and fill with glass fibre. Dampness in a cupboard can also be reduced by silica gel crystals placed in a de-humidifier container hung in the cupboard. In bad cases, a small lamp (Pygmy) with a 25 watt lamp and shielded with a perforated zinc or wire mesh, will help to keep clothes dry.

Banquette seating

This is space saving but is limited in its versatility (see Figure 26). It can be attached to the wall as a permanent fixture, but it may be more practical to have it movable. It can be made up in sections abutting to each other, which makes use of corners in a room. It can also be used as a room divider or to make bays and give an atmosphere of privacy for group seating. It is extremely practical in large areas where large numbers of people may have to be seated, for example, air and rail termini, waiting rooms at hospitals, college common rooms. In refectories, it is practical as it prevents the movement of chairs and offers compact seating. However, it can be more expensive to recover a banquette seat than one damaged chair, so it is not necessarily practical where there is a danger of vandalism.

Chairs

Next to the bed, the chair is the most important item of furniture. A chair has to take the weight of the body and give support to the back. The angle of the back in relation to the seat will depend upon what the occupier is doing.

For working or eating at a table the chair should be at a height at which the occupant can sit to reach the top of the table with the forearms at right angles to the elbow. There should be adequate knee room under the table. In student hostels an adjustable typist's chair would be useful.

For relaxing in lounges or common rooms, the average size is 40–42 cm (floor to seat) high and 42–50 cm deep (from back to front). The backs of the chairs should be slightly splayed, but this depends on the position of the legs. A chair with the top of the back extended well over the back legs will fall over if leaned upon. The elderly or infirm will require a higher chair which they can sit on easily with the knees bent at right angles to the thighs. The legs of chairs should be supported with stays or cross stretchers, which are not placed in such a position that they will be used as a foot rest.

Chairs in lounges should relate to the height of the tables: low chairs at low tables.

Stacking chairs need to be strong and they are usually made of tubular metal and with a plain or padded plastic shell seat and back. They are used for meetings and conferences, so remember that the occupant is captive for several hours. The width of the space between legs should be greater than any part of the chair. The bottom of the legs should be protected with rubber or plastic ferrules. There should be a space between the seat and the back for cleaning purposes, but it should not be too great or there will be no support for the lower part of the spine. Lecture-room chairs may have a writing rest for note-taking. It is preferable to have these detachable and reversible for adaptation for left-handed users.

Tables

Restaurant tables should be of a height comfortable for customers to sit at: 70–84 cm, with a knee clearance of 18–20 cm.

Table tops on which cloths will be used should be covered with a non-slip material, such as white felt or simulated felt. Polished topped tables should be protected by heat resistant place mats. They are usually treated with a heat resistant polyurethene varnish.

In canteens, refectories and fast food areas, table tops are usually of laminated plastic, fibre glass or polypropalene. The latter have the advantage of having curved moulded edges, whereas the laminated plastic has an edging which can break off. While heat mark resistant, none of these are resistant to cigarette burns.

Lounge table tops can have a variety of finishes; laminated plastic, glass, simulted marble, marble, slate. The legs should never protrude beyond the edge of the table. Lounge tables and chairs should be grouped in relation to their respective heights. Banqueting and conference tables are often supplied with frames on which a variety of tops can be placed. Avoid units which have loose nuts and bolts or clips. The legs should be looked after. If they are wooden they should be polished, and any roughness smoothed to avoid snagging tights or trousers. Round tables are more versatile; legs do not get in the way of those seated.

It adds interest to a dining room or restaurant if there is a mixture of square, oblong and round tables. Square and oblong tables should all be of the same height and of related dimensions so they can be placed together to make a large table.

Some square tables have crescent shaped flaps which produce a round table when raised, increasing the size of the table. Banqueting tables, and restaurant tables which may be put together, should have legs inset from the edge of the table top so when two pieces are put together, there is knee room.

All canteen furniture should be cheerful and easily cleaned with hard-wearing surfaces and strong structure. Chairs and tables which can be stacked are useful for thorough floor cleaning, or for easy storage. Vinyl seat covers are not advisable because they will deteriorate with the grease from overalls.

Clocks

Electric clocks should only need attention after a power cut, or at the beginning and end of British Summer Time. They keep good time unless there is a fluctuation in the voltage.

Battery clocks keep good time and need little attention except to change the batteries. This is necessary when they start to lose time.

Quartz clocks are similar to battery clocks.

Pendulum clocks usually have a visible pendulum. The drive for the pendulum comes from either a wound-up spring or weights. They therefore require to be wound up regularly and to be hung or standing quite level. They should not be moved or knocked otherwise the balance of the pendulum will be upset. One person should be responsible for winding the clock. This duty is often performed by the night porter.

Clock cases should be treated as for furniture of the same materials, bearing in mind that a pendulum clock is likely to be old, and may be an antique.

To prevent dust entering the works of clocks, they should be well sealed, especially in dust laden areas.

Where a large number of clocks require attention a clockmaker may be asked to come in and attend to them at regular intervals.

If it is necessary to move a pendulum clock for purposes of redecoration, call in an expert to do this. Grandfather clocks or long case clocks should be fixed to the wall. Wall clocks should be fixed at top and bottom, so that they are not moved while being wound or dusted. Clocks should never be hung on or stood by a damp wall.

Long case clocks should have the door kept locked, to prevent curious people investigating, or even hiding things inside the clock case. It has been known for cleaners to leave their favourite cleaning brushes and dust pans in a clock case!

Pianos

Pianos are often found in establishments. While a piano is strictly speaking a musical instrument, its casing can be regarded as a piece of furniture and should be treated according to its age and style.

The instrument parts inside the casing are made of wood and felt. Pianos made before 1945 need more attention then newer models because the glues used before 1945 are not so strong.

Pianos are damaged by extremes and changes of temperature, humidity, or extreme dryness. A piano should never be placed against a damp outside wall, a radiator or warm air vent. Bottled gas or oil heaters which produce moisture should not be used. Unless the piano is standing on some insulating material such as felt, it should not be left in a room with underfloor heating. Avoid moving the instrument unless it is mounted on a cradle with smooth running wheels or castors.

To avoid condensation and rusting inside the piano, an electric light bulb (60 watts) can be hung inside. A moth repellant will stop moths attacking the felt dampers. The casing should be treated for wood worm as for other furniture.

A professional tuner should be called in to tune a piano regularly, regardless of how little the instrument is played. Members of the following associations are regarded as professional: Association of Blind Piano Tuners; Institute of Musical Instrument Technology; Pianoforte Tuners Association.

The arrangement of furniture

When arranging the layout of furniture and lighting in any area, it is important to think of how the room and furniture will be used by the occupants and the staff.

This is where the study of ergonomics enters the realms of hospitality management. Ergonomics is a relatively new science which deals with the way that people are affected by their environment. The rooms must not only look right but be

right for use. Table and standard lamps should be placed to illuminate the activity area. Space must be left for movement of the occupants, to use the furniture. Doors and drawers have to open. Chairs have to be pulled out in order that one can sit at the table.

When planning the layout, there should be a plan of the room and scale plan shapes of furniture. These can be moved around on paper more easily than furniture round a room.

Hiring furniture

Hiring or leasing furniture is a growing trend. The advantages are that capital is not required. When starting a new business, this enables money to be available for working capital until the business is profitable. The payments will also clearly show running costs and be assessed against income. In addition, if repairs and maintenance are included in the contract, the responsibility is lifted from the lessor.

The disadvantages are that the choice is limited to the furniture selected by the leasing company. In most cases there has to be a uniformity of design and the establishment lacks a personal or individual touch. In some cases the responsibility of the manufacturer ceases once the contract has been completed and the lessor is dealing only with a finance company.

Furthermore, leasing can often be more expensive than borrowing money from the bank to buy furniture outright.

It is now fairly easy to hire tables, chairs, marquees, etc. for outside catering. In offices and residential establishments, companies are only too pleased to arrange terms on the rental of such things as typewriters and televisions.

Further reading

Conran, T., *The House Book* (Mitchell Beazley).

Useful addresses

The British Furniture Manufacturers Federated Association, 30 Harcourt Street, London W11 2AA

The Furniture Information Council, 11–14 Gough House, 57 Eden Street, Kingston on Thames, Surrey.

Furniture Industry Research Association, Maxwell Road, Stevenage, Herts SG1 2EW

8 Floors and floor coverings I

Floors and floor coverings are very expensive items so careful selection is of the utmost importance.

Aspects to consider when choosing a suitable floor or floor covering

Wear
Think about how much wear the flooring is going to receive. For example, is it to be laid in a bedroom or an industrial kitchen?

Warmth
A carpet will normally be laid in a bedroom in European hotels, but perhaps in very hot countries another type of flooring (such as tiles or terrazzo) might be more suitable.

Comfort
Hard floors are known to be cold and tiring – one of the reasons why professional chefs tend to wear laced-up boots at work. Walking on carpets all day tends to make the feet very hot and swell up, unless good shoes are worn.

Safety
Slippery finishes are dangerous, especially when heavy articles are being carried. Loose rugs that may cause people to trip are equally a hazard, especially for the elderly and children.

Noise
Tiles and stone floors can be very noisy, especially in modern buildings where the noise is carried very easily.

Choice
Choice often depends on the budget available, but a floor may be thought of as an investment – in some cases floors are forever. If a cheap floor covering is purchased, then it can usually be assumed that it will only have a short life span.

Planning
When planning the décor of the room an interior designer will often start with the floor. Thought must be given to the sub-floor; will it be suitable as a base for the floor or floor covering chosen? The colour and texture of the chosen floor covering must be well planned in conjunction with the complete room so that the décor is well balanced.

Maintenance
Before making a final decision, thought must be given to the cost and problems involved with repairs, maintenance and cleaning of the floor or floor covering.

Cost
Although last in this list, cost is often the greatest consideration. If capital is limited, a less expensive floor may be selected and the ensuing maintenance and replacement costs be taken over a number of years. On the other hand if capital is available, the most durable flooring or covering can be installed and the replacement costs will be less.

Types of floor

Solid floors
These are built directly on the ground. A layer of concrete is laid into which is sandwiched a damp proof membrane of PVC or bitumen. Solid floors do not allow for pipes or cables to pass through,

unless through a conduit. With underfloor heating there are electrically heated elements in the last layer of concrete.

Hollow floors

These have under them a space of about 30 cm from the ground in which there is free circulation of air. Air bricks built into the exterior walls allow for this, and if they become blocked dry rot can occur. There are joists across this space on to which is attached the actual floor.

Floor surfaces

Slate

Slate is sometimes found in foyers, lobbies and entrance halls. It can be of either a sawn or polished finish and is found in two main colours: Welsh slate is dark blue/grey and Westmorland slate is green/grey.

Advantages: Good appearance, hard-wearing and easy care.

Disadvantages: Very expensive, noisy, cold and hard. To add warmth, rugs or carpet squares may be laid on top.

Care: Sweep, dry mop or vacuum and wash. An emulsion polish or water-based seal can be used occasionally but care must be taken not to make the floor too slippery. Linseed oil and turpentine may also be used.

Ceramic tiles

These are made from clay. Sometimes they have a non-slip finish and can be purchased in a wide choice of colours, patterns, finishes, textures, sizes and thicknesses. They can be ideally used in coffee shops, canteens and bathrooms as they are easy to clean and add colour.

Advantages: Hard-wearing, waterproof and easy to clean.

Disadvantages: Cold, noisy, tiring underfoot and can sometimes crack under very heavy weights.

Care: Sweep or dry mop or vacuum then wash.

Quarry tiles

These are made from a special type of clay which is fired until it is very hard. They are usually brown, grey or buff-coloured. The tiles are square, but corner pieces curved in shape can be purchased, making them ideal for kitchens, stores, wash-up areas and toilets.

Advantages: Waterproof, resistant to grease, hard-wearing and easy to clean.

Disadvantages: Cold, hard, noisy and slippery when wet or greasy. Textured or non-slip quarry tiles exist but they are difficult to clean. Adhesive pads may be stuck at intervals on smooth quarry tiles, but they do come off with wear and cleaning. Duck-boards may be used around wash up sinks, so the operator is not standing on a slippery wet surface.

Care: Sweep or dry mop, wash or steam clean.

Marble

This is usually found in luxury establishments, in foyers and halls. It comes in various colours. White marble tends to discolour in time.

Advantages: Good appearance and hard-wearing.

Disadvantages: Expensive, cold and hard to walk on.

Care: Sweep and dry mop or vacuum and wash. Avoid acid cleaners. Where marble is used in bathrooms it should be washed and dried. Hard water deposits removed with white vinegar and water rinsed and dried.

Simulated marble tiles

These are lighter than marble and less expensive. Wall facings, claddings and columns can be custom made to match. Pure marble aggregates are set in a resin-bonding agent producing a material which looks and feels like marble, though it is less cold to the touch.

Care: It should be swept with a soft brush or vacuumed and washed with a mild detergent and water.

Terrazo

This consists of marble chippings set in cement, and is often found in entrance halls where it is laid in large slabs, and in bathroom and wash and toilet areas.

Advantages: It is very hard-wearing and easily cleaned.

Disadvantages: Cold, hard and noisy and in time cracks may appear. For this reason brass strips are often used between the slabs to cover the joins.

Care: Sweep or dry mop or vacuum. Wash but do not polish or else it will become slippery. Avoid acid cleaners which attack the marble.

Mosaic

This consists of small pieces of tiles or glass silica. It is suitable for use in the same areas as marble and terrazzo, especially in older buildings.

Advantages: Same as those of ceramic tiles.

Disadvantages: Cold, hard and noisy, and dirt can collect in the grouting.

Care: Sweep or dry mop or vacuum and wash.

Brick

Brick can be obtained in various colours and is used for entrance halls, covered walkways and patios.

Advantages: Long lasting and can be used inside and outside. A warm and rustic effect is created.

Disadvantages: The bricks can crack under heavy weight or uneven pressure. Over the years they do wear with tread. Unless treated they absorb dust and grease and dust collects in the crevices between the bricks.

Care: Sweep and wash, using a detergent as soap will leave a white deposit. Brick floors used indoors should be sealed and polished.

Stone

This is often found in very old dwellings and sandstone, limestone and granite are the most popular varieties.

Advantages: Hard wearing and long lasting.

Disadvantages: Hard, cold and noisy.

Care: Sweep, dry mop or vacuum and then wash. Stone may be sealed to make care easier but sometimes the colour will be changed by the seal.

Granolithic

These floors are made from granite chippings mixed with cement, and are often found as workshop or factory floors.

Advantages: Hard-wearing.

Disadvantages: Not really suitable for guest areas.

Care: Sweep and wash over.

Granwood block

These floors are made from cement tiles with wood chippings and linseed oil. They are sometimes found in sports halls.

Advantages: Hard-wearing and not as cold as many of the floors previously mentioned.

Disadvantages: Very expensive.

Care: Sweep, dry mop or vacuum and then wash. Polish may be applied occasionally.

Screed or seamless

These can be laid over a variety of subfloors. The type and thickness of screed will depend upon the use the floor will be given. Screeds consist of resins and fillers. Both ingredients having specific qualities suitable for different areas. Manufacturers will advice on the suitability of their products. Screed floors can be plain, coloured or mottled. They are relatively non-porous and non-absorbent and immune to attack by fungi and pests. Some claim to provide some sound insulation, and those with an abrasive ingredient are made non-slip. Manufacturers instructions on care and maintenance should be followed.

Concrete floors

These are often used in basement areas and cellars and externally for patios and paths. Internally they can be painted and sealed to make them less dusty and easier to clean.

Advantages: Fairly cheap and durable. Easy care.

Disadvantages: Hard and cold. In wintery conditions external tiles become slippery and crack because of water absorption.

Care: Sweep and scrub. Some concrete floors are painted and then polished with an emulsion polish. Repainting is necessary as it does wear off.

Wooden

Wood is the traditional flooring, and is still used in many buildings.

Strip and board

These consist of strips or planks of wood about 10 cm wide nailed to the joists. In older buildings the boards may be 17.5 cm wide. *Hardwood strip floors* usually have boards joined by tongue and groove, and fixed to the joists by secret nailing. *Softwood strip floors* have abutting boards, so dust and draughts can enter the building if the boards shrink. Softwood floors are usually covered.

When sanding hardwood strip floors, care should be taken because the nails are not visible. Hardwood strip floors are often used for dance floors because they are sprung.

Wood block

The blocks are made in a variety of sizes. They are generally laid on a sand and cement screed or on a concrete base and secured by mastic or bitumen emulsion mixed with rubber latex. They can be laid in several pattern ways but the herring-bone and square basket are the most usual. This is an expensive flooring and nowadays is usually made as a decorative feature of a room, though previously they were used in schools and public buildings.

Parquet and mosaic floors

These are made from specially selected decorative hardwoods: oak, mahogany, teak and maple. They are formed in panels. They can be fixed individually to a smooth even floor with adhesive or secret pinning. Wood mosaic flooring is similar to parquet flooring except that the blocks of decorative hardwood are smaller. Sanding of this type of flooring should be done carefully using nylon mesh discs, which will remove the top surface with minimum abrasion.

Parquet tiles

These are small strips of plywood with a hardwood veneer, made into squares with a backing.

They are laid as tiles over any type of smooth dry floor. They should be sealed and never sanded because the veneer is very thin.

Hardwood floors have the advantages of good appearance, resilience and toughness if maintained, and they improve with age and constant polishing. Their disadvantages are that dry heat can cause wood to shrink,while damp causes it to swell and rot. It is very expensive. Checks should be made from time to time for fire hazards – hardwood can smoulder for a long time without any signs of burning.

Wood floors should be vacuumed or swept or dry mopped. If sealed they can be spray polished with a non-slip polish. Old wood floors which have not been sealed should be treated with a wax polish sparingly applied and thoroughly buffed.

Chipboard

This is laid in the same way and as an alternative to wood strip floors. Panels of chipboard are laid by tongue and groove and secret nailing on battens to which polyurethene foam has been fused. This gives a certain amount of resilience to the floor. The chipboard flooring should not touch the wall or skirting board. Contact between the two will produce flanking sound transmission. The surface is treated with a polyurethene seal.

Dance floors

These must have a certain amount of give, to deal with the weight and movement they will be subjected to. They are called sprung floors. Treatment is the same as polished floors and 'slip' is given for dancing by sprinkling with French chalk or talcum powder. When not being used for dancing, they should be treated with non-stick polish. Frequently they are covered with a section of carpet which is lifted when required for dancing.

Portable dance floors can be placed over an existing carpeted or non-smooth floor. They are of polished wood tiles or laths. Tiles are mounted on stable backing of hardboard or similar material – in square sections which clip together. The outside of the portable floor is protected by long strips of wood with the outside edge bevelled.

The sections clip together or fit into each other, jigsaw fashion. Loose clips should be avoided as they get lost. These floors can be made up in different sizes according to the number of sections used.

Another type of portable floor consists of laths or strips of polished wood with a flexible backing, which can be rolled up when not in use. Both types of flooring should be stored in neither too dry or too damp conditions. They should be laid on an even surface. They should be treated as a permanent wooden dance floor.

Floor coverings

There is a wide range and ever increasing number of floor coverings. They are laid over the structure's existing floor when it is not suitable to be left exposed.

Some floor coverings should not be laid over wood floors, but in all cases the basic floor surface should be even and dry. Water should not be allowed to get underneath, either through the joins or at the edges. Non-porous coverings (such as cork) should be treated to render them waterproof.

Floatex (trade-name)
A PVC sheeting with a nylon pile. It is commonly used on the domestic market and also in some hospital wards, care units and geriatric units.

Advantages: Hard-wearing, waterproof, easy to clean, non-slip, fire resistant, warm. Good appearance and reasonably inexpensive.

Disadvantages: Bleach will damage it. Because of its semi-porous nature it does absorb certain substances such as urine. It also collects fluff on its tiny fibres.

Care: Vacuum and shampoo.

Altro flooring
This is a vinyl sheeting with abrasive grains of aluminium evenly spread throughout the surface giving a non-slip finish. It is suitable for use in some kitchens, wash-up areas, service areas, stores etc.

Advantages: Non-slip, hygienic, waterproof, non-flammable with a built-in smoke inhibiter.

Disadvantages: Rubber heels will mark it and cigarette burns make irremovable scars.

Care: Sweep, vacuum and use a scrubbing machine as for any other similar floor.

Safety floor
This is a modular honeycomb system built in special rot-proof non-slip polyethylene. It is supplied in 0.25 metre square sections by 20 mm deep. Each section interlocks with floor anchoring cells for mechanical fixing if required. Because of its cellular structure and the inherent properties of polyethylene, honeycomb flooring is tough, flexible and adaptable to uneven floors to give a stable walkway.

Linoleum
This is often called 'lino' and has largely been superseded by vinyl floor coverings, but because of its durability is still found in some establishments. It is made from a mixture of resin cork or wood-flour pigments and mineral fillers, with a jute canvas or bituminized paper felt backing. The latter is used for the less expensive types. It is produced in many colours and either printed or in-laid patterns. Embossed lino is more slip-proof than plain, but unless the lino is of good quality, patterns and embossing will wear off where there is constant tread.

It is suitable for floors requiring a clean, smooth surface. It should be laid with a paper felt underlay on a smooth sub-floor. Joins should be avoided in a maintread area, and there should be minimum gaps at the walls.

Advantages: Hard-wearing and reasonably warm.

Disadvantages: It can tend to curl at the edges, causing cracking. If water gets beneath the lino, it will rot the backing and damage the whole flooring.

Care: Sweep, dry mop or vacuum. When washing avoid excess wetting, and use a neutral detergent as lino reacts badly to alkalis and acids. Use the polish recommended by the manufacturer. Excess wax polish will render it slippery.

Rubber flooring

This is made from natural rubber or synthetic substitutes, combined with 'fillers' of china clay and pigments. The synthetic substitutes have the advantage over natural rubber in that they are resistant to oils, grease and acids. It is produced in sheets or tiles which can be cut square or in interlocking shapes rather like jigsaw pieces.

Rubber flooring is suitable for use in hospitals, hotels and hostels, especially in corridors and bathrooms. Because of the grease and acid resistance of the synthetic type, it is suitable for use in cafeterias and some kitchen areas.

Advantages: It is more flexible than lino. It is durable, quiet and resilient to the tread. It is produced in bright and attractive colours and is amenable to in-lay work, so that the logo or name of the establishment can be in-laid in constrasting colours. It is hygienic, resistant to moulds and bacteria. If correctly maintained it is slip-proof, especially the embossed type. It is warmer to the touch and gives better thermal insulation than lino. It is non-water absorbant and immune to pest attack.

Disadvantages: It is more expensive than lino or vinyl floor coverings and requires expert laying. The embossed type is more difficult to clean. Non-synthetic rubber reacts adversely to grease and acids.

Care: It should be swept daily or vacuumed to remove loose particles and wet or dry mopped. A little neutral detergent can be used in the wet mopping. To prevent deterioration from oxygen and sunlight it should be sprayed with a water emulsion wax polish, then buffed with a very fine pad on the polisher. Scuff marks can be removed by using a mild abrasive paste or a nylon pad.

Flexible PVC

This is a blend of polyvinyl chloride and polymer with pigments added. In the past asbestos fibres were added, but because of the health hazard of asbestos it is no longer manufactured. However, it may still be found in use, in which case, it should be replaced. Flexible PVC is obtainable in tile and sheet form and has largely replaced linoleum. It may be backed with felt, hessian, plastic foam, cork or fabric. When purchasing PVC tiles or sheeting, note the thickness and the type of backing. A poor quality will have the minimum thickness and a paper felt backing.

Tiles should be laid on a sub-floor of concrete or asphalt, which must be thoroughly dried out. Patterned tiles are not suitable for areas where there is heavy traffic. Sheet PVC is especially suitable for use in hospitals, since it can be heat-welded, preventing crevices in which bacterial growth could take place. It can be bought up a few inches on the wall, forming a skirting, and making for easier cleaning.

Advantages: It is waterproof, resistant to oil, grease and chemicals. It is relatively quiet and warm, and depending on the backing, resilient to the tread. It is immune to fungal attack. If suitably maintained it is non-slip. If the heat does not exceed 27°C and a suitable adhesive has been used, it can be used where there is underfloor heating.

Disadvantages: Gel polishes should be avoided. Vinyl tiles tend to shrink. Discoloration will occur unless a neutral cleaning agent is used. Seals should be avoided as it will be necessary to continuously strip and reseal in heavy traffic areas. It is easily damaged by heat and by certain spirit solvents. If left wet, or if grease is not thoroughly cleaned off, it is very slippery.

Care: After laying the covering should not be washed for seven days. After dry mopping or vacuuming, wash with a neutral detergent, and polish with a water emulsion wax polish. Remove scuff marks with a gentle abrasive pad (such as Scotch Guard). It should be washed periodically with water and a mild alkaline detergent, then rinsed with a solution of vinegar and water. Leave to dry thoroughly and apply two coats of water emulsion wax polish. Do not use solvent impregnated mops which will cause deterioration and produce a slippery surface. Soap should never be used for the same reason. Scouring powders will damage the surface.

Linoleum, vinyl flooring and cork carpeting should not be relaid after lifting because they will become brittle. These materials should never be stored in too moist or too dry conditions. They should be rolled, not folded, and never have any weight placed on them while stored.

Cork tiles and carpet

These are made from granulated cork and synthetic binders. Tiles have a firm synthetic backing and carpet canvas or pliable paper felt backing. Both are suitable for bathrooms, corridors or playroom floors. Tiles are applied to an even screed sub-floor with an adhesive and sealed. They can be sanded down and re-sealed. Water seepage will cause lifting. Cork carpet is similar to linoleum but thicker. It should be laid on a smooth even sub-floor with an underlay of paper felt. It too should be sealed with a solvent-based seal and treated with the manufacturer's recommended polish.

Advantages: Warm to the touch, quiet and resilient to tread, sound absorbent and gives good thermal insulation. It has an attractive natural colour.

Disadvantages: It is more expensive than linoelum and vinyl PVC. Excess wetting will cause rotting. Soap deposits will leave a white film unless removed promptly. Sunlight will cause fading and the tiles can chip and crumble at the edges.

Care: Seal with a polyurethane seal. Dry mop and wash. Avoid over-wetting.

Vinyl cork tiles

These are cork tiles which have been coated with a layer of laminated vinyl, which renders them more hard-wearing and non-porous.

Care: Dry mop and wash.

Raised floor tiles

These are useful for outside areas, such as patios and around swimming pools, where water may lie. They are polyethylene raised interlocking tiles, with an open perforated surface through which the water will pass. They can be lifted for mopping up the floor beneath.

Advantages: They produce a non-slip surface and provide insulation over a cold surface. They are resilient and insulate against impact sound transmission.

Disadvantages: They should not be left to cover a multitude of sins – dirt and stagnant water, for example.

Care: Brush and hose down to keep them fresh and clean.

Thermoplastic tiles

These are made from synthetic resins and vinyl. They are a common and inexpensive floor covering laid on a smooth screed in preference to wood.

Advantages: They are inexpensive, tough, resistant to abrasion and easily cleaned.

Disadvantages: They are cold, non-resilient and not completely resistant to great heat. When wet they are extremely slippery. Suitable for linen and service rooms, stores, etc.

Care: Sweep, dry mop and wash. It is not advisable to apply polish to these tiles since they can become very slippery. Remove scuff marks with fine steel wool or Scotch Guard.

Floor seals

These are necessary to fill or cover pores in a floor so rendering it non-porous. They should be used on porous floors such as cork, concrete, wood, unglazed brick and certain types of stone. Once sealed, the floor will be easier to clean. Dirt and germs will also not be able to penetrate the seal and collect within the floor itself. A seal should penetrate the floor in order to reinforce it. Also, by adding to the wearing surface, the seal will extend the life of the floor and protect it from dirt and stains. Seals are applied to some floors in order to enhance their appearance as well as to add to their ease of cleanliness and protection. A seal should never be applied if it is going to be difficult to remove. It will have to be removed periodically when it becomes worn in places.

Types of seal

Oleo-resinous

This seal is made from oils, resins, thinners and driers. It is used on wood floors, but mainly on the domestic market and in older establishments as it takes up to ten hours to dry. When it is dry it is tough and flexible and worn areas need only be touched up. It tends to be dark in colour.

One pot plastic seal

As this seal does not contain any oils it only takes about four hours to dry. Polyurethane is the main ingredient and the seal dries by chemical reaction or evaporation of a solvent. Again it is used on wooden floors and gives a good finish when dry.

Two pot

This type of seal is uncommon as it is exceptionally difficult to remove. It r st be perfectly laid and maintained but once down it has a very good quality. It comprises two components, a base and a hardener. Rather like the well known adhesive Araldite, these must be blended together. It should be applied to wooden floors only.

Pigmented seals

These seals give a floor a much better appearance and are widely used on concrete floors, thus making them easier to clean.

Water-based seals

Water-based seals are the ones most commonly used in commercial and institutional establishments, as they are easy to use and can be applied to almost any type of floor apart from wood. They are also relatively cheap.

Floor polishes

There are two types of floor polish or wax: solvent-based and water-based.

Solvent-based polishes consist of waxes suspended in solvents and they are available in either paste or liquid form. They are used on wood or wood composition floors but should never be used where a water-based seal has been applied. They should, therefore, not be used on thermo-plastic, rubber or PVC, as the solvent will cause deterioration.

Water-based polishes are also known as *emulsion polishes*. They are made from waxes and an alkali-soluble resin. They are more widely used than solvent-based polishes as they can be used for many more types of floor, including PVC, rubber, terrazzo, and lino. They may even be used on wood floors, if they are perfectly sealed, with no worn areas where the water may penetrate and damage the wood or make it dirty. Water-based polishes are also more heat-resistant. Some emulsion polishes are self-polishing and do not need buffing up. Others clean as well as polish and save time. Care must be taken with this type of polish to avoid build-up which causes unsightly marks along the edge of a floor.

Note   Floor maintenance is a specialist area and it is far better to seek professional advice from manufacturers or suppliers for a given floor surface, than to experiment. Companies such as Dimex have their own laboratories where they test out various chemicals. They are also willing to help sort out any problems and to offer training sessions for staff.

General procedure for stripping and re-sealing/polishing a floor

1   Sweep or vacuum the floor and then dry mop to ensure that all dust particles have been removed.
2   Apply the prescribed stripper, using a mop especially kept for this purpose. Any stubborn marks on the floor may be removed by a Scotch-brite type of pad.
3   Allow the stripping solution to work. A scrubbing machine may be used to help speed up the action.
4   Rinse the floor using a mop and plenty of cold water.
5   Use a neutralizing agent, such as a small solution of vinegar in water, to give the floor a final thorough rinse.
6   Allow the floor to dry. A wet vacuum may be used to speed up this action.
7   Apply the seal, using clean equipment specially kept for this purpose.
8   When the floor is dry, use a polishing pad and buff up the sealer. A clean dry mop may then be used to remove any surface dust.
9   Apply a finish/polish using a clean mop. Apply two coats, allowing each one to dry thoroughly before applying a further coat.
10   Buff up to obtain a high gloss.

Further reading

Conran, T., *The House Book* (Mitchell Beazley).

Useful addresses

Baskerville Technical Services,
Bigods Hall,
Great Dunmow,
Essex

British Ceramic Tile Council,
Federation House,
Stoke-on-Trent,
Staff ST4 2RU

British Floorcovering Manufacturers' Association,
125 Queens Road,
Brighton BN1 3YW

The Chipboard Promotion Association,
7A Church Street,
Esher,
Surrey KT10 78QS

Contract Flooring Association,
23 Chippenham Mews,
London W9 2AN

Cork Industry Federation,
30 Glenham Drive,
Gants Hill,
Ilford,
Essex IG2 6SG

National Federation of Terrazzo/Mosaic Specialists,
City Wall House,
14–18 Finsbury Square,
London EC2Y 9AQ

RAPRA (Rubber and Plastics Research Association),
Shawbury,
Shrewsbury,
Shropshire

9 Floors and floor coverings II

Carpets and rugs

Carpets have traditionally been a symbol of luxury. However, modern technology has made carpets a practical floor covering. The carpet is usually the most expensive single item of furnishing in a room. It covers a large area, and is an important feature of the décor. Aesthetically it produces an impression of comfort and luxury. It prevents the generation of noise at floor level without decreasing the effectiveness of projected sound, thus helping concentration and reducing irritation. Carpets reduce the hazard of slipping, and reduce the danger of injury, should a fall occur.

Although the capital outlay is greater than for some other floor coverings, and the life may not be as long as say, linoleum, the maintenance is relatively less expensive in labour and materials. Carpets simply require regular vacuuming and periodic shampooing. A study by the Industrial Sanitation Counsellors Inc. of Louisville, Kentucky found that the cost of maintenance of hard surface floors, when maintained at a comparative standard, was nearly double that of carpet. In addition, the finish of the subfloor need not be expensive, so long as it is smooth and level. Carpets reduce heat loss from the floor, and cut out draughts, resulting in reduction of heating costs of between 5 and 13 per cent. A carpeted floor never gets very cold so there is seldom condensation.

The resilience of a carpet makes for greater comfort for walking. The durability varies according to the quality and type of carpet. They can be treated *in situ* or at the factory to render them fire-resistant, moth-proof, anti-static and impervious to spillage. Moth proofing is usually done concurrently with dyeing.

Terms used in the carpet trade

It is useful to know the following terms.

Warp The yarn which goes lengthwise down a woven carpet.

Weft The yarn which is inserted across the loom and forms part of the backing structure. In conjunction with the warp, it binds in the pile tufts.

Pitch The number of tufts of pile per unit length across the loom (weft).

Shots The number of rows of pile along the length of woven carpet (warp).

Frames The racks or trays mounted behind jacquard Wilton looms, which hold the bobbins or spools from which pile yarns are fed into the loom.

Gauge The distance between the needles in a tufting machine.

Stitches The number of tuft insertions per unit length along the length of a tufted carpet.

Count A number which gives an indication of yarn thickness and therefore quality.

Denier/tex Used to measure yarns and fibres – the lower the denier/tex, the finer the yarn or fibre.

Pile weight The weight of pile per unit area, e.g. the weight of the pile per square metre.

Piece dyed A carpet which is dyed to the required shade after being tufted with white, undyed yarn.

Primary backing A woven or spunbonded cloth, into which tufts are inserted and latex bonded. The fibres used are jute or polypropylene.

Secondary backing   The backing cloth which is commonly laminated on to tufted carpet after tufting. It is usually made from jute or polypropylene, but a foam rubber backing is often used.

Swing needle   A patterning technique where the tufting needles are moved from side to side. When different or multi-coloured yarns are used, it produces a zig-zag effect.

Manufacture of carpets

Carpets are basically tufted yarn with a backing. Oriental carpets and those made by specialist firms follow the original methods of carpet making. An example is hand knotting in which the tuft yarn is hand knotted through a woven backing. In pile wire weaving, a backing is woven and the pile yarn is introduced from warp to form loops over wires which are inserted weft-wise. When the wires are removed a loop pile is left, so the resulting carpet is known as *loop pile*. *Cut pile* carpets have their pile cut as they are drawn out.

Woven carpets, usually made of cotton, rough wool, sisal and cords, do not usually have a backing and are used for rugs or large mats. They are not suitable for wall-to-wall carpeting.

Other methods of carpet manufacture are described below.

Types of carpet

Axminster
Axminster carpets are woven and have a cut pile. The majority of Axminsters have many colours and patterns, because the coloured tufts are inserted into the weave from above, so making the pile.

Axminster looms can combine up to thirty-five colours in any one design, but the quality of the carpet depends on the type of fibre (usually 100 per cent wool) and the amount per square inch.

Wilton
Wilton carpets are woven on a loom and all three types of pile may be formed. The yarn is woven in continuous strands using up to only five colours. The threads run along the back of the carpet, giving extra thickness and strength. Wiltons are made from wool rather than any other fibre and only the most expensive are patterned.

Tufted
Tufted carpets are a modern invention, unlike Wilton and Axminster, which are both very traditional methods of weaving carpets. They can have either cut or looped pile, and they have two backings. Tufted carpets were first made from synthetic fibres and tended to be of a cheaper quality but now there is a wide range of tufted carpets in pure new wool. The woollen variety are either plain or patterned and like Wiltons, they often rely on their texture to produce an interesting pile. Printed tufted carpets are also available.

Hand-tufted
Hand tufting is only suitable for individual carpet squares or wall coverings. The yarns are tufted into a backing cloth by a manually controlled needle-tufting gun.

Cord
Corded carpets are made in a similar way to plain Wilton carpets. The pile is always left uncut, so producing a corduroy effect. Cheaper cords are made from man-made fibres, and the more expensive contain wool. *Hair Cords* contain animal hair and are very hard-wearing.

Needleloom/needlepunch
Needleloom carpets have a mixture of fibres, needled through the backing, forming a carpet without a pile. An acrylic resin is also used to impregnate the fibres in the backing. This tends to make the carpet hard. Nylon, jute and polypropylene are mainly used, so they are cheap. ICI have recently developed a heat process which welds together nylon and terylene fibres, making an adhesive unnecessary and producing a softer finish.

Fibre-bonded

Fibre-bonded carpets (or soft floor coverings as they are sometimes called), are made by carding a variety of fibres to make a web, which is layered so making a form of wadding. The wadding is then glued to a backing fabric to give a loop pile effect, although this type of carpet often has no pile. It can be printed with a pattern after manufacture.

Knitted carpets

The backing fabric is knitted and the pile yarns are interlooped with the backing yarns, making either a plain loop or cut pile carpet. Yarns such as bouclé can be incorporated into this type of carpet.

Flock pile

These carpets are made by placing short fibres electrostatically on to a pre-coated adhesive backing. A very durable, hard-wearing carpet is produced which is suitable for corridors.

Brussels

Brussels looms were developed in the eighteenth century so like Wilton and Axminster carpets, Brussels carpets are traditionally woven. They are made in a similar way to Wilton carpet but they have a looped pile and are patterned, due to the wide range of colours that may be introduced into the weave.

Berbers

Berber carpets were originally made from undyed Karakul wool, a rather coarse hairy fibre in natural colours, cream to mid-brown or grey. They are also produced from synthetic fibres or a mixture of wool and synthetic fibres. These are known as *Berber-style*. They are hard-wearing and have a 'home-spun' effect, and a pleasing natural colour. If the loops are too long they can be pulled.

Rush matting

Rush matting is made of plaited or woven rushes which are made into squares or circles by winding the plaited lengths round and round. Round or square sections of the wound plaits are joined together. This floor covering is suitable for a rustic/type décor and for covering uneven stone floors. They are comparatively inexpensive, they do not hold the dust, but can be lifted for sweeping the floor beneath. When heavily soiled the matting can be taken out of doors and hosed.

When selecting rush matting, look at the type of plait, and check its thickness. See that the ends are securely finished off, and that the sections are securely joined together. The sections should be of a dimension that will fit into the area to be covered, because they cannot be cut.

Rushes are seldom dyed, but their natural green/beige colour is very attractive. Under heavy traffic and especially in a very dry atmosphere, the matting will wear badly. People may easily trip over loose edges. If the matting is kept slightly damp, it will keep a better appearance and will last longer.

Carpet tiles

There is a wide range of carpet tiles, from hard-wearing fibre pile, to the traditional cut or loop pile. Instead of a pliable secondary backing, they have a rigid backing. The better quality tiles are self-laying, fitting snugly against each other, lighter weight qualities require securing with an adhesive which precludes relocation.

They have the advantage that they may be removed in case of damage or wear, and relocated to get even wear. They are easily removed for access to under floor installations. The tough animal or man-made fibre tiles may be taken up, scrubbed and dried away from direct heat, thus making them suitable for use where heavy soiling occurs.

The disadvantage of poor quality tiles is that they spread, curl and arch.

Types of fibre used in carpets

Wool

Wool is the most popular fibre used in carpets. Very expensive carpets are made of 100 per cent wool, but it is more common to find carpets made with a mixture of wool and man-made fibres, so combining the strengths of nylon (for example) and the advantages of wool. Wool fibres differ in length and colour and crimp according to the different breeds of sheep. They are frequently blended to achieve a particular type of yarn or carpet.

Advantages: Hard-wearing, soil resistant, dyes well, easy to clean, soft, good insulating and accoustic qualities.

Disadvantages: Expensive, needs to be professionally laid and cleaned and can give problems with static electricity. It will rot if incorrectly cleaned or if it is not dried properly.

Animal hair

Goat, calf, sheep and deer skins are used to produce small skin rugs but these are mainly used on the domestic market. Cow, horse and in particular pig hair is used in the production of hair cord carpets as well as some looped or cut pile carpet. It is usually blended with synthetic fibres for this purpose. Pig hair is often used in the manufacture of carpet tiles. The tiles last longer and give a better appearance if they are kept slightly damp. Hair cord carpets or tiles are useful in heavy traffic areas like offices.

Advantages: As the hair is usually blended with nylon, rayon or wool, these carpets or tiles are hard-wearing and do not attract dirt. They are rather harsh to touch but are reasonably priced. No underlay is needed.

Disadvantages: If stuck down, cord carpets may bubble up in places and turn up at the edges. They should be professionally laid.

Jute

Jute is a brown, hard fibre produced from a plant stem. At one time it was always used in the backing of carpets but many companies now use polypropylene for this purpose. Jute is however, sometimes blended with viscose rayon and used in the manufacture of corded carpets. It may also be used as the stuffer in woven carpets and as a secondary backing in tufted carpets.

Advantages: Good as a backing for traditional carpets, hard-wearing and cheap when used in the manufacture of corded carpets.

Disadvantages: Rots when damp and susceptible to mildew.

Sisal

Sisal is a plant fibre of biscuit colour. When combined with other fibres, it is used in corded carpets and carpet tiles. It is also used for door mats and larger woven rugs when it is sometimes combined with nylon yarn.

Advantages: Hard-wearing and cheaper than wool or hair.

Disadvantages: Rough, and difficult to remove stains.

Coir

Coir is a coarse coconut fibre darker in colour than sisal, often used for doormats.

Advantages: Hard-wearing and good for soaking up grease and dirt.

Disadvantages: Occasionally needs thorough cleaning, preferably with a pressure hose, as when the fibres become flat and clogged, the matting is useless.

Cotton

Cotton is primarily used in the foundation of some woven carpets, for bathmats and in the manufacture of dust control mats.

Advantages: Hard-wearing, easy to launder.

Disadvantages: Becomes dirty easily and therefore needs frequent washing.

Silk and linen

Both silk and linen are added to some of the more expensive carpet ranges. Silk is particularly used to make costly Chinese or Persian carpets, which are not normally found in commercial establishments. Small Persian carpets can sometimes make attractive wall hangings.

Advantages: Excellent appearance and a good investment.

Disadvantages: Very expensive and a security risk.

Rubber and metal

Natural or synthetic rubber is often used for door mats, with metal as a sturdy frame. Metal fibres are sometimes blended into synthetic carpets to help to cut out static electricity.

Advantages: Hard-wearing and easy to clean. Very effective in the removal of dirt from shoes.

Disadvantages: A floor well is necessary in order that dirt from shoes may be effectively collected. Usually expensive.

Acrylic

Courtelle is the best acrylic fibre for carpets as it has a wool like appearance. It can either be woven or tufted. It is used in less expensive accommodation establishments and areas without heavy traffic.

Advantages: Cheaper than wool carpets, wear well, warm, resilient, and available in a wide range of colours. Also fairly easy to clean.

Disadvantages: Soils easier than wool and is not always fire resistant although the use of Teklan enables the manufacturer to reach flammability standards required.

Nylon

Nylon is used under many brand names in woven and tufted carpets. It often has a foam rubber backing and can be mixed with wool or viscose rayon. Blended with cotton, and a rubber backing, it is used for dust control mats.

Advantages: Cheap, easy to clean, durable with good abrasion resistance and it blends well with other fibres.

Disadvantages: Collects static electricity, attracts dust and soils easily. Cigarette ends will melt it, leaving irremovable marks.

Rayon

Evlan, a regenerated fibre, is the most common rayon to be used in the carpet trade, but there are others such as Darelle and Fibro.

Advantages: Gives lustre to other fibres. Cheap, anti-static and easy to clean.

Disadvantages: Not particularly hard-wearing and should be avoided in large commercial establishments as it does get dirty easily.

Polyester

Polyester is used for lightweight carpets or blended with other fibres for heavier use. It is sometimes used, with cotton, in bathmats.

Advantages: Soft. hard-wearing, easy to clean and fairly waterproof.

Disadvantages: Needs frequent cleaning.

Polypropylene

Polypropylene is widely used as carpet backing in place of jute. Merkalon is one of the most hard-wearing. It is not affected by mildew, micro-organisms or moths, and has a low water absorption rate. It is, therefore, good for bathrooms. It is also used in corded carpets, needle punch, twists and velours.

Table 9 summarizes the properties of the most common fibres found in carpets.

Types of pile

Cut piles

Shag pile

This is a long, shaggy cut pile. When pure new wool is used, it gives an appearance of luxury. The strands are generally all the same length and carpets may be plain or patterned. Shag pile carpets are also available in nylon and other man-made fibres. They are not practical enough for general use and unless care is taken, articles such as hair pins tend to become embedded within the fibres. A vacuum cleaner with a special rake attachment head should be used for a high standard of appearance and hygiene.

Velvet pile

This is a rich velvety close cut pile and is sometimes known as velour pile. It is usually used in plain or two-tone colours.

Twist pile

This is a cut pile using yarn which has a twist or kink. The twist effect is used to create a pebbly appearance and it is normally used in plain colours. It is sometimes used in conjunction with other types of pile to produce a two-tone effect.

Table 9 *The advantages and disadvantages of common fibres*

	Wool	Polyamide/nylon		Acrylics		Polyester		Polypropylene		Viscose	
		Trade name	*Manufacturer*	*Trade name*	*Manufacturer*	*Trade name*	*Manufacturer*	*Trade name*	*Manufacturer*	*Trade name*	*Manufacturer*
		Anso	Allied chem	Acrilan	Monsanto	Dacron	Du Pont	Amoco PP3	Amoco Plasticisers	Evlan	Courtaulds
		Antron	Du Pont	Courtelle	Courtaulds	Grilene	Grilon SA	Charisma	J. Holm	Danuflor	Hoechst
		Bri-nylon	ICI	Crylor	Rhône-Poulenc	Kodel	Eastman	Danaklon	Don Fibres	Darelle	Courtaulds
		Cambrelle	ICI	Dolan	Hoechst	Lirelle	Courtaulds	Donfil	Polyolefine	Fibro	Courtaulds
		Celon	Courtaulds	Dralon	Bayer	Tergal	Rhône-Poulenc	Downspun	Filtrona	Rovan	Rhône-Poulenc
		Dorix	Bayer	Forticol	Courtaulds	Terital	Montedison	Filtrona	F. Drake	Supralan	Norway
		Enkalon	Brit. Enkalon	Neochrome	Courtaulds	Terylene	ICI	Gymlene	Montedison	Swelan	Sweden
		Grilon	Grilon SA	Orlon	Du Pont	Treviar	Hoechst	Meraklon	Plasticisers		
		Nylfrance	Rhône-Poulenc	Teklan	Courtaulds	Vestan	Bayer	'P.L.' Polypropylene			
		Perlon	Bayer			Wellene	Wellman				
		Timbrelle	ICI								
		Ultron	Monsanto								
		Wellon	Wellman								
Advantages	High resilience, Good appearance retention, Good abrasion resistance, Good thermal properties, Excellent resistance to soiling, Easily cleaned, Fire resistant	Excellent durability, High strength, Easily cleaned and shampooed, Fire resistant, Good resilience		Nearest to wool, Reasonable abrasion resistance, Good resilience and wearing properties, Dyes brightly, When modified, good fire resistance		High abrasion resistance, Easily cleaned, Excellent in 'wet areas', Good Stain resistance		Good abrasion resistance, Excellent resistance to soiling, Easily cleaned, Relatively static-free, No moisture uptake, Excellent in 'wet areas'		Low price, Good bulk, Reduces static	
Disadvantages	Price variance, Supply, High moisture uptake, Prone to static	Prone to static, Tends to melt, Prone to soiling		Tends to melt, Prone to soiling		Can be difficult to dye, Moderate resilience		Can be difficult to dye		Poor abrasion resistance, High moisture uptake	

Sculptured pile

This is normally a cut pile. The yarn is cut into different heights, giving a sculptured or carved effect. Plain colours are generally used and this type of carpet is normally found in Wiltons or tufted carpets. Cut and looped pile is also used for sculptured pile.

Looped piles

This is formed by a continuous series of loops or uncut pile. The texture of the carpet depends on the length of the loop and the type of yarn.

Cut and looped pile

This is a mixture or cut pile and looped pile arranged in such a way as to form numerous attractive patterns.

Carpet backing

A soundly constructed backing is essential to provide a secure anchorage for the pile and to keep the carpet dimensionally stable.

The backing of Wilton or Axminster is woven at the same time as the pile. Traditionally, the weave is made of cotton and the weft made of jute, but polypropylene and polyester are sometimes used. In addition to the basic primary backing on which the carpet is formed, tufted carpets require secondary backing to give dimensional stability.

Primary backings are made from polypropylene or jute. Jute backings are always woven. Polypropylene may be woven from split film or bonded from non-woven fibre. The primary backings must necessarily be lightly constructed to allow for the penetration of tufting needles, so the firmness relies to a great extent on the secondary backing.

Secondary backings are laminated to the back of the carpet or formed directly on the carpet. Textile backings are usually jute plain weave or polypropylene. Foam rubber is also used as secondary backing; the higher the density the better the quality. Sheets of foam may be laminated on the back as for secondary jute backings. Cheap, low density foams break up if carpet is relocated.

Knitted carpets require similar secondary backings as tufted carpets. A firm backing is usually applied as an integral part of the manufacture of bonded carpets, so no secondary backing is required.

Design and colour

Carpets can be produced to individual requirements, colour and pattern. However, this is expensive and only economically viable if a large quantity is required.

Patterns can alter the apparent size and dimensions of the room, and as with patterned wallpaper, the effect of it on a large area should be seen. Most manufacturers illustrate this alongside their samples.

Because of the large area of carpet in relation to the wall surfaces, the carpet is a very important feature. The lighting of the area will affect the colour of the carpet. When selecting a carpet, view it under the type of lighting prevailing in the area where it will be laid. Light is reflected from the fibres of the pile. Cut pile carpets provide many facets from which the light is reflected, giving a sheen to the carpet and where the pile has been depressed, the carpet will reflect a different light.

When selecting coloured yarn from samples, it is important to view the end of the tufts for cut pile carpets and the side of the yarn for loop pile. Loop pile carpets have less lustre since there are fewer surfaces of the yarn exposed.

The pattern and colour of the carpet chosen should depend upon the environment and nature of soiling. In an area where spotting will be a hazard, a small pattern should be used because it will show up the soiling less than a plain carpet. In an area where light-coloured dust will be prevalent (for example, sand in a seaside hotel), choose a light-coloured carpet, which will not show up the dust. A dark-coloured carpet in a bathroom will show up the talcum powder. The often quoted generalization that dark carpets show less soiling than light coloured carpets is incorrect.

Dark carpets reflect less light so extra energy may be required to achieve the required luminance.

Carpet quality

The quality of carpets depends on the type of fibre; the amount of fibre or density; and the height of the pile. The British Carpet Centre has set five main carpet classifications. The classifications are worded in broad terms, as no two purchases will give exactly the same wear. The categories of carpet form the basis of the British Carpet Classification Scheme (BCCS) and of the equivalent International Carpet Classification Organization (ICCO). An increasing number of carpets are being registered under these schemes and carry the British Carpet Mark label or its international equivalent (see Figure 27). It is essential that the label should be looked at before purchasing any type of carpet. If a carpet is likely to be subjected to exceptionally heavy wear, then it is better to choose a carpet of a higher category.

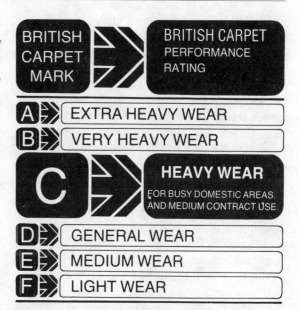

BRITISH CARPET MARK

BRITISH CARPET PERFORMANCE RATING

A EXTRA HEAVY WEAR

B VERY HEAVY WEAR

C HEAVY WEAR FOR BUSY DOMESTIC AREAS. AND MEDIUM CONTRACT USE.

D GENERAL WEAR

E MEDIUM WEAR

F LIGHT WEAR

Figure 27   *British Carpet Mark label*

British Carpet Performance Rating (BCPR)

Extra heavy wear
For locations where very high standards are demanded.

Very heavy wear
The heaviest domestic use and most contract areas.

Heavy wear
For busy domestic areas and medium contract use.

General wear
For most domestic areas and light contract use.

Medium wear
For domestic areas not subject to concentrated use.

Light wear
For domestic areas with the minimum of use.

Carpet wear

The life and wear of a carpet depends on the quality of the carpet; whether it has been laid on a smooth surface; whether it has a good quality underlay beneath it; and whether it is cleaned properly. However good the carpet, eventually parts will begin to wear. For this reason, plenty of spare carpet should always be kept in stock, so that patterns may be matched when repairs need to be carried out. Carpet should be stored safely in a roll. The store should be clean, dry and airy and supplied with a good secure lock. Avoid repairing a carpet with brand new carpet. Use some carpet from a room or an area that has had some use, but not as much as the one requiring attention. If new carpet is used alongside one that has been down the renovation will be conspicuous.

Where carpet is laid in lifts, it is a good idea to have at least two sets of carpet so that the panels may be exchanged for cleaning and repair without causing lift passengers too much inconvenience.

Underlay

When purchasing a carpet of quality it is also essential to buy underlay. The best quality of underlay that can be afforded should be purchased, as the purpose of underlay is to give the carpet a base or a cushion to help it to withstand heavy traffic and to lengthen its life. In old buildings with uneven floors, a thick underlay is essential if the carpet is not to show signs of wear on flooring ridges. For similar reasons, an old carpet should not be used as an underlay – the new carpet will simply settle into the worn patches of the old carpet and wear out in a similar manner. The pile of the undercarpet will also tend to move with tread, producing an unstable base for the new carpet, which will gradually shift.

Cheaper carpets have their own built-in underlay, which usually takes the form of a foam rubber backing which has been bonded on to the carpet. Some corded and needlepunch carpets are stuck to the floor surface, and do not need underlay.

Where carpets are purchased and laid in narrow widths, a felt underlay should be used, as rubber underlay tends to push up the seams, making them wear out more quickly.

An underlay should have adequate tensile strength. After a settling down period, there should be little change in the resilience. Underlays can be treated against moths, rot and fire, but check that there is no objectionable smell as a result of these treatments.

Needle felt

This underlay is made from hair, jute, matted cotton, wool or a combination of these and other fibres. It may be purchased in various qualities and thicknesses. This type of underlay is comparatively inexpensive, but it does flatten and lose resilience with wear. It can harbour moths and is attractive to vermin who may use it to line their nests. It also absorbs the dust from the carpet – yet another reason for buying new underlay for a new carpet.

Cellular

This is made from rubber or a polymeric foam and bonded on to the fabric, plastic sheet or hessian.

Rubber crumb

This is made from fibres and polymeric materials bonded to plastic or fabric sheeting.

Composite

This is made from fibres and polymeric material. For example, it may consist of foam rubber laminated to felt. Underlays which have a plastic sheeting surface give added strength and also prevent dust penetrating the felt or foam. Foam rubber underlays tend to make loose carpets creep, unless the carpet is properly edged or temporarily fixed down to the floor surface.

Carpet laying

It is essential that fitted carpets are laid professionally in order to get the maximum life. It is worth using a company with a good reputation. There are several methods of laying carpets. The turn and tack method is often found in older premises. About 5 cm of the carpet is turned under and tacked down at 10 cm intervals around the room. Plain carpets, in particular, show tack marks and if the carpet shrinks, after shampooing, it may be torn by the tacks.

The ring and pin method is not very common. It uses spiked rings, secured to the floor with tacks, which grip the carpet backing. Alternatively, the rings may be sewn to the carpet backing, which is then laid on to pre-positioned tacks.

The tackless method is the most common, as it is neat and efficient. A tackless strip of wood or metal is fixed to the floor surface with gripper pins pointing upwards. The 'smooth edge' is secured around the edge of where the carpet is to be laid.

The underlay is laid up to the inner edge of the strip, and the carpet laid so that the gripper pins grip the backing. A tiny gap is left between the strip and the wall, so that the very edge of the carpet may be tucked away out of sight, leaving an excellent finish.

Special grippers are available for foam-backed carpets, but these are often secured at the edges by double-sided tape. As with some of the other soft floor coverings, they may also be completely stuck down to give a stable fitting. They are sometimes secured by a narrow wooden beading placed over the edge.

Carpet seams are often heat-bonded. Although this is quick and easy the seams eventually come apart after frequent shampooing. Where carpet is used in very heavy traffic areas, it is better to have the seams hand-sewn, despite the additional cost. Loose carpets should be either hand-bound at the edges, or finished with plastic edging to prevent fraying.

Carpet dyeing

Occasionally it may be necessary to dye a carpet, or part of a carpet, usually because the colour has faded or the carpet has been stained. If the carpet can be taken away it can be vat-dyed. Alternatively it can be spray-dyed *in situ*.

Woollen carpets dye most satisfactorily, because the wool will absorb the dye. Mixtures of wool and man-made fibre will absorb the dye in varying strength, creating a mottled effect. Light colours will accept a darker colour, but dark colours will not take a lighter colour.

Stained carpets should be cleaned before dying. Stubborn stains or bleached areas will remain lighter or darker than the overall colour.

Care of a dyed carpet is the same as for a normal untreated carpet. However, mixed fibre dyed carpets may fade, and should be protected from strong sunlight. They are better used in a passage where the light is not strong and any unevenness in the dyeing less obvious.

Choosing a carpet

Before choosing a carpet, it is important to assess the use of the building and to consider what type will be most suitable. Afterwards, examine the carpets on offer, bearing in mind the following points.

Surface pile
Assess whether the pile appears soft, harsh, kempy, hairy or lustrous and whether shadowy stripes are present. Obtain information about the pile fibre and find out whether it will lose colour owing to flattening in the case of a lustrous pile, or whether it will give rise to surface fuzzing in the case of a hairy surface. If stripes are visible, one cause could be bad blending.

Rub the pile surface to see if the fibres are easily removed. Assess whether these are short, or, in the case of cut pile, V-shaped. Particular attention should be shown to semi-worsted spun yarns. Loss of pile fibre, particularly if V-shaped, can indicate poor fibre bind, resulting from poor back finishing.

Feel and smell the surface layer to detect the presence of excessive quantities of lubricants and additives from processing. The presence of such additives could result in excessive soiling.

Observe the surface pile and assess whether the surface is evenly and cleanly finished and if the tufts are well defined. Note also whether the density is such that the pattern is clearly visible. Poor surface definition in the original carpet could result in a rapid and unacceptable appearance change.

Observe whether untwisting of the yarns has occurred or is likely to occur, particularly where semi-worsted yarns or undyed (natural) yarns have been used. Twist stability is the major influence on texture change of a carpet. Poor yarn setting, under- or over-twisting will lead to loss of surface definition and thus appearance change.

In the case of multi-height carpets ensure that there are distinct differences between heights of pile, showing clearly the pattern of the carpet, particularly in plain coloured structures. Multi-height structures show the effect of flattening more than a level pile. Therefore a distinct pattern is important in order to anticipate the appearance change.

In the case of tip-sheared or cut/loop pile structures assess whether the areas of cropped or cut pile are excessive in proportion to the rest of the pattern and lack density. Cut pile has a different rate of change from that of loop pile and therefore the correct balance is again essential to minimize appearance change.

Avoid carpets, underlays and, indeed, any floor covering which have a strong moth ball odour. If they smell strong in a warehouse or store it is likely the odour will be more pungent in a small closed-in room. Di-butyl hydnoxy tolvene (BTH) is often added to polyurethane foam. It is an irritant which can cause distress to some people.

Design and colour combinations

Observe whether there are light or dark colours together or colours where cross staining is likely to occur, or whether there are stripes which could result from yarn of different dye lots being used.

Observe whether there are colours of similar hues side by side which are likely to become viewed as a single colour when flattened in use, or whether there is any frosting or lack of penetration of dyestuff.

If light and dark colours are placed together, check wet fastness. If there are large areas of pale shade, check oil content. Frosting or lack of penetration of dyestuff are associated with printed carpets and will affect pattern definition and clarity.

Backings

Assess whether there has been over- or under-penetration of latex or backsizing. Under-penetration of latex or backsizing will lead to 'tufting out' or excessive fibre shedding. Over-penetration on certain pile structures can result in premature wear; it will also reduce the pile on the surface of the carpet.

Observe the degree of firmness or stiffness, ensuring that it is firm but flexible. Excessive firmness or stiffness may lead to brittleness and cracking of the backing.

In the case of tufted carpets, check that the adhesion between the primary and secondary backing is adequate, particularly in poly-propylene fabric. Good adhesion is required to avoid delaminiation of the secondary backing, particularly for carpets in high traffic areas where castor chairs are used.

Assess the odour, particularly in the case of latex primary and secondary backings. A low odour is desirable.

Assess the evenness, density, flexibility and resistance to crumbling of foams. In the case of Monocel or pre-foamed backings ensure that there is good adhesion between it and the carpet.

Observe that there is no contamination in the foam. Contamination is not detrimental to the performance of the backing, but it can alter the aesthetic appearance of the carpet.

Care of carpets

Maintenance will depend on the fibre from which the carpet is made. All carpets must by law, carry a label stating the fibre content of the pile. The BS label 3655 will also state construction and some cleaning guidance. Maintenance will also depend upon the area in which it is laid and the type of soiling it will receive.

Dust, crumbs, grit and dry matter should be removed daily by a vacuum cleaner or carpet sweeper. In dining areas this type of dirt should be removed between meal sittings. Grit is damaging because it can become embedded in the pile and wear both pile and backing. A brush and dust pan is necessary in places which are difficult to reach. Brushing should be done in the direction of the pile with slow smooth strokes into the dust pan. Vacuuming should be done with slow movement and the final stroke should be in line with the direction of the pile. An upright cleaner with rotating brush/agitator and height adjuster for different depths of pile will give best results. Shag pile carpets are best cleaned with a suction-only cleaner and kept fluffy with a pile rake.

Loose ends of fibres can be woven in or burnt off with a match. Man-made fibres melt and this will prevent further running. Never leave the long loop as this is dangerous and will continue to run and leave a bare patch in a very short time.

Carpets can be treated for anti-static, anti-soiling, and for fire resistance. Anti-static will reduce the soiling because static electricity attracts dust. Areas where there is heavy wear can be protected with clear vinyl sheeting with special carpet grippers on the underside.

Joins between two sections of carpet or different carpets (for example, in doorways) can be protected with metal nosing. Stair edges can be protected with angled metal nosing, which is obtainable in various colours to tone with the carpet. A white nosing is useful on stairs, since it will show up the edge, and can help prevent accidents. To prolong the life of stair carpet where nosings have not been used, leave extra carpet at the bottom of the stairs so that the carpet can be moved up occasionally to spread the wear evenly. This should be done before there are obvious signs of wear. Jogging is the term used for this. Stairs with nosings can have new pieces inserted invisibly.

Dust mats placed at entrances will remove excess dust. They can be supplied by a service company which collects and replaces them at regular intervals.

Removal of stains

It is most important to treat the damage as soon as possible. If the room is occupied by guests whom you don't want to disturb, apply emergency treatment, and deal with the stain later. Scrape up all the solids with a spatula or spoon, working from the outside of the stain towards the centre. A fork can be used to comb through the pile. Wipe the area with warm water and soak up with absorbent kitchen paper. Wine spillages should be sprayed with soda water.

Table 10 summarizes the suitable agents for removing common stains. If the stain cannot be identified, try warm water and mild detergent first. Before using stain removal chemicals, test for bleeding or bleaching on a spare piece of carpet, or a section that is inconspicuous. *First Aid Cleaning Kits*, which contain several solvents, are a useful asset. However, smoking should not be allowed near the area where stain removal is taking place, since many solvents are flammable.

Stain removal procedure

1 Always work from the outside edge of the stain towards the centre.
2 Apply suitable agent, correctly diluted, rinse and dry. Repeat if necessary. Apply only small quantities, to prevent over-wetting.
3 Blot with absorbent cloth or paper. Do not rub the pile.
4 Rinse treated area with clear water.
5 Blot dry using a wad of absorbent cloth or paper, weighed down with a heavy object. A hair dryer could also be used.
6 Avoid walking on the carpet and do not replace furniture until area is completely dry. As a precaution, kitchen foil can be placed under castors or chair legs for 24 hours.
7 If there is extensive spot staining, shampoo the whole carpet.
8 If the damage has not been successfully removed, consult a professional cleaner.

Salt and sugar should always be swept up quickly, otherwise they will dissolve leaving a sticky mess. Similarly, sweet drinks (including colourless drinks such as tonic water) should be soaked up and washed with warm water before they make the carpet sticky.

Carpet cleaning

There are four methods of *in situ* carpet cleaning: rotary brush shampoo, cylindrical brush shampoo, spray extraction cleaning and impregnated compound cleaning. These are supplemented by various spotting techniques, described in the previous section, plus pre-treatment of heavily soiled areas with chemicals and raking of the pile.

Rotary brush shampooing

This method uses a rotary brush shampooer and dry foam and it has been estimated that 85 per cent of professional carpet cleaners throughout the world use this technique. The principle of the machine is that shampoo in the form of a solution or pregenerated foam is forced into the pile by the action of the brush or brushes and the greasy soil is emulsified and loosened for subsequent vacuuming when dry.

Advantages: Extremely efficient surface cleaning is achieved. Compressed pile in wool carpets, caused by heavy furniture, regains its original shape rapidly with any wet treatment. It copes with both lightly and heavily soiled carpets.

Disadvantages: Skill is required to avoid over-wetting and pile distortion. There is a risk of the backing becoming damp and shrinking. Drying time is relatively long. Shampoo residues are left in the carpet which can in some cases build up with successive cleanings and can cause accelerated soiling.

Table 10   *Stain removal guide for wool carpets*

Stain	Carpet shampoo solution	Dry cleaning fluid	Clear warm water	Other method
Beverages (tea, coffee, soft drinks)			1	2 Enzyme detergent (2%)
Bleach	3			1 Cold water 2 Enzyme detergent (2%)
Blood				1 Cold water 2 Enzyme detergent (2%)
Butter	2	1		
Candle Wax		2		1 Absorbent paper & hot iron (but check fibre content for heat resistance)
Chewing gum				1 chewing gum remover (proprietary)
Chocolate	2		1	
Cooking oils	2	1		
Cream	1	2		
Egg	1			
Floor wax		1		
Fruit juice			1	2 Enzyme detergent (2%)
Furniture polish	2	1		
Grass				1 Methylated spirits
Gravy and sauces	2		1	
Ink (fountain pen)			1	2 Enzyme detergent (2%)
Ink (ball point pen)	2			1 Methylated spirits or proprietary remover
Lipstick	2	1		
Metal polish				1 Brush off when dry 2 Methylated spirits
Milk	2		1	
Mustard	1			
Nail polish		2		1 Nail polish remover
Oil and grease	2	1		
Paint (emulsion)	2			1 Cold water
Paint (oil)	3	2		1 Turpentine or white spirit
Rust	2	1		3 Rust remover
Salad dressing	1	2		
Shoe polish	2	1		
Soot	2			1 Vacuum
Tar		1		2 Eucalyptus oil
Urine (fresh stain)	2			
(old stain)	1			
Vomit	2			
Wine			1	2 Enzyme detergent

1, 2, 3 – the order in which stains should be treated.

Cylindrical brush shampooing

This technique uses a cylindrical brush in which pregenerated dry foam is brushed into the carpet pile. Some of these machines incorporate a wet suction pick-up for removing dirty foam and loosened dirt in one operation.

Advantages: Less pile distortion. Less danger of shrinkage caused by over-wetting. Decreased drying time. Minimum skill required by the operative.

Disadvantages: It is not suitable for heavily soiled carpets. Minimum mechanical action at the base of tufts can result in tightly held dirt not being removed. Pile distortion can occur when machine is stopped with brush running. As with the first method, shampoo residues are left on the carpet.

Spray extraction

This method is based on the spraying of water, under pressure, at 40–95 °C into the pile to the base of the tufts and the almost simultaneous removal of this water and soil by powerful suction.

Advantages: There is minimum pile distortion, as no brushes are used. Embedded dirt is removed better than almost all other *in situ* cleaning methods. Hardly any residue is left and, therefore re-soiling is kept to a minimum.

Disadvantages: Operator skill is required to achieve optimum results and avoid over-wetting. This is also a very popular method of shampooing carpets.

Impregnated compound cleaning

This technique is based on the application, by brushing, of a solvent-impregnated soil-absorbent powder and its subsequent removal by vacuuming. The powder base usually consists of ground corn husk, wood flour, or a fully synthetic powder.

Advantages: It gives very short drying time (between 30 minutes and three hours). No damage is caused by moisture. There is minimum pile distortion.

Disadvantages: It is not suitable for heavily soiled carpets; in fact, it supplements, not replaces other methods. The powder must be applied to the pile manually, which can lead to uneven results. It is relatively expensive. Some compounds have an objectionable odour.

Factory cleaning

Factory cleaning is more effective than *in situ* cleaning, but can only be implemented if the carpet can be removed easily, quickly, and economically. This is usually only possible in the case of squares.

Cleaning chemicals

Because some cleaning techniques leave residues of shampoo in the carpet, it is essential that the shampoo should conform to certain minimum requirements. The most important requirements are that it should leave a dry, powdery, preferably crystalline residue; it should have a pH between 5.5 and 7.5, and it should not contain bleach or fluorescent brightening agents. Carpets can be vacuumed after shampooing to remove this residue.

Oriental carpets

It is useful to be able to identify an oriental rug, because a rug or carpet of uneven shape and design could be discarded as being valueless, when it may in fact be as valuable as a piece of antique furniture. As the name implies, oriental rugs and carpets come from Turkey, Iran, Iraq, Afghanistan, India and China. They are woven with natural fibres, with jute or cotton backing. High quality Chinese carpets have a silk pile. Some rugs (known as Kelims) are woven with no pile, and are reversible.

Oriental rugs have traditional patterns. Slight unevenness in shape is an indication that they are hand made, and only the width of a loom that can be handled with ease. The unevenness of shape and pattern are not indicative of inferior quality, and repairs visible on the reverse side may indicate that the rug is an antique. A modern, new city-made carpet may have man-made fibres included, and the colours may be harsher because chemical dyes are used instead of the natural vegetable dyes.

The fringes of a rug are the ends of the warp thread and they may be of natural wool or cotton. The fringes of rugs made by nomadic tribes or in remote villages are usually of natural wool and are uneven, and often embroidered, knotted or plaited. The cotton fringes in newer rugs are usually of even length.

At the back of the rug the weft thread, of uniform colour separating each row of knots, will be seen. In finely woven rugs this is almost obscured by the closeness of the weave. The pile in city-made rugs will b fine, short and even, showing up the design clearly. A village weaver usually makes a heavy, tight, deep pile for warmth. Beware of strong pile effect and a high gloss on a new rug, this is an indication of machine treated wool lying flat, which is not good for durability, and may indicate the addition of man-made fibres.

Oriental rugs can stand up to hard wear and sun. They are often exposed to the bleaching effect of the sun when being made. They need not be confined to use on the floor, but can be used as wall hangings, or to cover a table.

Care of Oriental rugs

When vacuuming, avoid tangling the fringe in the roller of an upright machine – a purely suction cleaner is kinder. Once a week they should be lifted and the floor underneath swept, to protect the rug against moths.

Edges and fringes show signs of wear first, and they should be repaired as soon as signs of damage appear. Since they are expensive, they should be handed over to a specialist.

They can be freshened by wiping over with a tightly wrung-out damp cloth. They can be washed with a green soft soap or mild detergent in warm water. Test a small piece first to see if the colours are fast. Rinse well, and dry off with a clean dry cloth.

Oriental rugs may slip on polished floors and 'creep' on carpets. Taklan Anticreep and Cling Adhesive will prevent this. The adhesive is a water-based resin applied to the under-surface of the rug to which the Anticreep underlay is stuck. Another method is to have rubber strips stuck on the under-edges of the rug, but it is important that a recommended adhesive is used so that the rug is not damaged.

Care of skin rugs

Animal rugs (such as sheepskin), are generally used as scatter rugs, on polished floors or on carpets. They need attention to see that they do not harbour moths and that they do not slip or 'creep'. To prevent moths, they should be dusted from time to time with an anti-moth powder which should be rubbed deeply into the fur or wool, and then brushed out. To prevent 'creep' or 'skid' they should have applied to the underside strips of a proprietory anti-creep material (see Oriental rugs, above).

Cleaning skin rugs is usually carried out by professional cleaners but they can be cleaned *in situ*. The dust should first be removed by shaking and brushing with a fairly soft brush. Use a proprietary shampoo or prepare a solution of 2 teaspoons each of borax, olive oil and glycerine, and 10 ounces of soap flakes in 1 pint of water. Boil for 1 minute. Dilute with 1 pint of cold water. Rub this into the hair surface, attending to a small patch at a time. Rinse off with a clean cloth wrung out in clear warm water. It is necessary to finish off each patch before going on to the next. Hang outside to dry (never dry by direct heat).

If the back of the skin shows signs of drying out and hardening, rub gently. If the skin still does not respond to this, replace some of the natural oils that it has lost by rubbing in a little liquid lanolin oil or olive oil.

Gently brush the hair or comb it with a wide-toothed comb along the way the hair lies naturally.

Sheepskin rugs can be shampooed, taking care not to rub the fleece too harshly, as hard rubbing would make it mat. Rinse and dry away from direct heat, and if the back remains hard, treat it as for the skin rug.

Further reading

Conran, T., *The House Book* (Mitchell Beazley).

Van Dishoeck, C. A. J., *Carpets from the Orient* (Merlin Press, London, 1966).

Useful addresses

Simon Boosey,
Oriental Carpet Expert,
The Tun House,
Whitwell,
Hitchin,
Herts SG4 8AG

The British Carpet Manufacturers Association,
Margam House,
26 St James's Square,
London SW1Y 4JH

The Carpet Cleaners Association,
97 Knighton Fields Road West,
Leicester LE2 6LH

The Carpet Clinic,
Portman Carpets,
7 Portman Square,
London W1

International Wool Secretariat,
Wool House,
6–7 Carlton Gardens,
London SW1

10 Bathrooms and sanitary areas

Bathrooms have an intimate atmosphere and are psychologically important. They should always be scrupulously clean and easily maintained to this standard. There should be no sharp corners, and curved coving between ceilings and walls and floor and walls are preferable.

They must be adequately ventilated and warm. A cold, clammy bathroom atmosphere where condensation abounds is not conducive to comfort, and can create mould growth. Windows should have louvred fittings or extractor fans.

Planning bathrooms

It must be remembered that in addition to the area taken up by the fittings there must be activity space. In some small bathrooms to be used by two people (for example, a private bathroom serving a twin-bedded room) there is sometimes not enough floor space for two people to move. The usual dimensions of bathroom fittings are as follows:

Basins   600 × 400 mm
800 mm or 900 mm high
Activity space: 1000 × 700 mm

Baths   1700 × 700 mm
500–600 mm high
Activity space: 700 × 1100 mm

Showers   800 × 800 mm or 900 × 900 mm
Tray must be at least 150 mm high
Activity space: 400 × 900 mm for showers enclosed on one or two sides; those enclosed on three sides: 700 × 900 mm

Bidets   700 × 400 mm
400 mm high
Activity space: 800 × 600 mm and this should extend back to the wall to give leg and elbow space.

WC pans   700 × 800 mm
400 mm high
Activity space: 600 × 800 mm

The disabled require much more activity space, especially round the shower and wc and in the centre of the room so that a wheelchair can turn, and to allow for a helper. The activity spaces given above are a minimum. When planning a bathroom, attention should be paid to the following safety features.

1 Grab rails
2 Disposable tooth beakers instead of glass
3 Textured floor covering and absorbent bath mats
4 Good lighting and ventilation
5 Shaving sockets marked 'For Shavers Only'
6 Alarm bells in old people's and disabled people's homes
7 Providing receptacle for used razor blades
8 Seeing the bath and shower tray are non-slip

Sanitary fittings

The range of sanitary fittings is great and consequently confusing. Research should be made before selection, and a visit to The Building Centre, 26 Store St, London WC1 and the Bathroom and Shower Centre, 205 Great Portland Street, London W1 will be of great help. All sanitary fittings should be smooth, impervious to water, with no exposed unglazed surfaces when the fitting is installed. They should have simple contours with no dirt-trapping nooks and crannies. Wash basins, lavatory pans and bidets should be cantilevered from the wall. This makes for easier cleaning and laying of floor coverings. Dark colours are more difficult to maintain since deposits from hard water are difficult to remove. Some types fade, and some colours are fashionable for a short time and soon become outdated.

Baths

The British Standard bath is 1700 mm long and 700 mm wide, but other sizes are available. Heights range from 450 mm to 550 mm. American baths are shorter and wider.

Cast iron porcelain enamelled

These baths are strong and durable but heavy. Because of their weight, they are unsuitable in some buildings. If chipped they are difficult to repair and attract stain from a dripping tap. After long use the surface can become pervious. They are slow to heat up, but retain the heat longer.

Pressed steel vitreous enamelled

These baths are less expensive than cast iron, lighter and easier to install. They can be obtained in various qualities, depending upon the gauge (thickness) of steel from which they are pressed. They are finished with a coating of vitreous enamel, not so thick as porcelain, but still durable. They can be resprayed.

Acrylic plastics

These baths can be obtained in a variety of shapes and colours. They are light and easy to install. They heat up more quickly than cast iron or pressed steel baths, and lose heat more quickly. They can be damaged by abrasives and cigarette burns, and some makes fade. Scratches can be polished out because the colour goes right through the material. They are not very stable and should be fitted on a cradle, and may require a rubber flange or plastic filling between them and the wall. They are resistant to chipping and the deposit from a dripping tap. The in-built non-slip dimples on

some makes do not render them reliably non slip.

Glass fibre reinforced plastic (GRP)

This material is similar to acrylic plastic, but it is more stable (less flexible). It is more brittle and can chip, but can be repaired. The colour is on the surface only, so scratches are not erasable. In all other respects they are similar to acrylic baths.

Baths are usually supplied with holes for the taps and water outlet. They can be supplied with or without side panels, so panelling can be made to match the rest of the bathroom. In all cases a section of the bath side should be removable for access to the plumbing. The base of the bath should be flat and have a non-slip surface. The slightly roughened surface is more effective than the dimple effect. For baths without a non-slip surface area self-adhesive appliqués are effective and can be decorative, but have to be replaced after about a year. Suction held rubber mats may be used, but they need special care in cleaning and sanitizing because of their uneven surface. A toe recess at the external base of the bath is a guard against toes being stubbed.

Special baths

For the disabled there are baths into which the person can be lifted, or step in, through a side of the bath which opens. A seat is moulded into the shape of the bath. The selection of baths for the disabled is limited, but there are manufacturers who specialize in bathroom fittings for the elderly and disabled. A lift can be used where a special bath has not been installed.

Corner baths take up more floor space than the traditional bath, but in some situations they can be more suitable. It is more difficult to site the shower if one is going to be incorporated with the bath. Some corner baths have a seat moulded into the shape.

Sunken baths seem exotic, but for the infirm, very young and shortsighted they can be dangerous and difficult to get in and out of. If the illusion of a sunken bath is desired, a normal or corner bath can be installed and a platform built round it with a step leading up to it. This eliminates the risk of anyone accidently stepping or slipping into it.

Sunken and corner baths are difficult to clean. Staff should never step into the bath without a rubber mat to stand on.

Whirlpool baths have water jets incorporated to provide underwater massage. They are expensive because a pump and special plumbing is required. Bubble bath liquid should never be used in these baths.

Where space is limited a short, sit-in bath may be fitted. Much less water is required, and they are also suitable for the elderly or infirm who would not be safe in a bath of usual dimensions.

Showers

These are much more economical on water and fuel than baths, and also save time for the users.

Before a shower is installed it should be ascertained that there is an adequate head of water. The distance between the base of the tank and the shower rose should be at least 1 metre. Without this distance, a booster pump may be installed or the tank raised. It is also important that the hot and cold water should be at the same pressure. The more sophisticated shower appliances have a thermostatic control valve to keep the water at a constant temperature preventing a surge of hot water should the pressure of the cold vary. There are also units with an in-built instantaneous electric heater which takes cold water directly from the main, and heats it as required.

The simplest and least expensive unit combines the shower with the taps serving the bath. There may not be a very good head of water and consequently reduced or variable pressure affects the temperature of the shower flow. Most of these types are manually manipulated to alter the flow from taps to shower. Some models, however, have an automatic flow diverter, which automatically redirects the flow to the bath after a shower has been taken. It is advisable to select a shower with controls which can be manipulated without the bather having to stand beneath the rose.

The controls on some showers are difficult to decipher and manipulate. In children's and old people's homes the temperature should be set. Showers in the bath are practical and less expensive to install, but not suitable for the infirm who may find it difficult to step into the bath. Protection from splashes is given by shower curtains or perspex screens round the bath.

A minimum floor area of 91 cm is required for shower cubicles. Complete shower cubicles in moulded plastic are available. Fully enclosed units of enamelled steel are more durable. Alternatively, a cubicle can be purpose-built in a suitable space, such as an existing alcove or cupboard. They should be tiled on the floor and three walls, with a door or curtain on the fourth wall. This type can give showering facilities in an existing bedroom in an old building.

Shower trays are available in the same colours to match the range available for other bathroom fittings, in pressed steel, stainless steel, porcelain, moulded plastic, or glazed fireclay (the latter inexpensive and suitable for schools). They can also be built in the normal building materials and tiled. In all cases they should be completely waterproof and to reduce condensation, a top to the cubicle should be fitted.

Inside any shower cubicle, or adjacent to any shower, there should be a soap receptacle at elbow level.

Shower heads come in a variety of types. The fixed head is found in older buildings, usually placed above head level, or at shoulder height. They should be positioned at an angle of 30 degrees to the wall. This type is suitable for schools and communal shower rooms. The variable type is attached to a rail, along which the head can be moved. The angle and direction can also be varied. A hand held shower head at the end of a flexible metal tube, which with constant use is liable to damage. They are attached to the bath tap unit and can be part of the variable type. They are useful for hair shampooing and rinsing the bath. Electric impulse shower heads produce pulsating hot and cold jets of water which tone up the muscles. They are found in keep fit clubs and health clinics.

The roses should be removable for replacement, cleaning and descaling. Metal shower heads will corrode because of the mineral salts in the water, so plastic heads are more durable. It is better to choose a shower head which drains off the residual tepid water, in which bacterial cultures could flourish.

Shower curtains should be easily drawn with large rings on a sturdy rail. If someone should slip in the shower he or she is likely to grab the curtain. The material may be plastic, fibre glass or polyester and cotton. They should be long enough to go beyond the edge of the shower tray or bath, and weighted along the hem. A concertina door is an alternative to a curtain, but water, soap scum and hard water deposits will penetrate all ledges, making cleaning difficult. This also applies to sliding glass panelled shower doors.

Care of showers is the same as for baths of the same material. Special attention should be paid to the shower heads which should be dismantled regularly, rinsed with a mild disinfectant and descaled (in hard water areas). They should be soaked in a suitable descaler solution.

Taps

Common sense and practicability have been sacrificed for decorative effect in the design of taps. Old brass taps used to have an 'H' and 'C' in relief, so one could feel which was which. Today they frequently have a tiny red or blue dot or ring, which is invisible to those who have removed their spectacles (which is customary when washing!). Mixer taps have the advantage of producing water at the correct temperature, so saving heat and water.

For the disabled, taps at the side of the wash basin or the lever type are more convenient. In hospitals and consulting rooms, the lever type are necessary so that after 'scrubbing up' the tap can be controlled by the arm and not the hands. The simplest design is best for easy cleaning. There should be enough space under the front of the tap and the surface below to get a cloth through for cleaning.

Plugs

The rubber or plastic plug and chain is the most

common. A link chain is more easily repaired than the round bead type. The plug should be well fitting. The flat disc type which lies over the hole is frequently shifted by the force of water.

'Pop up' plugs are not ideal, although they are commonly used. They can go wrong easily as the nuts in the simple mechanism become loose and get lost. They need careful attention when cleaning.

The electronic beam can dispense with the need for a plug. This controls the flow of water, by turning on the taps when it is broken by hands placed between them. This is a hygienic means of getting water, and limits the flow so that plugs are not necessary. However, it is limited to wash basins and handwashing. In some models, after the beam has been broken, the flow of water is controlled by a timing mechanism. Where this type of water flow is in use, notices should be displayed explaining what the system is.

Toilets

Lavatory pans are made from glazed fine clay or earthenware, or, more commonly, vitreous china which is strong, durable and resistant to acid. Lavatory pans or bowls may be either of a pedestal or cantilevered type. The pedestal variety is the traditional model, cantilevered bowls are found at airports, motorway service stations and so forth, where there are long rows of public conveniences. Floor cleaning is easier with the cantilevered bowl, as it is not fitted to the floor. Where vandalism is a problem, stainless steel bowls may be introduced.

There are two types of flushing systems: the wash down, and siphonic.

Washdown

This is the more common type. It is cleansed by the force of water of its flush driving the contents of the pan and the trap down the outlet pipe (see Figure 28). Failure to do this may be caused by a misshapen pan; the flush pipe being incorrectly placed; a defective cistern, failing to deliver water with sufficient force; or inadequate water pressure. Washdown systems are simple and cheap, but they do tend to be noisy which may be a

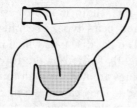

Figure 28   *Wash-down WC pan*

problem in a modern building where building materials are thin and noise travels.

Siphonic

The contents of the trap are withdrawn by suction, the flush being used to start the siphonic action and to wash the sides of the pan (see Figure 29). These pans are quieter than the washdown type and usually empty the complete contents of the trap and the pan in one flushing. This is of great importance where lavatories are being used continuously at peak periods. The outlet is narrower than that in the washdown type and more liable to become chocked if misused, causing blockage and bad smells. The height of the pan is usually 35–40 cm, but lower models are obtainable for children and the elderly. The siphonic WC is initially more expensive to install and usually has the low-level cistern store.

Some other nationalities have different toilet habits from the British, and use a squatting WC basin. In some hotels, it may be necessary to install these for the convenience of foreign guests.

Cisterns

Cisterns are an integral part of the lavatory.

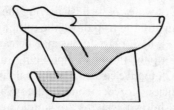

Figure 29   *Syphonic WC pan*

They contain the water for flushing, and have a capacity of 2 gallons. In time of water shortage, capacity can be reduced by placing a brick or similar object in the cistern to reduce the cubic capacity. Some cisterns have a half-flush capacity.

Cisterns may be of cast iron (found in old buildings, usually the over-head type) or of vitreous china or plastic. The latter is vulnerable to burning from lighted cigarettes – never place an ashtray on this type of cistern. The cheaper plastic cisterns are flexible and joints and seals can be loosened if it is leaned against. Of the plastic types, polypropethene is preferable. The cistern can be concealed behind a duct concealing the supply and outlet pipes, leaving the handle only exposed. In public buildings a foot operated pedal for flushing is more hygienic and sometimes the lavatories are flushed automatically by a time set mechanism.

There are two types of cistern, siphonic and piston. In both cases the inlet is controlled by a floating ball which should be of plastic material. The ball is raised by the cistern filling up with water, and it closes the inlet when enough water has entered and stops the inflow of water. There should be an overflow outlet to the soil pipe or to the exterior of the building in case the ball-cock valve ceases to function. Where there is not an adequate water pressure an overhead cistern will increase the head.

Bidets

These are appliances for ablutions after using the toilet. They should be connected to the soil pipe, and placed alongside the WC. They are usually made of vitreous china and match the WC.

The simplest type is a low floor standing pedestal with hot and cold taps and a waste plug and chain. More sophisticated models have a flushing rim, round which the water is discharged into the bowl, and have the advantage of warming the rim on which the user will be sitting. This type usually has a pop-up waste control from between the taps. Some bidets have the added refinement of a douche or ascending spray, rather like an inverted shower.

Advice should be sought before installing a bidet as some water boards have special requirements for their installation, aimed at preventing back siphonage and contamination of the water supply. Bidets can be floor standing or wall hung.

Wash basins and sinks
Wash basins are found in bathrooms, bedrooms, public conveniences, communal facilities and in food preparation areas for the purpose of hand washing. Sinks are found in kitchens, sluice and any other working area.

Pedestal wash basins are supported on a stand and tend to be very stable in design. The stem or stand hides the pipes, so the appearance is good, although a little extra cleaning time must be allowed for to clean the pedestal and the area behind (which is harder to reach).

Cantilevered wash basins are bracketed to the wall and may become loose in time. They also tend to be susceptible to vandalism. Supply and drainage pipes are sometimes visible with this design of basin, but floor cleaning is made easier as there is no pedestal.

The vanitory unit is the most common installation in private bathrooms of modern hotels. The unit doubles as a dressing table with the basin placed in the centre. The guest may place toiletries and the hotel may display such items as face flannels and tooth glasses on the shelving.

Corner wash basins are useful where space is limited, especially in lavatory cubicles.

Ceramic
Vitreous china is the most common ceramic material used for wash basins. It is a special clay, cast in a plaster mould which is then glazed in a kiln. Vitreous china basins are strong, durable, easy to clean and resistant to acids and abrasion. They can however be vandalized and can chip and crack, in which case they should be replaced.

Glazed fire clay is a much stronger material and is used mainly for sinks. It has the same advantages as vitreous china but it is also liable to chipping.

Metal
Stainless steel is used for both wash basins and sinks. It is very hygienic but hard to keep up a good appearance as it is marked by water.

Pressed steel is mainly used for domestic kitchen sinks. It is coated in enamel, which eventually wears away and becomes unsightly.

Plastic
As with baths, wash basins may be acrylic or fibre glass (glass reinforced plastic GRP). They are easily scratched and can be damaged by cigarette burns, and nail varnish cannot be removed. They can, however, be purchased in attractive colours and are cheaper and lighter than the traditional basin. A moulded vanitory unit with the wash basin incorporated eliminates any crevices.

To comply with health regulations an adequate number of wash basins should be placed in food preparation areas for the use of all food handlers, including waiting staff. These wash basins should be supplied with hot and cold water; a plug; soap; a nail brush and towels (disposables are usually preferred, in which case a suitable receptacle is necessary). In a kitchen, a used towel receptacle should have a lid. Public toilets in a restaurant must also have wash basins, soap and towels.

Accessories

Toilet-paper holders need to be conveniently placed, adjacent to and slightly in front of the lavatory pan. Select a strong one, uncomplicated with no sharp edges, which can be firmly secured to the wall. Those which have an ashtray incorporated can avoid damage to other fittings. The simplest type, suitable in hotels, is a bar, attached at one end only, from which the roll can be slipped on easily. For public or communal toilet areas, there are giant rolls available in vandal-proof casings. The advantage of using a giant roll or multi-pack system is that there should always be paper there, but they are conducive to wastage. If extra paper is used it may block drains. The alternative is to supply a double holder. In public toilets the toilet-paper holders should be locked to prevent theft and misuse.

Soft toilet tissue is more hygienic than the stiff sort. When purchasing toilet paper check on the quality and quantity in the pack: the more expensive pack may turn out to be more economical.

Automatic roller towel dispensers produce a portion of clean towelling on a roller at fixed intervals. The disadvantages are that the portion of towel is often too small and it is impossible to assess how much is left on the roll. All too often a dismal tail-end of soiled towel is left dangling.

Paper towels in a dispenser are hygienic, but the quality of the paper varies. The soft tissue type is the most absorbent but also the most expensive. They are often used extravagantly. There should be adequate baskets into which soiled towels can be placed.

Hot air hand dryers, are hygienic, but not a popular method of drying. They can be operated by a press button on a time switch, or by placing hands in a recess which breaks an electric beam which activates the mechanism to produce hot air. It is a slower method of hand drying and can cause hold-ups in a busy communal toilet area.

Giant paper towel rolls can be used where consumption is heavy and the aesthetic value unimportant.

A combined hot air and paper towel dispenser can eliminate some of the disadvantages of a single system.

Hand drying facilities should be placed adjacent to the wash basins so that the minimum distance has to be covered by someone with dripping hands. Towel dispensers and hot air hand dryers should be situated where they will not impede access to wash basins.

Sanitary bins should be provided in all ladies' lavatories. They should be metal or plastic so they can be washed and sanitized, and a bin liner should be used. Bins should be emptied daily by house cleaners. A sanitary pad disposal service is offered commercially, whereby the disposal unit in each cubicle is replaced at regular intervals. This dispenses with the capital cost of installing an incinerator, and the house cleaners' distasteful task.

Sanitary bags should be provided, ideally dispensed from a container. A notice requesting women not to throw sanitary pads or disposable nappies down the toilet, should be prominently displayed.

Sanitary machines selling tampon and sanitary towels should be in every ladies' toilet/cloakroom area. The machine should have a transparent panel, through which the level of the contents can be seen. They should be filled up and the money emptied regularly, to prevent coins getting jammed.

Other dispenser machines are found in public toilet areas, selling aspirins, disposable toothbrushes, contraceptive aids etc.

Tissue holders are found in luxury bathrooms and cloakrooms. They should be attached to or inset in the wall.

Mirrors should be plentiful and positioned in such a way to avoid congestion. They should be well lit, so that the light falls on the viewer. It is not necessary to have mirrors over wash basins, except in bathrooms for the use of wet shavers.

In cloakrooms, there should be a shelf with a mirror over it, with hooks for hand bags. A full-length mirror is an asset. The conventional plate glass mirror is satisfactory in bathrooms, but they should be of good quality. Precautions should be taken to ensure that the damp does not penetrate to the silvering on the back. A soft rubber or plastic foam strip stuck all round the edge of the back of the mirror will help, and also cushion it against the wall. Large mirrors should be hung with great care, as unequal stresses will lead to cracking.

Shaving mirrors with a light incorporated on a flexible arm are practical but may not be aesthetically acceptable. Coloured mirrors may be used as a flattering and decorative device in luxury bathrooms or cloakrooms, but they can be disastrous for women making up!

Soap dispensers are useful in communal toilet areas. One dispenser can be placed to serve two basins. Dispensers may contain liquid soap or soap leaves, but the latter are more messy. In some situations a dispenser of barrier cream may also be supplied.

Shaving sockets should be provided in all bathrooms and in some communal cloakrooms. They should be placed next to a mirror and not above a washbasin. There should be a notice prominently displayed, explaining that the socket is for electric shavers only, to prevent fuses being blown.

Lighting should be at a general level, and include the cubicles in communal toilets. In bathrooms the switch should be either on the external wall or a cord inside the bathroom.

Towel rails should be provided in all private bathrooms. They should be firmly secured to the wall, and within easy reach of the basin, shower or bath. The ring type might hold a small towel adjacent to the bidet.

Coat hooks should be placed on the back of every toilet door or on the wall.

Ashtrays should be provided in every toilet cubicle and above urinals. In private bathrooms an ashtray will be placed on the vanitory unit or on the shelf. A book of matches and a night light may also be placed on it in case of an electric power failure.

Soap dishes should be provided for baths, showers and wash basins. They are often included in the design of the unit or inset into the wall. Separate soap dishes should be deep enough so the soap does not slide out, and the sides should be grooved or it should have holes in the base so the soap does not lie in a pool of water.

Grab rails should be adjacent to bath and shower, firmly secured to the wall. Additional rails are necessary for the handicapped, at the side of the lavatory, and emergency bells by the bath in homes for elderly or disabled.

Drip dry lines or racks should be placed over the bath, to prevent wet swim suits or pieces of washing being draped over radiators and ruining the wall covering.

Bottle openers attached to the wall in a private bathroom can prevent spillage on the bedroom carpet. They should be placed over the waste bin, or have their own box to catch the caps.

Waste bins should be of coated metal or plastic so they may be easily cleaned. Both have disadvantages; metal rusts, and plastic is melted by cigarette ends. Paper roundels can be purchased to save the bottom of the bins becoming damaged or messy.

Laundry baskets are found in most private bathrooms of luxury hotels. They should be of plastic, and with a lid to avoid them being used as waste bins.

Toothglasses should be supplied in all private bathrooms and communal wash basin areas. The most hygienic type is the disposable beaker taken from a covered dispenser. Small wall-mounted dispensers are available for use in bathrooms. If real glasses are supplied, they should be spotless, and preferably sent to the wash-up for sterilization in the washing up machine, rather than cleaned in the bathroom or service room.

Shelf space should be provided in bathrooms and communal washing areas. It can be supplied by the vanitory unit, or by window ledges, or by the boxing of pipes. Glass shelves offer the same hazard as the toothglasses.

Hair dryers are found in most modern luxury hotels. They are usually wall mounted, near a mirror. A hot air hand dryer may have the facility of an air outlet which can be positioned to dry the face or hair.

Many hotels provide 'give aways', such as soap, bubble bath, and shower caps. In more luxury hotels one may also find razor blade boxes or envelopes, shampoo, toothpaste, after-shave lotion, perfume, mending kits, spot/stain removers. When supplying these one must not overestimate the advertising value, and they should be built in to the overall cost of the accommodation.

Bathrobes may be found in luxury hotel bathrooms, as well as the towels. In some establishments, to discourage guests from packing them, a discreet notice can say that they can be purchased by asking at reception. If they are to be sold, they should not bear the hotel logo.

Group toilet facilities

The standards of building and décor of group toilet facilities are frequently crude and below what they should be; these consequently induce crude behaviour and vandalism. Group toilet facilities are required where large numbers of people may have to be accommodated continuously or at peak periods. It is more practical to have them grouped in one area, with men's and women's adjacent to avoid families being split, and for the convenience of planning, water and drainage supplies. To prevent bottle necks, it is useful to have an 'in door' and an 'out door'. Lavatories should be nearest the in door, then washing facilities, drying and mirrors and shelving for make-up.

Cubicles

At least one cubicle should be large enough to accommodate a disabled person. These should be located nearest the entrance. The pan should be the correct height for the disabled and be so placed as to have space at the side for the wheel chair with a hand basin. These cubicles should be fitted with suitable grab rails.

The walls and doors should be at least 15 cm clear of the floor for easy cleaning, and to see if an occupant has fainted or is ill. A plastic finish makes for easy cleaning.

Wash basins

These should be grouped along a wall. The vanitory surround makes for easier cleaning, offers space for gloves, handbags etc., and prevents soap being dropped on the floor. It is not advisable to have a mirror in front of the basin because people will linger too long and hair will fall into the basin, eventually causing a blockage in the pipes.

The wash basins should be of the toughened china fire clay type. Towels, electric hand dryers or paper towel dispensers should be placed near the wash basins one at either end of the row and possibly on one wall in the centre.

The basins should be cantilevered to leave the floor clear for easy cleaning, or boxed in with a toe space. A knee-controlled tap placed below the basin level can give a water flow of 30 seconds. This is useful for disabled people. It is also a hygienic method for use in toilets since soiled hands do not touch the tap.

Urinals

The stall-type of urinal which has the outlet at floor level has the disadvantage of underfloor pipes, and there is often a wet floor problem from splashes and flushing. Flushing is always by automatic flushing cisterns operating periodically.

The bowl type urinals have largely superseded the stall type. The drainage pipes go out behind the wall above floor level, making for easier cleaning and access for maintenance.

Some urinals incorporate an electronic beam which, when broken by a stream of urine, releases a flow of water for automatic flushing. Ashtrays should be provided in a suitable position in front of the user, so as to prevent cigarette butts being dropped into the urinal drainage holes where they may get trapped and cause a blockage.

Urinals are made from vitreous china and should be thoroughly cleaned in a similar way to toilet pans.

Further reading

Maurer, I., *Hospital Hygiene*, 3rd edition. (Edward Arnold 1985).

Snow, A. and Hopewell, G., *Planning your Bathroom* (Design Centre 1976).

Tucker, G., and Schneider, M., *The Professional Housekeeper* (Cahners 1982).

Useful film

The Maid Cleaning the Bathroom, available from

Training Films International Ltd,
St Mary's Street,
Whitchurch,
Shropshire

11 *Wall coverings*

Wall coverings have been in use for hundreds of years, dating back to the original cave paintings. They brighten up a dull room and give it character. They can also hide defects, such as cracks. They assist with sound and heat insulation, and give the impression of altering the shape of the room, if the colour and pattern are chosen well.

Wallpapers

Lining paper

This is a plain absorbent paper, applied to bare walls before hanging the top paper. It is not essential but does give a first class finish. It can be obtained in various weights and thicknesses and the thicker the paper, the better the cracks or deformities in the wall are hidden. Lining paper should be hung horizontally and it is essential that the edges should not overlap. A pitch/bitumen-coated paper is available for use on walls to prevent penetration of dampness.

Anaglypta

This is made from a cotton fibre with an embossed design. It can look a little like plaster when applied to walls or ceilings. It is normally used in older properties, where surfaces tend to be uneven, but it can be used for decorative purposes.

Wood chip/ingrain/donkey paper

This has small wood chips or sawdust added to the paper when it is still in pulp form. It disguises uneven surfaces, is very hard-wearing and is usually white or grey in colour. It requires painting and can quickly be refreshed by applying a fresh coat of paint.

Machine-printed paper (ordinary wallpaper)

This is either plain, patterned or embossed or a mixture of all three. The colour is printed on to a white background. The thinner the paper, the cheaper it is and the more difficult it is to hang, because it tends to stretch when wet. Generally speaking, this type of wallpaper is quite straight-forward to hang as it does not require special adhesives. It is difficult to keep clean, however, as it is neither grease nor water repellent. The more expensive machine-printed papers are printed on to a coat of colour. Embossed paper is better when hung on top of lining paper and care must be taken not to flatten the surface during the hanging.

Hand-printed paper

This is made using stencils, screens or wood or lino blocks. Designs can be specially produced and for this reason it is normally very expensive to buy. It is not normally used in commercial establishments unless in the luxury class.

Washable paper

This was the forerunner of vinyl paper. It is ordinary paper covered with a matt or glossy coating and is sometimes found in domestic bathrooms. It is water repellent and can be washed using a sponge and mild detergent and then dried with a soft cloth.

Moiré

This is paper embossed to give the appearance of watered silk. It is sometimes found in older properties.

Marble paper

This has marble patterns printed on. Care must

be taken to order plenty of stock as the pattern does not repeat and each consignment tends to be different. Marble paper is sometimes available with a vinyl finish.

Flock

This has a velvety pile of wool, silk or nylon fibres, applied to paper, giving a pattern, toning or contrasting with the background paper. It gives a luxurious effect, especially in 'period' rooms, and is, in fact, one of the oldest types of wallpaper. It is suitable for large rooms where it will not receive knocks or scuffing, which crushes the pile. It does, however, collect dust and smells.

Hessian

This is a jute cloth, usually backed with paper for ease of application. Backed hessian is hung like wallpaper, and is more expensive. Since the dyes used on jutes are not light proof, they fade. Natural or oatmeal colours are safe; other colours are suitable for corridors where there is not much natural light. It is hard-wearing and does not scuff, but it does absorb grease, and is not suitable for moisture-laden areas. It is suitable for conference and meeting rooms and studios, since it does help with acoustics. It should not be used in areas where there are children, since there is a great temptation to pull out the strands of jute. Hessian may also be painted over with emulsion paint. If it is backed, it does help to hide wall defects.

Japanese grass cloth

This is made of dried grasses sewn closely together and glued to a paper backing. It withstands a certain amount of scuffing but does fray and is difficult to clean apart from gentle vacuuming. It is suitable for an area where an Oriental atmosphere is desired, and the subtle colouring provides an attractive background against which pieces of furniture or objets d'art can be shown to advantage. A similar type of wall covering may be obtained with bamboo instead of grass.

Vinyl

This is the most common type of wall covering found in modern commercial hotels. It is very hard-wearing, waterproof, washable and even scrubbable. It consists of either paper or a cotton cloth backing with a PVC finish. It needs a special fungicidal adhesive to prevent mould from growing between the paper and wall, since it does not allow for the evaporation of moisture. It should be hung by professionals as it tends to be very heavy. Vinyl is suitable for all areas, particularly those which get hard usage and those liable to moisture. It should never be put up where the walls are damp as the adhesive will not necessarily be able to cope with mould growth and the vinyl will peel off. All vinyl coverings have a flame test rating and a smoke density rating. The specification will be stated on the back of a sample and this should be checked before purchase.

For commercial use, vinyl wall coverings come in three different weights: standard, service and heavy. Vinyl tends to be expensive but is durable and long lasting.

Vinyl textured papers simulate tiles, rush matting, etc. The pattern is repeated, however, making them distinguishable from the 'real thing'.

Foil

Foil is made from silvering sprayed on to a paper or polyester backing. A hand-printed pattern with plastic paint on metallic mirror paper, reflects light and gives depth to small areas. It is suitable for bathrooms. It should not be used on walls where there is any dampness or acidity in the plaster. Foil paper should not be allowed to come in contact with any electric wires. Great attention should be paid round light switches and plugs.

Lincrusta

This is made from linseed oil and fillers, bonded to a flat or embossed backing paper. It is very durable, and has been in use since the latter part of the nineteenth century. It is often embossed to resemble wood panelling, tiles or hessian. Old lincrusta has strapwork designs or medallion designs and may be considered an antique worth preserving. Today it is available finished or ready for painting. It is suitable for covering defective walls, as a substitute for panelling, and for walls that receive hard use.

Cork

Cork is available in different forms. Cork tiles can be applied direct to walls, or thin strips of cork glued to a paper backing which is hung like grass paper. Thick cork tiles applied to walls provide a pin-board surface. Cork has good heat insulation and acoustic qualities. It is suitable for corridors, conference rooms, studios and well ventilated bathrooms.

Textile wall coverings

Various fabrics are used, including hessian, linen and silk. Silk for example, is usually applied to a paper backing, but most other fabrics are bought by the metre (not by the roll) and then fixed to a framework of narrow battens which are attached to the wall at the ceiling and skirting board. Pictures must also be fixed on to battens so as not to damage the fabric. Fabrics used must not stretch or distort. They are usually hard-wearing and should be gently vacuumed or taken down for laundering or dry cleaning. They are extremely attractive but expensive. There are also papers to which dried leaves are applied. They are quite unique and the subtle colouring on metalic paper makes them exclusive.

Felt used as a wall covering can give a luxurious appeal. It is warm and useful for sound insulation. It is particularly useful for dining clubs, and conference rooms and is easily cleaned by vacuuming. Dirty marks may be removed by dry cleaning fluids.

Most wallpapers are 530 mm wide and 10.05 metres long. To calculate the number of rolls necessary, measure the room, counting the number of widths required to go round it. Measure the height of the room, add up the lengths required and convert into rolls. Doors and windows are usually counted in as wall area to allow for extra paper for inevitable wastage. Where there is a drop in the pattern repeat, the length of the drop should be added to each length of paper required.

Table 11 *Wall paper symbols*

Symbol	Meaning
～	Spongeable
≋	Washable
≋	Super-washable
▥	Scrubbable
☼	Sufficient light fastness
☼	Good light fastness
↘	Strippable
↘	Peelable
⊔	Ready pasted
🖌	Paste-the-wall
➤ o	Free match
➤ ◄	Straight match
➤ ◄	Offset match
50 cm / 25	Design repeat Distance offset
⎮⎮	Duplex
⧚	Co-ordinated fabric available
↑	Direction of hanging
↓↑	Reverse alternate lengths

Table 11 shows the standard wallpaper symbols which are found on labels and in pattern books.

Apart from those marked 'ready pasted', it is essential that the recommended paste is used. General adhesives when used should be diluted according to the thickness of the paper: the thicker the paper the stronger the adhesive. Thick papers should have the adhesive applied and left to soak in before hanging. Non-porous papers require a fungicide in the adhesive. This should be used with care, avoiding splashes in the eyes or breathing in the dust. Wash hands after using. Overlap adhesive is used where vinyl paper must overlap or where paper has lifted.

Other types of wall covering

Mirror

Mirrors can be plain, patterned or have pictures printed on them. They are useful in a dark room, to reflect light and give an illusion of space to a small room. Mirrors can be used as panels or as a complete wall, but care must be taken to prevent people from walking into them.

Stainless steel

This can be purchased as sheeting or in tile format. It is ideal for kitchens, as it is hygienic and easy to clean. It can also be used as a kickboard on a swing door leading from a restaurant to the kitchen. Steel is expensive but is durable and hard-wearing. Matt or mirrored tiles may be used to give a modern look to public toilets.

Plastic laminate

Plastic laminate or formica is often used to protect a wall in heavy service areas, such as maid service or room service areas. It is hygienic and easy to clean, but must be of a good thickness and well secured to the wall. A dado using plastic laminate is quite effective.

Ceramic tiles

These may be purchased in many attractive colours, patterns, sizes and textures. They must be applied to a dry, smooth wall and if used in a food area an anti-bacteria grouting should be used, especially if the tiles are to be used as a working surface. White ceramic tiles with a smooth glaze are ideal for kitchen walls but they should never be painted over, as paint eventually peels. Coloured tiles brighten up canteens or fast food areas as well as bathroom and toilet areas. Should textured tiles be used, care must be taken to see that they are thoroughly cleaned to prevent dirt and germs from harbouring in the ridges.

Strong adhesives have eliminated the use of plaster and made the process of tiling much speedier.

Dark colours tend to show soap and wet spots more than the pale pastel colours, especially in hard water areas.

Polystyrene

This is available in tile form or on a paper backing. It has insulating properties, but it is soft and vulnerable to rough treatment, so it should be papered and the final surface painted. It is suitable for covering uneven walls and where sound and heat insulation is required. It requires a fungicidal non-flammable heavy duty paste. Before using it in a commercial or institutional establishment, a check should be made with the local fire officer to see whether this type of application is suitable. Polystyrene is known to give off harmful fumes when burnt.

Soft board

This is compressed paper and is suitable for notice boards, offices, childrens' rooms and study bedrooms. It can be covered by felt or hessian or simply painted in bright colours.

Wood panelling

Traditional wood panelled walls are usually found in old buildings, up to Edwardian times. They are of polished hardwood or pine, stripped or painted. They add extra insulation and give a great deal of character to a room. Modern panelled effect can be attained by covering the walls with large sheets of simulated wood, or plain coloured laminated sheets. It must be ensured that the joins of these panels are securely sealed to prevent moisture or dust penetrating. Where wood panelling is used today, it is usually made from birch or beech veneered on to plywood. Smooth birch can be sealed for a better appearance. Wood panelling can be used for ceilings as well as walls. It is normally fixed to the walls with battens and must be treated with a fireproof agent.

Low maintenance finishes

Owing to the high cost of raw material, labour and cleaning, many economy-conscious establishments use low maintenance finishes such as bare brick. This may be easily cleaned by vacuuming and, of course, never needs re-decorating. To a certain extent it is also damage-proof and vandal-proof.

Care of wall coverings

The manufacturers will give instructions which should be followed. Textured and textile wall coverings can be vacuumed using a small soft brush attachment. Protection against spotting or damage can be afforded by the following precautions.

1   A vinyl protective coating available by the litre and applied directly.
2   An aerosol spray of vinyl coating.
3   Applying a transparent film of *Contact*.
4   Covering a susceptible area with transparent perspex sheeting.
5   Protecting corners with stainless steel edging or heavy duty plastic.
6   Using a dado of heavy duty wall covering for the bottom half of the wall and a lighter variety for the top.
7   Affixing a bumper guard (usually wood) at chair back or trolley wheel level.

When treating a stain, use the correct solvent and start from the outside of the stain towards the centre, using a circular movement. This prevents the stain from spreading. Always test the solvent on a spare piece of wall covering or an unseen part before use. If the wall covering cannot be washed, general soiling can often be removed by a rubber/eraser or piece of bread. Grease marks can often be removed by talcum powder or French chalk, which will absorb the stain.

Spongeable papers should be treated with a moist sponge, wrung out in warm soapy water (with a mild detergent). Vinyl wall coverings and other washable walls should be cleaned as follows. Brush off the dust using a lambswool applicator or the soft brush of a vacuum cleaner. The dusting motion should be upward, as dust tends to cling at a downward angle. Make up a solution of warm mild detergent and test out on a small part of the wall. Wash the wall in small areas at a time, rinsing immediately. Water should be changed as frequently as possible so dirt is not rubbed back on to the wall. A circular action should be used and the washing process should start at the bottom and work towards the ceiling. This will prevent heavy dirty water making tracks through unwashed soil and so leaving marks. If dirty water should trickle down on to a clean area, there is no problem rinsing it off.

As vinyl is semi-absorbent, it will soak up a certain amount of soil, and after a while may become discoloured. Stains such as shoe polish and biro will be absorbed very quickly, so an attempt at their removal should be immediate.

Paint

When painting in an occupied residence, areas should be closed off, dust sheets used and 'inconvenience signs' displayed. The smell and the drying time depends on the type of paint being used.

Oil-based paints

Oil-based paints are thinned and cleaned off brushes etc. using white spirit.

They are composed of natural or synthetic resins, such as polyurethane, colour, oils, and white spirit. Owing to the oil content, they generally take longer to dry but a white oil-based paint tends to keep its colour better than an emulsion equivalent. Oil-based paints should be applied on a clean dry surface, using a matching or slightly lighter undercoat plus one or two top coats. All new surfaces need a primer. Gloss paint is the most common oil-based paint.

Advantages: Washable and very durable and hard-wearing: the glossier the paint, the more hard-wearing it usually is. Available in a wide range of colours. Helps to stop moisture penetrating the surface beneath.

Disadvantages: Takes longer to dry than emulsion. Has a very strong smell, so plenty of fresh air is required. Gloss paint shows up defects in surfaces beneath. Condensation is attracted especially by gloss paint.

Emulsion paints

Emulsion paints are made from synthetic resins and colour suspended in water. The water evaporates during drying, leaving a resinous film as a surface. Some paints are made from acrylic while others are made from vinyl. Vinyl paints give a smoother finish, whereas acrylics are more water-proof. Emulsion paints are also used as undercoats. Water is used to thin them, to clean brushes and splashes.

Advantages: Easier to use than oil-based paints. Quick drying paint with little smell. No special undercoat needed and can even be used on freshly plastered walls.

Disadvantages: Not as hard-wearing as oil-based paints and cannot be as easily washed. Not really suitable for metal or wood surfaces and therefore are primarily used as a wall paint.

Primer paints

Primers can be oil-based or emulsion. They are used to seal porous surfaces so that the top coat of paint remains on the surface and protects it, rather than being soaked in. A thinned-down coat of emulsion paint will serve as a primer but it is better to seek professional advise as there are many different types for the many different surfaces.

Undercoats

Undercoats are used under oil-based paints. Similar to primers, they are designed to provide a non-porous surface in order that the top coat retains its colour and shine. Undercoats and primers should be allowed to dry, then they should be rubbed down, wiped with a clean dry cloth and painted immediately in order to prevent dirt or dust establishing itself.

Textured paints

These have more elasticity and are suitable for covering poor surfaces.

Special paints

Water repellent and fire resistant paints are available for special areas. The latter should never be used in an unventilated area, since the fumes are potent and have been known to activate smoke fire alarms.

Bitumastic paint

This contains particles of aluminium. It is suitable for damp areas, and gives a silvery sheen finish.

Floor paints

These are available for use on dry concrete, wood and steel floors. They are unsuitable for heated surfaces. They are resistant to repeated and regular washing with water and detergent. Some have a semi-gloss finish, which is not resistant to spillage of oils or dairy food products.

Suede deck and floor paint gives a low sheen and contains an anti-slip ingredient. It can be subjected to heavy wetting but not to spillages of solvents, chemicals, cutting oils, dairy produce and foodstuffs.

Quick-drying enamel

This is a modified alkyd resin-based paint, pigmented with non-lead pigment. It is suitable for use on metals, equipment, whitewood furniture and fittings, where a hard, glossy, protective, quick-drying coating is required. It can be used on primer or on good previously painted surfaces. It is heat resistant up to 100°C and resistant to grease and water.

Epoxy paints

Epoxy primer and finish are sold together and mixed before use. They are resistant to a wide range of chemicals and therefore suitable for laboratories and hospitals. For all special conditions, advice should be sought from the manufacturer's technical service.

Paint strippers

Ammonia is the simplest stripper. Care should be taken to protect the skin and eyes of the operator. Inhalation of the fumes can be dangerous. There are several proprietory brands of paint stripper and the instructions should be carefully followed. One brand is spread over the paint to be removed, left to dry and then peeled off. Another common method of stripping is by burning off with a butane gas lamp.

Choosing paint

The correct paint for the surface should be selected for the décor effect and the wear to which it will be subjected. Gloss paint is tough and washable, but should not be used in areas where there is possibility of high condensation. It is resistant to knocks and marking and relects light. Silk finish and eggshell paints have a modest sheen. Eggshell is washable, but not so resistant to knocks or abrasion. Both eggshell and silks reflect light and colour. Matt paint has a flat non-sheen surface. It soils more easily than other types and is less easily washed. It gives a purer colour since it does not reflect light, shadow or colour.

It is difficult to select a paint from a small colour chart and some manufacturers produce miniature 'trial size' tins of paint which can be tried out *in situ*.

Safety points

Paints are highly flammable and toxic and should be treated with great care and attention. Read the instructions carefully paying attention to the flash point (at which the paint could ignite). No paint work should be carried out in an unventilated area. If a cupboard or an enclosed area is being painted, a mask should be worn.

Paints should be stored in a cool place and away from any source of ignition. Waste disposal should never be down a drain. It should be buried in earth with their lids removed or burned in a suitable spot.

If a fire should occur, use a foam type of extinguisher or a dry agent such as sand or soil. If there is a fire in the vicinity, the paint containers should be kept cool by spraying with water.

If paint is inhaled, move the victim to fresh air and give nothing by mouth. If paint is splashed in the eyes, flush with water for at least ten minutes, holding lids apart. If splashed on skin, remove contaminated clothing and wash skin with soap and water. If symptoms persist, seek medical advice.

Wherever painting is being done, smoking should be prohibited.

Useful addresses

Décor and Contract Furnishing,
Westbourne Publication Group,
Crown House,
Morden,
Surrey SM4 5EB

Incorporated Institute of British Decorators and Interior Designers,

162 Derby Road,
Stapleford,
Nottinghamshire

National Federation of Master Painters and Decorators of England and Wales,
37 Soho Square,
London W1V 6AT

12 *The linen room*

The linen room is as important as the kitchen to a residential establishment, and it should not be tucked away in some odd spot, such as the basement. It should have the following qualities:

1 Situated on the ground floor, within easy reach of a trade entrance where there is parking nearby, especially when laundry is cleaned off the premises.
2 Large enough to accommodate baskets of laundry and the equipment it will contain.
3 Well ventilated and damp free.
4 Adequately heated and lit.
5 Water and drainage facilities and a hand basin.
6 Cleaning material storage space, and a cupboard for its own cleaning material and equipment.
7 Light coloured, washable walls and ceiling.
8 Smooth floor for easy sweeping, vacuuming or washing.
9 Lockable doors and windows. Direct sunlight into the linen store should be avoided because sunlight can fade and rot certain fabrics.
10 Doorways wide enough to allow for easy access of hampers and bundles of laundry.
11 Close to the housekeeper's office.

Contents of a linen room

There should be a number of tables or working surfaces of a pastel colour upon which white linen will show up. Underneath these there should be adequate space for linen baskets, bins or bundles. The shelves should be of a height under which an opened linen basket can stand. This is a good height at which to work when standing. Cupboards should be fitted or free-standing, and there should be at least one set of safety steps. Office equipment is also necessary: a desk, chairs, filing cabinet and telephone.

As well as dirty linen containers, there should be separate bins for Chef's whites, washable uniforms, dry cleanable uniforms, rags/cloths, and linen to be written off.

A full length mirror can be attached to the wall or back of a door. The dirty linen area should be separated from the clean linen.

It is wise to have a selection of household equipment, separate from that used by the maids. It would include brushes (hard and soft), dust pan, carpet sweeper, vacuum cleaner, mop, bucket, dusters and sundry cleaning cloths and rags.

A hair dryer is useful for drying out wet patches as well as hair. A bedboard could be kept in the linen room.

First aid kit

Complete first aid kits are supplied by pharmaceutical firms but the housekeeper should have available a wide range of items in the linen room, while each other department should have a kit available for minor cuts etc.

The kit should include tweezers, scissors, spatulars, clinical thermometer, pencil, torch, finger stoles, rubber gloves, two small kidney dishes (enamel for sterilizing), two small enamel bowls, safety pins, witch hazel, burn spray, elastoplaster rolls and dressing strip, smelling salts, Listerine or Dettol or TCP, bicarbonate of soda, hydrogen peroxide, vinegar, vaseline and antiseptic ointment or jelly, pain reliever, eye bath and eye lotion, medicine glass, medicine spoon. In the cupboard there should be a bedpan, a urine bottle and a plastic draw-sheet.

Emergency cleaning kit

The housekeeper can buy proprietary carpet first aid kits but he/she should prepare his/her own kit containing the following items:

ammonia, methylated spirit, white spirit, biro solvent, salt, chewing gum solvent, carbon tetrachloride, turpentine, vinegar, soda and bicarbonate of soda, carpet shampoo, upholstery shampoo, disinfectant (not too strong a smell and already diluted), hydrogen peroxide, nail varnish remover, unscented talcum powder, 1 bowl, 1 bucket, newspapers, matches, glues or adhesives, scissors, needle and cotton, anti-static spray, Scotch Guard, starch, air-fresheners, pre-wash spray for stains.

Having all these items in one spot saves much time in an emergency.

Tool kit

The linen room should contain a tool kit to deal with small emergency repairs. The tools and the box should be marked for easy identification (splash of paint or nail varnish will assist in easy identification when they have been borrowed). The kit should include:

two hammers of different weights, pliers, wire cutters, set of screw drivers, bradawl, gimlet, set of spanners, wrench, bed spanner, Stanley knife, paint scraper, set of electrical screwdrivers, flex cutters/stripper, jars containing nuts, bolts, nails, tacks, screws, curtain hooks and rollers, washers; spring rule, masking tape, insulating tape, adhesives, sand paper, emery paper, light-oil can.

Housemaids' trolleys

These are fitted with receptacles for waste, soiled linen, cleaning equipment and materials. When selecting these, attention should be paid to the loaded height and ease of mobility in relation to those who are going to use them.

Sewing machines

The greater the versatility of the machine, the greater chance of things going wrong with it. Choose a simple machine, preferably electric, with a hand attachment and a swing needle for zig-zag stitching and darning. Keep the machine covered when not in use. Have it periodically serviced by the supplier, but in between remove any fluff that has accumulated round the bobbin and oil as indicated in the instruction book. After oiling leave a piece of fabric beneath the needle.

Ironing boards

These should be adjustable for height, firm standing, with the iron stand suitable for a right and left handed user. The pad should be of non-flammable material with a high heat resistance. It should have a separate cover for when not in use.

Irons

A lightweight iron may be better for general use. Avoid steam irons: if not properly attended to, these can create rust marks. A fine plastic plant spray will dampen the clothes adequately.

Washing machine

Where there is not a laundry on the premises, a strong domestic or small commercial machine is very useful. A fully automatic one will save the operator's time. Alongside it should be a tumble-drier from which there should be an outlet for the air from the back of the machine and a fine filter.

Linen room administration

The purpose of the linen room is to issue and control stocks of linen and other items, at established times. It services the food and beverage department (supplying tablecloths, napkins etc.) and the housekeeping department (supplying bed linen etc.). Sometimes the linen room will be responsible for supplying items requested by guests, such as bedboards, cots, toothbrushes etc. Staff room linen will, of course, also be stored in the linen room.

A linen keeper or linen room supervisor will be

in charge of the smooth running of the linen room, perhaps assisted by one or more attendants. In large establishments, a seamstress will be employed.

The following definitions are important in the linen room administration.

Circulating inventory The amount of linen in service in an establishment.

Minimum circulating inventory The minimum amount of linen that is required to service an establishment, taking its laundry schedule into consideration.

Linen reserve The new linen which is stored (in housekeeping or general stores) to be issued by requisition to replenish the circulating inventory (1 par).

Par The amount of linen required to meet the needs of an establishment for a 24 hour period at 100 per cent occupancy including the auxiliary linen supply of 10%. For example, ten beds with two sheets per bed equals twenty sheets, plus 10 per cent equals twenty-two sheets (par 22).

Auxiliary linen supply Linen required for late check-outs, rollaway beds, accidents and unusable linen which may have been delivered to the guest floor. This is normally 10 per cent of par.

Laundry work schedule The number of hours when a laundry operation is fully manned, producing clean linen to maximum output.

Stock book

The stock book should contain details of the following.

1 *Linen in stock* New, unused linen which is normally locked away in a separate stockroom, commonly known as the linen reserve.
2 *Linen in circulation* Otherwise known as the circulating inventory.
3 *Losses* Linen which has been lost, stolen or worn out and discarded.
4 *Remarks* Linen which has either been damaged or which is beginning to wear out. A record has to be kept of an item of linen which was purchased for one purpose and now has been remade into something else.

All stock is recorded in order to facilitate inventories and budgeting.

Laundry book

Where laundering is done off the premises or where hired linen is used, a laundry book keeps records of: linen sent out, linen received, shorts and stained and damaged linen. Duplicates should accompany the linen as it travels in and out.

Linen inventories (stocktaking)

The intervals between stocktaking will vary, but it should be done at least once a year and preferably at six-monthly intervals. It should be started after the linen for the day has been dispensed, but great care must be taken to avoid items being counted twice.

A list of the items should be made, together with a note of where each item should be. In some establishments, this will include a list of items in reserve, as well as those in use. At the end of the day, all inventory sheets are collected and the figures entered into a stock book. In large establishments, representatives from the accounts department will make spot checks on the stored linen and check figures from the stocktaking.

The purpose of a linen inventory is to keep control over the linen and identify where stock is being misused or stolen or wearing out, so that preventative action may be taken.

Par levels

By keeping proper par stock levels, the housekeeper will ensure that sufficient linen is in circulation. In the majority of seasonal establishments, where linen is changed on average three times per week, a par of three is sufficient. In hotels where linen is changed daily and the laundry operation is run on a 6-day basis, then 4.2 par is recommended.

Table 12 shows the stock requirements for linen

Table 12 *Linen par requirements*

Sheets	Beds	1 par	In circulation	Reserve (1 × par)
Double	228	502	1506	502

used on double-bedded rooms. It shows that the hotel has 228 rooms containing double beds. The par for 228 double beds is 502 sheets (two sheets per bed + 10 per cent auxiliary supply). In circulation there should be three times par, equalling 1506 double sheets (one par on bed, one par in laundry and one par in linen room). In addition the stock room should hold one par in reserve.

Figures also have to be worked out for all other linen used. Restaurant linen par requirement must be calculated taking into consideration the number of sittings or covers per meal time. Items such as blankets, bedpads, underslips and bed-spreads do not need such high par requirements as they are not changed on a regular daily basis.

The greater the variety of linen types, sizes and colours, the larger the stock will have to be. It is therefore much more efficient to maintain one basic colour and the minimal number of sizes and styles.

Linen rooms in hospitals

Overall responsibility for linen in hospitals is held by the district laundry manager. Linen room staff are responsible for packing 'greens' prior to sterilization. 'Greens' are the green overalls worn by operating theatre staff. Dirty bed linen in a hospital is collected by the porters who take it to a sluice area, where it is collected by laundry staff.

The linen operation in boarding schools

The housekeeper/matron will be responsible for the clothes of the pupils, and often their bed linen supplied by parents. There should be protected clothes rails and individual drawers or boxes for underclothes in the linen room. A drying room is necessary for wet clothes and sports towels, and ample washing facilities for sports clothes, even when the rest of the laundry is sent to a commercial laundry. Marking pens and adhesive name tape will be required.

The linen operation in university or college halls of residence

Each hall should have its own linen store supplied from the central point to which the linen is delivered. It will be necessary for porters with trolleys to collect the week's supply. Each hall will require a senior maid to supervise the collection on the spot. This is not such a formidable task since the bed linen will only be changed one a week.

In halls of residence and boarding schools, it is quite common to only change one sheet per week. The top sheet is used as a bottom sheet, the bottom sheet is laundered and a clean sheet and pillow case are supplied to each student, the clean sheet being used as a top sheet. In colleges, students are normally expected to make their own beds and they are often encouraged to supply their own linen. Laundrette facilities will normally be found on the university campus. If linen is supplied to the students, the amount necessary could be estimated as three sheets and three pillow cases per head.

If university halls are used for conferences and holiday lets, beds should be made up as in a hotel, although linen will only be changed weekly or on check-out.

Linen room routines

Linen change

In some establishments soiled linen will be brought to the linen room for direct exchange for clean. Banqueting linen is different and should be given out on a list presented by the waiter, which should tally with the lists of functions presented by reception or the banqueting manager each week. Hospital linen is usually collected directly from the wards. Heavily soiled linen should be kept separate in all cases.

The times of exchange of linen should be staggered to avoid queuing. The housekeeper should be informed of the daily departures by the receptionist. Any special requirements or requests known to the receptionist should be indicated on the departure list.

Sorting, packing and unpacking

On receipt, soiled linen should be sorted ready for counting to go to the laundry. Ideally linen should be repaired before laundering but this is not a pleasant job. Badly damaged linen could be put through the in-house washing machine before repairing.

Damp linen should be dried out before being packed. Bad stains should be given 'first aid' treatment and/or then sent separately to the laundry with a note for special attention.

The linen should be counted into units of ten, and entered into a duplicate laundry book. The top copy is sent to the laundry and the duplicate kept for checking.

Roughly fold the soiled linen to take up less room in the containers. Do not use a sheet for making a bundle. Use (if necessary) a large refuse sack clearly marked 'linen' or 'laundry'. Keep different fabrics separate and try to keep similar articles together. Do not send to the laundry any items which are going to be written off. Wash those on the premises.

Unpacking

Count the linen in tens, checking with the copy list which has been retained. The linen should be inspected for repairs, stains, bad folding, damage at the laundry and items from other establishments being sent in error. Any discrepancies or damage should be reported at once by telephone to the laundry, followed by a letter.

Storage

Linen should be stored on slatted shelves, supported at intervals, because the shelves are going to take heavy weights. The cupboard should ideally be 'walk-in' with shelves all round and down the centre if large enough. It is difficult to reach the back of wide shelves so they should be just a little wider than the items they are going to hold. The distance between the shelves should not be too great, as piles which are too high will topple over. The shelves should be raised from the floor to a height which enables the floor to be swept.

Linen should be protected from bright sunlight. All folded items should be stored with the fold to the front for easy counting.

Blankets should be stored in mothproof bags, or a polythene bag folded and taped at the top.

Woollen blankets should be dry cleaned, while cotton cellular weave blankets can be laundered as for cotton sheets. All blankets will benefit from being shaken in the open air. Worn blankets will cut down for ironing pads and bottom blankets on open spring beds to protect the mattress from wear from the wire spring.

Eiderdowns and duvets should be stored in plastic bags. Those with man-made fillings can be laundered, but down and feather fillings should be dry cleaned.

Care of linen

In large establishments staff may be employed to inspect linen for stains and damage, but this should be evaluated against wages and saving on linen.

All staff should be encouraged to return any damaged item without using it. Repairs can be done in the linen room, or sent out to a seamstress or to a mending room in large establishments. A record should be kept of linen sent for repair.

Because of rising costs, marking is usually confined to the more durable items. The marking may be done with the name or logo of the establishment. In some cases, the date is included. In hotels it is more discreet to have a cipher for this.

Linen will last longer if it is sometimes given a rest. To ensure even wear of stocks, when stacking the clean linen, place it underneath the linen already there.

Withdraw from use any linen not up to standard and keep for inspection by someone with the authority to write off. This may be suitable for use on staff accommodation or for remaking into other items. From luxury establishments, it may be sold, if possible, after removing identification.

Staff uniform should be hung up on protected rails or in a hanging cupboard. To prolong the life of towels and sheets, hem down the selvedges. Pulled loops in terry towelling should be darned in or cut off.

Glass and kitchen cloths with holes in them should never be allowed to be used. It is extremely dangerous.

To protect linen being stored for a long period.

Place an old sheet on the shelf – with edge to the front of the shelf. Stack the linen on this, then draw the surplus sheet from the back – over and down the front of the pile and tuck it in at the front.

Uniforms and protective clothing

Uniforms are issued to most people who work in the hospitality industry. Although there are many people who dislike wearing uniforms of any kind, they do have their advantages. The advantages to the company are

1 The staff can be easily identified.
2 Uniforms help to set the scene and create atmosphere: for example, uniforms may be worn either to match the décor or the theme.
3 Uniformed staff feel part of the team and their work improves.

The advantages to the staff are

1 They save money on working clothes, and perhaps on laundry costs.
2 Staff can get more involved in a messy job if they know their own clothes will not get dirty.
3 Some uniforms are protective.
4 Some uniforms confer prestige on the wearer.

When choosing uniforms, it is important to consider the work and environment of the employees. For example, short sleeves are more practical for room maids. Some uniforms, for example the headwear of kitchen staff, fulfil an important hygiene function.

It is also important to think carefully about the style. Choose a style that will look equally good on the fat and the thin, the short and the tall. Sometimes it is a good idea to have overalls or dresses of different styles, but the same colour and material, so that staff have an element of choice. In any case, consult the staff before selecting a uniform. All uniforms must suit the décor of the establishment, and the company's image.

All uniforms must be practical. It should be washable, and preferably drip-dry. Ensure that the material is flame resistant, and that there are no loose parts which might catch on door handles.

Porters, whose work takes them outside, should have a sufficiently warm uniform, while waiters should not be expected to wear heavy tailored jackets in the summer, while their customers are in short sleeves. Make sure that each uniform has enough pockets – for pens, bleeps, money etc. as required by the job of the wearer.

In certain situations, the employer is obliged by the Health and Safety at Work Act 1974 to provide protective clothing. This includes items such as rubber gloves and safety shoes which protect the wearer, and hats or scarves for kitchen staff, which protect the customer.

Purchasing uniforms

In large establishments, there is usually a separate budget for uniforms. In some hotels, the uniforms are bought and looked after out of the housekeeping budget, but the costs are then charged to each department.

When drawing up a uniform budget, consideration should be given to staff turnover, life expectancy of the garment, seasonal requirements, anticipated changes in décor and cleaning/laundry requirements. As a general rule, staff should be supplied with at least two or three outfits. Kitchen staff require at least four sets of whites, more if they enter the restaurant. Before drawing up the budget, consult individual department heads about their requirements, and check the existing uniform inventory.

Off-the-peg
Uniforms can be bought from a local department store. This is possible in small establishments, and the prices will be competitive and the garments quite fashionable. The disadvantage is that stocks change rapidly, and on a rare occasion guests may turn up wearing the same clothes.

Professional suppliers
The more traditional establishment will often have a contract with a regular uniform supplier. A company may have its own design and colour, and uniforms can be made-to-measure. Having an established supplier makes re-ordering much easier. The drawback is that, although

hard-wearing, these uniforms may be very expensive.

Shopping around

The housekeeper can seek tenders from a number of different suppliers. This ensures variety and choice, as well as competitive prices. However, it is very time-consuming.

Hiring

By hiring uniforms, the establishment avoids the need to worry about repairs or replacements, or even laundering. A wide variety is often available. However, delivery is not always reliable, and it will be difficult to maintain a distinctive company identity with hired uniforms.

Linen

'Linen' is a term which now includes cotton, terylene, and nylon, as well as pure linen – in fact any fabric used as bed sheets and pillow cases or table clothes, serviettes, etc. Chapter 6 examines the qualities of the various fabrics available.

Bed linen

Robert Brooke described 'The cool, kindliness of sheets that soon smooth away troubles and the rough male kiss of blankets'. No doubt he was thinking of pure linen sheets! It is worth remembering that sheets also protect blankets from the sleeper.

Sheets

'Single', 'double' and 'king' size can be misleading terms, so when purchasing sheets, the actual measurements should carefully be noted. The mattress should be measured and an allowance made for shrinkage, turnback and tuck-in. The cheaper the sheet, the looser the weave, the greater the shrinkage and the narrower the hems. Careful inspection of these aspects must be made.

Hems should be well finished so check the corners especially. Hem stitching is an indication of the overall quality of the sheet. On commercially used linen, hems should be the same width at either end: this increases the life of the sheet

because its position on the bed will inevitably be varied. Sheets usually wear out faster at the knee or foot area.

Selvedges should be firm, even and closely woven. The weave should be close and even. The number of threads per square inch or centimetre is known as 'the count'. The higher the number, the better the quality. Cotton may shrink from 5 to 8 per cent after laundering unless it is marked 'pre-shrunk'.

Fitted sheets have four mitred corners to fit snugly over the corners of the mattress. The top sheet has two mitred corners. They give a neat finish to the bed and save time by eliminating tucking in during bed-making. However, the corners frequently tear and the bottom sheet gets more wear than the top. They are difficult to fold, and to iron. They are not suitable for use with duvets.

Coloured sheets are attractive but only pastel shades are practical. Dark colours lose their colour and it is difficult to remove stains. White sheets are essential where staining is likely to occur and bleaching may be necessary. Polyester/cotton sheets should be coloured as it is very difficult to keep them white, because they cannot be boiled. Apart from duvet covers, patterns should be avoided as they fade and often do not match room décor. Similarly, frills and lace should be avoided because of laundering problems. Many guests will not like them.

Linen often has to be ordered well in advance, especially if it has to be made to a colour or size specification or has to be marked with a date or logo. Sheets should last for at least 250 washes, but they usally last for 400–800 washings.

Pillow cases

Pillow cases are made from the same fabrics as sheets. The usual size is 50×76 cm, slightly larger than the average pillow. It is advisable to check the pillow size and buy cases that will cover the pillow and underslip comfortably.

The open end case is the easiest type to deal with, but it must be at least the width of the broad hem longer than the pillow. The housewife style has a fold-back (pocket) inside the case, into which the end of the pillow is tucked. The pocket often becomes unstitched.

Frilled, embroidered and hemstitched cases, used mainly for the top pillow, are expensive and require careful finishing to look smart. They are only suitable for up-market establishments.

Pillow cases will last for about 450 washes.

Dust sheets

The linen room should have a stock of dust sheets for covering floors, furniture etc. when a room is being redecorated or spring-cleaned or when a room is not going to be in use for some time. They can be written off sheets, but without holes or fraying edges and not shedding lint. Heavy-duty plastic is better for covering carpets since it does not 'kick up'.

The dust sheets should be laundered after use. A dirty dust sheet defeats its purpose. Unbleached calico purchased for the purpose may be needed where there is extensive use required.

While plastic is a non-porous material through which spillages will not seep, it is slippery and can be a safety hazard. The thicker the gauge, the less dangerous it is.

Pillow covers

These are covers which are used under the pillow case. Their use is not so necessary when plain white ticking is used, and where the pillows are easily washable. However, they are essential where the pillows have striped ticking, which shows through most pillow cases. Covers made from written-off sheets or slightly substandard pillow cases can be used. Where heavy soiling is likely, protective covers made from polyester melded fabric should be used. They are washable and prevent staining and grease penetrating the pillow or mattress.

Valances

These are like a sheet wth a deep drop which is frilled or pleated to cover the sides of the divan base. They are placed on top of the base and under the mattress and improve the appearance of the bed when the bedspread is removed or when a duvet only is used.

Duvet covers

These are available in cotton, cambric, polyester and cotton, terylene and cotton, dacron and percale, usually to match the sheets and pillow cases. Pastel colours will withstand laundering. It is essential that the material is light, absorbent, porous and flame-proof. The opening should be large, preferably the whole length of one side, and secured with velcrum in preference to studs. Materials can be bought in bulk and made up on the premises. The size should be at least 18 to 20 cm longer than the duvet itself.

Mattress covers

Waterproof mattress covers should be fitted, to prevent wrinkling, and have a matt finish to prevent condensation. These are essential in hospital, geriatric and pediatric homes.

Other mattress covers protect the mattress and are usually made of unbleached calico. The opening should be wide and it is usually secured with tapes or velcrum. There should be openings for the flat loop-handles of the mattress so that it can be turned easily.

Underblankets

This is placed under the bottom sheet (over the electric blanket if one is used). If offers warmth, and protection to the mattress. Flannelette sheets or portions of written-off blankets can be used for this purpose where economies have to be made. Underblanket pads with elasticated corners are preferable to a loose flannelette sheet or blanket.

Towelling

Towels are usually made from cotton Turkish towelling. Turkish towelling is made from terry cloth, a cotton pile fabric made usually from uncut loops, although the pile may be cut to give a more velvet feel.

Towels are available in a range of sizes from bath sheets (122×182 cm) to bath towels (76×152 cm) to hand towels (ranging from 60×122 cm to 30×45 cm). The closer the weave, the better the buy, as the towel will be more absorbent. Coloured towels must be fast and hems or edges must be well finished.

Bath towels are usually of cotton or cotton and man-made fibre terry weave which has a loop pile on both sides. Some better quality towels have a cut pile on one side and this gives a soft and velvet like pile. The loop pile exposes more absorbent fibres. The loops are woven into a foundation cloth which may be of terylene to give extra strength to the towel.

A terry ratio gives the length of the weft thread in relation to the width of the material. For example, a terry ratio of 4:1 means that a towel 20 cm wide has a weft thread $4 \times 20 = 80$ cm. The higher the ratio generally means the better quality of the material, giving longer loops and consequently a deeper pile. A terry ratio of 2–1 would give a loosely woven towel with a shorter tuft. If a very fine thread is used, the towel might have a high ratio, but not much bulk, so weight in grams per square metre is a better indication of the quality of the towel.

Avoid towels which have a loose foundation cloth. About 1 cm of the foundation cloth will be visible at the selvedges. Avoid towels with a broad end border or fringed ends: these serve no useful purpose. Sculptured pile reduces the drying properties of the towel. Avoid dark colours for the same reasons as dark table and bed linen.

Indian towels are cheaper, but they are woven from the shorter cotton fibre, and tend to shed fluff.

Bath sheets are usually only found in luxury hotels because of their expense. Bath sheets are very large and are usually too heavy for elderly or infirm people to use.

Should there be a swimming pool in the hotel, then separate towels should be provided. Chlorine and sun tan lotion can damage towels and there will be extra wear and tear from people lying on them on a beach. Ideally there should be a small kiosk at the entrance to a private beach or pool where guests may borrow pool towels, so that there is less risk to bathroom towels.

Towels supplied for the bidet, especially abroad, are usually made from huckaback. Huckaback is a fancy weave of cotton, linen or a mixture of both fibres. In England it is only found in up market establishments, especially in cloak-rooms where an attendant issues personal towels. Huckaback is usually white and requires good laundering and ironing for a high standard of appearance. Some roller towels are produced from a type of huckaback weave and teatowels or glass cloths may also be made from a cotton huckaback.

Towels usually have the logo of the establishment woven into them. If folded correctly, the logo should show. A date mark may also be woven into the towel at the same time, for inventory purposes.

Face flannels are often lost, stolen or misused. Consequently they are usually only found in good class hotels where often two flannels per person are issued. If flannels are purchased, it is better to buy them with a hem rather than an 'oversewn' edge as the hem will wear better.

Bath mats

For ease of laundering, a very heavy terry cloth or candlewick mat is best. A man-made long pile mat with latex backing can be machine-washed, but is not as durable as cotton terry. Many establishments use disposable bath mats.

As with towels, bath mats should be changed daily, or upon every departure.

Table linen

As with bed linen, there are many substitutes for the traditional linen made from flax. Table cloths, napkins etc. can be made from damask (linen, cotton, or a mixture), bark weave (cotton or cotton and man-made fibres), seersucker (usually cotton) or gingham (cotton).

Table linen can be purchased in a variety of colours, and some suppliers will arrange for a bolt to be dyed to the customer's requirements. If an establishment buys a bolt (about 80 or 90 metres) the table linen can be made up in-house. Table cloths should be given a drop of 30–45 cm. Banquet cloths should have a longer drop, because they will often be required to cover an unoccupied side of the table. Each cloth should be marked at each corner, with its length and breadth, to avoid having to unfold it to see the size. Banquet cloths for tables with semi circular ends should have rounded ends, to avoid corners trailing on to the floor where they can be tripped over. Alternatively some D-shaped end cloths will overcome this.

Napkins should match the table cloths and are obtainable in the following sizes: 36 cm², 40 cm², 45 cm², 50 cm².

Place mats, trolley cloths and tray cloths are all obtainable in the same fabrics as table cloths. Often it is more practical and economical to have these made on the premises for individual requirements, from material bought in bulk or from the good parts of partly worn larger items.

Slip cloths are square cloths smaller than the main table cloth, laid diagonally over the main cloth. They can be made of the same as the main cloth or contrasting. Easy care material is suitable for these cloths, and the colour can complement the décor.

Waiters' cloths are of union or all cotton. They should be thicker than table linen (between 30 and 38 threads to the centimetre). They have either a twill or basket weave, and a coloured line round the edge or down the middle. If waiters cloths are made up from remakes in the linen room, they should be of double or treble thicknesses to withstand the heat from plates. They too should have a few rows of coloured machine stitching round the edge to distinguish them from other table linen or casually used cloths.

Glass cloths

These should be of a linen cotton union or linen only. Cotton alone is not sufficiently absorbent and leaves a lint on the glass. Linen has greater absorption qualities, since it is a hollow fibre. Some cotton has been treated with non-fluff finish, but it is still not so absorbent as linen or a union.

Glass cloths should be distinguished from kitchen and other cloths by a different coloured check or stripe. All glass cloths must be laundered before using for the first time, so keep a supply of ready washed clothes available to be brought into use. Buy as large a size as the budget will allow, since the laundering cost of a large towel is the same as for a small one. Glass cloths/

teatowels issued to room maids must also bear a different coloured stripe for inventory purposes.

Kitchen cloths, tea towels and kitchen rubbers are usually of union or cotton, thicker and with rougher threads than glass cloths.

Oven cloths

A close weave of hessian or unbleached cotton or union is suitable. It must be as large as possible. Oven gloves are used in large scale kitchens and they should be industrial specification. The normal domestic oven glove is not suitable, as many of these are very loosely woven and the bundle of weft threads separate.

Baize and felt

This is a woven woollen cloth with a brushed finish, giving it the appearance of felt. Traditionally it is green. It is used to cover service doors in stately homes to deaden noise, to cover card tables, notice boards and the deal tops of restaurant tables and conference tables.

It can be obtained in varying widths and is best bought by the bolt and cut to the required lengths. A good drop is required for conference tables – to the ground on one side and with about 30 cm on the side where the chairs are placed. If green baize is used as an underlay for table cloths, the colour will run if there are spillages. Melton cloth is cheaper than baize as a substitute for the above uses.

Modern conference and restaurant tables are frequently already covered with a light coloured felt. Used in place of baize or Melton cloth, it shrinks rapidly if wetted, and neither washes or dry cleans satisfactorily. It is a help if the varying lengths are marked on tape and sewn on to the individual pieces of baize.

Buying linen

When purchasing linen, it is necessary to shop around, once you have drawn up a comprehensive list of requirements, including numbers, sizes, etc. It is worth going to a reputable firm, who will give good advice and deal with any complaints efficiently. It is also worth considering approaching an agent.

Before buying anything, ask for samples of small items and swatches of material. Give these a test wash, and look for shrinkage, discoloration, deterioration of appearance and ease of stain removal. Test the swatch by rubbing it between the fingers. Some manufacturers add a starch-like filler to give body to the material, which will come off when rubbed.

Order in good time for peak periods, and ensure that you know the delivery dates. Try to order a year's supply in advance, to take advantage of bulk discounts. If the budget will not allow this, some suppliers will hold the stock order and it can be drawn and paid for at intervals (for example, quarterly).

In large organizations, linen purchase is usually done by a specialist at the headquarters, a senior administrator, or an outside consultant. This brings the advantages of buying in bulk, but the comments and recommendations of staff in the individual establishments should be noted.

Linen hire

Because of the higher capital cost of equipping an establishment with a stock of linen, linen hire has become more popular. In establishments where there is already a good stock, it is difficult to change over. So if the hiring of linen is being considered, stocks should be run down. Sometimes only one item such as sheets is hired. If there is an overlap, linen of a different colour from that used by the establishment can be hired.

Besides avoiding capital outlay the repairs to hired linen are not the responsibility of the hirer, and the cost of linen can be easily calculated against revenue. Extra linen can be hired for a short period, for special occasions or for high seasons. Less storage space is required.

However, there are disadvantages. There is a more limited choice, and linen hire contractors frequently have their linen marked with their name which obviously does not relate to the identity of the establishment. Standards may not be maintained in the quality of laundering and

repair, and there are no partly worn items for remaking or for rags.

Disposables
Rising labour costs and technical advances have resulted in a greater use of disposables. Some of the disposables replacing traditional linen items are table napkins, table cloths, sheets in hospitals, uniforms (chef's, aprons, head protective caps, kerchiefs, etc.), kitchen cloths, drying cloths, hand towels, razor cloths, lavatory cloths, continuous roll towel (replacing roller towels), bath mats, glass mats, place mats, banqueting cloths, conference table covers, dish cloths, bedpan covers, draw sheets.

The choice is infinite and should be considered carefully, having in mind the use and cost. For table cloths dunicel (a thick disposable material that closely resembles a fabric) can be purchased in a variety of colours and sizes and by the roll from which any required size can be cut. Sheets are also available on the roll, in different widths.

The advantages of disposable linen are:

1 Labour saving: eliminates sorting, repairing, laundering.
2 The cost can be less than using traditional linen: the cost of a disposable item may be the same as the cost of laundering its linen counterpart.
3 More hygienic since they are only used by one person.
4 The storage of soiled linen awaiting collection is eliminated. Immediate disposal, as in hospitals, avoids cross infection.
5 Conference and private parties can choose their own colours.
6 Pilfering and spoilage of linen is eliminated (disposable items are cheaper to lose).
7 Uniform headwear is light and cool to wear.
8 Some bonded fibre items are washable. They are flame retardant, chemical resistant, porous, absorbent of grease, bateriostatic, lint-free.

The disadvantages are:

1 They do not reflect the correct image in luxury and traditional establishments.

2 They require large areas for storage since to be economic, they should be bought in large quantities.

3 There should be ample receptacles for collection of used items, and facilities for prompt disposal.

4 They can be misused.

5 The colours are not fast and if inadvertently left with linen and laundered, they can stain linen.

13 The laundry

In all accommodation establishments, a good system of laundry service is essential. Bed and table linen, in particular, should be laundered professionally to safeguard both hygiene and appearance. Efficient and careful laundering will also ensure that fabrics last for as long as possible.

There are three options open to most establishments: an on-site laundry, a contracted out laundry or hired linen. Hired linen, which is laundered by the owners, has been dealt with in Chapter 12.

Contracted out

When an establishment owns the linen, but sends it out to a private laundry company to be cleaned, it is said to be 'contracted out'. Hospitals rarely choose this option, because much of their linen may be excessively soiled, and they need to have close control over hygiene standards. However, many hotels and educational institutions of various sizes, use contract laundries.

The main advantage is that space does not have to be found on the premises to house a laundry. In a hotel, it may be more economical to use this space as a conference room, which will bring in money. Labour costs are also saved. The disadvantages are that the establishment has less control over standards, and there may be delivery problems, especially in bad weather. The linen room staff need a good system of stock control, so that items do not get lost. Contracted out laundries can be expensive.

In-house

Many hotels, especially large hotels, have in-house laundries. Hilton International, for example, have laundries on most of their properties. Hospitals usually have a central laundry for a district covering several hospitals. The main advantage for the establishment is complete quality control. This affects not only standards of cleaning, but the way the linen is presented and folded, and the type of cleaning agents used. A study has been done in the USA which proves that linen washed on site actually lasts longer than contracted out linen.

The main disadvantage of this system is the cost, especially the capital cost for an establishment which is starting up. A room has to be found and equipped with specialist machines. The running costs are also high, and include labour, machinery maintenance, heat, light, power, purchase of detergents. All these costs have to be assessed against the charges that a contracted out service would make.

Procedures

If it is decided to have an in-house laundry, the system adopted and the standard of care must be high. Figure 30 shows a flow chart which summarizes the different stages that a laundry procedure must go through.

Collection

Large Hotels have a laundry chute which runs through the entire height of the building down to the laundry, which is usually situated in the basement. The maid or the linen porter simply puts the dirty bed linen and towels down the chute via an opening in the floor service area.

Small hotels and other establishments carry dirty linen to the laundry in trucks, trolleys, bas-

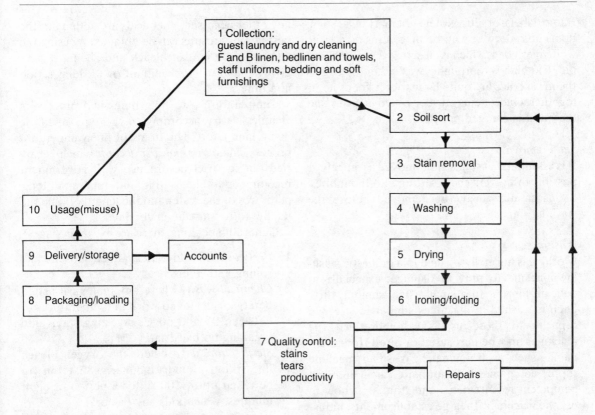

Figure 30   *Laundry flow chart (in-house)*

kets or nylon sacks. It is of great importance that any receptacle used to transport clean or dirty linen is used solely for that purpose, to prevent further soiling or damage.

Food and beverage linen is normally taken to the laundry or linen room in trucks or bundles in order that it may be exchanged on a one to one basis.

Staff uniforms and soft furnishings are taken individually to the linen room and exchanged on a one to one basis.

Guest clothing should be collected by a valet runner, maid or other person designated. It is common for guest clothing to be collected by 9.00 a.m. in order that it may be cleaned and returned the same day.

The soil sort area
When the dirty linen arrives in the laundry it is sorted out according to size, type, extent of staining, colour etc.

Bed linen is sorted into types, e.g. double sheets, single sheets, pillow cases etc. Care must be taken to check that there are no foreign bodies such as soap, razor blades, night dresses mixed up with the bed linen. Foul linen must be dealt with separately – it could be sluiced and then soaked. Table linen must also be sorted according to size, type and colour.

Great care must be taken to keep the soil sort area clean. It can be a haven for cockroaches as it is warm, often damp and there are plenty of food particles, especially from the food and beverage linen.

Soft furnishings are often dry cleaned and may be contracted out. Chef's whites must be washed and boiled separately.

Guest clothing is marked with an Indian ink

stamp, labels, or ultra violet light markings. Small items of underwear can be placed inside a large white mesh bag, which is closed with a numbered pin. Clothing is thoroughly washed in the bag as the mesh holes are quite large, but it keeps items together. Guest items must be noted in order that the guest is charged per item.

Stain removal
It is essential that stains are removed as quickly as possible to prevent them setting into the fabrics. Stains should always be removed before the washing stage.

Washing
Clothing is normally washed in a domestic washing machine to prevent damage, especially to delicate fabrics. In a small establishment, dirty linen is washed in machines similar in size and capacity to those used in laundrettes. The machines may be purchased or hired from companies such as Coinamatic. Washing machine supply companies will normally calculate exact equipment requirements and train staff how to use the machines. In large establishments, industrial equipment is used. Whatever the type of machine, for maximum efficiency, it must be loaded and operated according to the manufacturers instructions.

Industrial washing machines are front loaded and the drum is split into three compartments in order that the weight of the linen may be equally distributed so as not to unbalance the machine. The modular system of loading is the simplest. Each item of linen has a known weight, so they are counted out into piles to the appropriate total weight. For example, if it is known that the weight of a sheet is 500 grams, and the capacity of each compartment is 25 kg, then 50 sheets are counted out for each compartment.

Alternatively, bundles of linen can be weighed before putting them into the compartments. If the operator goes by volume and loads the compartments to capacity, it may result in an inadequate wash.

Washing takes place by the rotating action of the clothes in hot water. Soaps or detergents and any other necessary chemicals are added but the best laundry results can be obtained by using the *minimum* amount of bleach and chemicals and giving the *maximum* amount of washing action and time.

Temperatures, washing times and processing chemicals vary according to the type of fabric being laundered. The items of linen undergo a process called *thermal disinfection* which is carried out in strict accordance with government recommendations, setting out minimum temperatures of the water and the length of time the temperature must be maintained.

Generally speaking, there are five main stages:

1 *Pre-wash* in cold water, which loosens any soiling and stains.
2 *Chemical wash*, where any biological action detergent begins to work in temperatures of between 0° and 60°C, digesting stains and breaking up bacteria.
3 *Sterilization stage* where the oxygen bleach does its job. Laundry is boiled at 82°C but can be taken up to 100°C for a period of eight minutes, which kills any bacteria.
4 *Rinsing* is done using hot and cold water, which is usually recovered and re-cycled during the last rinse, in order to save water.
5 *Extraction* removes at least 50 per cent of the water used in the rinsing process. Hydro-extraction must be kept to a minimum to prevent pronounced creases setting into the fabric.

Drying
Drying takes place in tumble driers. Only towels and poly/cotton items need to be dried fully. Cotton is simply shaken out after extraction and then ironed.

Ironing and folding
Towels do not need ironing, they should emerge from the tumble drier in a soft and fluffy state, whereupon they may be folded by hand or machine. Poly/cotton is not designed to be ironed; it should be simply folded on an industrial folding machine, or by hand. However, older

poly/cotton items may be pressed or ironed to improve their appearance. Cotton items should be ironed on a flatwork iron or callender, which also folds the linen, and in some cases counts and stacks it into piles. The ironing process will kill off any remaining bacteria as temperatures go beyond 100°C.

Guest clothing and uniforms are finished on various steam presses and then either folded and packaged, or put on to clothes' hangers. They may be covered in polythene.

Quality control

The control stage is very closely linked with the ironing and folding section of the operation. It is essential if good quality appearance and productivity output are to be maintained.

Linen is inspected for stains and tears. The stained linen is returned to the stain removal section and once again is processed. Torn linen should be sent to the linen room for repair.

Once the linen has been cleaned and folded they can be counted, to measure and keep a record of the productivity rate in the laundry. The control supervisor may also check to see that: towels, bath mats and napkins, are folded in such a way as to reveal the company logo, in order that their display may aid advertising. All items should be folded in such a way that they aid the productivity rate of other staff in the establishment. For example, table cloths should be folded in a manner to facilitate the waiter to change a cloth quickly, napkins should be finished so that special folding is quick and easy and sheets should be folded to enable the maid or nurse to make a bed as quickly and comfortably as possible.

Packaging/loading

Linen may either be loaded on to trolleys or into bags and baskets and taken to the linen room, where it will stay until required. Bed linen and towels, however, are often taken direct to the floor service cupboards, where they are locked away.

Whatever the linen is loaded into, must be spotlessly clean and free from rust. Normally a set number of items or pieces will be loaded per trolley to aid control systems. Great care must be taken when loading, so as not to crease clean items.

Delivery/storage

Guest clothing is normally delivered back to the room in the early evening. As soon as it has been delivered, the charge for laundering, dry cleaning or pressing should be forwarded to the front office cashier, in order that it may be added to the guest's bill.

If a trolley containing the correct working par is distributed to the floor service area, the trolley may simply be locked away, thus saving time by not transferring linen from trolley to shelf.

Use and misuse

Use and misuse of linen is the responsibility of every supervisor. All staff should be made aware of the expense of purchasing and laundering linen. If staff are not trained or properly supplied with such items as: waiter's cloths, shoe cleaning facilities, kitchen rubbers, rags, dusters, tea towels, and bath and toilet cloths, there is the temptation to use the first thing that is at hand, which can lead to damage and wastage of valuable items.

Laundry staffing

Laundry manager

In some cases the responsibility of the laundry is that of the housekeeper and there is not a separate laundry manager. The responsibilities include:

1 Liaison with other departments to ensure that laundry is supplied in correct quantity and quality.
2 Staff recruitment, training and welfare.
3 Order of supplies.
4 Arranging machine maintenance.
5 Cleanliness of the laundry.
6 Efficient laundry production.

Assistant laundry manager

He/she will assist in the supervision of practical

work within the laundry operation, as well as aiding the laundry manager with administrative duties.

Dry cleaner

He/she is a section head, supervising the collection, cleaning and delivery of guest clothing and staff uniforms and dealing with any soft furnishings that need to be cleaned. He/she works together with the *valet runner* who collects and delivers guest laundry and dry cleaning, and also *guest laundry and press operators* who sort and tag, launder and then finish articles of clothing and other items.

Head washman

He/she is usually in charge of sorting dirty linen, stain removal, loading the machines and ensuring that the correct washing programmes are adhered to. He/she may have washmen in assistance.

Folding supervisor

He/she is responsible for checking the quality and productivity control of the linen. He/she is in charge of the folding/ironing operation and supervises the staff who operate the machinery concerned.

Laundry equipment

Purchasing laundry equipment involves a tremendous amount of capital outlay. For this reason, smaller establishments often prefer to rent equipment. The type of laundry equipment to be used may include the following

Washer/extractors
Tumble driers
Flat work iron or callender, alternatively a folding machine would be required for poly/cotton linen
Steam presses
Dry cleaning equipment
Water softening plant
Water boiler and steam plant
Tables
Sinks, drainage and adequate water supply

Clothes rails/hanging space
Trucks and trollies
Office facilities and equipment
Floor cleaning equipment

Permission must be obtained from the local authority for the removal of such large quantities of waste water. Large laundries come under the legislation of The Factories Act Section 174, while smaller laundries with a staff of more than five come under the Laundry Welfare Order. These documents cover such aspects as the working conditions of laundry employees. The design of the laundry premises must consider health and safety and fire precautions.

Before considering the installation of an in-house laundry, it is essential to seek professional advice and to complete accurate cost comparisons of all possible methods of laundering, in order that the most cost effective method is chosen.

Valet work

Valet work includes guest laundry, dry cleaning and pressing. The majority of hotels today do not have guest laundry and dry cleaning services on site, but the short-stay guest often appreciates an express service, and if marketed and properly organized, a good valet service can be a profit-making concern.

Owing to high labour costs, the hotelier should consider contracting out valet work. It is essential to have a well organized system whereby the guests complete their own laundry and dry cleaning list. It is a good idea to have brightly coloured lists and separate laundry bags to avoid accidents, such as items of dry cleaning being laundered.

Machines

Trouser presses can be placed in all rooms, and shoe shine machines in corridors or hallways. It should be remembered that the well travelled guest will often bring a travelling iron with him. However, these can cause damage and therefore thought should be given to a housekeeping policy for the provision of irons and ironing boards supplied to guests. Most reputable hotels will lend irons and boards to guests and sometimes a charge is made to deter pilferage. There must be a good control system to prevent loss and the possibility of fire.

The 'tidy-dry'
This is an expandable washing line over the bath. Tidy-dry lines can be installed easily in both commercial and resort hotels and help to discourage guests from hanging their clothes out on balconies to dry.

Amenity kits
Sewing kits or shoe shine cloths can be provided. If these are given away they should be costed into the room rate. Even if they are not used by the guest, they may be taken as a souvenir – which can help with advertising!

Further reading
Perdue, G. R., *The Technology of Washing* (British Launderers' Research Association).

Useful addresses
The Association of British Launderers and Cleaners Ltd,
Lancaster Gate House,
319 Pinner Road,
Harrow HA1 4HX

British Launderers' Research Association,
The Laboratories,
Hill View Gardens,
Hendon,
London NW9

The British Textile Rental Association Ltd,
Lancaster Gate House,
319 Pinner Road,
Harrow HA1 4HX

14 Beds and bedding

The bed is the most important item of furniture in any residential establishment. The occupants of bedrooms, dormitories, and hospital wards spend longer in bed than using any other piece of furniture. Yet the selection, care and maintenance of a bed usually receives less attention than that given to a chair.

The structure of the bed and quality of materials used in mattresses and divan bases are hidden by the cover which can be very deceptive, so one needs to know something about the way beds are made and the types of material used before one can make an informed choice. Reputable manufacturers produce brochures which give detailed information on how and from what materials their products are made. They also invite purchasers to visit the factories and offer training sessions.

Raw materials

Steel is the basic component of all spring mattresses. It is bought in a wide range of thicknesses or gauges, with varying tensile strengths. High tensile carbon steel is used in the better quality mattresses.

Coir fibre is the fibre from the outer shell of the coconut. It is tough and resilient and is a good insulating material. It is needled into hessian, so a pad is obtained which covers the springs of the mattress or divan base.

Sisal is a grass fibre and used in the same way as coir fibre and has similar qualities. It is more expensive and imported from East Africa.

Cotton felt is made by teasing and forming raw cotton into sheets of wadding and used as a surface upholstery material.

Softwood is used for divan base frames, but *hardwood* should be used for the load-bearing surfaces, castor blocks and corner supports.

Horse or hogs' *hair* is less commonly used now, but is used in good quality mattresses in the same way as sisal and coir fibre, or in its loose state as a soft surface upholstery pad, or to produce soft edges and corners on bases and mattresses.

Calico was used in most pocket spring mattresses, but has been largely superseded by a man-made material of even greater strength. It is still used as a covering material on the exposed underside of expensive divan bases.

Hessian is used in conjunction with hair, coir and sisal for insulating pads and in the manufacture of firm edge divans where the springs are lashed together with webbing, and for the undersides of the less expensive divans.

Synthetic fibres and materials include *polyether* foam, which is used in blocks for mattresses as an upholstering material. It is also used for edge to edge quilting where it gives a dimpled effect which is attractive in appearance and soft and yielding to the touch.

Latex foam (Rubber) is more expensive but used in the same way as polyether.

Terylene and dacron are strong and resilient, light in weight and are replacing wool or cotton felt for the soft outer layer.

Structure

When the springs have been secured, an insulating pad is stapled to the edge coils at top and bottom. The surface is covered with surface filling of cotton wool, dralon, terylene or low density foam wadding. On mattresses this is placed on top and bottom of springs, in divans to the top only. Sometimes the wadding is machined to the cover of the mattress or divan, giving a quilted effect.

In some mattresses, known as tufted mattresses, the springs are kept in place by strong cords passing through the mattress and kept in place on the surface by toggles or tufts. This makes for a firmer mattress.

A traditional bed is basically a base or divan raised on legs or castors and on top of which a mattress is placed.

Bases

Wire mesh
There are various types of link-wire mesh bases held in a metal frame. The better quality bases have springs at the ends to allow the mesh to 'give' from the ends rather than straining the links themselves.

Open spring
Coil springs are fixed on to metal bars. They are not covered and are therefore dust collectors. They have advantages in hostels and similar establishments, for they are less expensive than upholstered types, less likely to harbour parasites, and more easily sterilized.

All metal bed
The frame is a welded square section tube, and the legs of tubular steel (crush-bent at the angles). The mattress panel is of metal and the whole bed is robust, and complies with the strictest fire retardent regulations BS 476 Class 1. These are very suitable for camps and schools.

Wooden frame
This has a box-like base with either wooden slats across from side to side or a perforated wooden sheet across the bottom. Into this open box base the mattress is placed. It is modern in appearance and less expensive than upholstered bases.

Polypropene base
This is made up of interlocking perforated polypropene sections which fit into a moulded frame.

These are light in weight, tough and modern in appearance.

Upholstered divan base
This is usually constructed in the same way as a spiral spring mattress, except that the springs are fixed to wooden slats fitted across a wooden frame. There are four types of divan

Sprung edge   A fully sprung platform with coils right up to the edges. This is the best type because every portion of the mattress receives equal support.

Firm edge   The springs are surrounded on all sides by solid wood. This type uses fewer springs. Because the mattress rests on the timber edges, there is less 'give' at the edges and it is often selected for establishments where the beds are often sat upon, as in bed-sitters and hotels. The constant pressure of the mattress on the firm wooden edge can reduce the life of the mattress.

Solid top   This type of divan consists of a solid platform with a padded top but no springs. Often the space where springs would have been in other types is used for storage. It can have drawers, or a hinged top (ottoman), so that the base is like a box with a padded lid. This makes for a very firm bed, and can be used where the user might require a bedboard.

Hinged divan   A double sized base (135 cm × 190 cm) should be hinged for ease of movement, and have six or eight legs or castors.

Mattresses

Palliase or pallet
This is a thin mattress of ticking filled with cotton waste (flock) or horsehair. Regrettably these are found still in some boarding schools where a mattress should be supporting growing bodies. More modern types are of foam rubber or polyether at least 15 cm thick. They are inexpensive to replace, and can be cleaned.

Continuous springs
This is composed of a single unit of springing which looks like knitted wire. This woven web is

held in place by a wire framework. Posture sprung mattresses are a type of continuous sprung mattress which is made under licence. The woven springs are designed to distribute the body weight evenly.

Pocket springs

These have a series of coiled springs, each held separately under tension in a fabric container or pocket. The number of springs per mattress depends upon the quality. This type of springing enables more springs to be placed together, up to 1000 in a double mattress compared with 350 open coils. Each part of the body is supported, and in a double bed two people of different weights each have their own contours catered for, without affecting the other. Each spring operates individually. These mattresses are the most expensive.

Open springs

As the name suggests, this has a series of springs fastened together but without the individual fabric pockets. The helical wire that joins the springs together is designed to help to spread the weight of the body more evenly over the bed. The better the quality of the wire the more expensive the mattress. They are the most common type.

Foam mattresses

These are made of latex or polyester foam. A firmer mattress incorporates a centre core of high density foam. These mattresses should be placed on well-ventilated bases because of condensation. Latex foam is more expensive than polyether but better quality, and suitable for people who are allergic to the usual mattress fillings. It is a good idea to have one or two foam mattresses available for guests who may suffer from an allergy or asthma.

Foam and spring

A series of coiled springs are bedded into a deep sheet of polyether foam. This type of mattress is often refered to as an orbit spring mattress. It is clean, hygienic and light in weight, but tends to be very firm.

Upholstery spring

This has a series of open springs covered with two layers of upholstery material, as for upholstered furniture.

In all these mattresses the firmness of the mattress depends upon the density of the foam and the gauge of the wire used for the springs.

Special beds

Space savers and convertibles

These are practical in areas where a bedroom has another use, e.g. in bed-sitters and studio bedrooms in hostels. In hotels, a settee which is convertible gives extra sleeping accommodation in suites or family bedrooms.

Space savers include bunk beds, stacker beds, divans fitted with storage space, and 'Zed beds' (which, as the name suggests, fold up into a closed Z shape). Convertibles include bedsettees (or sofa-beds) and chunks of foam latex or polyether, which can be used as low chairs or seats and when laid out and placed edge to edge, can be used as a mattress. Air beds or inflatable mattresses can be easily stored and are suitable for children.

Fold-away beds save space because they are folded away into the wall when not required, leaving space for other use. A bedroom can therefore be used as a private dining room or set up for a small meeting or seminar. The lower surface of the bed can be made to fit into the décor of the room, frequently with panelling, simulated cupboard doors, or mirrors. The manipulation of the bed must be easy and the bedding firmly secured, so that it does not fall about when the bed is lifted at an angle of 90° to be folded up against the wall.

If there is not a recess into which the bed can be folded, cupboards and a desk or dressing table unit can be built out so that when the bed is folded away the face of the bed base is level with that of the cupboards or desk. The bed must be made up carefully preferably with fitted sheets so that there is the minimum of tucking in.

The pillow should be held in place with velcro

straps. Extra pillows if required can be stored in a cupboard during the day.

The cost is greater than that of the conventional bed, but the outlay may well be set off by the greater versatility of use of the room.

Mobile beds can be stored in an upright position and moved on castors underneath a headboard. The bed is wheeled into position wherever it is required and eased down from the perpendicular to a horizontal position. The bed can be stored already made up (but covered to protect it from dust).

It is very important that any unconventional bed should be of an excellent quality, so that the occupier may not feel he/she is sleeping on something make-shift.

Cots

These should have open mesh bases and a firm mattress. The open rails on the side should be set far enough apart for the child not to get his/her feet or hands stuck and not wide enough to put his/her head through. It is essential that the drop side catch is strong and quite child-proof. For the occasional hotel visitor, it might be useful to have a cot of each type (rails and solid sides) and ask the parents which they prefer. In a nursery dormitory, solid sides could prevent the child from being distracted by the activity around it.

Waterbeds

These were considered for some time as merely a gimmick or required solely for orthopaedic use, but now they are becoming more popular. To dispel the visions of what could happen if the guest had a perverted sense of humour, an apparently indestructible waterbed has been produced. It is a water-filled PVC mattress with a wooden frame and headboard. Waterbeds are claimed to relieve pressure on the body and help back pain sufferers. It may be wise for a far-sighted hotelier to have one waterbed suite to meet the needs of the occasional user.

Vibrating beds

These have a vibrating mechanism operated by an electric impulse controlled by a switch like that on an electric blanket. They are claimed to have a soporific effect and are found in some luxury hotels or on massage or solarium couches.

Hospital mattresses

These are usually manufactured to specifications required by the DHSS. The depth of the mattress is usually less than that of the normal mattress and designed not to be turned. The other specific requirements are that they should be fire resistant, water repellant, stain resistant, odour resistant and have anti-bacterial properties.

Air beds

There is an inflatable mattress usually used on medical instruction and made to medical specification.

Special firm beds and mattresses

These can be made to individual specifications.

Single/double beds

Some single beds can be joined together to make a king-size bed. The base should be linked firmly with metal bars and the mattresses can be zipped together.

Choice of beds

There is a bedding centre and space-saving bed centre in London where beds from the leading manufacturers are exhibited and where selection and comparison can be made and advice obtained. The use, wear and tear to which a bed will be subject is the most important factor in selection. Table 13 shows the various bed sizes available.

Schools

The bed should be strong, easily cleaned and the frame almost indestructible. It should have a firm mattress, preferably of moulded foam or rubber, with a fire resistant and water repellant cover.

Holiday camps

These have the same requirements of a bed as schools. It may be practical to have disposable

Table 13   *Bed sizes*

American bed sizes	
King	76 in × 80–4 in
Queen	60 in × 80 in
Full double	54 in × 75–80 in
Extra long twin	39 in × 80–4 in
Twin	39 in × 75 in
English bed sizes	
New standard double	150 × 200 cm
Small double	135 × 190 cm
New standard single	100 × 200 cm
Small single	90 × 190 cm
Compact single	75 × 190 cm

mattresses after each season – a synthetic foam mattress would be cheap to replace.

College and university halls of residence

A wooden frame base or a firm edge divan is practical and a firm interior sprung mattress suitable.

Hotels

The quality of the bed depends on the standard of luxury and comfort being offered to the guests, and the expected revenue. In all cases, buy the best quality the budget will allow. Larger beds are now being required, and, if space will allow, consider this when selecting. The capital outlay on furniture and fittings is usually written off after five years, so consider renewing beds in the same way as other items. Reputable manufacturers will recondition their beds and give advice where required.

Hospitals

When selecting beds for hospitals or nursing homes, one should follow the requirements laid down by the DHSS.

Points to look for:

Legs of divans should be screwed into a *hardwood* cross piece at the corners. Beds other than single should have six or eight legs. Note the depth and thickness of the screw. Castors take less strain than legs, but the divan is only a few centimetres from the floor which makes cleaning under the bed more difficult if the room space will not allow for easy moving of the bed. Glides instead of castors at the foot of beds used with wall-mounted headboards, will prevent the bed being pushed away from the wall when the occupant is sitting up in bed.

Divans which have drawers or storage space should have a toe-recess at the base to prevent toes being stubbed. There should be enough space at the side of the divan for the drawer to be pulled out. One manufacturer does have sliding doors and another places a drawer at the bottom of the bed.

Bunk beds are space savers, but thought should be given to:

1 Height between the lower and upper bunks. Can the occupant of the lower bunk sit up in bed?
2 How firmly the top bunk is secured to the lower.
3 How secure the ladder is.
4 A protective rail for the occupant of the top bunk.
5 Whether the beds can be used independently as two separate beds.

Slide-under beds can save space but there must be enough space in the room for the lower bed to be pulled out, leaving room for walking round the bed.

Bed settees should be considered equally as bed and settee. Mattresses should have a special hinge-spring in the middle or at the $\frac{1}{3}$ and $\frac{2}{3}$ folds. A normal mattress should never be substituted and folded. These should be selected for the ease of folding and making-up and suitability for the place where they are going to be used.

Metal frames should be easily taken apart. Avoid any with loose nuts or bolts.

The height of the bed is important. In a small room a high bed will dominate the room. High beds are not suitable for children's homes and old people's homes – they will be difficult for the occupants to get in and out of. In studio bedrooms the height should be at chair seat height. Hospital beds are often adjustable, a high bed is required for attending to the patient and for ease of making.

The main point to consider with a bedhead is that it will take pressure by being leaned upon, so it should be firm in itself and securely fixed to either the bed frame or divan or to the wall. The latter is more secure and enables the bed to be moved easily from the wall. Upholstered bedheads will attract grease and dust, and the same consideration should be given to these as for upholstered chairs, settees and bench seating. Plain wooden bedheads should have a good natural polish or a silicone finish so that grease does not penetrate the wood.

Care of beds

Apart from when it is made, a bed often receives little attention. Mattresses should never be folded. When turning a mattress, it should be kept straight, which requires two people. Turn, not only from side to side, but from end to end. Some makers have attached to the mattress a label with alternate months of the year printed on each side of the mattress, to encourage seasonal turning. Mattresses should not be subject to cleaning with a powerful suction cleaner, since this can move and alter the distribution of the upholstery material and loosen tufts. This does not apply to non-upholstered beds. Brush upholstered divans and mattresses or use a small dustette-type of suction cleaner.

Metal and open-spring types of bases should be brushed with a special spiral brush and rubbed over with a spray polish or turpentine. The latter was used when bed-bugs were a menace. Careful cleaning is necessary to avoid the accumulation of fluff and dust which can harbour moths' larvae and other pests.

Check for and secure loose headboards and secure bolts on metal frames. Check that divan legs are screwed in tightly. Check that mattresses are not developing a hollow or the base is sagging.

Open-spring should be protected by an underlay of padded hessian or unbleached calico. This should be secured to the base at the corners and the middle, with stout tapes. Mattresses should be protected by a cover or an overlay, waterproof in some cases, especially in institutions for children and the elderly.

In some hotels, twin-bedded rooms are let as singles and one bed may be used more than the other, so it is useful to change the beds over once a year.

Wherever possible, the bed should be aired before it is made. The body gives out 125 ml of body moisture every night and if a person is exceptionally hot or ill then the moisture output will be even greater.

Where possible, try to dissuade people from sitting on the edge of the bed as this will weaken the edge of the mattress as well as the base. An easy chair should always be put in a bedroom.

Beds should be regularly cleaned by brushing or vacuuming. Much of the dust found in a mattress is dead scales of human skin (humans shed approximately 500 g of skin a year). Dust mites live of these dead scales and the mites themselves can cause allergies. Ideally the bed should be cleaned every time the mattress is turned. This not only ensures that the mattress wears evenly but also gives the maid an opportunity to check for damage or unwanted pests such as bed bugs. Secondhand beds should never be purchased as the purchaser will not know how the bed has been treated in the past. One and a half million people in Britain suffer from head lice and one million people suffer from scabies or the itch mite.

Try to dissuade people from smoking in bed. This is one of the most common causes of hotel fires.

Always check that bedboards have been removed after a guest's departure. Not everyone suffers from bad backs and consequently a lot of people do not appreciate a firm mattress.

If a mattress becomes stained, act as quickly as possible to prevent liquid seeping into the mattress – the longer it is left, the more difficult it will be to remove. Strip off all bed clothes and stand the mattress on its side. This will help to prevent seepage deep into the mattress. Sponge the stain with clean cold water and mop up with excess liquid with a clean towelling rag. Use other stain removal agents as necessary. Finally, dry off the mattress with a fan heater or hair dryer. *Do not* use an electric blanket or hot water bottle.

If a mattress is badly soiled, infected or infested, it is best to burn it or take it to a disposal dump.

The life of a mattress depends on its quality and the use and care it receives. Ten years is considered the life of a bed in constant domestic use but in the hospitality industry it may only last from five to seven years. When not in use, spare mattresses, rollaway beds and cots should be stored in a suitable area and covered with a protective cover or dust sheet.

Pillows

These are usually 74 × 48 cm or 69 × 46 cm. Continental square pillows are 66 × 66 cm. It is also possible to buy triangular and crescent-shaped pillows. For general use it is better to choose the longer of the rectangular pillows

(74 × 48 cm) since pillow cases are usually made for this size.

Fillings

These are many and varied, but can be divided into two categories: man-made fibre and natural fillings.

Natural fillings

Down is the soft fine feathers taken from the breasts of ducks or geese. Goose down is of better quality and of course more expensive. Down is soft, light, luxurious, very buoyant, durable and very expensive.

Down and feather (must contain at least 51 per cent down) produces a good quality pillow.

Feather and down (must contain at least 15 per cent down) produces a pillow of reasonable quality and price.

Water fowl produces a reasonable pillow, but one which is much heavier than those previously

Table 14 *British Standards for pillows with natural fillings*

Type of filling		Minimum weights for pillows measuring	
		74 × 48 cm *g*	*69 × 46 cm* *g*
Curled poultry feathers	Artificially curled feathers	1135	910
Curled poultry feathers and goose or duck feathers	At least 50 per cent poultry feathers	1135	910
Duck or goose feathers	May include up to 10 per cent other feathers	1025	825
Duck or goose feathers and down	Mixture with not less than 15 per cent down	850	740
Duck or goose down and feathers	Mixture with not less than 51 per cent down	680	595
Duck or goose down	May have up to 15 per cent small, fluffy feathers	570	485

Figures taken from BS 1877 Part 8 and BS 2005.

mentioned as it consists only of duck or goose feathers with a natural curl.

Land and water fowl again produces a heavier pillow, which contains duck and chicken feathers. A strong ticking is required to prevent the feathers from escaping through the fabric or the seams.

Curled poultry is of poor quality and contains purified and artificially curled chicken feathers. The feathers can be 'spiky' and therefore a strong ticking is required to prevent discomfort.

Table 14 indicates the standard weights of pillows made of the various natural fillings.

The advantages of natural fillings are that they are soft, light, and resilient and the better qualities have a special comforting feel. However, the natural oil in feathers does, in time, stain the covers, and some people are allergic to down and feathers. They are not so easily laundered as man-made fillings: they can be machine washed and tumble dried, but dry cleaning is usually recommended. Feathers break down in time and the pillow loses its resilience. A 'tired' pillow when laid over the arm will droop sadly – if it is unable to support itself, it is not going to give much support to the head of the sleeper. The feathers seep through the ticking, as does the dust from the breaking down of the feathers. Because they are animal material, if stored without care, they can attract moths.

Man-made fibres
Terylene and polyester fillings are soft and resilient, light in weight and washable. They do not require stiff covers since they do not seep through the cover.

Polyester filled pillows retain their 'bounce' longer than terylene. Polyester is a 'hollofil' fibre. They tend to become a little harsher than down and the feel difference can be described as the difference between the feel of silk and an artificial silk.

Latex or plastic foam has been superseded by terylene and polyester, as foam is rather too solid for most people.

Foam chips are usually found in very inexpensive pillows. They can be washed. Sometimes they are mixed with feathers.

Kapok is a plant fibre similar in appearance to terylene and polyester which have largely superseded it. It is very soft and light and does not affect the cover. It is not washable and does, in time, lose its resilience.

Flock (waste cotton) filled pillows may still be found in some old neglected establishments. They are heavy and lumpy and because of their obvious age, should be replaced.

Care of pillows
Pillows should be removed from their fine polythene wrapper after purchase. In hospitals, however, they are often covered in a waterproof material to prevent excessive staining. Pillows should always have underslips, which may be specially purchased with ties, or made up from old pillow cases. Underslips protect the pillow and help to prevent any stains from seeping in. The underslips should be changed regularly as unsightly stains sometimes may show through the pillow case. A badly soiled feather or down pillow should be burned as cleaning is difficult and expensive. Pillows made from man-made fibres and latex may be washed or laundered. A pillow which has aged and whose ticking is slightly stained may be re-covered. Pillows should be shaken daily to fluff the feathers up. They should never be pounded and pillow fights should be discouraged as this will break up and damage the feathers.

Blankets

Blankets keep the body warm by trapping air, which is a poor conductor of heat, between the fibres. They are available in two sizes: single 180×240 cm, and double 240×260 cm.

Wool
Wool traps air well and this quality is enhanced by the wool in blankets being loosely woven and teased. Wool gives the warmest feel and retains its fluffiness and shape if carefully laundered. The warmth and weight depends upon the wool content. At one time, it was considered that the heavier the blanket, the better the quality.

However, it has been found that the body relaxes better under a light weight, so light blankets and duvets have become more popular.

Man-made fibres

These have been produced with similar qualities to wool. The difference can be detected by rubbing between thumb and finger – the wool fibre is a little softer than the man-made fibre.

Mixture of wool and cotton or wool and man-made fibres

This has the advantage of being less expensive, lighter and more easily laundered. All man-made fibre blankets have a tendency to flatten and lose some of their softness.

Cellular blankets of wool or man-made materials

These are woven with large holes, and some have a honeycomb effect. They tend to lose their shape and rings and fingers can get caught in the holes or threads. They are not suitable for children's beds or cots. They are light and warm but not so cosy as the traditional blankets.

Cotton/cellular or honeycomb weaves

These are practical for hospital wards, residential homes for the elderly and children because of easy laundering.

Merino blankets

These are extremely expensive but very warm and light. They need careful laundering and dry cleaning would be advised.

Blanket care

Blankets should be laundered or dry cleaned at least once a year, but preferably more often. Maids should be trained never to pile the blankets on the floor when making the bed. Instead, they should be placed on a chair, to avoid picking up unnecessary dust and dirt. Luxury hotels use a top sheet over the blanket. This results in extra laundering charges, but it is more hygienic and saves the blanket from getting dirty. Wool blankets should be moth-proofed and all blankets should be neatly folded and stored in plastic bags.

Continental quilts/duvets

Since duvets are being used more in homes, they are becoming more acceptable in hotels and other residential establishments. Before introducing them throughout an establishment, it is advisable to do some market research. It is useful to introduce two or three and monitor customer reaction during a period of a few months, before deciding to replace blankets with duvets. It is cheaper to purchase a duvet than two blankets, an eiderdown and a bedspread, and they make bed-making easier. The covers can be laundered easily but the natural filling duvets, although they can be laundered, will take a long time to dry. Man-made fibre filled duvets can be washed. Quilts also have the advantage that they do not shed fluff or collect dust in the way blankets do.

The main disadvantage of duvets is that some customers may not find them acceptable, so it is unwise to dispense with all blankets. The covers may not fit in with the décor in some establishments. Some people may be allergic to natural fillings, but the man-made fibre fillings will not cause these problems.

Fillings

Duvets have some of the same fillings as pillows: the natural fillings used are down, down and feather, or feather, and there is a wide range of man-made fibres. As with pillows, if the duvet is filled with feathers, these should be small and the cover should be of a finely woven material, so that the quills do not stick through. Synthetic fillings and covers have a low vapour transmission and tend to cause sweating.

Structure

Weight is not a criterion of warmth: the efficiency of a duvet can be affected by the structure, i.e. the channels in which the filling is held. Some channels are stitched through both sides of the cover, but those with walled sides give greater insulation, since the filling is less depressed, and there is no heat loss through the stitching. Some have off-set overlapping walls which are diagonally slanted (see Figure 31).

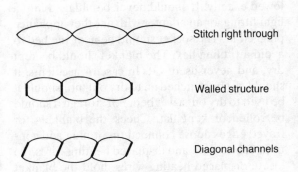

Stitch right through

Walled structure

Diagonal channels

Figure 31   *Duvet structures*

Efficiency rating

Duvets are given a 'tog rating' which measures the insulation provided by the quilt. This is measured by keeping one side of the quilt at body temperature and the other side at 20 °C. The heat loss through the quilt is measured and the top value is equal to ten times the temperature difference in degrees centigrade between the two faces of the quilt, when the flow of heat is equal to 1 watt per square metre. The higher the tog value, the greater the insulation. Values range from 4 to 13.5. BS 5335 stipulates that a quilt must have a rating of 7.5 before it can be called a continental quilt. However, the Shirley Institute Research Association maintains that this is too high for a centrally heated room and that a tog rating of 5 or 6 would be more appropriate. At the time of writing, the accuracy of tog values is being investigated.

Some manufacturers make twin quilts, one has a tog rating of 4 and one of 7.5. These can be fastened together with velcro giving a tog rating of 11.5 for winter use and 7.5 or 4 in summer. Table 15 shows the tog values of different fillings.

Sizes

Generally the quilt should be at least 45 cm wider than the bed, and the sizes available are:

Single	135 × 198 cm
Small double	180 × 198 cm
Double	200 × 198 cm
Long single	135 × 220 cm
Long double	200 × 220 cm
King size	230 × 220 cm

For King size beds it might be practical to have two single quilts, perhaps with different tog values for two individuals' personal preferences. Quilts for bunk beds are made 115 cm wide.

The British Standard 5335

This requires the following information to be labelled on all quilts.

1   Trade mark/or name of manufacturer.
2   British Standard number 5335.
3   Description of filling per BS2005/BS1425.
4   Care labelling information.
5   Length and width measured in centimetres.
6   The BS warmth category.
7   Weight per square metre.
8   The description of the content of the casing material.

Table 15   *Tog values*

Man-made fillings	Tog value
Superloft	9–11
Hollow polyester	10.5–11.5
Superloft fibre	9.5–11
Terylene superloft polyester	10.5
Terylene FRX (flame retardant)	7.5
Dacron hollowfil	10.5
Terylene	7.5–8.5
Terylene P3 fibre	8.5
Polyester	8.5
Natural fillings	
New white goose down	13.5
White goose down	13.5
New goose down	13.5
Goose down	12.5
New duck down	12.5
Duck down	12.5
Goose down and feather	10.0
New duck down and feather	11.0
Duck down and feather	10.5
Duck feather and down	10.5
Dual quilts	
(Goose down and feather)	10.0 ⎫ 14.5
(New white goose down)	8.5 ⎭

Electric blankets

These are frequently found in hotels, clinics nursing homes and some hospitals.

All electric blankets should have the BS label 3456 and the British Electrotechnical Approvals Board Mark of safety (BEAB). The control switch should be illuminated when on. They should be fitted with a thermostat control, with three grades of heat, low, medium and hot. The grade should be indicated by raised markings so that they can be felt as well as seen.

Underblankets

These are placed under the bottom sheet and preferably under the underblanket. Electric blankets are usually coloured and can show through the bottom sheet. The underblanket will give extra protection from soiling to the electric blanket, which should be secured to the mattress by tapes to prevent rucking. They should be so placed that the top of the blanket comes about the width of the pillow from the top of the bed. There is no point in having the heat generated under the pillow.

Blankets come in various sizes, and a short one should be placed at the level at which the heat is required. Some double blankets have two heat controls so that each side of the bed can be controlled to suit the needs of each occupant of the bed.

This type of electric blanket should never be used where there is a chance of them being subject to wetting. Unless they are of the low voltage type they should be switched off before getting into bed. There are low voltage blankets which can be left on all night and these are suitable for the elderly or sick. Underblankets should never be used on top of the occupant.

Overblankets

These are light and can be washed, left on all night, and are not dangerous if subjected to wetting. They should never be used as underblankets.

Care of electric blankets

The manufacturer's instructions should be followed exactly. It should never be plugged into a light fitting, or an adapter with another appliance plugged in. The socket should be near the bed to avoid a trailing flex. The blanket should be kept dry, and never used wet. In case of accidents, it should not be switched on to dry out, nor should it be used to dry out a wet bed. For storage it should be rolled or kept flat. Check the blankets for frayed edges, loose connections at plug and controls, fabric wear and displaced heating wires. To locate displaced heating wires, hold the blanket up to the light – the wires should be evenly spaced and not touching anywhere.

The blankets should be serviced regularly. Hot water bottles should never be used in addition to a blanket. In hotels instructions should be shown for the use of the blanket. The maid may switch them on when preparing the bed for use at night, but it is pointless to turn the covers back, and allow the heat to escape. If air conditioning or central heating is working correctly, electric blankets will not normally be necessary in a hotel. If they are issued, care must be taken to warn guests of the dangers.

Heated pads

American guests especially will often request a heated pad, which is about the same size as a hot water bottle and does a similar job. As they are electrical appliances, they should be treated in the same way as electric blankets.

Bed pads

A bed pad acts as padding between the mattress and the sheet, giving the guest additional comfort, especially where the mattress is buttoned or tufted. It is also an underblanket, giving additional warmth and soaking up excessive body moisture. It protects the mattress from any spillages or soiling. In modern hotels, a bed pad is a flat, quilted cover which goes over the mattress. They are made from white cotton with a terylene filling, thus making laundering easy. Bed pads should be laundered regularly for high standards of appearance and hygiene.

In hospitals very often the mattress protector is

waterproof. Waterproofs or wet blankets should be available in all residential accommodation in case of incontinent or disabled people as well as for children. If advertised diplomatically, guests will not be embarrassed to ask for them and money, time and face will be saved. In the older establishment, a mattress protector may be a cotton or calico cover which engulfs the mattress and is secured by tapes, or is simply a flat cover, tied on with tapes. An old blanket will suffice as an underblanket on top of the mattress protector.

In old people's homes it is common to have thermal underblankets which are made of a fleecy man-made fibre and have excellent warmth values.

Eiderdowns

Eiderdowns were originally made from the down of the eider duck. Although they have been largely replaced by duvets, eiderdowns may still be found in older establishments, where they are used in conjunction with blankets. Establishments which still use eiderdowns usually have synthetic fillings – usually terylene, which is easy to launder. The feathered variety should be cared for in the same way as duvets or pillows.

Bedspreads

Throw-over bedspreads require less material than fitted covers. Most material suitable for curtains can be used for bed covers, and when calculating the quantity required any pattern drop should be taken into consideration.

The material required for a single bed is twice the length of the bed + twice the height of the bed from the floor + turnings. A complete width of the material should be placed down the centre of the bed and the remaining width cut in half as the drop on either side. All measurements should be taken with the bed made up. A small saving of material can be made if the end of the bed is against a wall, of if the bed has its own bedhead. The bottom corners of the bedspread should be rounded to avoid corners trailing on to the floor, which is highly dangerous.

For *double and king size beds*, three times the length may be required, and more than a half width may have to be joined to the centre panel.

Fitted bedcovers have a centre panel, the size of the bed surface, and a valance pleated or gathered on to it. The depth of the valance should be the height of the bed from the floor plus turnings, with the pattern going vertically. The length of the valance should be four times the length of the bed and twice the width of the bed for fullness, assuming that there is no valance required at the top. By having only pleats at the corners of the bed, material can be saved. A gusset at the top of the cover will allow for the pillow, or an extra flap added at the top can be folded back to cover the pillows.

When selecting bedspreads, choose those which are easy to launder. They should be crease resistant – people often sit or lie on the beds during the day time and hotels rarely change the bedspread for every new arrival.

A soft, loose woven fabric is not ideal as it will easily become shapeless. A shiny satin type of fabric will crease and slip off. The material should be fire resistant – especially with the danger of people smoking in their bedrooms.

Further reading

Conran T., *The Bed and Bath Book* (Mitchell Beazley).

Useful addresses

National Bedding Federation,
251 Brompton Road,
London SW3 2EZ
Tel: 01-589 4888

Relyon Beds,
Price Bros & Co. Ltd,
Wellington,
Somerset TA21 8NN

Snuggledown of Norway (UK) Ltd,
39 Burners Lane,
Kiln Farm,
Milton Keynes,
Bucks.

15 Décor and design

Décor is defined in the *Shorte. Oxford Dictionary* as 'Beauty, ornament, the scenery and furnishing of a theatre stage'. Nowadays it applies to all buildings and homes, but it is worth remembering that décor originally referred to the stage; it can be thought of as setting a scene. The behaviour and attitudes of human beings are known to be affected by the atmosphere produced by décor. This is true not only in luxury establishments, but also in institutions, where suitable décor can create a less institutional environment. Hospitals, schools and nursing homes will seem brighter and happier if colour is used well. Hotels and restaurants help to create their image from the décor – customers pay not only for their room or meal, but also for the atmosphere. Restaurants and other public places can often afford to be more adventurous in their use of colour, pattern and lighting – after all, the customer has come for a change from the home environment.

When choosing a colour scheme, it is necessary to consider the type of building, and the customers or clients who use it. The character of the building is also important, and the features it already has. The amount of light coming into the rooms, for instance, will affect what colours and patterns you choose. Consider, too, whether the rooms have any disadvantageous features which should be camouflaged or compensated for.

There are many sources of advice on decorating and interior design. Manufacturers of wall paper, fabric and paint offer advisory services, and magazines can also be consulted. When visiting any consultant, take a plan of the room concerned, with measurements and samples of existing materials that will be retained. Make a note also of what direction the room's windows face, and how much sun they get. A consultant may be able to visit the site, but if he or she is to draw up any detailed plans, make sure he/she is properly briefed about the atmosphere desired and the budget constraints. It is useful to make up small samples of the fabrics and paint colours etc. being considered and putting them together in different combinations. Never choose anything in isolation – always compare each item (carpet, wallpaper, soft furnishing, paint, curtain) with the other items.

Room dimensions

It may seem that the size and shape of the room are there to stay once the building has been completed. However, effective use of colour and pattern can change the apparent dimensions.

To give height to a room

Remove or camouflage any horizontals, e.g. picture rails. Use striped wallpaper or one with a pattern which is vertical (see Figure 32). A pale

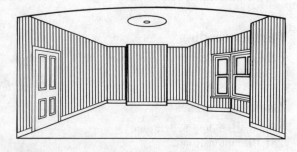

Figure 32   *Giving height to a room*

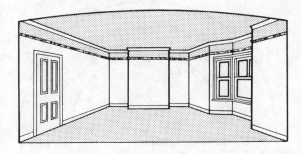

Figure 33   *Reducing the height of a room*

ceiling, and a light coloured carpet will make the floor and ceiling recede. The furniture should be low and non-dominant in pattern.

To reduce the height of a room
Paint the ceiling down to the picture rail (if any) with a fairly deep colour (see Figure 33). Avoid a very dark colour because this will make the ceiling disappear. The carpet should match the ceiling, thereby drawing the ceiling and floor together. Pick out any horizontal features, picture rail, dados, cornices so that they take the eye round the room.

To increase the size of the room
Pale cool colours will give the illusion of space (see Figure 34). Keep the walls uncluttered with dado, picture rail. Paint or paper cupboard doors to match the wall and use matching curtains – if these are the same pattern as the wallpaper, this

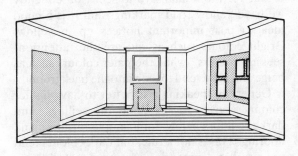

Figure 34   *Increasing the size of a room*

will add continuity. Heavily patterned papers should be avoided. Hard and glossy textures, mirrors, slate, marble, ceramic, chrome and glass all create an illusion of space. Splashes of rougher texture and warm pinks and golds will take the edge off any coldness.

To reduce the size of a room
Break up the walls with pictures and pick out any architectural features, or add borders or trompe d'oeil panelling. Make a feature of the fireplace, which will attract the eye to a focal point, and away from the vastness of the room. Rugs will break up the floor area, large furniture can be accommodated, and the room may be divided by folding doors or full length curtains.

To create a warm atmosphere in a dull dark room
North-facing rooms or basements need warming up and this can be done by using warm pinks and yellows. They should not be used indiscriminately or in too intense shades. Bare brick terracotta, rush and hessian are natural textures which add to the feeling of warmth. A light painted wall outside a basement window will add some reflected light. White drapes will hide an unsightly view and add light to the room.

To reduce the length of a long narrow room
Have the end walls in a darker colour than the rest of the room. Book-shelves along these walls will add width to the room and tend to reduce the length of it. Light walls and vertical pattern or stripes along these side walls will help with the optical illusion of reducing the length.

General principles of décor

Too much pattern is disturbing – with a patterned carpet have plain walls and plain upholstery. The floor colour or covering itself can be brought up the wall to reduce the height of the room or to produce a continuous effect bringing the eye up to a focal point. Bar fronts, for example, are frequently carpeted, but the effect is less attractive after a time, as the floor area gets more wear and looks shabby alongside the bar front. A skirting board painted the same colour as the carpet is less distracting to the eye than having it a contrasting colour.

Doors can be treated as part of the wall and be papered or painted the same if attention does not need to be drawn to them. Panelled doors are often attractive features in their own right and can be painted a contrasting colour and framed by the architrave. Polished hardwood doors, skirting boards and window sills cost more initially but do not need much attention and repainting.

Pipes and radiators – not things of beauty in themselves – should be painted to blend with their surroundings.

Colour schemes

Using colour is the easiest way to transform a room. Large international hotel chains usually employ their own interior designers or at least have an interior design consultant in order that this very specialist aspect can be dealt with in a professional manner. In a small establishment, however, the task of selecting suitable colour schemes may be that of the housekeeper.

Colour often tends to be a personal matter but there is an established colour wheel (see Figure 35) and four main types of known colour schemes (see below).

Primary colours are the fundamental colours which we need in order to make up other colours. They are red, blue and yellow. *Secondary colours* are made by mixing equal parts of two primary colours, for example

    blue + yellow = green
    red + yellow = orange

Tertiary colours are made by mixing a primary colour together with a secondary colour until the exact shade required is achieved, for example

    red + orange = russet

The colours on the left of the colour wheel are known as cold colours. The blues and greens remind us perhaps of cool water. On the right

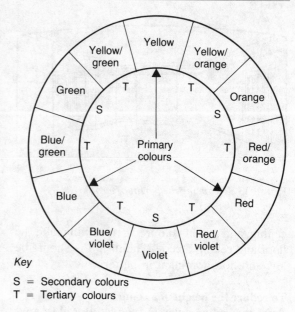

Key

S = Secondary colours
T = Tertiary colours

Figure 35   *Colour wheel*

hand side, the colours are warm – the colours remind us perhaps of the sun and warm fires.

Colours have a psychological effect on people. Green, for example, has been found to be the most restful colour to the human eye. This is why very often hospital wards are decorated in a pale green colour. Even blackboards in schools are no longer black, but dark green. The seating in the house of commons is green and it is quite common to put green baize on the table in board rooms or for standard meeting/conference room set ups. Yellow has been found to be the easiest colour for the human eye to see. Consequently we have yellow road markings and it is a good idea to post important notices up in yellow. Bright colours such as red are the 'attention-seeking colours', while the paler colours such as beige and fawn tend to fade into the background.

Generally speaking it is better to have lighter colours above, for example for ceilings, and darker colours below, for example furniture and flooring. This is not a rule, but dark colours tend to be rather depressing and even claustrophobic when situated above eye level.

Types of colour scheme

The triad scheme

All three types of colours are used, primary, secondary and tertiary, but one is the main colour and the others complement it. The main colour may be in bright bursts, while the other colours may be in softer or paler shades.

The complementary scheme

The colours are normally taken from opposite sides of the colour wheel. For example, red and green are often used for decoration at Christmas or even used to garnish food – a salad of lettuce and tomatoes.

Split complementary scheme

One main colour is used together with either its contrasting colour (opposite on the wheel), or the two colours on either side of its contrasting colour. For example violet might be used with yellow or with yellow/green and yellow/orange. These types of colours are often found for decoration at Easter.

Analogous or related colour scheme

Colours situated side by side on the wheel are used. For example, blue is used with turquoise. Often one colour would be darker or stronger, while the other softer or paler to complement it.

Apart from colour and patterns, *textures* also give atmosphere to a room. Different wall coverings, carpets and furnishings have different textures which can be combined imaginatively.

Lighting

Lighting plays a very important part in the décor of a building. Like colour, texture and pattern it has a psychological effect on people, but the housekeeper should also be concerned with its safety and efficiency.

The lobby, foyer, reception

This area should be adequately and unobtrusively lit, with good general lighting, and brighter but concealed lighting at the reception desk, where guests and staff can see to read and write.

Lounge and reception

Pools of soft light from table lamps make these areas welcoming and attractive, by creating small focal points in what otherwise might be a large and forbidding area.

Bars and lounges

The buffet should be well illuminated with neutral coloured lamps so as not to distort the colour of the food. The tables should be lit with a small table lamp with a steady base and no trailing flex, yet the overall effect may be of subdued light, creating an intimate atmosphere.

Restaurants

These are often dimly lit to create atmosphere, but there should be attractive pools of light. An overall dimness is oppressive, and the human eye takes 30 seconds to adjust from normal daylight to a low level of light.

Fast food restaurants and cafeterias require a brisk atmosphere for a fast turnover, the lighting should be quite bright but not harsh or glaring, and adequate to see that the tables, china and cutlery are clean. A hotel restaurant or luxury restaurant requires soft lighting for a relaxed atmosphere. Individual lamps on the tables or candles give adequate task lighting to read the menu and see the food on the table. The lighting should not distort the colour of the food or the skin colour of the customer. Individual table lamps should have shades which protect the eyes of the customer from the glare of the bulb. Lowered suspended lamps should be adjustable, to protect the customers' eyes, and illuminate the table but exclude the rest of the room.

Function rooms

Since these are used for a variety of purposes: conferences, meetings, exhibitions, private parties, dinner dances, etc. they need to have flexible, decorative and functional lighting. A source of good general light can come from concealed cornice, wall, or ceiling lighting. Standard lamps might complement the décor, together with track and spot lights. Dimmer switches will reduce the light from standard and ceiling lights when a subdued light is required.

Cloakroom and toilet areas

The lighting should be overall of such a level that one can see it is clean, but it should not be glaring or stark. Mirror lights and shades should be neutral in order not to distort make-up colour.

Standard and table lamps

In general, standard and table lamps play an important part in the décor of most rooms, the stands and shades adding shape and colour and pools of light. They should be tried out on site if possible. A royal blue lamp shade may be perfect to tone with the carpet or curtains in daylight, but look quite different when lit up. Shades can be made up from the customer's own curtain or furnishing fabric where suitable. Cane and wicker shades look attractive when not lit up, but peculiar shadows are produced when the light is on.

Pendant lamps

Pendant ceiling lights are not found in many new buildings, but where they do exist they should be made a decorative feature.

Cornice lights

These give some general light, reflected from the ceiling or wall, and draw attention to an attractive ceiling or moulded cornice.

Spotlights and architectural tubes

These can be used to draw attention to focal points, architectural features, archways, alcoves, pictures sculptures, floral decorations and objets d'art. They also create some general light. Special lamps are available which will help plants to grow and flourish in the absence of daylight.

Exterior lights

These should create a welcoming atmosphere, illuminating car parks and paths. Mushroom lights are attractive and less distracting than plain reinforced glass lamps. Old street lamps, which can sometimes be purchased from local authorities, make attractive outside standard lamps.

Light/lamp shades

These are used primarily to conceal the bulb, prevent glare, and direct and diffuse the light.

Shades should be tried out in the room for which they are intended. As well as ensuring that the shade matches the décor, check that the spread of light is sufficient and that undesirable shadows are not created.

Always use the bulb with the recommended wattage – too strong a bulb will burn the fabric or melt plastic shades. This is particularly important with ceiling or wall shades which completely conceal the bulb. Even if the shade does withstand the heat, the plastic coating of the wiring can be melted and create a fire hazard.

Care of shades

Most plastic, glass and fabric shades should be doused in warm, soapy water, rinsed and hung up to dry after wiping off superfluous moisture. If they are hung up to drip dry, a water mark is often left. Crystal chandeliers may have to be washed *in situ*, each piece being washed separately, or taken down carefully and washed in warm soapy water in a plastic bowl or a bath lined with an old towel or blanket. They can be dried with a blow hair drier. If any crystal drops are lost or broken, spares can be purchased individually and replaced. A proprietory brand spray is available for cleaning.

Bowl-type shades should be cleaned frequently as they do collect dead flies and moths. Both lights and shades should be cleaned regularly, since the dust they collect reduces the efficiency of the light source. The 'fish bowl' type of lamp shade can be effectively washed in a dishwasher.

Candles

Candles give a very soft, flattering light, but they are more properly thought of as part of the décor than a light source. They are most frequently used in restaurants, and they should be placed so that guests can still see each other across the table.

Candle lamps, which protect the flame with a glass shade and raise the candle automatically as it burns, are a suitable alternative. These avoid the danger of wax spillages, or of the candle falling over. Candles should be snuffed out, or blown with the hand behind the flame to stop wax falling on to the table. They should be placed carefully in candlesticks, so that they are well balanced and the wax can drip into the lip. They can be held in place with Blu-tac or similar adhesive, or with foil filling up any gap in the holder.

Perfumed candles should be used with discretion. Candles are not cheap, and their burning times should be compared before purchase. Candle ends can be sold for recycling.

Windows

The curtains, or other window coverings, are obviously part of the décor, but so is the view from the window. If the view is unattractive, it can be obscured by net curtains or blinds, or by special dark glass, which allows light to enter but obscures the view. If there is a blank wall in front of the window, it can be painted – either white to reflect the light into the room, or with an attractive mural. Plants or flowers could also be hung on a blank wall. An attractive view from the window can be framed by curtains.

Pelmets

A pelmet is a frill or valance for covering curtain headings or tracks. Sometimes strip lighting can be put behind the pelmet to light the curtains when drawn. Pelmets in Georgian or Edwardian houses are usually made of plaster, and incorporated in cornices. In more modern buildings they are usually wood or hardboard. They can be painted or papered to match the décor, or covered in the same material as the curtains.

Blinds

Blinds are used where it is difficult to hang curtains (for example, in dormer windows) or to hide a view. Dark blinds are used in lecture rooms for black-outs. They are shielded with a pelmet on each side to give greater light-proofing. Special blinds with a thin film of aluminium on the outside are available. These reduce heat loss in winter (by 30 per cent according to the manufacturers) and keep rooms cool in summer, while still allowing in a diffused light.

Roller blinds

These are available in a variety of fabrics and materials, to fit in with the décor.

Pinoleums

These slatted blinds, made from wood or quill woven together with cotton are suitable for garden rooms or where an area of a room needs to be screened from view. They give an Oriental effect.

Venetian blinds

These are made of slats of metal, wood or plastic slotted on cords which operate their opening and closing. Another set of cords raises and lowers the blind. The amount of light entering the room is adjusted by the slant of the slats.

They are difficult to clean, but a special brush is available. They tend to collect dust and grease.

Vertical louvre blinds

These are rather like Venetian blinds hung vertically. By altering the angle of the slats more or less light is allowed to enter. The slats can be of wood, stiffened silk canvas or man-made material. The slats are about 10 cm wide, so care should be taken to see that curtains (if used as well) are hung far enough from the blinds to allow for the slats to be opened.

Balastores

These are made of strong pleated paper. They are less expensive than Venetian blinds, but do not allow for variation in the admittance of light.

Pleatex blinds

These are similar to balastores, but made of wet-stretched kraft paper in plain colours, and are not so durable.

Silent gliss lamella system

This is a sophisticated decoration or room divider which hangs like a curtain but acts on the principle of the Venetian blind. The strips can be of plastic laminate or simulated linen and it is available in a large range of colours and textures. The strips can be angled to filter the light and the system can be hand or electrically operated. It is suitable for filtering the light and for screening very large expanses of glass.

Curtains

Curtains are often the most expensive item of soft furnishing. They should enhance the floor and wall covering, and complement the rest of the furniture and furnishings. Besides contributing to the décor, they have a number of other uses. They insulate a room against noise and cold. They are often used to cut out light during the day, especially in hotels where people are sleeping in the daytime (in airport hotels especially). Some furnishings are damaged by too much sunlight – and many people find sunlight uncomfortable – so curtains can be used to shade a room. Net curtains can stop a room being overlooked, especially in a built-up area. Sometimes curtains are used to divide a room. They might separate the sleeping and living area in a bed-sitting room, or screen a storage area in a banquet room – and, of course, they divide a stage from the rest of the theatre.

Choosing curtains

It is unwise to select too expensive a material and be unable to afford lining, or to have to skimp on the fullness – so consider the budget allowance. Choose the style and material while considering the effect they will produce in relation to the rest of the room. The most expensive materials are not necessarily the most effective. The amount of wear they will receive or how much sun they may have to withstand is important. Some materials, for example rayon, rot quickly if exposed to strong sunlight. Consider how frequently they will require washing or dry cleaning – remembering that dry cleaning is more expensive than washing. Ensure that the fabric is suitable for the

environment – for example, velvet curtains in a small dining room will absorb the smell of food and hold the dust. This applies to other rough textured fabrics. All curtains should be flame resistant.

Good quality printed fabrics will have, on the selvedge, the maker's name and the colours incorporated in the pattern. This is an aid in selecting other colours for the décor, which will blend with the material. The drop of the pattern repeat is very important because it will affect the length of fabric required. The pattern will have to match when two lengths are required, and the pattern must match when the curtains are closed. In a room with more than one window, the pattern should be at the same level in all the curtains. Similarly, curtains matching the wall paper should have the pattern at the same level as the paper. Materials should be looked at against the light. Velvet, in particular, when hung at a window looks quite different to what it looks like with the light on it.

Types of curtain

Drapes are fine net, lace or tulle. They are hung at the windows behind draw curtains. They give a semi-opaque screen to the window, affording some privacy from the outside, or screening an unsightly view from the window. They are available in a large variety of patterns and designs. They protect the draw curtains, collecting dust and smoke which may enter by the window. They are easily laundered.

Sheers can be used in a similar way to drapes, but they usually replace draw curtains, giving privacy, but allowing light to enter the room. They are often of coarse cotton and a loose weave.

Draw curtains, as the name implies, are drawn across windows at night. They can be sill length or floor length.

Café curtains are hung, ungathered, on rings from a rod usually placed about halfway up the window. They require less material than gathered curtains.

Black-outs cut out all light when drawn. They must be lined with a dark lining, be headed with a pelmet and have a good overlap at the centre and at the edges of the window.

Curtain tracks

The track must be suitable for the weight of curtain hung from it.

Tudor-style wooden and brass poles Solid poles along which wooden or brass rings slide. The rings are either sewn to the curtain or attached with hooks on the curtain.

False wooden or brass poles The track has a false face resembling a solid pole, but behind this there is a plastic or metal track accommodating runners and hooks from the curtain.

Plastic track These have runners with loops, through which the curtain hook is fixed. The track should be fairly rigid – a poor quality will 'whip' and bend, and even sag with the weight of the curtain. A track for drapes can be incorporated with the track for draw curtains.

Brass tracks These have brass runners and are very durable and found in older establishments. They tend to make a noise while curtains are drawn and occasionally the runners get stuck. A squirt of spray polish on the track will ease the runners, and at spring cleaning time boiling the hooks and runners in water to which washing soda has been added, will clean them up. Spray with polish before replacing.

Aluminium track These have nylon runners or glides and are most suitable for commercial establishments. They are capable of supporting heavy curtains. In no way should they be cleaned like brass; soda causes irreparable damage to aluminium.

Expanding plastic-coated stretch wires These are sometimes used for hanging net drapes. They are not recommended for prestigious establishments, but they are cheap and easy to fix, requiring only a small hook screwed into the wire, and an eye into the window frame.

Curtain drawing can present a problem. Curtains should not be regularly clutched in the same place to draw them. It helps if staff are trained to take hold of the lining or loop attached rather than the material itself. There are three systems by which curtains can be drawn.

1 A cord attached to the rollers in such a way that if the cord is pulled both curtains are drawn. Problems arise when curtains with this system are drawn by hand.
2 A pole attached to the top of each curtain is used to draw the curtains.
3 Electronically, by which curtains are drawn by pressing a button remote from the window. This is expensive to install.

There should be enough space between the draw curtains and the drapes, so that the latter are not disarranged when the curtains are drawn.

The type of curtain hook used depends upon the type of tape and heading. Plastic hooks perish and break in time, especially those supporting heavy curtains.

Curtain headings

The heading of the curtain is made by using different kinds of tape. The tape is sewn to the top of the curtain, and the cords pulled to make the gathering, pleating etc. The ends of the cords should then be neatly secured. The heading should be released for laundering, where it is not stitched in place.

Gathering A gathered heading is often hidden under a pelmet. The tape should be placed about 1.5 cm from the top of the curtain. The curtain width required is 1½ times the length of the track (see Figure 36).

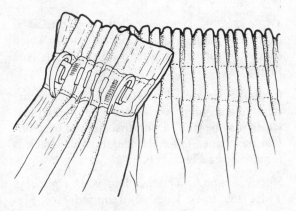

Figure 36 *Standard gathering*

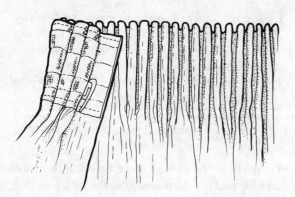

Figure 37   *Pencil pleating*

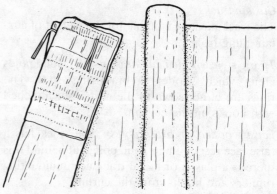

Figure 39   *Cartridge pleating*

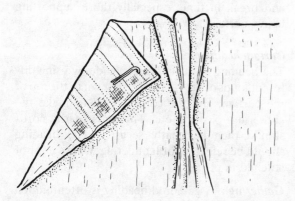

Figure 38   *Triple pinch pleating*

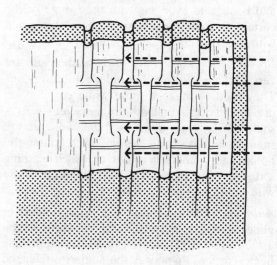

Figure 40   *Smock heading*

Pencil pleating   This is suitable for any material and requires 2 or 2½ times the length of track (see Figure 37).

Triple pleats   Twice the length of track is required. These require special hooks which should be stitched in place with the pleats (see Figure 38).

Cartridge pleating   This is suitable for heavy curtains at large windows. It gives a full found pleat which may be stuffed with tissue paper to maintain the shape. Twice the length of the track is required (see Figure 39).

Smock heading   This heading is 10 cm deep. Twice the track length is required (see Figure 40).

Assessing the amount of material required
Plain fabrics require the length from the top of the track to 1.25 cm above the window sill plus turnings, or 15 cm below the window sill plus turnings, or 2.5 cm above the floor plus turnings.

Patterned fabrics require extra material depending upon the pattern. Allow an additional pattern repeat for every width of curtain after the first, for example, if five widths are required then four pattern repeats are needed.

At least 20 cm should be allowed for turnings:

headings and hems for shrinkage. The width of the curtain should allow for overlap at the side of the window and at least 15 cm at the centre. The tracks should take care of this, so the length of the track is usually taken as a guide (see types of heading).

Curtain linings require the same amount of material as the curtains, except when the curtain material is patterned. Detachable linings require less material.

Hems of curtains may be weighted to give a better hanging effect. Weights can be sewn into the hems or a special weighted bead-cord laid along the hem fold.

Linings

Most curtains need to be lined, with the exception of those materials which have interwoven lining, backing or insulation material. The life of the curtains is prolonged by having linings since they are protected from the damaging effect of the sun's rays. Lining material is usually of mercerized cotton which better withstands the effect of the sun's rays. Linings provide better heat insulation. Air trapped between the curtain and the lining provides a bad conductor of heat from the room, and the extra weight given to the curtain is a protection against draughts. The curtains usually hang better when lined and lined curtains exclude more exterior light. From the exterior of the building lined curtains give a uniformity of appearance.

However, linings do increase the initial cost of outlay on material, and lined curtains are more expensive to make up. Unless linings are detachable there may be uneven shrinkage between the lining and the curtain fabric.

Detachable linings can be washed frequently, so they look fresh from the exterior (window side) without the more delicate furnishing fabric being subjected to frequent laundering. Detachable linings require less material (usually one and a half times the width of the track is adequate) and they can be interchangeable betweeen different curtains of the same size. Detachable linings are also useful if the lining material wears out more quickly than the rest of the curtain.

Non-fabric curtains

Bead, bamboo, and grass curtains can be used to screen windows and doorways or used as room dividers. Heavy-duty, clear, flexible plastic strips are also used in hospitals, loading bays, store rooms etc. They are particularly good in warehouses.

Hot air curtains are jets of warm air supplied by a fan heater over a doorway. They are excellent for entrances where there is a draught problem and air curtains have been found to prevent flies etc, from gaining easy access.

Ceilings

Traditionally, ceilings are lathe and plaster with a smooth skin of fine plaster which is covered with an emulsion paint. In some older buildings the ceilings have plaster mouldings, or have been covered with an embossed paper simulating mouldings. Nowadays plaster replicas of old cornice mouldings are available. Polystyrene mouldings are a fire hazard.

Modern ceilings can be skimmed with a plaster type material and 'decorated' by swirls made by the trowel or a serrated board. This adds a little interest to the ceiling and can be used to camouflage an uneven surface. Otherwise, they can be decorated to harmonize with the décor: painted, papered or covered with fabric swathes or mirror.

Ceilings can be lowered by suspending a false ceiling of opaque glass sheets, behind which lights can be placed.

Plastic or wooden trellis work can be carried across the ceiling with plants trained to grow over it. Vine ivy does this with alacrity and it is very suitable for lounges, garden rooms or leisure areas around swimming pools.

There are many tiles available to fit on to suspended frames to hide air conditioning ducts and wiring etc. The tiles are usually textured and act as sound insulation.

Ceilings should be cleaned and kept free from cobwebs by brushing with a special cobweb brush or vacuuming using a soft brush attachment.

Flowers and plants

Flowers are a useful part of the décor, and indicate a personal, caring attitude on the part of the establishment. When buying flowers, it is useful to select a reliable supplier or nursery, who can be used regularly. A retailer may be prepared to give a special price to a regular customer.

However, it is wise to avoid regular deliveries, since these might arrive while the old flowers are still fresh, leading to unnecessary waste. Bulb and tuber flowers should be bought in bud, so that they last longer. Never buy flowers which are spilling pollen – these are past their best. Fresh and crisp leaves are an indication of freshness, while flowers with slime on the stem are old.

Flower arrangements

The arrangements, and the flowers chosen, should be suitable for their environment. For example, wild flowers and grasses are more at home in a country inn or tea shop than sophisticated, hot-house carnations. Large quantities of flowers are not necessarily the most attractive – sometimes a single bloom in a vase is more effective. Grasses, twigs and foliage should also be used – they back up an arrangement and tend to last longer than the flowers themselves.

Choose colours that blend or complement each other as well as the décor. As a general rule, blues and dark reds do not show up well in artificial light, while apricots and pale pinks look well, so take the lighting into consideration as well. Avoid flowers, such as mimosa, to which many people are allergic.

Before arranging the flowers, soak them in water up to their heads. Oasis should also be soaked. Pick them over carefully for any dead leaves or flower heads. Cut the stems at an angle and crush woody stems to expose a greater surface to the water. Remove leaves from the lower part of the stem which will be submerged in the water. Drooping flowers can sometimes be straightened by wrapping their whole length in damp newspaper. A sugar lump or proprietory flower food can be put in the water to prolong the life of the flowers. Some flowers are 'allergic' to certain foliage, so check in a specialist book first. The flower arrangement should be given daily attention. Dead heads and leaves should be removed, and the water changed or topped up.

Flowers should not be arranged in an area which is used for the preparation of food. Newspapers or plastic should be used to protect the floor or work surface.

Restaurants

Table arrangements should be low, and should not dominate the food. The shape of the arrangement should follow the shape of the table. Flowers can be incorporated with candles. Some candlesticks have a ring round the base or special holders.

Flowers are best not placed on buffet tables, as there is always the danger that insects may wander into the food. They can also seem to be in competition with the food and distract attention from it. Avoid strong-smelling flowers, whose scent does not always mix with food smells.

Reception rooms

Bold arrangements are acceptable in large areas, and can command a dominant position. Where there are going to be large numbers of people, the arrangements should be at eye level or they will be lost. They should not obliterate a picture or some special feature of the room. Arrangements placed in front of a mirror will add emphasis.

Bedrooms

Avoid strong-smelling flowers – they can be oppressive in a small room. For the same reason, avoid large and dominating arrangements. Put the flowers somewhere practical – the bedside table is not a good place.

Wedding flowers

At the booking interview the colours of the bride's and bridesmaids' dresses and flowers should be ascertained, and the flowers in the room selected to maintain the theme. The bride might also be asked if she has a special vase or box in which she would like to have the flowers for the cake arranged. A small china shoe makes a pleasant change from the inevitable silver vase. The flowers for the cake are often ordered by the bride and left to the housekeeper to arrange.

Guests' flowers

In hotels or residences where flowers have been sent to greet the guests, make sure a suitable bowl or vase, florist's wire mesh or oasis, scissors and newspaper are discreetly available so that the recipient may arrange them. Ask if the guest would like a member of the staff to do this for him/her. If the guest wishes to take them away, provide a plastic bag.

Vases and containers

These should be water-tight and non-porous. Unconventional containers can be used, such as teapots, jugs and glasses, but not those in regular use in the establishment. The containers should relate to the environment and the flowers used. For example wild flowers would not look at home in a crystal or silver vase. Copper and brass urns and coal scuttles filled with flowers and foliage look well in fireplaces during the summer. Another idea is to paint metal cigar capsule containers and attach them to painted surfaces to contain small sprays of flowers at strategic places.

Pot plants

Plants add to the décor and atmosphere in the same way as flowers. They can also be therapeutic – in old people's homes, or hostels, the care of plants can be given over to some of the interested residents. Before buying plants, seek specialist advice so that they are suitable for the environment. The temperature, humidity and draught-proofing of the establishment will all affect a plant's welfare. Also ascertain how often the plant requires watering – it is not advisable to have plants grouped together if they require watering at different intervals.

Earthenware pots are better for the plant, but remember that they are porous, so the furniture on which they stand will have to be protected. Plastic pots also have the advantage that they do not break, and they will do less damage to any surface they may fall on. The pots can be arranged inside another container, such as a basket or a trough. This can be lined with foil for added protection.

Plants collect dust in the same way as other surfaces. Their leaves should be dusted regularly with a damp cloth, and they should be sprayed. There are many books on plant care, which should be consulted. However, as a general rule, ensure that staff do not over-water plants, or allow stale water to collect in the container.

Rental services

Owing to the cost of purchasing fresh flowers and plants, together with the cost of time taken to arrange them, care for them and replace them, many establishments use artificial arrangements, rent fresh plants or do a combination of both.

Plastic flowers are now out of fashion and silk flowers are becoming popular. Although no imitation can ever replace real plants or flowers, silk is a very good second choice. Silk flowers and plants may be purchased from any florist and arranged on site, but many establishments, especially smaller hotels and restaurants prefer to have a contract with a florist who specializes in rental of silk flower arrangements. The arrangements are quite inexpensive to rent on a weekly basis and various sizes of arrangements can be made up to suit different locations. Colours can be chosen to suit the décor. With a regular contract, the florist usually changes the arrangements every week so no one has the opportunity of becoming bored with them.

Fresh plants can also be hired from specialist companies. Although plant hire is expensive, the housekeeper must consider the many advantages:

1   Plants are well cared for, so the appearance is always excellent. The plants are usually watered and weeded and leaves are dusted on a daily basis.
2   As and when necessary, they are automatically replaced. Without rental services this could be a costly business as some of the more exotic plants are very expensive.
3   Plants and flowers can be ordered for a special

occasion and can transform any area even if only for a day.

Other decorative features

Books
Books add interest to a room. They can even be purchased by the metre, in which case they can be antique-bound books or reproductions or even hollow artifacts. A collection of paperbacks will add colour as well as make an interesting feature. They can be bought cheaply at jumble sales and markets and if 'borrowed' are cheaply replaced.

Open fires
Fires are often considered part of the décor because an open fire can create a live and positive feature to a room, as well as providing heat. Simulated open fires produce the same effect.

Mirrors
Mirrors increase the size of the room and the light in it. Mirrors or mirror tiles placed opposite a window can bring the view into the room, on what might otherwise be a blank wall. They require frequent and careful cleaning and are expensive.

Framed mirrors can be used as decorative items on their own, or so placed to reflect some particular article, such as a china figure, flower arrangement or light from candles.

Pictures
These should be hung on a plain background which does not compete for attention. Unless large and imposing, they should not be hung singly but in groups. The frames should suit the picture and the style of the room. The mounts can pick up a colour used in the décor.

The pictures themselves should also relate to the environment. Small pictures with great detail should be hung at eye level so that their quality can be appreciated.

Other artefacts
The arrangement of vases, and other artefacts creates interest and atmosphere in any establishment. They may be carpets, oriental rugs, tapestries, statues, busts, sculptures or small items like boxes, thimbles or even matchboxes. Small items look best in groups – the most humble item attracts attention in a group or a collection.

Refurbishment

To 'refurbish' means to renovate, and 'refurbishment' covers replacement of furniture, fixtures and fittings which have become worn out or obsolete. It should not be confused with redecoration, which simply involves renewing paintwork, wallpaper etc., or spring cleaning, which is the thorough clean which should take place once a year.

The frequency of refurbishment depends on the budget of the establishment, and the amount of wear the interior is subjected to. Some of the luxury class hotels budget for refurbishment over a period of seven years, while other establishments would like to replace their furnishings regularly, but cannot because of the high cost.

Before a programme of refurbishment is embarked upon, a number of questions should be asked and answered.

Evaluation
A physical inspection should be carried out to ascertain if the project is really necessary. A sheet like the one shown in Figure 41 should be completed.

A work sheet should then be prepared in detail. This is normally done in conjunction with the chief engineer or the head of the maintenance department (see Figure 42).

Availability of time
When considering the work and the costs involved, the expected completion date must be planned. The work should be carried out during a period of low occupancy or at the most convenient time.

Budget
How much money is available for the project? There may have to be a compromise between

Physical inspection sheet				Date:		
Room no.	Carpets	Walls	Furniture	Fittings	Ceilings	Bathroom
401	X	O	✓	✓	X	O
402	X	O	✓	✓	X	O
403	X	O	✓	✓	X	O
404	✓	✓	✓	✓	X	X
405	✓	✓	✓	✓	X	X

Inspected by _____

Key:
✓ = Good for another year
O = Good for another six months
X = In need of urgent attention

Figure 41 *Physical inspection sheet*

what actually needs doing and what can be afforded and the budget adhered to.

Theme
If the original theme of the establishment or area is to be changed, the suitability of the newly chosen theme should be researched and a feasibility study and market research carried out. The project should be financially viable.

Design
The project should be ergonomically sound, possibly using work studies and all the practicalities of hygiene, cleanliness and comfort considered.

Décor
Suitable fabrics, finishes and colours should be chosen. It would be ridiculous to have burgundy velvet curtains and seating in a MacDonalds type of restaurant. The fabrics and finishes, should be hard-wearing, fire resistant, vandal-proof, easy to clean, and give the right kind of atmosphere.

Staffing
The project work may be carried out by direct labour or contractors, and a cost comparison made. If refurbishment takes place, there should be the necessary staff to maintain the new image. Consideration must also be given to new uniforms, recruitment and training.

Equipment
The equipment to do the work concerned may need to be purchased or hired and availability checked.

Raw materials
Suficient supplies should be ordered and facilities made for reordering. The best possible purchase price should be obtained allowing for sufficient secure storage space.

Inconvenience
Provision should be made for the inconvenience to guests, staff, suppliers, etc. while project work

Project work sheet   Room no: . . . .   Room size: . . . .

Action

Order of work	Date	Recommendations

Costs

Order of work	Date	Carpets	Walls	Furniture	Fittings	Ceilings	Bathroom	Total

Remarks

Figure 42   *Work sheet*

is in process. Temporary arrangements may need to be made.

Procedures

All the correct company and statutory procedures should be adhered to:

1   Planning permission
2   Fire regulations
3   Health and safety aspects
4   Licensing laws
5   Trades description
6   Company policy

Control

All aspects of control should be finalized.

1   Financial controls
2   Purchasing
3   Solicitors
4   Insurance

5   Contracts
6   Inspection
7   Records kept

For the housekeeper, record-keeping is, perhaps, the most important aspect of control. He/she should keep documentation in the form of a rooms history card, so that he/she has details of all work carried out, for the purposes of future planning.

Redecoration

The housekeeper would not be involved in applying paint or putting up wallpaper. However, he/she should be able to oversee the process, and ensure that a high standard of work is maintained. There should be a written contract with outside decorators, including starting and finishing dates. The contract should clearly state the work that is required, and the order in which it is to be carried out. The housekeeper should discuss with the foreman how best to do the work with the minimum of disruption to staff and guests.

The housekeeping staff will have to prepare the rooms for decorating contractors. They should:

1 Strip beds and remove all bedding.
2 Remove small items of furniture, pictures and artefacts to a safe place.
3 Take down curtains.
4 Have chimneys swept if there is an open fire.

Other preparations are also necessary, and if the housekeeping staff are not doing them, it should be stated in the contract that the decorators are responsible:

1 Take up carpets, or cover with polythene dust sheets, with the edges tucked under.
2 Drain and remove radiators.
3 Disconnect light fittings and remove from the wall.
4 Cover remaining furniture with dust sheets and put in the centre of the room. (The housekeeper should have ample supply of clean dust sheets.)
5 Remove any wall fittings such as shelves.

Further reading

BSI, BS 1192 *Building Drawing Practice*

Hessayan, D. G., *The Houseplant Expert* (PBI publications 1980).

Sandwith, H., and Stainton, S., *The National Trust Manual of Housekeeping* (Allen Lane 1984).

Smith, D., *Hotel and Restaurant Design* (Design Council 1978).

Weaver, G., *Home Decoration Using Light*. (Marshall Cavendish Publications 1975).

Useful addresses

Interior Design,
Westbourne Publications,
Crown House,
Morden,
Surrey SM4 5EB

16 Pests

A pest is any thing or person which is destructive, noxious or troublesome. A horrible child or a vandal is often described as a pest, but in this chapter we shall only be concerned with non-human pests.

Pests can be divided into six categories, although many will come under more than one.

1　Pests which cause physical damage: wood-worm, moths, carpet beetles, mice and rats.
2　Those which contaminate food and the environment: cockroaches, flies, wasps, mice and rats.
3　Those which are comparatively harmless, but repulsive to many people: spiders, silver-fish.
4　Those which attack food stores: flour beetles, bacon beetles.
5　Parasites, which directly attack human beings: bed bugs, head lice, fleas.
6　Seasonal nuisances, or casual intruders from outside: ants, earwigs.

Reasons for pest control

Legislation
Pests, by definition, cause harm to buildings, the environment and human beings. This is good enough reason to try to eliminate pests, but there is also legislation which imposes a legal obligation on establishments to protect the public.

1　The Prevention of Damage by Pests Act 1949. This states that establishments are bound to keep premises free from rats and mice. The act is not only concerned with protecting health, but also preventing loss or damage to property and its contents by pests. It includes insect infestation of premises used for food.
2　The Food and Drugs Act 1955.
3　The Food Hygiene Regulations 1907.
4　The Health and Safety at Work Act 1947.
5　The Control of Food Premises Act 1976.
6　The Public Health Acts of 1936 onwards cover very many aspects of housekeeping standards including pest control, waste disposal, etc.

The Animals Cruel Poisons Act of 1962 is also relevant. This prohibits the use of such poisons as strychnine, because they cause pain to pests such as rats and mice.

Contamination
This second reason is linked closely with the law. Good pest control reduces the risk of contamination of food and lessens the risk of illness and of contaminated food having to be destroyed.

Reputation
The hospitality industry depends for its success or failure very much on its reputation. This can be ruined if pests are sighted or if guests can trace food poisoning back to the establishment. Loss of reputation results in loss of revenue. Prudent owners will have in their insurance policies cover against food poisoning, and the loss of business ensuing from such a case. Even if the establishment is not the source of the contamination and food was contaminated before arrival, adverse publicity will result.

Depreciation
The physical damage done to property and its contents by pest and fungi is considerable if they are not dealt with in the early stages. It is better to

spend money on regular pest control operations than larger sums on repairs and renewals or suffer the depreciation.

Principles of good pest control

The housekeeper should be able to identify pests or evidence of their presence. He/she should know under what conditions they thrive and the measures necessary to stop them flourishing. Pest sightings should be monitored, and a 'Pests book' kept to record sightings, treatments and dates. Pest control contractors, such as Rentokil, can be employed to inspect premises and carry out any necessary treatment. Local authorities employ environmental health officers, who will offer free advice. They may also run short training courses.

Exclusion

The first principle is to keep the 'beasties' out.

1 Defective roof slates/tiles will allow water, birds and insects to enter.
2 Blocked gutters and pipes cause dampness leading to mould and rot and conditions suitable for some insects.
3 Broken lead flashings round chimneys and windows should be repaired.
4 Unused chimney stacks and ventilating pipes should be capped.
5 Defective paintwork on window sills, door frames encourage rot.
6 Inadequate damp coursing or covered damp courses allow rising damp.
7 Uncovered water tanks in lofts are an attraction for pests and can be contaminated by their dead bodies.
8 Broken air bricks and grilles should be replaced, and any spaces in brickwork through which waste pipes or ducts pass should be filled.

Restriction

1 Do not allow accumulations of paper, felt or fabrics, carpets in little used areas.
2 Do not leave empty bottles and food cans around.

3 Dispose of all waste food, crumbs and spilt liquid.
4 The dustbin area should be kept clean – hosed and brushed down with a disinfectant.
5 Dustbins should have tight fitting lids and should be placed away from kitchen windows.
6 All organic refuse should be put into plastic bags which are sealed before being put into bins.
7 Food in kitchens and larders should be kept covered and edges of carpets and all floor coverings and skirting boards should be kept free of dust and fluff.
8 Blankets stored should be kept in moth-proof bags.
9 Ornamental pools and plant troughs should be inspected and stale water not allowed to accumulate.
10 Insect trays and fly killing devices or screens should be inspected to see that they are still functioning and not harbouring dead pests. Ultra violet tubes must be replaced annually.
11 Storage areas, boiler houses, cellars should be regularly inspected and debris not allowed to accumulate.
12 Wardrobes, clothes and linen cupboards, drawers and all crevices should be kept free of dust and fluff and inspected regularly.
13 Periodic moving of furniture and equipment prevent dust and dirt accumulating behind them.
14 Check that woodworm is not brought into the building in plywood, softwood or wicker containers, or secondhand furniture. Upholstered furniture might also have moths.

There is always a risk of refuse awaiting collection attracting pests. It is possible in some areas to ask and pay extra for more frequent collections. Burning refuse is the best way of disposing of it and the installation of an incinerator is desirable, if budget and space allow. Any incinerator should be of the smokeless type. A small incinerator for the disposal of organic refuse only is useful. A paper shredder and a tin crusher reduce the bulk of refuse.

Pests which cause physical damage

Woodworm (the furniture beetle)

Recognition
Small round holes about 1 mm in diameter are evidence of this insect. These have been produced by a wood-boring beetle which flies. It is about 5 mm long, dark brown in colour and attacks not only furniture but roof joists, floors and any wood used in the structure of buildings. It prefers softwood and plywood but will attack hardwood furniture and joinery. Many of the holes seen in old furniture are signs of an old attack. Some less reputable antique dealers have even been known to fake woodworm holes in order to make their wares appear more authentic!

Life cycle
The beetle lays her eggs in cracks, splits or rough areas of the wood surface, but it is the larvae which actually do the damage. As the eggs hatch, the larvae burrow into the wood and feed on it for a period of from two to four years, when they emerge as adults having burrowed their way out of tell-tale holes. If small holes such as these are noticed one may simply tap the surface to check if the woodworm is active – a light wood dust will be evident if the attack is active or recent. See Chapter 7 Furniture and fittings.

Prevention
Regular cleaning and dusting of furniture, especially rough and unfinished surfaces. Use a woodworm-killing wax polish on all polished wood and occasionally apply it to the unpolished surfaces such as the back, feet and drawers.

Eradication
Small areas in furniture, can be treated by the injection into some of the holes of a proprietory brand of woodworm killer using the applicator supplied. This must be backed up by brushing the woodworm killer liberally over *all* surfaces of the item. Large areas, timbers, panelling etc. are difficult and the specialist should be brought in.

Reputable companies offer a free survey, report and estimate. Some give a 30 year guarantee and one offers an insurance scheme against woodworm.

Another wood-boring insect is the *deathwatch beetle* which attacks damp timbers found in old buildings. Evidence of its presence is the noise it makes by tapping its head against the timber, most noticeable in the silence of the night. It is a distinctive short, sharp click. Specialist advice and attention should be sought.

The carpet beetle

Recognition
It is round in shape, about 3 mm long, slightly smaller than the ladybird. The hard wing cases are mottled black, white and yellow, but it is the larva which is more easily recognized – a small golden brown grub with hairy tufts on its body, thereby giving it the rather endearing name of 'woolly bear'. It is found around carpet edges or in airing cupboards where there may be wool fluff and/or blankets being stored.

Life cycle
The eggs are laid in the autumn in old birds' nests or other undisturbed areas where there is suitable animal protein. The larva eats the animal material, wool, fur and feathers. Added nutrient like spilt food or drink allowed to dry on a carpet or woollens add interest and flavour for the larvae.

Prevention
Moth-proof carpets and any stored woollens. Vacuum right up to the edges of carpets using the narrow suction appliance. Remove all spillages thoroughly. Check airing cupboards and linen cupboards. In upholstered furniture remove dust and crumbs from the deep folds and crevices. Check lofts for old nests, dead birds or other debris. Inspect stuffed animals and birds and also animal skin rugs.

The fur beetle has similar habits but the adult is black with a single white spot on each wing case.

Moths

Recognition
There are two types of moth which are very similar – the brown house moth and the clothes moth. The brown house moth is golden brown, with flat wings bearing black flecks. The clothes moth is silver/buff and folds its wings in a tent-like fashion.

Life cycle
They are active in the summer when they can lay the eggs in undisturbed peace on woollen clothes and blankets and furs which are not being used. The eggs are laid on the source of food (wool or fur). The whitish grubs make holes in the fabric or consume the pile on the material. They then form a silken-like cocoon in which to pupate. Soiling from food, perspiration or urine adds piquancy to the wool diet. The house moth will also consume cork, leather and dried fruit.

Prevention
Woollen clothes and blankets and furs should be

1 Cleaned before being stored for the summer and sprayed with moth-proof aerosol (after testing on a small piece of fabric). Special attention should be paid to pockets and folds where crumbs and fluff have accumulated.
2 Stored in clean plastic or paper bags. The ends should be folded over several times and closed with sellotape.
3 Kept in drawers, wardrobes, cupboards, linen cupboards which have been cleaned frequently and had fluff removed from corners and crevices. Drawers should be removed so that the runners and the recess into which the drawers slide can be cleaned and treated with a moth-proof aerosol.

Chemical crystals (paradichlorabenzene) can be sprinkled along the folds of goods being stored. The crystals evaporate slowly at room temperature and are a deterrent to moths and beetles. The smell is less unpleasant than napthalene formerly used for moth balls.

Rats and mice
Rats have always been considered sinister creatures. Buddha charged them with bringing death into the world and the Black Death was thought to have been caused by the fleas hosted by rats. Both rats and mice cause a great deal of physical damage to property, including buildings, cables, pipes, books, linen and blankets. They gnaw these to try to get at food, or to find materials for their nests. They also spread serious disease such as Weils disease in humans, and trichinosis in livestock, which can be spread to humans. Rats can live inside or out of doors. They will often be seen near rivers or streams and in outbuildings, and in cities they are found in drains, sewers and rubbish dumps. There are two types of rat found in the United Kingdom.

Black rat
This is smaller than the brown rat. It has a black pointed muzzle and large ears. The long thin tail is longer than the body. It seldom burrows, but climbs with agility. It is sleek and fast moving. It frequents walls, ceilings and roofs. Droppings are small and cylindrical with blunt ends.

Brown rat
It is grey-brown and longer, heavier and less agile than the black rat. It has a blunt muzzle and small ears. The tail is long and hairless and no longer than the body. It burrows and is found in cellars, drains and at ground level, but it can climb. Droppings are large and spindle-shaped, pointed at both ends.

Recognition of rats
Evidence of the presence of rats includes

1 The discovery of droppings.
2 Shredded substances such as paper.
3 Gnaw marks and footprints.
4 Sometimes a black streak seen along the skirting board – this comes from the rat's greasy fur as it runs along the edge of the room.
5 Noise of heavy scuttling under floors or above ceilings or behind wainscotting.

Prevention

The staff should be encouraged to observe all the hygiene requirements in storing food and disposing of rubbish. All dry food should be stored in containers with tight-fitting lids. Vegetable storage areas should be kept clean and the produce moved regularly.

All inlets to the building should be closed to rats and mice, either with traps or fine mesh wire. Unnecessary gaps should be stopped up with cement or plastic wood. Standing water can have disinfectant added to it to render it undrinkable.

Elimination

The three methods of destroying rats and mice are trapping, gassing and poisoning.

The spring 'break-back' trap can be effective for the odd mouse if it is placed near signs of mouse activity with the treadle at right angles to the wall and close to it. Cheese is the traditional bait but mice are partial to chocolate, especially the fruit and nut variety – their natural food is seeds, cereals, nuts and berries.

Sticky board placed across the mouse hole or rat run can trap some pests, but it does not control an infestation and is aesthetically unacceptable to staff.

Gassing should only be done by trained pest control operators and is not suitable for use in inhabited buildings.

Warfarin was for many years the only poison available to the public, but a breed of 'Supermice' developed which became immune to it. For mice indoors the following are now used as alternative to Warfarin:

1   Quick-acting alphachloralose baits.
2   Lindane contact dust (for professional users only).
3   New rodenticide baits, containing calciferol difenacoum or bromadiolone placed inside bait boxes, so reducing the danger of contamination by spilled bait.

It is advisable, however, to call on the services of the local authority's rodent operative or a professional pest control company, who will use either traps or poison as required.

It is known that rodents exist and are attracted to catering establishments, no matter how prestigeous, so there should be no hesitation in calling in these agents on early sightings before an infestation has developed. The law demands that premises are kept free from rats and mice.

Pests which contaminate food and environment

Flies

There are several species of flies which infest buildings. All are objectionable and potential sources of contamination and infection. The bluebottle is larger than the common housefly and metallic blue in colour. Its presence is often made known by its familiar buzz. The housefly (musca domestica) is dull grey with black stripes on the thorax.

Life cycle

The fly lays its eggs from spring to autumn in refuse dumps, manure heaps or other moist, warm environment, with some organic matter as a source of food for the larva. The eggs of the bluebottle are larger than those of the housefly. They are laid in clusters, cream in colour and about 1.5 mm in length. It takes from a few hours to three days, depending upon the condition of temperature and moisture for the eggs to develop into the familiar white maggot which soon pupates in a brown cocoon. The larvae or maggots take from forty-eight hours to three or four days to produce a mature fly. The female fly will make and lay eggs a few days after its emergence from the pupa, and can lay during her life up to 700 eggs in batches of five or six.

Habits

Flies are attracted to all kinds of carrion and faecal matter which contain disease-bearing organisms which they pick up on their feet and in their gut. They are also attracted to all kinds of food which they contaminate as they feed. When they crawl over any surface they deposit organisms causing intestinal diseases in human beings, including cholera, enteric fever, typhoid, dysentery, gastroenteritis or summer diarrhoea.

Prevention

It is vitally important to prevent the flies breeding, from entering the building, and if possible to destroy all the flies seen. Food should be stored carefully and refuse disposed of hygienically, as described above. Drains should be kept clean, by regularly pouring a solution of soda and hot water and disinfectant down them. Flies can be prevented from entering a building by putting a fine wire mesh over windows and vents to kitchens and larders. Flies also breed on human excrement, so toilets should be kept clean and in good working condition. In homes or hospitals where patients or residents are incontinent care must be taken to dispose of fouled linen and bedding immediately.

Elimination

Electrical ultra-violet lights are the best method of killing flies. The insects are lured by the light and electrocuted as they touch the surrounding grid. They fall into a collecting tray which should be emptied at regular intervals. These lights may be purchased or hired.

Aerosol sprays are available for both flying and crawling insects. They are excellent to use in housekeeping areas, but should be avoided in food preparation and food service areas, as the product may be harmful to exposed food. Sprays can also be supplied in the form of a machine, rather like air fresheners which emit a measured amount of flykiller at regular intervals. Care should be taken not to site these machines directly over food, as flies killed by insecticides may fall into the food.

Vapour strips are quite effective, but are not recommended for industrial kitchens. Sticky fly papers are unsightly and not suitable for food preparation areas.

Boiling water or a steam cleaning machine may be used effectively against an infestation of maggots. The source of fly breeding should be investigated.

Wasps

The wasp is easily distinguished by its waisted body and obvious black and yellow stripes. The sting is situated at the end of the abdomen. These pests do not have the same habits, nor do they offer the same health hazards as flies, but they are a nuisance and the sting can be very painful and even lethal to a few susceptible people.

Life cycle

The queen wasp constructs a few six-sided cells of a coarse paper-like material, which she makes by pulping wood fibres with her saliva. In each cell an egg is laid and while the first ones are hatching and maturing as larvae, other cells are being constructed and eggs deposited. The workers that emerge then take on the building of the nest and rearing the young. The grubs take two weeks to turn into pupae and emerge as adults. All the workers die off in winter, only the queens surviving by hibernating. While wasps feed their larvae on flies and insects the adults are attracted to sweet food and in late summer may invade kitchens and dining areas.

Prevention

The same preventative measures as for flies should be taken. If there is a great number of wasps, a search should be made in the building and grounds for a nest. A likely place is the roof loft or shed, but it may be in a wall, bank or underground. A nest may be spherical, up to the size of a football, or may spread between joists. It is creamy brown in colour, and papery in texture. The nest is abandoned in winter and is not used again, so there is no point in removing old nests. Nests in banks or holes in the ground can be dealt with at dusk by puffing a proprietory wasp nest killer into the entrance hole. The removal of a wasps' nest in a roof is not for the amateur and a pest control service should be brought in to deal with it. Isolated buildings plagued by wasps can be protected by special baits placed around their perimeter.

Treatment of wasp stings

Wasp stings should be treated promptly, by

applying something cold or a pocket aerosol containing anti-histamine. If there is any sign of distress, the victim should be taken immediately to the out patients' department of the nearest hospital. It is advisable to telephone the hospital in advance and give warning that the victim of a wasp sting is being brought in. Anyone who is allergic to wasp stings can suffer symptoms of shock, and one or two people die from the effects each year.

Cockroaches and steam flies

These are perhaps the most common pest found in catering establishments. There are two types found in the UK

1 The Oriental cockroach, which is often wrongly identified as the black beetle which it resembles.
2 The german cockroach or steam fly which is smaller and brown.

Neither is a beetle and they differ from beetles in structure and life history.

Recognition

The whole body is flat, about 1 cm long, and the insect moves very fast with characteristic scuttling movements. Their flat bodies can squeeze through the smallest gaps. They contaminate food and working surfaces and leave excreta and vomit together with a very persistent odour. An infestation can easily be started by egg capsules in goods brought into the building from infected buildings via laundry baskets, crates etc. They are more prevalent in old buildings with uneven places, skirting boards, panelling etc. They come out at night and one may be unaware of their presence unless an inspection is carried out at night. Tropical in origin, they like warm, humid areas such as boiler rooms, kitchens and heating ducts, as well as laundries.

Cockroaches live on small food particles and are also very partial to beer. Hence they are commonly found in cellars and bars, kitchens, stillrooms and service rooms. They have been known to carry salmonella, streptococci, staphylococci, dysentry, cholera and tubercle bacilli. Consequently they are potentially one of our most dangerous pests.

Life cycle

Cockroaches lay from sixteen to forty eggs at a time, secreted in an ootheca or egg capsule. The young (known as nymphs) are white for a short time when newly hatched and between moults and run about freely, maturing by a series of moults.

Prevention

All areas where they could secrete themselves, such as cracks, should be filled with cement or plastic filler or plastic wood. New buildings are free from infestation since their construction has smoother surfaces, and often solid floors, but the ducts through which services are taken are still an ideal environment for these creatures. A persistent insecticide with good residual properties is needed to deal with adults that may emerge after many weeks from hidden egg capsules. Boric acid powder is also useful.

Above all, any area where food and beverages are stored, prepared, dispensed and served must be kept spotlessly clean. Soiled linen areas and laundries are also vulnerable places for cockroaches and the same tight controls of cleanliness must be maintained here.

Elimination

For a small problem, a puffer pack of insect powder based on carbaryl and an aerosol based on diazinon or permethrin, should be used on the areas from which the creatures emerge. For the major infestation it is necessary to call on the services of a professional pest control officer.

Harmless but horrible

Spiders

The spiders found in the UK do not harm humans, but can cause fear and revulsion. However, they do eat other insects, snaring them into their 'parlours'. They tend to be more active in the dark among dust, and where there is water available, for example, bathroom overflows and outlets.

Prevention and eradication
They will be discouraged by premises being light, airy, dry and free from dust, and unlike Robert Bruce's legendary spider, by having their webs removed as soon as they have made them. Superstition often prevents people from killing spiders or seeing them killed. If necessary, remove them with an inverted jar or carton, sliding them on to a sheet of paper for extermination or release outside. They can be killed by an aerosol insecticide for crawling insects.

Silver-fish

These are a very common pest, but not such a health hazard as flies and cockroaches. The silver-fish is wingless, about 1 cm in length, silvery and cigar-shaped. It tends to dart about like a fish. Although they are comparativley harmless, their presence should not be ignored because it can be indicative of something wrong – damp or spilt food – which will attract other harmful pests.

Habits
They are found in cupboards near sinks and drains, and also in damp store cupboards. They feed on cellulose and starch material, so are attracted to spilt flour and cereals in cupboards. They can also attack wall paper and starched linen and cotton articles. They are active at night.

Prevention
Avoid loose wall paper, especially in damp areas, and leaving spilt cereals on shelves. As for all pests, thorough cleaning of all cupboards and shelves and rotation of goods in storage will discourage them. Check for plumbling leaks, condensation or rising damp.

Elimination
Treat areas away from food with an insecticide such as carbaryl powder or a proprietory crawling insect spray based on diazinon, carbaryl or permethrin.

Woodlice

These are unpleasant-looking grey segmented creatures some of which roll up into a ball when disturbed. They are harmless, but live on damp rotting wood, and indicate that there is something rotten in the state of the building, and the source of damp should be sought and cured. They are crustaceans and may enter buildings to avoid dehydration in dry weather.

Booklice

Booklice are not strictly speaking lice, but distant relatives of plant bugs. They are minute, fast moving insects 1–3 mm long, with rather soft bodies. They are harmless, but unpleasant when they appear in larders and on furniture. They do not confine themselves to books, but they do feed on the moulds growing on paper. They also live in food stores, barns, thatched roofs and compressed straw used for internal walls. If they have access to suitable food (e.g. flour or sugar) enormous populations can quickly build up. Booklice live for five or six months. The female can lay 100–200 eggs and they breed most rapidly at high humidity, especially in a centrally heated environment.

Elimination
An infestation can be difficult to eradicate, since they can spread over a wide area. In commercial premises the treatment will involve spraying or fumigation, carried out by a professional pest control contractor, who will carry out a follow-up service to clear the remaining pockets of the pest.

Dust mites

There are many types of these minute creatures, invisible to the naked eye. They are harmless to most people but they can cause allergies. They live everywhere where there are people; in bedding, soft furnishings, carpets. They live off scales of dead skin. They thrive in warm damp conditions, and multiply quickly. A recently discovered disease they cause in humans who are allergic to them is Kawasaki disease. The symptoms may be fever, swollen glands or a type of asthma. Small children are more vulnerable to this disease and research has shown that it can be contracted by children crawling on carpets.

Prevention
Nothing can prevent mites living in our environment, except keeping accommodation clean, airy, dry and free from dust.

Food pests

These do not always come under the control of the housekeeper, but s/he may be called in to advise.

Flour moths, flour beetles, flour mites
Any flour, oatmeal or fine cereal, not looking completely clean and free flowing should be suspect, and destroyed, or in the case of a newly opened pack, returned to the supplier. The cereal should be burned and the store cupboard cleaned and the surface sprayed with a residual insecticide for crawling insects. For infestation in commercial premises, professional treatment is necessary.

Weevils and beetles of various kinds sometimes occur in pasta, biscuits, dried fruit and cereals. The infected material should be burned, the receptacle thoroughly cleaned and the storage area treated as above.

Fruit and vinegar flies
These are so small they could easily be ignored, but they can be a menace in cellars and bars or where there is split alcohol and fruit juices, since they live on the dregs of fermenting liquor, or rotting fruit. The adults have large eyes and a characteristic slow hovering flight. The female lays her eggs on the smooth interior of bottles (or unclean decanters) and secures them to the surface with a cement resistant to steaming hot water and detergent. An attractive breeding ground is where empty bottles are stacked awaiting collection.

Cork moths
These can also build up an infestation undetected in an area where racks of bottles are stacked for a long time. Cork is also a happy breeding ground for the brown house moth and the white-shouldered house moth, which lay eggs in the cracks in corks, causing leakage and contamination.

Prevention
Areas where breeding may take place should be inspected and kept scrupulously clean, not allowing a sticky build up of fruit juice or spilt liquor.

Eradication
Should the pest become an infestation, a pest control service should be called in. They will use a low toxicity insecticidal fog which cuts across the life cycle, but involves no risk of tainting beverages.

Pests which attack humans

Fleas
Most present day infestations of fleas are caused by cat fleas which can breed all the year round in centrally heated premises. Cat fleas will also attack humans. They are particularly a problem in cheap furnished accommodation or hostels, but can be brought into luxury establishments by pets or feral cats. Although they abound in unhygienic conditions, they can be brought into a clean environment on clothing, secondhand furniture and carpets as well as cats.

They are grey-black and about the size of a pin-head with hard bodies, flattened from side to side. They are difficult to catch and squash. They jump great distances from one host to another or to and from clothes, bedding, carpets, etc. While difficult to sight, their presence is made known to people by the irritating bite with a small red spot where blood has been sucked.

Life cycle
Cat fleas' eggs are laid in fur, hair or bedding and in minute crevices with cellulose. The eggs and white thread-like larvae may abound in an animal's bedding and surrounding furnishings, but the life cycle may be completed in fluff, carpets and upholstered furniture in centrally heated

premises. Peak time for infestation is late summer.

Prevention and eradication

Scrupulous cleanliness, paying special attention to cracks and crevices is vital. Avoid storing old carpets and bedding in warm dark places especially if their origin is unknown. No matter how beautiful a cat is, it should be discouraged from using the lounge, upholstered furniture or finding a comfortable retreat in the linen room. Cats should be inspected regularly and given veterinary attention at first sign of infestation.

Bedbugs

Like fleas, bedbugs can be imported into a clean environment via laundry hampers, dirty clothing, secondhand furniture, carpets, bedding and people.

They are oval in shape, between 2 and 5 mm wide, flat and chestnut brown. They give off an offensive odour which is secreted from two glands. This is a defensive mechanism to ward off enemies. They cannot jump or fly, but walk from one host to another.

Life cycle

The female lays her eggs in the summer on suitable material; organic fluff, dust or material, in crevices, in bedsprings, mattress buttons – even behind wall paper or in books. The eggs are glutinous at first and readily adhere to whatever material they are deposited upon. There is no larval stage – the nymphs that hatch simply mature by a series of moults. They can live for long periods of time without food, which is human blood. Therefore, they can live in an uninhabited house or room and only make their presence known when it becomes occupied again. They live longer in a cold or cool environment. They are nocturnal and are attracted to the warmth and scent of human beings whom they attack at exposed skin areas, usually face, neck and arms.

Prevention

Scrupulous cleanliness and inspection of likely habitats will prevent infestation. Spraying with a crawling insect insecticide is effective, but if the problem persists specialist pest controllers should be brought in, since fumigation of bedding and upholstered furniture may be necessary.

Lice

There are three types of human lice: head, body and pubic. They live off human blood and are about 3 mm long. The eggs, known as 'nits' are cemented on to hairs or clothing and hatch out causing severe itching. Scratching to relieve the discomfort can introduce secondary infection. Lice are regarded as a medical problem and since they can be easily passed on to others medical advice should be sought. A fine tooth comb will dislodge the nits from head hair, and a special insecticidal shampoo should clear them up.

Elimination

A room used by someone with head or body lice should be spring cleaned, and the bedding laundered and the mattress cleaned.

Pests from outside

Ants

There are several types of ants. The most common in the UK is the garden or black ant, which lives and works in communities. Ants have long thin bodies with a pronounced waist, and are easily recognizable since they work as a team, and one seldom sees a lone ant. Flying ants are the winged males and females that emerge for their mating flight.

Life cycle

Their life history is similar to that of the wasp. The nests are found in the ground, in piles of dead leaves or trunks of old trees. A large community will often construct several nests in close proximity.

Habits

They will eat almost any kind of animal or vegetable matter, but they are particularly attracted to sweet foodstuffs.

Prevention

The usual hygiene measures taken in the kitchen and larder are the best precaution – keeping food containers clean on the exterior and covered, wiping up spillages etc.

Elimination

Boiling water poured into the entrance hole of the nest (if this can be located) is a quick first aid measure. A spray or dust containing lindane, carbaryl or boric acid is more effective, but should not be used near exposed food. Spraying with an aerosol of diazinon at points of entry, pipe runs and skirtings is a protection. Insecticide lacquers and liquid or jelly baits are available. Boric acid powder pumped into wall and floor cavities give long term protection.

In extreme cases, the services of the environmental health officer or a pest control company should be sought.

Pharaoh ants

The pharaoh ant is a tiny yellowish brown insect, about 2 mm long, which can penetrate into the smallest spaces. It cannot live out of doors in the UK and has established itself in many large centrally heated buildings where there is high humidity and plentiful food. It is an increasing problem in hospitals, where it goes for blood, soiled dressings and other organic matter. It is difficult to eradicate without specialist help. Some hospitals have their own trained team to deal with this pest.

Birds

Birds are not obviously pests, but directly and indirectly some species must be considered as such. Feral pigeons reside in towns on the ornate stone-faced buildings which resemble their natural habitat (rocky cliffs and caves) and are attracted by the easily obtainable food supply from humans. They deface and damage buildings, and the accumulation of feathers and droppings foul stonework, block drainage systems and carry diseases and parasites. The dust from dried droppings on window sills blown into buildings can carry such diseases as aspergilloris, histopharmosis and ornithosis. Mites and carpet beetles breed in the debris accumulated by the birds and in their nests.

Other birds – such as starlings, sparrows and doves become pests in certain areas. They can damage the mortar between bricks and foul premises and food if they enter the building. They can build nests in guttering, pipes, and unused chimneys and their noise may disturb occupants. They also may carry fleas or mites which can harm humans. The house martin carries a 'martin bug' which travels from the nest into bedrooms and has similar effects to those of the bedbug.

Prevention

To deter pigeons, window sills and ledges can be treated with soft plastic gel which gives the birds an insecure foothold. Pest birds must be humanely killed without risk to protected species. Contractors may use trap cages to collect the birds or use a stupefying bait and kill them humanely. Plastic nets can be fixed over alcoves, large openings and wells. Roofs and gutters should be kept clear of mosses and chimney soil pipe ventilators should be protected with wire mesh to prevent birds nesting or falling into them. Many 'ghosts' have been birds trapped in a disused chimney! Discourage guests or staff from feeding birds from window sills or ledges near the building. Stuffed birds can also harbour moths and should be inspected.

Residents' pets

Pets have been included in this chapter, because they can easily become pests to the housekeeper. In all establishments the admission or exclusion of pets will be a policy decision of those in authority. The housekeeper may be required to give his/her knowledge of the effects of having animals in the building. The following should be considered.

1   Is there an adequate area outside the building for the animal's natural functions, without fouling paths and recreational areas?
2   Once the building is closed for the night, can the clients be given facilities for going out to exercise their animal early in the morning or late at night?

3 Subsequent guests could be allergic to animal hairs and dust – even with the most sophisticated cleaning methods, it cannot be guaranteed that all evidence of an animal's presence can be removed.

4 If dogs and cats are admitted to bedrooms, drinking and food bowls, suitable covering for the carpet, and, on occasions, a basket and blanket will have to be provided.

5 Animals can bring pests into the hotel, especially fleas or other parasites.

6 It is highly recommended that pets should not be allowed into dining rooms or other public rooms because they can be highly objectionable to other users of these rooms, and the most docile creature can be suddenly very antagonistic towards another animal. Should such an incident occur, a soda siphon is an effective weapon.

Housekeepers should report any contravention of the policy concerning pets. They are often smuggled into hotels, and even if pets are allowed, reception should be informed so that a charge can be made.

Some common pest control chemicals

These chemicals can be purchased under a wide range of proprietory brand names. The main active ingredients are listed on the packaging and can be checked for the suitability of their use.

For flying insects　Diazinon, dichlorvos, pybuthrin, pyrethrin, permethrin.

For crawling insects　Arprocarb, bendiocarb, bromophos, carbaryl, chlordane, dieldrin, fenitrothion, iodofenphos, lindane (gamma HCH), malathion, firimiphos methyl, pyrethoids (permethrin).

For wood-boring insects　Dieldrin, lindane (gamma HCH), permethrin.

For textile pests　Dieldrin, lindane (gamma HCH), paradichloroberzene, permethrin.

Fumigants　Aluminium phosphide, methyl bromide.

For rats and mice　Alphachloralose, brodifacoum, bromadiolone, calciferol, coumateretralyl, chlorophacine, diphacinone, difenacoum, norbormide, warfarin.

Note　It is imperative that all pesticides should be used with great care, strictly to the manufacturer's instructions. When using aerosols do not walk into the spray, but start at the far end of the room and walk backwards away from the spray.

Further reading

British Pest Control Association, *A to Z of Household Pests*.

Coggins, C. R., *Decay of Timber in Buildings* (Rentokil Library 1980).

Cornwell, P. B., *The Cockroach*, Volume 1 (Rentokil Library 1968).

Cornwell, P. B., *Pest Control in Buildings* (Rentokil Library 1979).

Hicken, N. E., *Household Insect Pests* 2nd edition, (Rentokil Library 1974).

Lucas, G. C., *Hygiene in Buildings* (Rentokil Library 1982).

Munro, J. W., *Pests of Stored Products* (Rentokil Library 1966).

Useful addresses

The British Pest Control Association,
Alembis House,
93 Albert Embankment,
London SE1

The British Wood Preserving Association,
Premier House,
Southampton Row,
London WC1B 5AL

The Health Education Council,
Middlesex House,
Ealing Road,
Wembley,
Middlesex HA0 1HH

The Hotel Catering and Institutional Management
Association,
191 Trinity Road,
London SW17 7HN

The Institition of Environmental Health Officers,
Chadwich House,
Rushworth Street,
London SE1 6RB

Ministry of Agriculture, Fisheries and Food,
Government Buildings,
Hook Rise,
Tolworth,
Surbiton,
Surrey ET6 7NK

The Rentokil Advice Centre,
Felcourt,
East Grinstead,
West Sussex RH19 2JY

The Royal Institute of Public Health and Hygiene,
28 Portland Place,
London W1

Wellcome Industrial (Pesticides),
The Wellcome Foundation,
Berkhamstead,
Herts

17 *Heating, ventilation and damp*

Heating

Heating is perhaps the most important factor in the provision of a comfortable environment. The actual plant and heating system is not directly the responsibility of the housekeeper, but it is usually he/she who receives complaints about room temperature or non-functioning of radiators. Some knowledge of the heating system and appliances and how they function is useful because a minor problem can often be speedily rectified.

In large establishments where there is a maintenance staff which can be called upon immediately, there is no problem. However, in small establishments, often isolated, with no maintenance person and some distance from a heating engineer, the housekeeper needs to know how to sort out the minor problems.

The two basic types of heating are central heating and local heating. The type of heating used depends upon:

1. The average temperature acceptable in different areas and the type of occupants.
2. Times of occupancy.
3. Control of temperature.

Most public buildings are heated indirectly from a central source, with ancilliary local heating.

Room temperatures

The Offices, Shops and Factory Premises Act 1963 states 'The statutory minimum temperature is 15 °C or 60.8 °F after the first hour. People add heat and moisture to the atmosphere of the room so where a large number of people are expected, the temperature should be comfortable when they arrive, and the control can then reduce the temperature during the period of occupancy.

Hospitals and clinical establishments in which the elderly are living should be warmer than those occupied by younger people, and where the occupants are active. Thermostats in hotel bedrooms can be regulated by the occupants, or by a time clock which will give heat at required times.

Solid fuels (coal, coke and wood)

Coal and wood are used mainly for open fires and seldom for central heating boilers. Natural gas has superseded coke and former coke-burning boilers have been converted to burn natural gas or oil.

The advantages of solid fuel are

1. Available in some areas where natural gas is not laid on.
2. The installation costs are lower than for oil.
3. Fuel can be bought from independent suppliers.
4. It can be bought in quantities at advantageous prices.
5. In country areas where wood is readily available or where coal is indigenous these fuels can be used to advantage for supplementary heating in open fires.

The disadvantages are

1. Labour is required for stoking, removal of ash, and declinkering in large boilers – all of which are dirty jobs.
2. Solid fuel is slow to react to temperature control.
3. A flue or chimney is required and both need attention and regular sweeping.

4 Unless smokeless fuel is used (compulsory in many areas) there is air pollution.
5 Storage space is required and the fuel will deteriorate if exposed to the weather for a long time.
6 Boilers are bulky.
7 Deliveries of fuel can be affected by labour disputes.

A solid fuel boiler requires skilled attention. To the uninitiated it may look all right – glowing red – but the base of the boiler may be filled with clinker which produces no heat.

Electricity

This is the cleanest and the easiest to control source of heat, but it is the most expensive. It is eminently suitable for local heating but is expensive for central heating.

Electric boilers are not common and the most economical way of using them is at night at 'off peak' tariff rate. The water so heated is stored in well insulated hot water cylinders for use during the day. The water is stored under pressure to enable its temperature to be maintained in excess of boiling point. Before circulating round the building, it is mixed with the returning cooled water to bring it to a temperature suitable for re-circulation. Bulky thermal storage tanks are required, therefore, so it is not a very practical method of central heating.

The advantages of electricity are

1 It is clean and requires no attention.
2 No fuel storage space is required.
3 There is no air pollution nor chimney or flue required.
4 No fuel deliveries or refuse collection problems.
5 It is safe and silent in operation.
6 It does not require air for combustion, so high draught proofing standards can be maintained.

Its disadvantages are

1 The high price.
2 The consumer is at the mercy of a monopoly supplier.

3 Inflexibility when a boost is required during peak hours.
4 The possibility of power cuts.

Oil

Oil is widely used for central heating, but it should not be used for local heating, because oil stoves or heaters present a serious safety hazard. There are many safety regulations to be followed if oil is used as a fuel.

1 The oil must be stored in a tank above or below ground level, but separate from the main building and protected by a brick or breeze block wall.
2 A fire extinguisher should be within range of the tank area.
3 There must be a thermostat in the flue or a photo-cell to shut off the supply of oil should the flame fail to ignite.
4 An automatic valve to shut off the supply of oil in the event of air pressure failure or in the event of water flow failure.

Regular inspection and maintenance should be carried out by maintenance staff or a contract service. The storage tanks must also conform to certain safety regulations.

The advantages of oil are

1 It is efficient, converting up to 75 per cent of fuel into useful heat.
2 Apart from regular servicing, it requires little attention.
3 Responds quickly to control.
4 Wide choice of boilers.
5 Fuel available from competitive sources.
6 Several weeks' supply can be stored.

Its disadvantages are

1 Noise levels in some boilers are higher than those from gas or solid fuel boilers.
2 High installation costs.
3 Outside storage space required.
4 A flue is needed.
5 Fuel prices are subject to fluctuation caused by external forces.
6 Stringent safety regulations to be followed.

Gas

Gas is a versatile fuel which can be used for cooking stoves, large central heating boilers, and local heating for which there is a great variety of fires and radiators. It must be borne in mind that many gas-fired boilers are dependent upon an electrical charge for ignition, for the operation of a pump which circulates the hot water or air, and for the forced draught required to take away the toxic fumes through the flues. So a failure in the electricity supply can affect the gas-fired central heating.

Moisture is produced with the combustion of gas, so flues should be lined with a non-corrosive material. Damp patches on internal walls can sometimes be traced to a faulty flue.

The advantages of gas are

1 Once it has been installed it is extremely versatile.
2 Needs little attention apart from regular servicing.
3 Automatic ignition.
4 Quick response to controls.
5 Moderate installation costs.
6 No fuel storage space required.
7 No waste removal required.
8 No labour costs for stoking.
9 The gas boiler is relatively quiet and clean.

The disadvantages are

1 Regular servicing is essential.
2 Gas is not available in all areas and the cost of bringing in a supply from a distance to an establishment is very high.
3 The price of the fuel is determined by a monopoly supplier.
4 A flue is required for all boilers and independent fires for local heating fires.
5 Correct ventilation is required for all gas installations, for example, air bricks or ventilators in rooms where gas fires are in use.

Butane gas

This may be used in areas where natural gas is not available. Because of the size of the bulk storage tanks it is not practical for central heating boilers of large buildings. On the other hand it is useful for a secondary source of heating in portable fires, and for cooking stoves. It cannot be used in appliances normally used for natural gas.

The advantages of butane gas are

1 It is readily available in most areas, and in cylinders of various sizes to tanks.
2 It responds readily to control.
3 It is clean and has the same advantages of natural gas, except that portable stoves carry their own source and do not need piping.

The disadvantages are

1 It is more expensive than natural gas.
2 The size of the bulk storage tanks.
3 It requires special burner jets.

Heat pumps

Heat pumps are in the process of being further developed and accepted. They are based on the principle that energy (heat) is used or released on the change of state from solid to liquid and from liquid to gas. A quantity of heat is used when ice changes into water, and water into steam. On the reverse change of state heat is released, which can be used. Heat pumps are possible because the output energy available for heating is greater than the input. In other words, the energy required to drive the heat pump is less than the energy produced by the change of state of the water. A heat pump is best used as an auxiliary form of heating as it is capable of providing full requirement during the spring and autumn only. The hot water output of a heat pump is typically 45–55 °C, whereas that of the domestic boiler is usually 65–75 °C. Where a heat pump replaces a traditional boiler, the lower temperature will mean reduced heat output, at full load, from the existing radiators. However, in some cases this may not be a serious problem if radiators are not being run at their full capacity.

In new, well insulated buildings low temperature emitters may be adequate, and heat pumps are particularly suited to underfloor heating systems because of the large effective surface areas. The noise made by evaporator fans and other outdoor components in even the quietest of machines can be disturbing, and acoustic fans may be required to reduce the noise entering open windows.

Solar heating

The sun, which is the source of all heat and energy, can supply direct heat to a building, and to the interior, via the windows. Developments have been made whereby he: from the sun (solar heat) is directed to heat water in solar plates and thence to a hot water system, or central heating system. In Britain, it is at present only practicable to supplement other conventional types of heating. When considering the installation of a solar heating system, a solar heating consultant should be called in to assess which of the many systems is best suited to the particular needs of the establishment.

Heat recovery units

These, as the name implies, recover heat which would otherwise be wasted. Where there is refrigeration plant, boiler houses or kitchens, the heat generated can be utilized to supplement heating from other sources. This recovered heat can seldom replace existing systems, although in some cases, heat recovered from large refrigeration plant is used to heat warehouses. Such units should be placed in a front protected area, preferably where heat is being wasted in a boiler house or outside a refrigeration room. They cause no pollution and require little attention.

A potential disadvantage of any fuel is disruption in supplies caused by strike action or breakdown, from which no supply is immune. Therefore it is advisable to have two sources of supply, and some local heating from an independent source. It is unlikely that more than one source will be cut off at one time, and emergency heating, light and cooking can be provided for on a limited scale to provide the services required.

Large establishments such as hospitals have their own emergency power generators to supply essential equipment.

Central heating

When considering the choice of a central heating system the following factors should be considered

1 Availability of fuel.
2 Current cost of fuel.
3 Installation costs.
4 Maintenance costs.
5 Labour costs for running the system.
6 Cleanliness.
7 Smoke emission.
8 Replacements and specialized inspection and servicing.
9 Likelihood of breakdown, electricity failure, and speed of repair service.
10 Noise.
11 Storage space.
12 Suitability to the use of the building (for example, steam central heating produces pipes too hot to touch, so they are not suitable for use where there are the elderly or very young).

Hot water

There are two types of hot water central heating

1 *Gravity circulation* is the simplest method. The water is heated by the boiler and circulates to radiators by its own convection currents and possibly with the aid of an electric pump. This is a fairly antiquated system which has been superseded by the small bore system. The heat loss from gravity circulation is anything from 18–24°C.
2 *Small bore*. The hot water is assisted round the system by an electric pump, through pipes 85–110 mm in diameter. The heat loss from the smaller pipes is greatly reduced, and the volume of water heated is less.

In both systems air locks occur because the hot water contracts on cooling leaving pockets of air which will prevent the flow of water. This usually happens when the heating has been turned off for some time, or when the feed tank has run dry. The disadvantage of circulating hot water is the corrosion of pipes, radiators, and valves, causing leakage.

High pressure steam

Steam under pressure passes through the pipes. It is too hot for ordinary radiators, but suitable for unit heaters and fan convectors where air is drawn in to pass over the heated coils or pipes, and then passed into the room. The system is noisy.

Hot air

Air is heated at a central point and distributed by ducts through the building. The air passes over coils or tubes and is forced by a fan through ducts throughout the building. The cooled air is returned by ducts back to the central heating point. Filters are required to prevent dust particles entering the room. It is quick acting and there are no radiators or appliances visible. The ducting is unobtrusive and frequently incorporated in the decorative scheme, for example in skirting board grills. If the outlets are on the floor, carpets must not cover the duct openings, and they should be kept free of dust.

Air conditioning

As the name implies, this keeps the air at an acceptable standard of heat, humidity and cleanliness. To be fully efficient there should be no other means of ventilation and the windows should be double glazed (see section on ventilation below). From the housekeeper's point of view, it should present few problems so long as vents and outlets are kept clean and the windows shut.

Heating appliances

Booster hot air convectors   The air is sucked into an appliance, often inset in a wall, and then passes over hot water pipes before being forced back into the room. This is noisy but quickly effective.

Radiators   These, together with hot water pipes (unless the latter are lagged) radiate heat into the area in which they are exposed. The siting of radiators is very important. If placed under the window their effectiveness is partially reduced when full length curtains are drawn. The theory behind placing them under windows is that the cold air from the window will be warmed, but with double glazing this is not really valid. Large pieces of upholstered furniture placed in front of a radiator will reduce its effectiveness. If there is an open fire, a radiator placed opposite it will produce a more even distribution of heat.

Since radiators are not things of beauty they are sometimes camouflaged by being encased in a wood with a metal grill in front. Access should be made for cleaning. All radiators so encased are less efficient.

The wall behind a radiator can be covered with a metallic finished insulating material which will reduce the loss of heat through the wall, and reflect it into the room. Some radiators are fitted with thermostatic controls which enable the occupants of the room to control the heat.

Radiators can make the arrangement of furniture very difficult and in some cases it is more practical to have a long length of low radiators instead of several tall double banked radiators. The heating engineer should be able to assess the area of the radiator required in a room.

Radiator shelves   These direct the rising hot air into the room, and prevent soiling of the walls by the up-current of hot air carrying dust particles. The shelf should be close fitting to the wall and a foam strip along the back of the shelf will ensure a snug fit, especially if the wall is slightly uneven. Some radiators have the control knob and/or the bleeding valve placed on the top of the radiator, so a detachable shelf will make for easier access. Wooden shelves should be of well seasoned hard wood which will not warp. Veneered chip board or metal shelves with a simulated wood finish or plain surface (which can be painted to match the décor) can be purchased to fit standard size radiators.

Maintenance of radiators

Central heating systems should be inspected regularly for leaks at the joints connecting the pipes to the radiators. The hand should be run round the joints and vent nipples. Even a small leak will cause corrosion on the surface.

The signs of corrosion that should be looked for are

1   Radiators only heating in parts or not at all.

2 Black water drawn from the air vent or drain cock.
3 Radiators needing frequent venting and hydrogen being drawn off.
4 The pump becoming clogged.
5 Radiators leaking.

Corrosion is caused by any of the following

1 *Black oxide* sludge caused by electrolytic corrosion. It is heavier than water and falls to the bottom of the radiator. Because of its iron content, it can be brought to the outlet by applying a magnet to the base of the radiator.
2 *Hydrogen* build up is caused by corrosion processes where the water is broken into its component gases. The oxygen is used for the formation of metal oxides and the free hydrogen liberated. Presence of hydrogen in the system can be detected by ignition at the outlet.
3 *Bacteria* of the sulphur reducing type exists in some heating installations and produces hydrogen sulphide which is also ignitible and has the characteristic odour of bad eggs.
4 *Dezincification of brass.* Brass is a zinc–copper alloy. If the zinc is dissolved, the brass becomes porous and leakage occurs at joints.
5 *Electrolytic corrosion.* Dissimilar metals in intimate contact with each other and water, form a 'short circuited electrolytic cell'. So in a system where two metals such as copper and iron are connected in water, an electrolytic situation can result. This corrosion is accelerated in hot water.

Hard water is less corrosive than soft water but has the disadvantage of depositing scale inside the system which reduces its efficiency. Boilers should be descaled regularly. Scale build-up on the inside of pipes and radiators reduces the flow of water round the system and acts as an insulation, reducing the radiation of heat into the building.

It is possible to prevent corrosion by the use of a non-rusting metal such as stainless steel which is very expensive. The addition to systems of commercial chemical compounds will give protection against corrosion and scaling.

Air locks prevent the passage of hot water to radiators, and frequently occur after the central heating has been turned off. As hot water cools, it contracts and air collects in pockets. To release the air, the radiators must be 'bled' using a special key to open the valve nipple found at the top of the radiator. When the valve is opened the air will be released, and it should be kept open until water begins to flow. It is advisable to have a thick cloth underneath to collect any overflow. To completely free the system it is necessary to start at the radiator nearest to the boiler and work round the system. Bathroom hot water towel rails are also subject to air locks. The key is a very essential small piece of equipment and should be kept on a key ring, as it is very easily mislaid.

Other central heating components

Skirting heaters These consist of a metal 'skirting board' with hot water pipes passing along the back. The rear of the fitting should be insulated so that all the heat is directed into the room.

Radiant panel heaters In principle these are the same as skirting heaters. Panels are attached to the ceiling or walls as required. They are unobtrusive and the heat can be evenly distributed through the area.

Embedded panels A gridwork of pipes is embedded in concrete to produce underfloor heating. They can also be used in the ceiling or wall facing. They produce even heat, but are not suitable for rooms that are not in continual use since they are slow to heat up, and ceiling heating can be comfortable. They are very clean and safe.

Frenger heating Perforated aluminium plates are attached to the underside of a series of hot water or steam pipes, to produce a suspended ceiling. The pipes should be insulated on the upper side. The aluminium panels produce good acoustic effects suitable for large reception and meeting rooms and entertainment halls.

Local heating
Few establishments rely solely on local heating, but it is frequently used to supplement central

heating, to create a cosy atmosphere and to give a focal point in a room.

Meters for individual gas and electric local heating units are used in some establishments where users pay for the supplementary heating. Some are coin operated and can be connected to the wall or incorporated in the heating appliance. They can be damaged by individuals attempting to by-pass the meter, or breaking into them. Their disadvantages are that foreign coins or metal discs can be used instead of legal currency; and changes in tarrifs require alteration to the setting of the number of hours per coin.

Electric fires
These do not require a flue, and can be wall mounted or portable. They should be fitted with a 13 amp fuse.

The most common type of electric fire is a *single or multiple coil* (element) of high resistance wire, through which the current flows, producing heat. The element is usually backed by a highly polished metal reflector and has a safety grill in front. In some older models the elements are recessed in fireclay radiants.

Portable fires should be used with caution, since the extended flex can be tripped over, and they can be placed too near to curtains and furniture. Care should be taken to see they are not used indiscriminately by residents in homes and hostels. Wherever possible portable fires should be placed in a fireplace or hearth and protected with a fire guard. Period-style electric fires mounted in traditional fire baskets usually have one or two radiants and simulated wood or coal, illuminated with a red electric light bulb which sets in motion a small fan which creates a flickering fire effect. This can be used independently of the heating elements and does not give off any heat. These are safer than other fires since they are placed in recessed fire places.

Wall mounted fires should be protected so that furniture cannot be pushed against them, or people touch them accidentally.

Another type has an electric element encased in a *quartz tube* backed by a polished metal reflector, or incorporated in a light luminaire.

These heaters are usually wall mounted above head height and since the element is encased they are suitable for use in bathrooms and where there is high humidity.

Electric convector heaters have an element at the base of a metal container, which heats the air, which is then admitted into the room through grilles at the top. The air flow can be accelerated by a small fan.

Electric radiators are similar to central heating radiators in appearance, but they are mobile. They are oil filled and heated by an immersion heater. They are safe, and can incorporate a towel rail for use in bathrooms.

Electric tubular heaters used as skirting board heaters are similar to electric radiators.

Electric felt underlays are similar to an electric blanket. They are not suitable where there is heavy traffic and do not give much room heat.

Electric wallpaper has electric elements incorporated in the wallpaper. It gives the effect of embossed wall panels. The capital cost and durability of the wallpaper should be considered, as it may not be financially viable.

Night storage heaters The element is enclosed in heavy fire clay and encased in a metal box. The fireclay blocks are heated during off-peak, low tariff periods and the heat emitted during the day. They are extremely heavy and bulky so there should be adequate space to accommodate them, and the floor must be strong enough to take their weight. They lose their heat during the day, and if required they can be fitted with an override switch which will give a boost during very cold conditions or when they have cooled off. In some types the heat emitted can be controlled by a thermostat activating the opening and closing of louvres. Separate wiring to an 'off peak' meter is required so installation costs must be considered.

Hot air curtains are usually placed over entrances of shops, offices, and hotels. Air is heated either electrically or by hot water pipes from the central heating system. Fans direct a flow of hot air downwards. They give a warm welcome, eliminate draughts, and assist other heating systems.

Gas fires and radiators
Gas heating appliances are connected to a gas supply pipe. Radiant gas fires should be fitted in a chimney breast with the flue open for the exit of fumes. The gas jets heat fine clay radiants from which the heat is thrown into the room. The whole of the radiant face must be protected with a fixed guard, and where there are children or elderly people, a fire guard is also advisable. There is usually an automatic lighter which is generated by a battery cell and a thermostat control. Broken radiants should be replaced and the jets kept free of dust or debris. The controls are most convenient when placed on the top of the unit, especially for the elderly.

Radiant convector gas fires are similar to radiant fires, but they have an air passage at the back, sides and outlets for the warm air at the top of the appliance.

Simulated wood/coal gas fires   The gas flame can heat synthetic 'coal' or 'logs', from which heat is radiated. In addition there are free jets giving a white flame which is so realistic that frequently rubbish is thrown into the 'fire'. This flame is not the most efficient use of gas but the atmosphere effect is good. It is suitable for use in lounges and bars for effect and some suplementary heating.

Gas radiators are independent of central heating. The water in the radiator is heated by gas jets at the base.

Bottle gas heaters
A bottle of butane gas is connected to radiants similar to those of a gas fire, the whole encased in a metal box on castors with the elements exposed. The whole appliance is mobile and it can be placed in a fireplace. This fuel produces moisture.

Oil heaters
These are seldom used in establishments because of the fire hazard. They are highly dangerous. Attention should be paid to see that they are not brought into establishments such as student hostels or old people's homes.

Open fires
As well as being a decorative feature, open fires augment the background heat provided by a central heating system. An open fireplace is necessary and this requires ventilation, a clean chimney and a draught.

Its advantages are

1   The appearance is good.
2   In some areas the fuel is readily available (wood and/or coal, sometimes peat).
3   Aids ventilation and circulation of air.
4   Heats a specific area.

The disadvantages are

1   Needs attention.
2   Fuel storage space is required.
3   Can be a source of danger.
4   Smoke pollution.

Care of open fireplaces
Chimneys should be swept before being used if they have been unused for a while, as there may be an accumulation of soot, leaves, twigs or birds' nests. They should be swept at least once a year or twice a year for wood burning fires. They should be swept in the spring, when fires are no longer required.

If a chimney catches fire the fire brigade should be called. The fire in the grate should be extinguished immediately by using a powder type extinguisher or sand or soil. Keep doors and windows shut to reduce the draught.

The grate should be emptied so that an accumulation of ash does not impede the draught. Superfluous wood ash can be used on the garden. Some grates are fitted with a sunken ash pan into which the ash falls so that the grate need only be emptied periodically. This type of grate has an air inlet under the floor from the outside of the building and the air inflow is controlled by a lever on the hearth.

Never empty the ash into a plastic bucket or dustbin, use a metal one and place it on the hearth, as the hot ash can heat the bucket sufficiently to burn the carpet. Hot ash should never be carried on a shovel through the building to the dustbin, or emptied into a bin containing combustible material.

Open fires should never be left without a fire

guard. Open fires may be unsuccessful because of a cold chimney, an unswept chimney, or inadequate draught. An adequate draught may be achieved by raising the grate on bricks.

To light a fire, crumpled newspaper should be placed in the grate. On top of the paper put kindling wood then the cinders left from the previous fire then small pieces of coal. The paper should then be ignited or a gas poker used.

Scandinavian slow-burning wood stoves do not necessarily need a chimney, but must have a flue pipe leading to the outside. They can be situated in the centre of a room providing they are well guarded, and the flue has been professionally installed, according to the required fire regulations. They are very eficient and there is little ash residue to be removed.

Heat conservation

With ever increasing costs of energy, it is important to conserve fuel. Heat is measured in joules. 1 J is the amount of heat required to raise 1 kg of water through 1 °C.

1 watt = 1 joule per second

Heat loss from building materials is indicated by U values. The U value of a material is the rate of thermal transmittance based on the watts that escape through 1 square metre per hour for each degree centigrade difference between the inside and outside temperatures. The lower the U value, the better the insulation. This is transferred in three ways.

1 *Conduction* is the transmission of heat from particle to particle of a substance by contact. Good conductors of heat (materials through which heat passes easily) include metals, water and moisture-filled air. Good conductors are bad insulators. Bad conductors include still air, a vacuum, plastics, wool, mineral wool, paper, granules of vermiculate, fabrics, glass wool, wood and wood chippings.
2 *Convection* currents of hot air or water will carry heat from one place to another. When air and water are heated they expand, become lighter and rise, producing convection currents. They can be directed in some cases by baffles or shelves over radiators.
3 *Radiation* is the action of sending out or reflecting heat in all directions by a surrounding medium. Materials which reflect heat include highly polished metalized surfaces such as reflector panels behind electric elements and aluminium panels, placed behind radiators.

Heat is conserved by

1 Elimination of heat loss from the building.
2 Prevention of cold air entering the building.
3 Eliminating heat loss from surfaces inside the building where it will be wasted.
4 Efficient maintenance of heating appliances.

Roofs

Since hot air rises, the roof is the most vulnerable area from which heat can be lost. It can be insulated by covering the underside of the tiles or slates of the roof with roofing felt or hard board. The area between the rafters can be covered with vermiculite granules, mineral wool pellets, or sheet mineral wool. None of these materials should be pressed down since it is the trapped air which increases their insulating properties. These materials are rot and mouse-proof, do not hold moisture and are non-combustible. Because heat is being prevented from entering the loft area, water tanks and pipes therein should be insulated against frost.

Ceilings

These can be insulated with expanded polystyrene tiles but these are a fire hazard and should only be painted with a fire resistant paint. A gloss paint acts as a solvent of the polystyrene. Ceilings can also be insulated by a stretched textile material.

Floors

Heat loss from floors can be reduced by

1 Having closely fitting floorboards.
2 Covering badly fitting floorboards with hardboard, linoleum, vinyl floor covering, or cushion backed vinyl.

3 Carpet with its own secondary backing or underlay.
4 If matting is used, the floor beneath can be covered with newspaper or the felt paper used as an underlay for linoleum.

Walls

Heat loss from cavity walls can be reduced by filling the cavity with a bad conductor of heat. Air trapped in the insulator increases its efficiency.

Ureaformaldehyde plastic foam can be injected into the cavity walls and the holes sealed to match the external finish of the wall surface. Air bubbles are trapped in the foam which sets after injection and produces insulation against heat loss.

Polystyrene beads are pumped into the cavity and are suitable only for cavity walls in good condition. Since the beads are light and move with ease, they can escape through cracks and holes in the wall as the cavity is being filled. A development of this method is where the beads are bonded with a special adhesive as they enter the cavity and so bind into a self-supporting block which will be stable and will not shrink.

Mineral wool is blown into the cavity in the same way as the other materials. It has the advantage of remaining stable, there are no smells and it will not shrink.

Note Filling cavity walls is technically a breach of the Building Regulations and application for relaxation to do this should be made to the local authority. Special care should be taken to see that flues and ventilators do not get blocked during the installation of cavity fill.

In very old buildings, the walls are very thick and solid, constructed of bad conductors of heat (mud and twigs, hair etc.) and faced with plaster. In many cases they are panelled on the interior, or hung with tapestries. Solid walls can be covered on the exterior with rigid expanded polystyrene panels which are then coated with several layers of rendering, and finished with a decorative coat.

The interior of a solid wall can have applied a 9.5 mm sheet of plasterboard with a thicker polystyrene foam backing. This can be glued or nailed to the wall or fixed on battens if the surface of the wall is uneven. The joins are sealed with tape and the surface finished off by paint or paper. Interior walls especially in bathrooms, can be covered with a polystyrene insulating layer used behind wallpaper.

Pipes

Pipes carrying hot water from the hot water storage tank should be lagged to prevent heat loss into areas where it will be wasted. Pipes can be lagged with plastic, nitrile rubber or mineral wool insulating sleeves which are made to fit pipes of various thicknesses. They are slit and slipped over the pipe and clipped into place. Plastic pipes conduct heat less than metal pipes.

Doors and windows

Draughts from badly fitting doors and windows can be very largely reduced by applying draught excluder. Copper strip, plastic foam with a self-adhesive backing, toughened rubber with canvas, or a tufted barrier which springs up after shutting the door can be used. Draughts from badly fitting window and door frames can be reduced by filling rebates with mastic or rubber seal of which there are many proprietory brands. Draught proofing kits can be purchased.

In large buildings doors may be frequently used. The subsequent heat loss can be reduced by

1 Two sets of doors, electronically controlled, whereby the first doors are closed automatically before the second doors will open.
2 By having a heat screen – hot air forced down immediately behind the door.
3 By large pliable plastic doors which push open as one enters and then fall behind. They are a cross between doors and curtains.
4 Revolving doors prevent the direct entry of cold air and draughts. They allow only a segment of cold air to enter with each entrant and they are provided with draught excluder material to prevent draughts when they are not being used.

Windows

Double glazing is the obvious way to prevent heat

loss from windows, by preventing the entry of draughts round the frames and by having a sandwich of air or a vacuum between two layers of glass. The original window frames should be well fitting to eliminate the movement of air, and condensation between the two layers of glass. The space between the two sheets of glass should be not less than 12 mm and in some intensely cold climates the space can be up to 15 cm. Triple glazing affords even greater insulation and is usual in the cold climates of Scandinavia, USA and Canada. Double glazing is also an insulation against noise transference, but for complete sound proofing the space should be 15 cm.

Sealed double-glazing units consist of two separate sheets of glass hermetically sealed at the factory with space filled with clean dry air. They are used to replace the glass in existing window frames.

Coupled frames are two frames each with glass, joined together with hinges at one side so they can be separated for cleaning.

Double sash two sheets of glass in separate sashes, sliding either vertically or horizontally.

Secondary sashes are inner frames which fit over existing windows. The frames may be of aluminium or plastic and can be hinged, sliding or fixed. Some are held firmly closed with plastic clips which do perish in time. They may have to be taken down and stored in the summer.

A cheap improvization is to stick thick plastic sheeting or perspex all round the window frame.

When considering double glazing the following points must be borne in mind

1   Initial capital outlay and reduction of heating costs. This is not always as beneficial as might be expected – a 40 per cent reduction in heat loss may not result in a 40 per cent reduction in heating costs.
2   The size of the windows. Some types are not practical for large windows or where the windows are a series of smaller frames.
3   The ease with which outside and the inside windows can be reached for cleaning.
4   In old buildings with deeply recessed windows, it may be more practical to have the whole window area sealed with glass fixed in a frame.

Ventilation heat loss

Condensation can cause deterioration of wood and will eventually seep into the wall. Double glazing reduces condensation but does not always eliminate it.

Condensation is caused by the difference of temperature between the atmosphere on the exterior and internal surfaces, and the humidity of the air inside. Warm moist air inside the building condenses on the cold glass or metal frames connecting to the cold exterior of the building.

Ventilation is essential to prevent condensation, but care should be taken that it does not result in draughts.

Curtains can reduce draughts and prevent heat loss by conduction. The thickness of the curtain material relates to the insulation properties. Lined curtains and especially those incorporating an interlining of a fleecy material will insulate best. A material with a metallic finish known as milium, can be used to line curtains with the metalic surface placed towards the interior of the room. It will reflect heat back into the room.

Time clock switches

These are used to control the switching on and off of lighting, heating, air conditioning, sewerage, refrigeration plant etc. They are controlled by electricity and therefore any power failure affects them and they require to be re-set. There are many types of time clocks, but they usually have a clock with 24 hour numerals, usually a dial. The clock is set with the correct hour opposite an arrow, and the dial revolves. Round the dial are knobs or levers of different colours or numbers. These are set at the hour at which the power is to be switched on and off. Figure 43 illustrates the operation of a simple clock switch.

Knob *A* is placed opposite the time on the dial at which the motor is required to be switched on.
Knob *B* is set to the time at which the motor is required to stop.
Knob *C* is set at the time the motor is next required to start again.

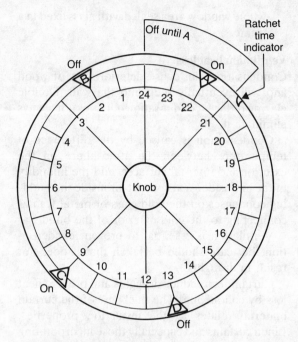

Figure 43 *From this setting, heat will be switched on at 2200 hours, off at 0200 hours, on at 0900 hours and off at 1230 hours*

Knob *D* at the time at which it is required to be switched off and so on.

At the side of the time clock there is a switch with three positions, *on*, *off*, and *override*. When it is *on*, the clock dial passes knob *A* and triggers off a switch which starts the operation. When it passes *B* another ratchet switches off the motor. Time clocks should be protected by an outer casing to avoid unauthorized alterations.

Ventilation

Ventilation is so frequently neglected that students in lecture rooms and delegates in conference rooms fall asleep, not because of the lecturer or his subject, but because of the physical conditions of the room. Restaurants and bars can become so polluted that the occupants are uncomfortable. Ventilation not only involves fresh air from the outside entering the room, but also stale air being taken away, reconditioned and recirculated.

Fresh air entering by windows has certain disadvantages:

1 It may be polluted by dust and noxious fumes from traffic or factory chimneys.
2 It can waste the energy taken to heat the room.
3 It allows external noises to enter the room which is as disturbing as the lack of fresh air.
4 Fresh air entering by a window can cause uncomfortable draughts.

Air can be changed by a number of methods

1 Sucking out the stale air and allowing a fresh source of air from another area of the building. The simplest form is an extractor fan in a window drawing out the warm stale air above head height or conversely sucking cool air from the outside.
2 Air inlets, air bricks or grilles fixed in the outside wall.
3 Stale air being drawn into ducts by means of fans and directed to the outside of the building.
4 Air conditioning, which either draws the air out of the room and replaces it with air from a fresh air inlet to the air conditioning plant which brings it to the controlled temperature and humidity; or draws the air out of the room along ducts to the reconditioning plant where it is cooled, dehumidified, cleaned, mixed with fresh air from an inlet and recirculated through ducts.

Fans

The desirable number of air changes per hour is given in Table 16. Although air change is very important, there are no statutory regulations controlling the rate, so the figures shown in Table 16 are only recommended. The cubic capacity of the room is found by multiplying the length, breadth and height of the room. If the cubic capacity is then multiplied by the recommended ACH, the total will indicate the capacity of the fan or fans required.

Fans should be placed above head height, in a window or wall furthest away from the air in-flow (door). If the exterior wall or window is in line with a prevailing wind, then the outlet should be in the ceiling and expelled from the roof. If there is a fuel burning appliance in the room, it should be ascertained that there is an adequate air in-flow. Fans can be installed in a hermetically sealed double glazing system if a special sealed unit is obtained from the double glazing manufacturer. The electricity supply to fans should be isolated from the lighting circuit and separately fused.

Fan extraction units should not be sited in positions where they might be exposed to water/liquid spray, nor subjected to temperatures in excess of 40°C. Fans and switches must not be situated where they can be touched by a person in a bath or shower. Only pull cord switches should by placed in bathrooms.

Types of fans available

1   *Punkah fans*   Large three-bladed horizontal fans suspended from the ceiling.

Table 16   *Air changes per hour (ACH)*

Situation	Changes
Assembly Hall	4–6
Bakeries	20–30
Banks	2–4
Banquet halls	6–10
Bathrooms	15–20
Billiards rooms	6–8
Boiler rooms	20–30
Cafés and coffee bars	10–12
Canteens	4–6
Club rooms	8–10
Factories	6–10
Hospital (general wards)	4–6
Hotel bars	6–10
Kitchens (commercial or school)	15–20
Kitchens (domestic)	10–15
Laboratories	4–6
Toilets	10–15
Living rooms	4–6
Offices	6–8
Photographic and X-ray dark rooms	10–15
Restaurants	6–10
School classrooms	2–3

Note   The higher figures should be used for smokey conditions.

2   Four blade *propeller fans* which stand on a desk or table or mounted on a wall bracket.
3   *Extractor* or *inlet* fans inserted in windows, operated electrically, which draw air in and out of the window.

Fan blades should be cleaned and the joints kept greased. The oil levels of the motor should be checked and kept to the correct level.

Air purifiers or filters
These should not be confused with air conditioning units. They free the air of dust, smoke and odours. Air is drawn into the machine, passes through a filter and then through an electrostatic plate. Odours are removed by a third filter of activated carbon, and the clean air is forced back into the room. The size of the unit depends upon the size of the area. Small ones are suitable for freshening a small waiting room similar to a sitting room in a house. A simple hood type can be serviced by the housekeeping staff, (for example, the type that may be found over the cooker). The glass fibre filter can be washed and the tray in which the charcoal granules is held between two wire mesh sheets can be refreshed by washing and drying off in an oven. The disadvantage of some types is that they are very noisy.

Humidifiers
These supply the atmosphere with moisture to replenish the drying effect of the heating. The simplest type is one that is hung over a radiator. It is a plastic socket in which there is a piece of material that holds moisture. This is kept wet and with the heat from the radiator the water evaporates into the air.

Air conditioning units
The units will operate in a room, are either wall mounted or portable, and are plugged into a 13 amp socket. They are useful in certain areas because they are cheaper than installing a complete system. They tend to be noisy and should be used with discretion, but are suitable for freshening a meeting or conference room after each session. They must be cleaned and maintained. There are suitable cleaners on the market,

capable of dissolving different types of pollutant from different environments.

Note   It must be remembered that air filters or air purifiers only clean the air, but do not replace the used oxygen as does an air conditioning system.

Damp

The housekeeper should always be on the look-out for signs of damp. If damp is left uncorrected, it will soon spread throughout a building and cause structural damage. For example, moisture entering a cracked window sill can flow down a wall, along floor joists and into a ceiling below. Eventually, the weight of the moisture will make the ceiling collapse suddenly. The signs of damp that should be looked for are

1   A damp room has a distinctive musty and slightly sour smell.
2   Excessive chill in a room can indicate the presence of damp. Moisture is a good conductor of heat, and damp floors and walls will conduct the heat away from the room. Moisture can be felt on walls, carpets and curtains.
3   Peeling and discoloured wall paper.
4   Crumbling plaster.
5   A cream-coloured encrustation on the brick or plaster surface.
6   Soft rotting wood, peeling paint or emulsion.
7   Lifting of linoleum or vinyl tiles.
8   Mould on any surface.
9   Moss or green discoloration of external brick work, and plaster, and obvious wet patches.

Possible sources of damp are

1   Rain penetrating defective structure or materials – leaking down pipes or gullies.
2   Faults in the flashing and flaunching round chimney stacks, parapets, windows etc.
3   Cracked window sills, badly fitting and rotten window frames.
4   Missing or broken roof tiles or slates, cracked asphalted flat roofs.
5   Blocked guttering and downpipes.

6   Bridged cavity walls.
7   Defective parapet or top of wall coving.
8   Defective barge-boarding.
9   Defective or absent damp course.
10   Damp course below ground level.
11   Old and defective mortar.
12   Leaking waste pipes and connections.
13   Bad ventilation preventing air circulation, causing condensation.
14   Creeper-clad walls where the bricks have become porous.
15   Use of paraffin oil heaters without adequate ventilation.
16   Hygroscopic salts in the building materials absorbing moisture from the air.
17   Birds nesting in gullies or chimneys.
18   Unused chimneys with blocked up fireplaces.
19   Unlined chimneys or flues formerly used for open fires and now used for gas fires or appliances.

Rising damp
As the name implies, rising damp is moisture that has penetrated the walls and risen from the ground by capillary action, because of a lack of or a faulty damp course.

Damp course
This is a water-proof membrane placed along a layer of bricks (or other building material used in the walls). The damp course must be a minimum of 15–22 cm above ground level and may be one of the following.

1   A plastic membrane or bituminous felt.
2   A metal (zinc or lead) sheeting placed along a layer of bricks, the required height above ground level.
3   Slates (two courses) bedded in the brick work.
4   Chemical injection – a newer technique used where there is no damp course or where the existing one has failed. Silicone or aluminium stearate (both water repellant) is injected under high pressure or by gravity into the walls. These materials do not block the pores of the bricks. They allow the passage of water

vapour outwards, while preventing the rising of moisture. This method is not suitable for basements. It is a remedial method for an old building without a damp course, rather than for new buildings where fresh mortar with a high alkaline content has been used. Difficulties may be encountered if this method is used on stone or flint walls.

5 Electro-osmosis was a popular method technique up to about 1980, in cases where there has been no damp course or the existing one failed. The difference between an electric charge between the damp wall and the earth is short-circuited by looping a copper strip into holes drilled in the wall at the height where the damp course would normally be. This strip is connected to copper covered rods driven into the ground. This method is effective for walls of any thickness and of stone or brick, but is more expensive and less reliable than silicone injection.

A reputable damp-proofing specialist will offer a free survey and give a 30 year guarantee on the work. An insulation specialist can often give advice on condensation problems.

Correction of damp
All defects in the structure should be attended to immediately they are noticed. Any soil which has accumulated above the damp course should be removed. Gutters should be regularly cleared of leaves and debris and air bricks and ventilating grilles should be kept clear. A damp area should never be dried out by heat alone (and never with an oil heater). There should be free circulation of air, so that the moisture-laden air can escape. Plaster containing hygroscopic should be replaced.

Any dripping overflow pipes on the exterior of the building indicate problems inside, and ball cocks in lavatory and water cisterns should be attended to. Dehumidifiers should be used in bathrooms or areas where the moisture content of the air is high, causing condensation. Increase the heat in areas where condensation occurs, so that there is not such a contrast in temperature.

Where flooding or spillages have taken place, the whole area should be completely dried out before carpets or floor coverings are replaced.

Bricks, which have become porous can be treated with two coats of silicone solution which will give them about ten years protection. Internally, the application of a special metal foil applied to a clean plastered surface, held in place with a waterproof adhesive will prevent damp penetrating to the surface. The protected wall can then be lined and redecorated. However, the source of the damp should be traced and dealt with. Where there is severe deterioration to a wall surface, the damaged wallpaper and plaster should be removed and the wall replastered, and treated with a water repellant primer. After it has dried out, a laminated water-proof material is applied, it is again left to dry out and then redecorated.

Furniture should be brought forward from damp walls, pictures removed and curtains dried off in the open air then cleaned. Gentle heat and ventilation will help to dry out a damp room, but heat *without* ventilation will only aggravate the condition.

Wet and dry rot
These two types of rot are forms of fungal decay owing to damp. They thrive on damp wood in conditions of poor ventilation, and can be detected by signs of warping or cracks in skirtings, windows and door frames. A penknife will sink easily into rotting wood.

Dry rot is the more pernicious of the two, as it will not confine itself to the original damp area, but spread to sound wood. The air-borne spores settle in damp wood (they require 20 per cent moisture content in the wood to germinate). Having exhausted the food supply in that area, the fungus leaves behind dry cuboidal cracked rotten wood (see Figure 44). In order to carry moisture to fresh wood it develops strands called rhizomorphs which carry moisture as the growth breaks down the cellulose in the wood. The strands penetrate wood brick and mortar, and under favourable conditions can spread at a rate of 3.6 metres a year. It can spread from cellar to

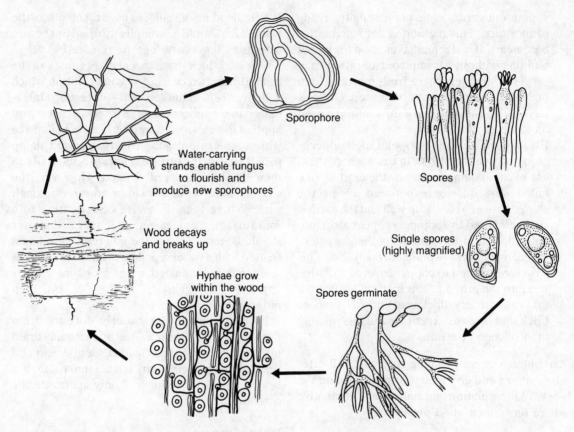

Sporophore

Water-carrying
strands enable fungus
to flourish and
produce new sporophores

Spores

Wood decays
and breaks up

Single spores
(highly magnified)

Hyphae grow
within the wood

Spores germinate

Figure 44 *Life cycle of dry rot fungus. Courtesy of Peter Bateman.*

attic. Advanced attacks of dry rot show matted whitish strands of fungus resembling cotton wool.

Wet rot is usually found in wet exterior joinery which has not been maintained, or where wood has not been allowed to dry out after being exposed to wetting. Door and window frames are most commonly affected, and floors under sinks where there may be leaks. Wet rot does not spread like dry rot, but if it is only partly dried out, the timbers may then be attacked by dry rot.

Prevention

Dry airy conditions are a deterrent to the growth of fungi. Under-floor areas should be well ventilated with ventilating bricks or grilles. Damp courses must be in good condition to prevent rising damp. Any leaks should be repaired as soon as they are noticed.

After accidental flooding the floors and walls should be allowed to dry out completely. Carpets, linoleum, carpet tiles should be lifted to allow the floorboards to dry out.

Woodwork should be painted regularly or treated with a preservative (Cuprinol or Rentokil). New timber should be pre-treated by vacuum pressure impregnation.

Eradication

Wet rot can be eliminated by cutting out the affected wood and replacing it. Then the surrounding and replaced wood should be treated with a special dry rot fluid. Dry rot requires specialist attention. Not only does the affected timber need to be cut out and burned, but the bricks and mortar through which the water carrying strands may have passed also need to be removed and/or treated. Correct diagnosis is essential, and immediately it is suspected that there may be dry rot, specialist contractors should be brought in.

Further reading

Gladwell, D. C., *Practical Maintenance and Equipment for Hoteliers, Licencees and Caterers*. Volume 1, Engineering. (Barrie and Jenkins 1974).

Useful addresses

Agrément Board,
PO Box 195,
Bucknalls Lane,
Garston,
Watford WD2 7NG

British Gas,
326 High Holborn,
London WC1

Department of Energy,
Thames House South,
London SW1

Electricity Council,
30 Millbank,
London SW1

Heating and Information Service,
The Building Centre,
26 Store Street,
London WC1E 7BT

Heating and Ventilating Contractors Association,
Coastal Chambers,
172 Buckingham Palace Road,
London SW1W 9TD

National Cavity Insulation Association,
178–202 Great Portland Street,
London W1N 6AQ

Solid Fuel Advisory Service,
Freepost,
Sunderland SR9 6AQ

Solar Trade Association Limited,
26 Store Street,
London WC1E 7BT

18 *Lighting and sound*

Lighting

Lighting plays a very important part in the comfort and safety of the occupants of a building. Like colour, texture and pattern, lighting contributes to the décor of a room. However, besides aesthetic considerations, the housekeeper also has to think about the efficiency and safety of lighting.

Light is transferred by rays. *Direct* lighting is where the light is directed straight from the bulb into the room. *Semi-direct* is where some of the light is directed into the room and some allowed to be directed and reflected from the ceiling. *Indirect* is where all of the light is directed on to a ceiling or wall from which it is reflected back into the room. *Diffused* lighting is where the bulb or light source is completely enclosed and the light diffused through a translucent shade or material. Curtains, wall or ceiling panels can conceal the light source.

Glare

Light is obviously necessary for carrying out any task, but glare should be avoided. Glare is defined as dazzling brilliance which can obstruct vision. It can also produce eye damage, and should be avoided. It is caused by

1 Natural sunlight streaming in through a window.
2 Reflected light from mirrors, shiny surfaces, even white paper at a desk.
3 Direct light rays from a naked light bulb or a spot light.

Glare can be reduced or eliminated by the use of diffusers – baffles covering electric light bulbs or flourescent tubes – lamp shades, sheers or venetian blinds, or vertical louvred blinds at windows. The correct positioning of lights will ensure that the source of direct light is well above or below eye level, and not directed on to a reflective surface. The level of general lighting should be sufficient to prevent shadows being cast on a task area.

Daylight

Only about 10 per cent of normal daylight enters a room. In spite of this it is brighter than artificial light. Colours look different in daylight and in artificial light. Daylight varies in intensity and colour throughout the day. A northern aspect gives a colder and less variable light and it is better for studios and areas where colour matching is important. Most large buildings need additional artificial light, even during the hours of daylight.

The advantages of daylight are

1 It costs nothing except the cost of providing windows.
2 It is natural.
3 Because it varies according to the time of day and passing clouds, it is soothing and kinder to the human eye, and possibly causes less fatigue than a constant uniform artificial light.
4 The windows and the changing light add another dimension to the room and the view from them can be refreshing.

The disadvantages of daylight are

1 The variation in the strength of daylight can change the mood or atmosphere of the environment.

2 Brilliant sunshine fades some colours and rots some materials.

3 The heat from the sun's rays can cause discomfort.

4 Daylight varies with the aspect of the windows and furnishings should be selected accordingly. A series of rooms which are identical in shape and size, but with different aspects, should have different colour schemes.

5 Daylight does not uniformly illuminate a room.

6 Windows should be kept clean to get the maximum advantage from daylight. Net curtains and sheers should be kept clean.

7 Large windows can cause heat loss unless double glazed.

8 Windows with a southern, eastern or western aspect will probably require blinds to reduce the glare.

9 Supplementary lighting is required, since daylight is not constant. A light sensor can be fitted by which the artificial light can come on when the daylight has fallen below a certain level.

10 Large windows with a southern or western aspect can make a room unbearably hot in summer (although the converse is the case in winter) and in some cases air conditioning is necessary.

Filament bulbs

The most common type of filament bulb is a glass container, with a vacuum or filled with an inert gas. In this container is a highly resistant filament element through which an electric current passes, heating it sufficiently to make it incandescent. The filament coil may be 'single coil' or 'coiled coil'. The latter maintains a higher temperature and emits more light, but it is susceptible to damage from knocks or vibrations.

The advantages of these bulbs are

1 Easy to install.

2 They give an acceptable light with little colour distortion.

3 The amount of light required can be altered by simply changing the bulb for one of greater or less strength.

Their disadvantages are

1 They are not of uniform quality, so maker and supplier should be reputable.

2 The light does not mix comfortably with daylight.

3 Except for the decorative types, they are rather ugly and the direct light is unpleasant, so they must have shades which will diffuse the light, or reflect it on to a surface from which it will be redirected into the room.

The bulbs are connected to the light with a bayonet fitting or an Edison screw fitting. Figure 45 shows various types of filament bulb. They can have different glass for various effects.

1 Clear glass, through which the filament is easily seen, is suitable where sparkle is required with crystal or crystal type perspex shades.

2 Pearl is glass frosted on the inside to mask and diffuse the glare from the filament.

3 Opal is a heavier white internal silica coating which diffuses the light more than the pearl. The filament is invisible and the shadow minimized.

4 Reflector lamps are used for spot lights and flood lighting. The internal silvered surface reflects the light with greater intensity towards a definite area. Since the spread of

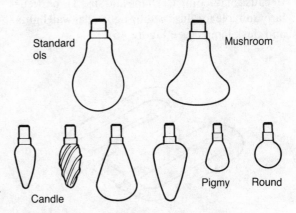

Figure 45 *Various types of filament bulbs*

light is less and the light rays restricted and directed towards one spot, greater heat is also directed.

5   Coloured bulbs can be used for decorative purposes, but seldom for general lighting as the loss of light and distortion of colour is considerable.

Tubular filament lamps

These work on the same principle as the filament bulb, except that the case is a tube about 2.25 cm in diameter along the length of which the filament runs. The tube can be of clear opal or frosted glass with a bayonet fitting at one end or with contact fittings at either end. They can be straight or curved, in lengths from 20 cm to 110 cm from 15 to 60 watts. They generate more heat than bulbs of the same wattage and the life is less than that of a fluorescent tube. Frequently used to illuminate bathroom mirrors.

The 2D Lamp

This operates on the discharge principle. It is not a filament lamp but can replace a 100 watt filament lamp.

It is a narrow U-shaped tube, length 134 mm width 134 mm and 27 mm in depth. The wattage is 21 and output 1050 lumens. The lamp unit incorporates an integral starter switch. The burning life of this lamp is 5000 hours so it is more economical on power consumption and in operational life than a comparable 100 watt bulb. Because of its compact shape and size it is particularly suitable for flush ceiling lights, flat wall lights and desk lamps (see Figure 46).

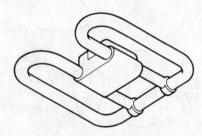

Figure 46   *Two-dimensional lamp*

Reflector filament lamps

Usually 100–150 watt, these have a silvered or aluminum inner reflector coating, used for spotlights and feature or decorative lighting. Since the light is confined and narrowly directed, and the wattage is high, a great deal of heat is generated.

Tungsten iodine lamps

These are used for exterior and floodlighting. They are also known as linear tungsten halogen.

Fluorescent tubes

Frequently referred to as strip lights, these are vapour filled with fluorescent powders. The light is produced by ultra violet radiations from an electrical discharge falling on the powders. Different powders produce different coloured light. They can cause distortion of the colours. This colour factor is known as colour temperature.

Fluorescent tubes produce a flickering light which is apparent to some people, especially the high wattage tubes. This flicker can be masked by external shields at the ends of the tubes where the flicker is most apparent, or they can be completely shielded by baffles or opalescent shields.

They can be placed behind pelmets at windows or in front of mirrors. The pelmet should extend in front and behind the tube, or the tube will be reflected in the glass or mirror. Baffles and shields attract dust and grease and should be cleaned regularly.

Fluorescent lighting will have a beneficial effect on plants. The tubes are much cheaper to use than filament bulbs and they have a much longer life. There are two types of fluorescent tubes: hot cathode tubes and cold cathode tubes.

Hot cathode tubes are the most commonly used, and from a light efficiency point of view are better than cold cathode tubes. They are slow to light up, and flicker before lighting fully. They are less expensive than the cold cathode tube.

Cold cathode tubes can be produced in a variety of shapes. They light up immediately without any flickering. They require a higher than normal voltage, and although they last longer, the initial expense is greater. They cannot be fitted with a

Table 17 *High efficiency fluorescent tubes*

	Colour temperature	Name	Effect
High efficiency tubes	3000	Warm white*	Blues appear violet, greens slightly yellow, yellows very bright, reds medium
	3500	White*	As above
	4300	Daylight*	Blues fairly bright, greens bright, yellows very bright, reds fairly dull
Better colour rendering fluorescent tubes	3000	Softone 32	Gives a warm appearance to the interior, and blends well with tungsten light
		Deluxe warm white*	As above
	3500	Plus white	Slightly subdues deep reds, but very efficient
	3500	Deluxe natural	Good on all colours but tends to emphasize reds
	4000	Natural*	Shows up decoration well, and blends quite well with daylight
	4000	Colour 84	Slightly subdues deep reds and yellows but is very efficient
	4200	Kolor-rite	Equal emphasis to all colours
		Trucolour 37	As above
	6500	Artificial daylight*	Used for critical colour matching to BS 950 Part 1
	6500	Colour matching northlight*	Colour matching only to reasonable accuracy, normally the interior 100 is too cool

* British Standard colours, others are trade names. The list is not exhaustive and manufacturers should be consulted for latest information.

dimmer control switch. The installation cost is greater because of the special fitting required.

Because of their longer life, they are suitable for inaccessible places, but they do get dirty, especially in kitchens where they become coated with dust and grease, so regular cleaning is required. Table 17 shows various types of fluorescent light.

Care of light bulbs

Bulbs should be dusted as a normal procedure. In large establishments it is usual for all light bulbs to be replaced at regular intervals irrespective of whether they have burned out or not. Bulbs deteriorate as they get old and when this is noticed, they should be changed.

A list of the lamps and the wattage of bulbs they require should be kept in the store room. The lamps themselves can be labelled unobtrusively showing the wattage of the bulbs they require. Casualties do occur, so there should be a few bulbs available in each department for emergency replacement.

All bulbs have a guaranteed life; any that do not attain their guaranteed life should be returned to the supplier to be replaced. The manufacturers are able to test the bulbs and ascertain how many hours burning they have had.

It is better to replace all the lamps in one area, noting the date, so that a check can be made on the burning life. This also saves odd lamps going out in succession. Moving a bulb from one lamp to another shortens the life, since the filament becomes brittle after some use and the movement causes the filament to break. Variation in the voltage from the mains can also shorten the life of bulbs.

Colour temperature

All artificial light has colour differing from daylight. The colour of different types of light influences the atmosphere and distorts colour.

Fluorescent tubes can be divided into two categories in relation to colour temperature:

1 *Warm white, white and daylight* These are highly efficient but produce colour distortion. They are suitable for factories and offices where colour distortion is not important. They are not suitable for guest areas, food preparation or service areas.
2 *De luxe* These are less efficient, but their colour distortion is less. The colour factor is indicated by a temperature number. The higher the colour value, the cooler the colour of the light. The warmer lamps give a light similar to that from a filament bulb.

The colour temperature of natural daylight is about 6500. Warm lighting with a temperature of 3000 or less is suitable for living areas, and cooler lighting with a temperature of 4300 is suitable for work areas and offices. A temperature of 4000 or more is suitable for critical colour matching and for commercial buildings. The colour temperature is shown on the details on the tube.

Because of the colour distortion and the adverse effect that the ultra violet rays can have upon paintings, picture lights should be filament tubes rather than fluorescent tubes.

Types of lighting

General lighting

The level of lighting is spread throughout an area and one may not be aware of its source. It is usually from above eye level, such as ceiling lighting, pendant fittings, cornice lighting or from wall panels. Whatever the source of light, the type of wall, floor and ceiling surfaces and colours affect the amount of effective illuminance. Dark colours and matt surfaces reflect less light than colours and glossy surfaces.

Concealed lights Filament bulbs or fluorescent tubes are concealed in the ceiling and diffused through opalescent panels, baffles or elaborate screens of glass, crystal or perspex, metal leaves or pendant pieces.

Pendant ceiling lights The bulb is suspended by flex from the ceiling, the bulb concealed to avoid glare and the light reflected on to the ceiling from which it is reflected into the room. Pendant lights can be adjustable, so they can be raised or lowered, and brought down over a desk or dining table.

Chandeliers These are suspended. There are usually several lower wattage bulbs and the light is reflected from the crystal drops, so there is no glare. Candelabra type chandeliers may have low wattage bulbs with small shades.

Spotlights Strategically placed in the room, they can be directed on to the ceiling and reflected into the room, or they can be recessed into the wall or ceiling. They can be uncomfortable for anyone sitting directly underneath them.

Task lighting

This provides illumination for reading, sewing, work, make-up and eating. It is provided by lights above working surfaces and mirrors, wall lights, desk and table lamps, standard and track lamps. Portable lamps should give a wide enough range of light to be practical. They should be positioned so that the base of the shade is at eye level.

Standard and table lamps should stand steadily with the base weighted if necessary. Trailing flex is dangerous and untidy and it can curl under the base and make it unstable. Surplus flex (if it is impractical to shorten it permanently) should be looped and left in place with a rubber band or special plastic loop.

Adjustable task lights are more functional than ornamental. The most common type is the angle-poise which can stand or be clipped on to a shelf, table or chair back where a strong light is required. The jointed stem of the lamp enables the light to be directed on to the task so that the glare is not directed into the eyes.

Track lighting can be fitted along walls or ceiling. The spotlights can be adjusted to throw light on wall or ceiling to give general or task lighting. It can also be used to illuminate special features in a room. The track is sold in metred sections with two or three spotlights per section. It is practical for use in studio bedrooms, offices and for displays.

Warning and/or safety lighting

All hazard areas, such as steps, stairs, exits, and fire escape routes should be well lit. Stairs can also be illuminated by strip lighting recessed in the handrail or by pendant lights. Low energy light tubing fitted into an aluminium extrusion can provide illumination for stair carpet edging. It is produced in straight sections according to specification.

A special nightwatch lamp is suitable for interior or exterior illumination. A low pressure sodium lamp with 43 per cent greater light output than a 100 watt tungsten lamp is encased in a moulded polycarbonate body and covered with an opal polycarbonate impact resistant cover. This type of lamp can be controlled by an automatic switching system.

Emergency lighting

This is required in all public buildings and is a requirement for a fire certificate. It is necessary in all hazard areas, and in homes for the elderly and children, may also be required in areas such as lavatories. Emergency lighting needs a source of power separate from the normal source, for example;

1 Wet or dry batteries which are charged from the normal source when it is in use.
2 A generator which automatically takes over when the mains supply fails.

Emergency lighting can be incorporated in a normal light fitting, or in separate fittings. Emergency lighting should be checked in the same way as fire fighting appliances. A test relay is available for on-site testing during planned maintenance on self-contained luminaires.

Exterior lighting

For safety, security, and advertising it is necessary to have the exterior of the building and the grounds illuminated. Exterior luminaires have special water-proof casings and suitable bulbs. They can be operated by a photoelectric cell which operates the switch automatically. Floodlit buildings look very attractive, but floodlights

Table 18 *Recommended lighting levels*

Area	Lux
Reception	300
Halls	150 at floor level
Stairs	100 at floor level
Landings	150 at floor level
Lounges	150
Dining tables	100
Food preparation area	150–200
Inspection areas	450
Bedrooms	50–100
Reading lamp	150
Bathrooms	100
mirror	150
Offices	300
Writing tables	300
Reading	150 at surface
Study area	50
desk	300
Sewing	300–500
Work environment	300
Fine detailed work	1000–1500
General overall lighting	50

Class of visual task	Example	Lux
Casual seeing	Safe movement	150
Task with large detail	General work	300
Ordinary tasks	Reading, writing	500
Fairly severe tasks	Sewing, drawing	750
Severe and prolonged tasks	Sewing with dark material	1000

shining into bedroom windows can be disturbing to the occupants, unless there are light-proof curtains at the windows. Similarly, strong spotlights from the building can be blinding to people approaching if they are directed along the path of entry. Neon lighting has a distinct 'hum' and should not be used around bedroom windows.

Measurement of light

Candles are no longer used as a means of lighting except for decorative effect, but 'candle power' is still the basis of the measurement of light. The amount of light thrown by 1 candle at 1 foot distance is known as a 'lumen per square foot'. In America this term is still used but in Europe the metric equivalent is a 'lumen per square metre', or lux.

A *lumen* is a unit for measuring the quantity of light emitted at the source and a *lux* is the measure of illumination level *at* or *on* the *surface* being illuminated.

The amount of light required depends upon the use to which the area is put; the tasks being performed and the décor effect required. Table 18 gives the recommended lighting levels for different areas and purposes. The décor aspects of lighting different areas are examined in Chapter 15.

Energy conservation

Lighting uses about 4 per cent of the UK's primary energy. It accounts for some 15 per cent of electrical energy and in large modern air conditioned buildings about half the annual consumption is accounted for directly by the lighting. While it is commendable and desirable to save energy, lighting should never be reduced at the expense of safety. Safety risk areas should always be well illuminated.

Economies can be made by the following

1   Keeping tubes, bulbs and shades clean.
2   When possible combining task and décor lighting by careful placing and suitable shades.
3   Switching off unnecessary lights, for example by having cupboard lights controlled by the opening and shutting of the door.

4   Avoiding having one switch to control the lighting of a large area. In a large room lights may be required in one area only.
5   Use of a gadget at the door of the bedroom into which the tag on the door key is inserted to switch on the main lights. As the key is removed when the guest leaves, the room lights are extinguished.
6   Switches should be as near as possible to the lights they control – cord operated ceiling switches are effective. Electronic controls (ultra sonic or infra red) are a future possibility, and a master control of this type would make wiring switches to walls unnecessary.
7   Changing bulbs and tubes when they show dimming indicating the approach of the end of their life – the same amount of current is being used to produce less light.

Time controls
If the occupation of an area effectively ceases at a definite time each day, a time controlled switch is useful but the facility to override this control should be provided.

Photo-electric controls
These are sensitive to the natural daylight, and suitable for entrance lights, path lighting and corridor lighting. They switch off the artificial light as soon as daylight is adequate.

Top-up control
The light output of fluorescent lamps is increased as the daylight diminishes.

Room surfaces
Greater efficiency can sometimes be attained by re-decorating or cleaning surfaces and having light colours from which the light is reflected more efficiently. Mirrors give the maximum reflection value.

Electricity

Electricity is lethal and must be treated with caution. Insulation of cables, wires and plugs is essential for protection – bare metal wires are highly dangerous. Electric appliances and wiring should never be tampered with, and if a fault is not eliminated by change of fuse, an electrician should be brought in.

The tools required for attaching plugs or changing plug fuses are:

Wire stripper
Wire cutter
Screwdrivers with insulated handles (2 mm and 4 mm)

A ring main circuit has two types of fuse as protection against overloading – a small cartridge fuse in each plug and a main fuse in the consumer unit or fuse board. A lighting circuit is protected by a main fuse only.

If an appliance stops working, switch off immediately (turn off appliance itself and the socket outlet if both have switches). Remove plug, unscrew top and take out fuse. Fit a substitute fuse or check existing fuse as described below and replace if necessary. Also check connections for loose or disconnected wires. Refit plug cover. If the appliance still fails to work and the main fuse is intact, get the appliance checked by an approved electrician. Fuses can be 3 amp, 5 amp and 13 amp. It is highly dangerous to use a fuse with more amps than recommended for the appliance.

Instructions and diagrams for wiring a plug are available from the electricity showrooms. Spare cartridge fuses should be kept for emergencies and the amps noted. Fuses 'blow' when the current is too great for the appliance, if there is a fault in the circuit or appliance, or when the appliance overheats.

Fuse boxes have miniature circuit breakers with a switch that falls down when the fuse has blown. When the fault has been located and remedied, the switch can be brought up again. Fuse boxes should be labelled, indicating the areas which each fuse controls. Always switch off at the mains or trip switch when carrying out any electrical repair or investigation. There should be a plan of the circuit throughout the building to which reference can be made by maintenance and electricians. The housekeeper should know where the fuse boxes are and the circuits which they control.

In larger establishments, where there is a maintenance or engineering department on no account should the housekeeper carry out electrical repair work. The housekeeper should simply concern her/himself with effective reporting systems, in order that maintenance and repair work may be carried out as quickly as possible.

However, there are emergency situations when a cartridge fuse needs replacing.

Electricity terms

Conductor of electricity is a medium through which current can pass. Good conductors include metals and water. Some metals are better conductors than others.

Volts measure the pressure of the flow of the current. Currents are usually 240 V or 415 V.

Ohms measure the resistance of the wire through which the current flows. Resistance to the flow of current creates heat. Copper and aluminium offer little resistance, while the heating elements in appliances are of a high resistance.

Amps (amperes) measure the rate of the flow of power passing through the circuits.

Watts measure the amount of current used by an appliance. Light bulbs indicate their consumption in watts. 1 kW is 1000 W.

Unit of electricity is the amount of current used by 1kW in 1 hour. Meters show the consumption of electricity in units and the charge is made at so much per unit. It is not a flat rate, but varies according to how much and when current is taken and the type of establishment.

Sound insulation

Sound is a transference of energy, so the principles of insulation of heat apply in part to sound. Sound like heat, requires air, water or some other medium for its transference. Like heat, it can be reflected and absorbed. While sound can be pleasing and harmonious, when it is too loud or undesirable it becomes noise, and a nuisance. Noise need not be loud. A low sound such as the hum of a motor or the low throb of a pumping machine can become a noise. Most people have a tolerance level to noise. Those who live with distant traffic or country noises, or within hearing distance of the sea, do not hear their normal environmental sounds, but will notice their absence. People can be more sensitive to noise than to heat or cold. It is easier to add a garment, or to discard one, than it is to cut out noise.

Measurement of sound

The ability to measure sound has resulted in improvements in building acoustics, and in an appreciation of the importance of reducing noise. There is, at present no legislation to control noise inside a building although there is legislation for the control of noise emitted from factories. However, the realization that excessive noise has an adverse effect, physically and psychologically, has led to efforts to reduce noise in places of work and in the home.

The number of pressure variations per second is called frequency of sound and is measured in cycles per second or hertz (Hz). The range of human hearing extends approximately 20 Hz to 20,000 Hz (or 20 kHz). The range from the lowest to the highest note of a piano is 27.5 to 4186 Hz.

The decibel is the smallest change in sound heard by humans. 0 decibels is the threshold of hearing and the threshold of pain is between 130 and 140 decibels.

Noise in and around buildings

When planning a new building, there may not be a choice of site, but care should be taken from the beginning to protect the occupants from internal and external noise, for example a service area instead of a bedroom next to a lift shaft.

Insulation against external noise

If the building is situated near, for example, a motorway, it can be designed so that windows are not facing the direction of the noise. Corridors, rather than bedrooms, should be positioned near the noise source. Boiler rooms, refrigeration motors and pumps should be separated from the main building, so vibrations are not transmitted through walls. Windows with small grilles will admit fresh air without having to be open. Double glazing helps noise insulation. The minimum space between the two panes of glass should be 150 mm.

Automatic window closure is a system not at present widely used. Where there is excessive noise intermittently, a microphone outside the building activates a hydraulic power pack which automatically closes windows when a predetermined level of noise occurs, and opens them when the noise ceases.

In general, the more solidly built the building, the thicker the walls, the better fitting the doors and windows, the better the sound insulation of the building.

Insulation against internal noise

It is a management responsibility to control noise as much as it is to ensure that the occupants of the establishment are not too hot or too cold, and are given fresh air to breathe.

Training staff to work quietly and the selection of quietly running equipment will help in this respect. A badly maintained piece of equipment will frequently be operating noisily. The use of laminates and plastic where practical will reduce noise. Metal on metal is very noisy. Trolleys should have wheels well oiled.

Partition walls should be solid and covered with an acoustic correction material. Where existing partition walls are of lath and board construction they can be filled with mineral fibre. This will not totally eliminate noise transference but it will help. Noise can be partly contained in a room by wall coverings. Book-filled book shelves will give insulation as will clothes and linen cupboards.

False or dropped ceilings, or ceilings of stretched textile material will reduce the passage of sound. Acoustic tiles applied to the ceiling will improve the reception of sound in the room and reduce the transference of vibrations. These are the more cosmetic methods, which will improve the acoustics probably more than the sound insulation. Sound will pass through the ceiling and along the space above and back into the next room, unless the insulated partition wall is extended into the loft space. Fire barriers in the loft areas are equally effective for increasing sound insulation.

Joist floors can have mineral or glass wool in blanket form laid across the joists and the floor boards in strips between the joists. A blanket of insulating material laid on a solid base beneath a floor will provide heat and sound insulation. It will not vibrate, so there is no danger of creaking floor boards. Second floors laid on top of the existing floor on hard board battens can have a sound insulating gap of approximately 5 mm between the wall and the second floor and a 3 mm gap between the skirting board and floor. The floor rests on joists with a resilient pad which acts as a buffer and prevents the vibrations extending. Floor coverings will reduce the noise of foot traffic.

The noise from air ducts and service pipes can be reduced by the use of isolators of canvas or rubber or plastic sheeting. Loose connections will produce noise, as will rodents which may have penetrated the ducting.

Door springs should be adjusted so that the doors close more slowly for the last few centimetres. Rubber or plastic roping round the jamb of the door will reduce the noise on closure.

Television and radios should be controlled from a central point by the management if possible. They should be placed away from a partition wall.

Refrigerators should be level, especially those in service rooms, bars, and dining rooms. They should be stacked so the contents do not rattle. Plant heating, refrigeration and sewage pumps should be timed to come on at times when they will give as little inconvenience as possible. For example, pumps switched on mid-morning will not disturb sleepers and will be partially masked by the every-day sounds of normal working.

Further reading

Warring, R. H., *All About Home Lighting*. (Argus Books Limited 1977).

Useful addresses

The Sound Research Laboratory,
Holbrook Hall,
Little Waldingfield,
Nr Sudbury,
Suffolk

Building Research Establishment Digest,
Advisory Service,
Building Research Station,
Garston,
Watford WD2 7JR

Management

19 Housekeeping management

The housekeeper is responsible for the care of a large capital investment in building equipment, furniture, furnishings and fittings, linen stocks, human and material resources. The professional housekeeper of today should be a person who can take an active role in the management team, whether the establishment be large or small, a going concern or a non-profit making enterprise. In the majority of establishments, it is the accommodation sector that produces the highest profit. However it also has a high payroll and needs high levels of investment if standards are to be maintained. It is therefore essential that the housekeeping management is committed to the business aspects of the operation. The professional housekeeper should have the following attributes

1 *A formal educational qualification* in the field of hotel, catering and institutional management.
2 *Relevant practical experience* – job experience, practical skills and techniques.
3 *Specialized job knowledge* – cleaning and maintenance, fabrics and finishes, pest control, purchasing, quality control etc.
4 *Management techniques* – planning, organization, delegation, problem solving, training, decision making, control.
5 *Human relations skills* – the management of people, motivation of self and others, social skills, communication and liaison, industrial relations, discipline, teamwork.
6 *Legal knowledge* – for example, employment law, health and safety.
7 *Other attributes* – first aid qualification, typing and other administrative skills, suitable

appearance, able to accept responsibility, honest and trustworthy, mentally and physically fit.

The housekeeper must always develop his/her management skills:

S   speech and communication.
K   knowledge.
I   interest in people (guests and staff) and in the work.
L   listen to other peoples' advice, ideas and points of view.
L   learn about new developments within the field.

Administration

Computers
Many large hotels have used computers for rooms management for many years but it is only recently that their use has been appreciated for other services within the acommodation unit. Mini- and microcomputers will be used in small establishments, but larger establishments making use of a main frame computer, will perhaps benefit the most as far as housekeeping administration is concerned.

Rooms management
This is obviously the most important area. The housekeeper will usually have a terminal in his or her office with a printer and a keyboard. The housekeeper will require the following information from the computer

1 Arrivals and departures as well as occupancy figures.

2   Occupancy forecasts.

3   VIP and other special arrivals, such as tour groups, conferences, airline crews, with check-in and check-out times.

4   Guest history and special requests (e.g. Bedboards, vases, water-proof sheet, disabled facilities, cot, rollaway bed etc.).

5   Out of order record giving reason (e.g. re-decoration, flood).

6   Room change (when a guest has moved from one room to another).

7   Room type change.

8   Complimentary or staff rooms.

9   Rooms sold for special purposes (e.g. syndicate rooms, interview rooms).

10   Day lets.

11   Suites sold as individual units.

12   Connecting rooms sold for friends or in a 'family plan'.

13   Sleep outs (where the guest has slept out).

14   Walk outs.

15   Stay ons (where the guest who was supposed to be leaving has decided to stay on).

16   Occupancy numbers per room.

Information such as this will be in a two-way flow from Reception to Housekeeping and vice versa. From the housekeeping side, information may be fed into the computer from the keyboard. If the computer is linked to the telephone system, information on room status may be dialed in directly by the floor supervisor (see Chapter 5).

Stock control

All types of housekeeping stock may be controlled by computer including

Linen inventories
Cleaning agents
Cleaning equipment
Uniforms
Guest supplies
Soft furnishings
Bedding
Spare carpet and curtain/upholstery fabric etc.

By keeping efficient stock control, purchasing and budgeting will be made easier and information on stock levels etc. will be readily available.

Room design

With a sophisticated computer, diagrams may be produced for studies of work flow, or ergonomics, including plans of bedrooms, restaurants and other areas.

Records

All housekeeping records may be kept in the computer, for example, room type with listed contents, design and colour scheme; suppliers, dates of purchase, cost and problems of particular items; and method of cleaning and maintenance.

Work methods

These should be identified for use in training periods or where special infrequent cleaning operations were carried out.

Files

Computer files take the place of traditional files reducing the need for filing cabinets.

Word processing

The computer used as a word processor takes the place of a traditional typewriter, so all correspondence could be prepared in this way. Standard letters could also be kept in the memory.

Planning systems

A well organized housekeeping department has several planning systems in operation. The computer is ideal for keeping such records and preparing forecasts for example on window cleaning, re-decoration etc.

Energy saving

Computers can be used to control heat, light, power and telephone usage.

As time goes on, more sophisticated programs will be developed and more computerized equipment is becoming available.

Office skills

Even where computers are installed, a certain amount of traditional office administration is required, including

Typing of letters and memos etc.
Filing
Following company procedures
Dealing with staff requests
Dealing with guest requests
Telephone technique
Planning and organization of work.

Work study

When calculating the time to perform a task, it must be borne in mind that it can vary in relation to the following factors

1 Time of day. Some cleaners work in the evening after having done a day's work. People tend to work less productively towards the end of a long shift or after a heavy main meal.
2 Age of the employee.
3 A new method or a new piece of equipment.
4 Interruptions.
5 Time wasted in waiting for supplies or the use of shared equipment.
6 Emergency situations, e.g. excessive spillages and soiling.

When assigning an employee's tasks for the day or shift, time must be allowed for the following

1 Reporting for work at central location.
2 Getting to the assigned area.
3 Collecting and getting ready equipment.
4 Break times.
5 Cleaning, changing, reporting back.

Work study is quite common in hospital housekeeping and to a lesser extent in the large international hotel companies. Studies are usually carried out by specialist members of the management/administration team. The main purposes of work study are

1 To establish labour productivity measurements.
2 To provide a basis for productivity bargaining systems such as bonus schemes.
3 To establish staffing levels.
4 To provide a basis for training systems.
5 To simplify work methods, making physical work less tiring.

6 To study and select the best work method for a given task.

Time study

In this study method work is measured by the use of a stop watch. The various methods of doing a particular job are first studied and the best method selected. The best method will be chosen for various reasons: shortest time, least physical effort or the quality of finished product/job. The job is then broken down into various elements or tasks. The job is timed, using the stop watch. A speed correcting rating is applied to the employee who is being timed. A rating of 100 is the 'standard rating' and will be the performance of a well motivated employee (perhaps on a productivity bonus). A normal speed would give a rating of 75. The observed time is multiplied by the rating of the employee and divided by 100, to give the basic time. For example, if the time taken by a maid to enter a room and put down the linen is 35 seconds, and he/she is on a rating of 80, the basic time will be 28.

$$\frac{35 \times 80}{100} = 28$$

Allowances are then added to allow for contingencies such as a sheet being torn or stained and having to be changed. Basic time plus allowances gives standard time.

Methods time measurement (MTM)

This is an alternative to time study and does not require a stop watch. It is a system of producing job times by considering the human motions involved in doing a job, for example, bending and stretching. MTM is used to build up standard times for commonly recurring elements in jobs such as dusting or wiping different surfaces, using spray polishes or other aerosols. MTM patterns are written for different methods of doing jobs and then averaged out to produce standard data times.

Alternative standard data times can be produced for routine cleaning in an occupied room as well as a more thorough clean of a 'checkout' room, thus making it possible for the

Table 19 *Method study questions*

Purpose	Why is it done?	What else could be done?	What should be done?
Place	Where is it done?	Where else could it be done?	Where should it be done?
Sequence	When is it done?	When else could it be done?	When should it be done?
Person	Who does it?	Who else could do it?	Who should do it?
Means	How is it done?	How else could it be done?	How should it be done?

housekeeper to judge the time differences needed for maids to clean different types of rooms and therefore allocate the work load accordingly.

Analytical estimating
Certain job tasks are so variable or peculiar to a particular operation that time study or MTM are inappropriate. Analytical estimating involves the process of breaking down each job into small elements and estimating each element separately. It is usually very accurate.

Method study
Method study is part of work study but is concerned with improvements in working methods, rather than timing a particular job. A method study goes through the following stages:

1 Select the method to be studied.
2 Record the method using charts, diagrams or video/films.
3 Examine the operation critically to find shortcomings, wasted time, etc.
4 Develop new methods where appropriate.
5 Install the new method.
6 Maintain standards by constantly checking.

Every event in the work method must be scrutinized and questions such as those shown in Table 19 should be asked and answered.

Other studies

Queue studies
Queues form if there are haphazard times of arrival of people and often inconvenience or com-plaints will emerge. On the other hand, time is wasted and/or lost during waiting periods in between the haphazard arrivals. Table 19 can also be used to overcome the queuing problem.

Activity sampling
This is a method of sampling the work of a group of people. The main objective is to find out how long it takes and how many people to do a job and to improve the way of doing that job.

Crew size studies
These are studies carried out to find out how many people are needed to perform a job in the most efficient manner. The two most popular techniques involved in this particular type of study are time study and activity sampling. Different numbers of staff are used to perform different tasks. For example, in some hotels, the maids work in pairs, whereas in others, they each have a standard number of rooms to clean. Besides doing a work study, the housekeeper should think of possible advantages and disadvantages of different crew sizes. The following list gives some problems that can occur if maids work in pairs.

1 Arguments over share of tips.
2 Unequal work load.
3 Unequal speed of work.
4 Unequal quality of work.
5 Drop in standards – maids tend to rush work or spend time talking.
6 Guest complaints – noise control caused by maids talking/shouting to each other.

Frequency studies

Studies can be carried out to test the exact cleaning frequency necessary. Such a study would aid the planning and organization of staffing, time, materials and inconvenience.

Cleaning systems

The room by room system

The majority of large international hotels use this system of room cleaning which simply entails maids being responsible for their own section of rooms and cleaning each one in turn. They are trained to complete one room before beginning the next and are requested to clean certain rooms before other types, for example VIP rooms might be cleaned first. This is the best method of room cleaning, as the maids take a certain pride in their work. This is because they are responsible for a set section of rooms and regard them as their own. If they have a few spare moments, they are most likely to spend a little time doing extra cleaning. The maids complete the whole product (a room) and so have visible evidence of their work, leading to greater job satisfaction.

The block system

The block system involves the maids completing the same task in all rooms for which they are responsible. Some smaller establishments prefer this method of room cleaning or use a combination of both methods. The block system is sometimes advantageous in a crisis situation for exam-ple a back to back tour or conference, where a large number of rooms are vacated at the same time. An army of staff can be organized to clean the rooms on a block system, for one person would strip all the beds, another would place all clean linen in the room, another would make all the beds and so on. It is unwise to continue this type of approach on a long term basis as it may develop into an 'assembly line' bringing all those related problems of boredom and carelessness.

Productivity

After a work study has been completed, a productivity rate per maid can be set, and maids trained to attain that rate.

Maid productivity is calculated as follows (see Figure 47):

1 Add together total room occupany for the week (obtained from reception's statistics). The number of rooms cleaned this week is 3188.
2 Add together the total number of full-time maids on duty. This week 190 maid-days were worked by full-time maids, but from Monday to Friday 4 hours overtime was worked each day giving a total of 20 hours overtime. This is equivalent to 3 maid-days (approximately), so the total number of full-time maids is 193.
3 From the total rooms cleaned, deduct the number of rooms cleaned by casual staff. In this particular hotel, casual staff are not

Housekeeping department   Week ending . . . .

Room occupancy:	369		474		470		524		466		431		454	
Date:	5 March		6 March		7 March		8 March		9 March		10 March		11 March	
	Monday		Tuesday		Wednesday		Thursday		Friday		Saturday		Sunday	
	Man day	Hours/ rooms	Man day	Hours/ rooms	Man day	Hours/ rooms	Man day	Hours/ rooms	Man day	Hours/ rooms	Man day	Hours/ rooms	Man day	Hours/ rooms
Job group Maids	27	4	31	4	30	4	31	4	30	4	26	0	15	0
Casual maids		8		16		16		50		14		163		185

Figure 47 *Maid productivity*

counted in the productivity as full-time manning is kept to a minimum. 3188 rooms − 452 rooms = 2736 rooms cleaned by full-time staff.

4   Divide the total number of rooms cleaned by full-time maids by the number of full-time maids 2736 ÷ 193 = 14.176. Throughout the week, each full-time maid cleaned an average of 14 rooms per day.

If it is felt that this amount of work is too low, then the housekeeper must take appropriate action, such as decreasing the number of casual staff employed during the course of the week.

Allocation of duties

When allocating duties, a knowledge and consideration of the staff's skills, ability and aptitude will make for a happier staff and greater efficiency. So after listing the jobs to be done, consider who should do what. One maid may not like making beds, but likes polishing and straightforward cleaning. He/she could do the corridors or a lounge. On the other hand, there must be a certain amount of flexibility and a corridor maid could come in to vacuum and dust bedrooms if there was a shortage of bedroom maids.

Records

Keeping records is an essential part of the housekeeper's job. In small or private establishments, checklists, report forms and schedules may not be provided in a standard format from head office, and it may therefore be necessary for the housekeeper to devise his or her own records in order that the department is maintained in an efficient manner. Housekeeping functions can be recorded in one of the following ways.

1   Wall charts.
2   Books.
3   Lists.
4   Computer files.

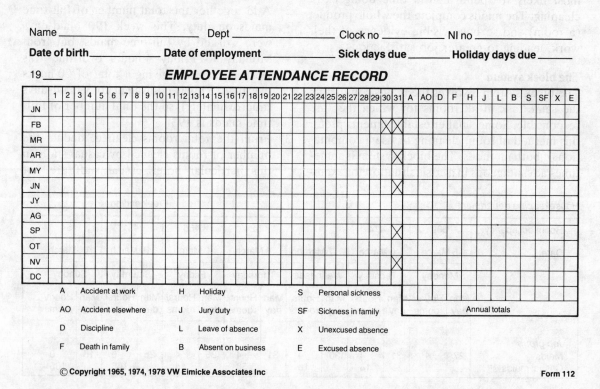

Figure 48   *Staff record. Courtesy of V. W. Eimicke Associates Inc.*

Other records the housekeeper should keep include:

1 Contract records, for example, floor maintenance, window cleaning, flowers, contract cleaning.
2 Special projects, for example, new building extensions.
3 Room records, for example, room inventory and colour scheme, room type, redecoration and refurbishment.
4 Purchasing and stock records.
5 Cleaning, spring cleaning, on-going and occasional cleaning, such as window cleaning, carpet and upholstery cleaning.
6 Work methods.
7 Staff records (see Figure 48)
8 Guest records
9 General information such as, house doctor, hospitals, local authority departments and services.

Guest complaints

The natural reaction to receiving a complaint is to be defensive. Suppress this reaction. It must be borne in mind that it requires effort and sometimes embarrassment to complain, and that there might have been a series of irritations before a very minor incident that may prompt the complainant finally to voice dissatisfaction. Complaints are received either verbally or in written form.

Verbal complaints

Avoid hearing a complaint in any public area – suggest that the two of you go to a more comfortable place to discuss the problems. In an office, avoid sitting with a desk between you and the guest. The desk sets up a physical and psychological barrier. Draw up a chair at an angle of about 45 degrees alongside the person. A cup of tea or coffee eases many situations, but do not offer alcohol, as this might be thought of as a bribe. Listen patiently and do not interrupt, as this will only irritate the person more. Nod and show that you are listening.

When the dissertation is finished, look sympathetic and thank the person for having brought these points to your attention, and regret that it has been necessary for him or her to go to this trouble. Ask if you may take notes of all the points that have been made, so that you can start making your investigations. By being allowed to make all the points (there is seldom only one) the guest will be feeling relieved and will then probably be much more rational. Never offer any monetary or other compensation in the first instance. This is a management decision, after investigation has been made. Never admit responsibility without having made the enquiries and inspection. However, if it is a small thing that can be rectified immediately, do it or have it done then. A complaints form will help in analysing the situation for a report to the management. Inspection is the first step, checking who was on duty and should be responsible for the fault. Ask the member of staff for his/her version and allow him or her to make any points relevant to the situation. The customer is not always right, so listen to another point of view and assess the situation. A piece of equipment may have been misused by the guest or instructions misread.

Always go back to the complainant and report progress made. The complaint may not always be of a physical nature, like lack of hot water, but one of the attitude of a member of staff. Complaints about services are more easily dealt with than complaints about attitude. Talk to the staff member and try to assess the situation, bearing in mind the attitude of the guest as well as the staff member.

Written complaints

These will probably be made to the manager. Carry out the inspection and questioning and make a report to the manager as soon as possible, as it is essential that the letter should be replied to immediately. If it is going to take time, the manager will acknowledge the letter and, after you report write again. A company may have its own complaints form, or the housekeeper can make out her/his own. A complaints form should include the following information:

1 Name of complainant.
2 Address and telephone number.
3 Time and date.
4 How it was made (verbal or written).
5 To whom it was made.
6 Nature of complaint.
7 Details.
8 Area.
9 Normally inspected by and when.
10 Responsibility of.
11 Fault inspected by and when.
12 Report of inspection.
13 Report of interview with staff.
14 Action taken.
15 Notes: attitude of complainant; assessment of validity; assessment of staff's reaction.
16 Recommendations.
17 Requests made by housekeeper.

Where standard forms are in use, analyses may be made identifying the main areas of complaint, so that corrective action may be taken.

Preventative measures

Step 1 *Provide a good working atmosphere*
If housekeeping staff have job security, job satisfaction and are confident in their work, any guest complaint that unfortunately occurs should be dealt with on the spot – before a mole hill turns into a mountain. Even if the cleaner or maid cannot handle the complaint alone, he/she should be trained to act positively toward the guest and call the supervisor straight away.

Step 2 *Good communication*
If there are good systems of communication, any guest complaints will be known about almost as soon as they have happened. They can then be dealt with in the most appropriate manner. Complaints may be communicated by means of the telephone, bleep, word of mouth, guest questionnaire, letter or memo. Speed of handling the situation is essential. A system for dealing with the complaint must be activated immediately, once the guest has been passified. Guests always appreciate knowing that action has been taken in respect of the complaint.

Step 3 *Speed and efficiency*
Naturally in some cases a serious complaint is valid, but as often as not, the majority are small ones that with a little bit of effort may easily be put right. If they are not dealt with speedily things will tend to snowball. Company policies must also be set up for certain serious complaints such as theft or damage to guest property.

Step 4 *Action and Follow-up*
The guest does not want to hear excuses. He is not interested, for example, to hear that there aren't enough staff or half of the maids are off sick. This is the housekeeper's problem! The complaining guest needs the wrongs put right, and quickly.

Step 5 *Fault analysis*
After the complaint, the fault should be studied objectively and discussed openly with all those concerned. Problem areas must be pinpointed and through the team effort, improvements should evolve in order to combat similar future complaints.

Communication and liaison

Effective communication is essential to the running of any business. Good vertical communication, between the department head and his/her staff, will ensure that jobs are done well and there is a good teamwork. Horizontal communication, between members of the management team, will ensure that the different specialists are putting the company objectives into practice in their own area. All communication must be two-way.

Communication with other departments
Figure 49 shows the lines of communication in a hotel, between the housekeeping department and the other departments. A similar chart is easily drawn up for other types of establishment.

Food and beverage department
All areas of the food and beverage service department have to be kept clean, and this may be the responsibility of the housekeeping

Figure 49 *Housekeeping communication chart*

department. Communication is necessary to ensure that this is done to the desirable standard and at convenient times. Uniforms have to be exchanged (this applies to all departments) and other items, such as table linen, waiters' cloths and glass cloths, will be supplied by housekeeping. The flower displays in the bar or restaurant may be the responsibility of housekeeping: the food and beverage staff may have to inform housekeeping if flowers and plants need attention.

The front office (reception)
Besides the cleaning and exchange of uniforms, which applies to this and other departments, co-operation with reception and housekeeping is necessary to ensure maids know which rooms are empty and cleaners know what they are preparing a room for (whether it is a conference or a banquet, for example). Reception will often receive guest complaints, which then have to be communicated to housekeeping. The two departments also have to co-operate when major spring cleaning or redecorating programmes are being planned. The hall porters are part of the front office department, but they are often responsible for the 'night cupboard' which con-

tains articles such as spare soap, towels, etc. These are supplied by housekeeping.

Maintenance or engineering
The maintenance department and housekeeping will be constantly liaising over day-to-day repairs, renovation programmes, care of equipment and budgets.

Laundry
The laundry may, indeed, be part of the housekeeping department. If not, a close relationship is necessary to ensure standards are adequate and stock control is effective.

Sales
All hotel staff are sales staff since they are all dealing with guests; their appearance, attitude and behaviour will impress the guests, for good or ill. Housekeeping has a special role because of its responsibility for the care of uniforms.

Accounts
Many of the records that the housekeeper keeps will be used by the accounts department, including staff records (for payment of wages), budget preparation, inventories and reports on room status.

Purchasing
A separate purchasing department will only exist in a large establishment, where purchasing is kept centralized in order to achieve economies by buying in bulk. The housekeeper must keep the purchasing department well informed of the department's needs, so that supplies are made available when required.

Personnel and training
The housekeeper will liaise with personnel over interviews and selection of staff, health and safety matters, cleanliness of staff accommodation, and training of the housekeeping staff.

Security
Only the large city hotels will have a separate security department. The housekeeper's responsi-

bility in this respect includes key control, lost property, selection of trustworthy staff, control of stores and equipment, and training of staff so that they lock up where necessary and report any suspicious people or circumstances.

General manager

The housekeeper is usually responsible to the general manager, and will discuss with him/her the objectives of the establishment, and the best way to put these into practice. Communication must be two-way: the housekeeper must find out from the manager what the company's policies are, and must be able to tell him/her of any problems encountered.

Communication with external bodies

Figure 50 shows lines of communication with outside bodies.

Guests

The housekeeping department is strictly speaking 'a back of house' operation, but there will be liaison with guests over matters such as complaints, special requests and lost property.

Contractors

The housekeeper will deal with contractors for pest control, window cleaning, and possibly laundry and dry cleaning services. Communication is necessary to ensure that these outside

bodies do their jobs to the desired standard and within the agreed budget.

Staff agencies

Not all establishments will have a policy of using agency staff, but if they are used the housekeeper will be in touch with the agency to make sure the workers do their jobs well, and billing is accurate.

Suppliers

Suppliers will often want to see the housekeeper to display new products. Although it is essential to keep abreast of new developments, it is important that time is not wasted listening to lengthy sales pitches. Salespeople can be given appointments for a defined period.

Housekeeper's associations/professional bodies

The housekeeper must keep up to date with new ideas, methods and products, and membership of professional bodies such as the Hotel and Catering Industry Management Association (HCIMA) or the British Institute of Cleaning Science, will ensure that he/she hears about developments. It is also beneficial to have a friendly relationship with competitors through a local housekeeper's association, or a more informal arrangement, whereby information on, for example, prospective suppliers or employees, is exchanged by telephone. In larger companies, regular meetings between housekeeping staff at different hotels will be organized.

Hotel and catering colleges

The housekeeping department and local catering college will benefit equally from a close working relationship. The local colleges will be looking for placements for industrial training for their students, who can have a great deal to offer. Talks and visits can be arranged by both sides, at which ideas can be exchanged. Sometimes the college will want to find a 'real life' problem for students to solve and a fresh answer may evolve.

Local authorities and services

Local authorities will have services to offer as will the following organizations

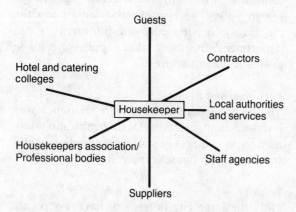

Figure 50   *External lines of communication*

1   Department of Employment.
2   Department of the Environment.
3   Health and Safety Officer.
4   Race Relations Board.
5   Regional Tourist Board.
6   Consumer's Association.
7   Fire Service.
8   Police.
9   Chamber of Commerce.
10 Schools.

Methods of communication

Listed below are some of the methods of communicating which are used in the hotel and catering industry.

Verbal
   Telephone
   Bleep
   Meetings
   Face to face
   Intercom – rarely used by a housekeeping department

Visual
   Computer – visual display/print out
   Rooms management system/rooms status indicator
   Written – lists, reports, minutes of meetings, memorandums, letters, forms, function sheets, messages, warnings/instructions
   Tent cards and other forms of advertising
   In-house movies
   Magazines
   Notice boards
   Graphs
   Photographs/pictures
   Role playing, e.g. for training purposes

Hotels and other establishments have many legal duties, which the above bodies can advise on.

There are many new methods of communication being introduced, from the intercom and 'bleep' to the computer. These bring advantages of economy and speed, but it must be remembered that communication is about people, and it is all too easy to lose the human contact. A spoken message contains more than the actual words: the tone of voice and 'body language' also convey information. Even a written message is somehow more personal than information from a visual display unit. Whatever electronic means of communication an establishment has, the housekeeper must always be in personal contact with staff, to listen to complaints and watch out for problems before they happen. All communication has three elements, all of which have to be successful if the message is to get through.

1   Transmitter (the person giving the message).
2   Message.
3   Receiver.

Communication will not take place if the transmitter hasn't thought about how to transmit the message, if the message itself isn't relevant and clear, or if the receiver is not listening or is unable to understand. Besides verbal communication (which includes tone of voice), posture, physical expressions (using hands for example) and facial expression are all part of conveying information. Above all, remember that listening and seeing are as important as talking – after all, we were all born with two eyes, two ears, but only one mouth!

Conclusion

If a professional housekeeper is doing his/her job properly, he/she must be capable of performing many duties. Housekeepers could therefore be labelled 'DRIPS'.

D   Diplomatic when dealing with all kinds of people.
R   Responsible even when things go wrong.
I   Information centre – to have certain job knowledge, but also to be able to find out other items of information.
P   Psychologist to be able to understand people.
S   Salesperson.

Further reading

Crawford, J. A. D., and Williams, C. S., *Study on Systems of Bedroom Cleaning*, Department of Applied and Life Sciences, Queens College, Glasgow.

20 *Personnel*

Good management of any organization depends on a balance between managing work and managing staff. If too much emphasis is put on the work, the staff will be dissatisfied and the work will, in turn, suffer. Similarly, if staff relations are emphasized too much, the quality of work will suffer. Most of this book has dealt with management of work, but this chapter deals with managing staff.

Managing staff has three main aspects

1 Organizing work for people: distribution of work through rotas, arranging physical resources such as equipment, etc.
2 Organizing people for work: manpower planning, recruitment and selection, training, etc.
3 Motivation: wages and salaries, bonus systems and other benefits, discipline and counselling, etc.

Manpower planning

Manpower planning involves deciding how many staff, and what sort of staff, an establishment needs. In a new housekeeping unit, a specialist known as an operations analyst will be called in, but in a small establishment, the local management will do their own manpower planning. The following questions need to be answered

1 What work needs to be done?
2 When does the work need to be carried out?
3 How long will it take to do?

The answers to these questions will depend on the nature of the establishment, the standards required and the type of user. A work and method study will help to determine how many

staff are needed (see Chapter 19). The management then need to determine what qualifications and skills are required to do the specific jobs. A manpower planning exercise also needs to take into account what staff will be available. This will depend on the following

1 Location.
2 Availability of transport.
3 Times staff are required.
4 Whether full-time or part-time staff are required.

Manpower planning is as necessary in an existing department as in a new unit which is just being established. The housekeeper should be continually reviewing staffing levels in the department. Any establishment evolves and its needs change. If a different type of customer is coming to a hotel, the staffing needs may change. The introduction of new technology may eliminate or reduce the need for some workers. The establishment may be going 'up market' and need more staff and higher standards – although it must be borne in mind that higher standards may be achieved by the same staff and greater productivity. The housekeeper should review staff turnover, in case this is causing problems. Staff records can be used to see if a number of people have left for the same reason, which might indicate a problem to be tackled. If most of the staff leaving are about the same age, perhaps this indicates that it is better to recruit staff of a different age-group.

Recruitment and selection

Before embarking on recruiting staff, one should

look objectively at the situation beforehand. The following questions may be asked

1 What is the purpose of this job and is it really necessary?
2 Could this particular job be combined with another job or could job tasks be re-allocated to make better use of people?
3 Has anything been learned from the person who has just left this post?
4 Could this vacancy be filled by (a) a college student on industrial release, or a young person on a governmental training scheme (b) an existing member of staff being redeployed or (c) internal promotion.
5 Is it possible to train someone already employed to do this job?
6 Is it easy to recruit locally or can the nature of the job be altered to make local recruitment easier?

Step 1 Assess the job

Before recruitment begins the job should be assessed and analysed. The job specification should be looked at, so that the manager can draw up a personal description which specifies the type of person suitable to do the job:

1 Skills.
2 Personality qualities.
3 Age group.
4 Physical qualities.

A Job/personal specification for a bedroom maid could include the following

Job title	Bedroom maid
Area	Block A six suites
Education	Must be able to read and write English. Preferably completed a City & Guilds 1 year course
Experience	None necessary but some preferable
Knowledge and skills	Basic knowledge of principles of cleaning. Able to follow instructions. Observant and attentive to details
Physical requirements	Must have reasonably good health record. Must be mobile and able to stoop. Not allergic to common cleaning agents or dust
Personal requirements	Neat and clean appearance. Preferably non-smoker. Able to work with people. Pleasant manner.
References	Must be able to produce these readily
Availability	At times required. Have adequate transport
Promotion	Potential for promotion
Training	Training given in certain areas and for promotion

Step 2 Advertising

Having decided what type of person is required, one must decide where to advertise, taking into consideration the readership of daily and weekly newspapers, magazines, journals or the board in local newsagents, college notice boards or local radio stations. When advertising for senior members of staff who are required to take responsibility, the professional journals, national catering trade publications or *The Lady* might produce the professionally qualified or experienced applicant. Contact with colleges with which one may have been co-operating in training and work experience can produce a newly qualified candidate.

There are many places to advertise for part- or full-time cleaning staff including

1 Local evening, daily and weekly papers, and weekly information sheets, including those delivered free of charge. Starting the advertisement with the first word beginning with a letter near the beginning of the alphabet is helpful. A potential applicant may have selected a job before reaching 'W' for 'wanted'.
2 The local newsagent's shop. Here there is also scope for advertising the establishment by incorporating a photograph of the area in which applicants will be working. It is unlikely that there will be written applications to this

type of advertisement, so state times at which it will be convenient to call or telephone and to whom the enquirer should ask to speak.

3   The local radio station. This is a relatively new and useful medium, though rather expensive.

4   Word of mouth. The age-old way of recruiting staff is to tell existing staff that someone is required and ask if they know of anyone or have a friend who would like to work with them.

The advertisement should do some of the selection, stating

1   The personal qualities, skills and qualifications required.
2   The type and location of the establishment.
3   Grade/status, salary.
4   To whom application should be made and by what means.

When the advertisement is about to appear warn the telephonist or receptionist that calls will be coming in and the details given below should be recorded perhaps on a special form. It will help if the receiver of the calls sounds interested and appears to know about the vacancy.

Name and address of caller
Telephone number
Previous experience
Hours of availability
Date/time of call
Comments

From this candidates can be selected for interview but always acknowledge all calls and keep names and addresses for future reference. It is useful to have such a form permanently in the office so any enquiries for jobs can be recorded and a file of applicants for work can be kept for reference when a vacancy occurs.

In a small town, for a local applicant, it is helpful to call at the house and deliver the letter for the applicant to come for interview. This will reveal what standard is maintained in his/her home, and the attitude of the applicant when not keyed up for a formal interview. The applicant also has the opportunity to see the person by whom he/she may be employed. In a larger establishment this somewhat informal manner is not possible, and all applications for employment are sometimes dealt with through the personnel office or an assistant manager in charge of personnel.

The advertisement is placed and applications are invited by letter, telephone or personal caller. It is advisable to issue a job description at the same time as an application form, so that the prospective employee may see what kind of work will be expected of her/him, before completing the application form.

Step 3   **The interview**

Prior to the arrangement of selection interviews, a certain amount of 'weeding out' usually takes place in order to get the list of candidates down to a reasonable size. By studying the completed application forms, the interviewer can easily identify 'possibles' and 'rejects'. Rejects should be dealt with by a polite letter. The other applicants may then be invited for interview. If this is done by post, it is advisable to enclose a brochure of the establishment. This will enable the applicant to be a little more familiar with the place where he/she is intending to work as well as serving as sales promotion. Many companies enclose this type of literature when originally sending off the application form. It is wise to have a relatively simple form.

Interviews arranged for housekeeping staff are usually based either on a one to one or two to one basis, although for housekeeping management it is not uncommon to have panel interviews. If the interviewer has not met the applicant before, it is helpful to walk through the room, unannounced, and see how he/she looks when relaxed. This can give an indication of the type of person. At the interview put the applicant at ease. Tell him/her about the establishment and the work involved. It is useful to ask a member of staff to show him/her round the department. This gives the applicant a chance to ask questions he/she may not care to ask the interviewer.

Basic questions that should be asked by the interviewer are

1 Previous employment and experience.
2 Does the applicant require permanent, full or part-time work.
3 What hours is the applicant available.
4 What is the husband/wife's employment (this is relevant because it could have bearing on the availability of the applicant).
5 If there are children, what are their ages, what provision is made for their care out of school hours and holidays.
6 What holiday commitments may have been made.
7 If previously employed, reason for leaving and who will provide a reference.
8 Reasons for applying for the job.

After the interview, it is wise to ask the applicant to think over the situation and to let you know if he/she wants to be considered for the job. Frequently applicants for part-time work or those who have not worked for some time are nervous at the interview, and accept the job if offered on the spot, but then later take fright and do not turn up. Beware of the applicant who discredits a former employer. It must be remembered that the applicant is the one who should do most of the talking at the interview – the interviewer will assess the candidate largely on what he/she says.

Since the employee in the houskeeping department will be in contact with customers, residents and their personal possessions, it is necessary to take up references from previous employers, or anyone who can testify to the applicant's honesty. Previous employers may give more frank references over the telephone than in writing. It may be the company's policy to take out fidelity bonds on staff – in which case the insuring company will make the necessary enquiries.

The following checklist summarizes the points to get out of an interview

1 *Education* Assess from reply to advertisement and/or give a job description to read and comment on. Ask for any certificate alleged to have been received or check with college.
2 *Experience* The type of establishment at which the applicant presently works will give an indication to type of experience the applicant has had and whether relevant to new job.
3 *Knowledge and skills* Show a work schedule and ask for comments. Ask what applicant has noticed while waiting, what he/she liked about it. Ask what he/she likes doing at work and at leisure.
4 *Physical requirements* Ask discreetly about general health. If a medical check-up is required by the company, this must be acceptable.
5 *Personal requirements* Appearance at interview. Notice if fingers are nicotine-stained. Does the applicant stand when you enter the room and attempt to open the door? This will indicate manners. Take into account that the applicant may be nervous. Ability to get on with people can be assessed by asking questions about school life or previous job and colleagues.
6 *References* Check these by telephone, and the status of the person giving them. Have referees been asked to do this by the applicant?
7 *Availability* Ask about family commitments and spouse's work if applicable. What mode of transport is available for arriving and returning from work?
8 *Promotion* Does he/she have ambition?
9 *Training* Is there a positive reaction to the possibility of training?

Step 4 Placement

Once an applicant has accepted the job, he/she is normally sent a letter giving details of starting date etc. The selected applicant should be given a contract of employment stating clearly

Hours of work
Remuneration and intervals of payment
The name of the person to whom he/she is directly responsible
Holiday entitlement and holiday pay
Terms relating to incapacity to work due to sickness or injury
Amount of notice of termination of employ-

ment required to be given by employee and employer

Any other details deemed relevant by the employer

A part-time member of staff working more than 16 hours per week has the same rights as a full-time member of staff, under current law.

Induction or *orientation* is one of the most important areas of recruitment and selection. The purpose of induction is to help the new employee settle into his/her new working environment as quickly as possible. One of the highest staff turnover points is within the first two weeks of employment, leading to a great deal of wasted time, effort and money in starting recruitment again. Induction is intended to minimize this danger. On starting employment, the employee should be issued with the following as appropriate

Contract of employment
Identification card
Locker and locker key
Uniform
Clocking in card
Staff house key (if applicable)

A medical examination is sometimes given at this point.

The following items should be included in the programme

1 Tour of housekeeping department and the whole establishment.
2 Introduction to the general manager and as many department heads as possible.
3 A film, slide presentation or talk on the organization.
4 House rules, usually accompanied by a staff handbook.
5 Health and safety session which should cover what to do in the event of a fire and/or an accident.
6 Clarification of contract of employment.
7 Explanation of duties, hours of work, meal breaks etc.

The follow-up interview

Within the first month of employment and preferably at the end of the first two weeks, the new member of staff should have an interview with his/her department head. The objective of the follow-up interview is to clarify any aspects of work that the employee may be concerned about. Any problems may be put right at this stage.

Other types of interview

Many people make the mistake of losing interest in their staff once they have safely been installed into the work situation, but many behaviourists have proved that work productivity and the working climate will be improved if there is a genuine interest in staff. There are however a number of interviews which take place between the employee and the department head during the course of employment.

Appraisal interview

The purpose of the appraisal or evaluation interview is to control the standards of staff work performance. These interviews may be carried out by the housekeeper

At the end of a training period
Prior to a pay rise, promotion or transfer
In conjunction with a management by objectives policy, when performance evaluations are done on a yearly or six-monthly basis (usually only for senior staff)

This interview is not designed to criticize the member of staff, but to help him/her to identify strong points and to discuss how these strengths may be maintained, and, on the other hand, to help him/her to identify weaknesses and discuss how these problems may be overcome. Tact is required if the member of staff is not performing adequately. No member of staff is perfect, not even the executive housekeeper, so when assessing the performance of a member of staff think how you would like to be told of your shortcomings.

Counselling interview

Counselling interviews are held in order to discuss and give advice on problems that staff may have at work or at home. The range of problems may be enormous and often the housekeeper has to accept the role of information centre if he/she cannot give all the answers. The secret to this type of interview is to allow the employee to solve the problem him/herself but at the same time offer support. It may be necessary to suggest that the member of staff seeks alternative advice from such bodies as the Citizens Advice Bureau, a doctor or a professional counsellor.

Grievance interview

Within the United Kingdom, all establishments must have a grievance procedure which is stipulated in the contract of employment. The purpose of a grievance interview is to enable an employee to air a grievance. The housekeeper must discover and try to remove the cause of dissatisfaction. This type of interview may begin as a grievance interview and end up as a counselling interview.

Disciplinary interview

As the name implies, this interview is to inform an employee of his/her shortcomings, to correct mistakes and bad behaviour and to prevent them from happening again. Discipline is a serious matter and may have to take a formal route. At the time of writing, an employer is required to issue one verbal warning and two written warnings within a reasonable period of time and in relation to a similar wrongdoing, before an employee may be dismissed, unless the offence is serious enough to warrant summary dismissal.

Termination interview

A termination interview may be a very emotional affair, but it is of utmost importance that the housekeeper should 'keep cool' and deal with the matter in a correct and efficient way. In a large establishment, she may be only partly involved in such an event, in conjunction with the personnel manager.

Dismissal procedure is complicated, and many problems can be avoided if the correct procedures at the commencement of employment have been carried out, and the employee has been given clear and detailed information and training. It is unwise to overlook mistakes, shoddy work or misdemeanours, since if they are not corrected they will be considered acceptable and become more serious. A careful log should be kept in the staff records of mistakes and procedures followed. Misconducts or letters should be at least in duplicate as the employee is entitled to receive a copy.

Exit interview

The purpose of an exit interview is to discover the real reason why an employee is leaving. If the member of staff has been asked to leave, then an exit interview is not necessary. The exit interview cannot be carried out by the department head as it is he/she who received the resignation in the first place and the employee would naturally wish to stick to his/her original reason for leaving. Ideally, such an interview should be carried out by the personnel manager, his/her aim being to identify staff turnover problems or climate problems in the housekeeping department.

Conduct of interviews

Homework should be done before any interview:

1 Study the employee's job, and what constitutes a satisfactory performance and review the standards attained.
2 Review the interviewee's background, experience and training.
3 Identify where the employee is failing.
4 Anticipate the possible tension and anxiety of the employee, remembering your own and trying to reduce that as well as his/hers. Be friendly, helpful, unhurried, objective but firm.
5 Arrange for uninterrupted privacy.
6 Be natural, and frank, about how his/her failures affect you and the customer. Be frank if you see that you may have failed (e.g. in not having given or arranged for adequate training).
7 Compare the employee's appraisal with your own but do not allow yourself to be sidetracked.
8 Be objective and stick to facts.

9 Ask the employee to determine in what areas improvement is needed.

10 If the employee cannot, or does not want to, improve, ask in what area he/she may be happier, and then say you need time to consider the proposal.

11 If he/she does think the standards in the area in which he/she is working can be attained, then give words of encouragement and assistance.

12 Tell the employee what he/she needs or wants to know regarding the organization, policies and how the employee's performance, development and advancement tie in with this.

Motivation

The majority of people work in order to receive monetary benefit in return for their efforts. Wage policies vary from establishment to establishment. Health service employees are currently covered by the Whitley Council Handbook which states not only wages but also terms and conditions of employment. Employees in the hotel and catering industry come under the Wages Councils, the main one being the Licensed Residential Establishment and Licensed Restaurant Wages Council. However, if hospital domestic work is put out to contract, staff will not come under the Whitley Council and it may be that the catering Wages Council will also be abolished at some date in the future. At present, however, they set minimum rates of pay and conditions of work, although employers in the private sector have the authority to give better wage rates and conditions of employment. Conditions of employment also cover sickness and holiday pay. There are other items offered to staff as additional benefits, which are considered below.

Tips

This is a controversial topic and there is usually a company policy relating to this. What an employee receives from a customer is his/her own business and it is his/her responsibility to declare tips to the Inland Revenue. However, if one person (a head watier or housekeeper perhaps) receives the tips and distributes them, the responsibility of seeing tax is paid can fall on that person. Ascertain from the management the policy on tips and follow this.

Where tips are distributed by the management and entered on the wages sheet, tax is deducted before the employee receives the money. This will happen when the service charge is added to the bill, as the money has gone into the company's accounts.

Guests will often give maids gifts rather than money. It is important that the housekeeper has a policy of issuing staff with a package pass to clear the maid of theft when he/she takes the item out of the building. Package passes can also be used for any other item which a maid is entitled to take out of the building, such as items of lost property which have not been claimed after the designated period of holding or items of old stock.

Pension scheme

Many companies offer a company pension scheme which is additional to the one offered by the state.

Private medical care

Medical care such as BUPA is usually a privilege offered to supervisory and management staff.

Transport

In remote areas of the country or where the need arises for staff to work late at night or early in the morning, free transportation may be offered.

Living-in facilities

Living-in facilities or staff houses are available in some hotels, especially those in remote areas, and in hospitals, boarding schools, halls of residence and residential homes. In advertisements the salary is quoted together with the sum which is deducted for the accommodation provided. Sometimes the net salary is quoted but this may seem lower than expected since people will not calculate the cost of renting accommodation and other benefits in kind. In some cases accommodation is provided with self-catering facilities.

Uniforms and protective clothing

Uniforms are usually supplied to all housekeeping staff. In some establishments safety shoes and tights are bought in bulk and made available to staff at cost price.

Social club

Some establishments have thriving social clubs, with events organized by a committee of enthusiastic staff. It might include sports facilities, dances, games, outings, visits, charity events, parties and so on. Often there is a club room with a television where staff may rest in break times.

Company privileges

Larger companies in the private sector usually offer all staff benefits such as complimentary accommodation in hotels within the group, fifty per cent food and beverage rates in company properties apart from the establishment where they are currently working, free or reduced travel facilities and discounts in other company outlets such as shops.

Bonus schemes

Bonus schemes tend to be more common in the welfare sector of the industry and are usually related to productivity.

Awards and competitions

Awards and competitions are designed to maintain standards and increase motivation and morale. If run properly they are very effective and staff appreciate tangible prizes.

Crèche

In some establishments it is advantageous to offer a child-minding service in order that women may come to work. Such a service could also be utilized for the beneit of guests. It is essential to have properly trained staff to care for children.

Work attitudes

Attitudes at work can be greatly influenced by the housekeeper. If often falls to the housekeeping staff to do some quite unpleasant jobs, but the housekeeper can set a good example by showing how to tackle these with minimal display of distaste or revulsion, and as practically as possible to reduce the unpleasantness. Appreciation of work well done should be expressed.

When a reprimand is necessary, try to find something which has been done well, mention this, give a word of praise, then come on to the points that need correction and make a comparison between what has been done well and that which has not.

Assess the abilities and skills of the staff and try to give to individuals what they can do and like doing best. If two people are not compatible then see that they do not work together.

Be positive about the work. While pointing out the necessity for evening work, for example, do not say 'Im afraid you will be required to work some evenings', but put it positively; 'Working some evenings will enable you to have the day free to do shopping and have time with your family'. That advantage may not have been thought of. Never speak negatively or disparagingly about any job but when there are disadvantages do not ignore them.

Rotas and work schedules

Duty rotas are necessary

1 To ensure that there are sufficient staff on duty at any given period in order that work may be covered.
2 To ensure that staff work the correct number of hours, as stipulated in the contract of employment.
3 To ensure that days off are as regular as possible giving staff adequate rest periods and ensuring that work output remains at a constant level.
4 To plan days off for staff in a fair manner.
5 To aid preparation of attendance and payroll reports.
6 To know who is on the premises in case of fire.

Duty rotas should be posted up on a notice board

for all staff to see, at least one week in advance in order that they may be able to arrange their private lives. During induction, the duty rota should be explained clearly to the new employee. Sometimes it is necessary to make last minute alterations to the rota but these should be explained to staff and not just announced. In most establishments, if staff require the occasional special day off then it is usually in the housekeeper's interest to allow it, for example a maid may ask for a Saturday off in order to attend a wedding. If there is a certain amount of flexibility within the department it will lead to a smoother running operation.

Before completing a duty rota it is necessary to ascertain

1 The coverage hours (those working hours when the housekeeping department is operational).
2 The number of full-time and part-time staff on the payroll.
3 Whether casual or agency staff are available.
4 The number of hours worked per day/week per person.
5 Meal and coffee breaks time allowances.
6 Expected productivity rate per employee per day/working period.
7 Staff requests such as special days off or holiday periods. Periods of illness must also be taken into consideration and sometimes provision has to be made for last minute sickness or absence.

Maids Duty Rota Date: Week ending 27 July

Occupancy	150	150	150	150	150	150	150
Name	Mon.	Tue.	Wed.	Thur.	Fri.	Sat.	Sun.
Anne	off	off					
June			Off	off			
Silvia					off	off	
Mary						off	off
Jane	off						off
Elaine		off	off				
Pamela				off	off		
Ann P.						off	off
Evelyn	off	off					
Margaret			off	off			
Rosemary					off	off	
Debbie	off						off
Joanna		off	off				
Jennie				off	off		

Figure 51 *Maids duty rota*

8   Quantity of expected work load per day.
9   Special operational factors, e.g. spring cleaning or refurbishment projects.

Figure 51 shows an example of a duty rota for a hotel where

1   Day maids are required to work from 7.30 a.m. until 3.30 p.m. including a half-hour meal break for lunch.
2   Each full-time maid works a 40 hour week.
3   The hotel has 150 rooms and is fully booked for the week in question.
4   Each maid is expected to clean 15 rooms per day.
5   There are 14 full-time day maids (no part-time or casual staff are available).
6   Mary is beginning her holiday on Saturday and June has requested Thursday off so that she can take her little boy to the clinic.

This is just a simple case study. Where the daily occupancy rate varies on a daily basis, duty rotas have to be planned more carefully. The previous night's occupancy rate is the expected work load in the housekeeping department for the following day, i.e. if the hotel is full on Monday night then there must be maximum staffing on Tuesday morning in order that all rooms may be cleaned ready for another full house on Tuesday night.

The majority of staff usually prefer to have both of their days off together, but this is not always possible. Where split days off are necessary, then it is advisable to allocate them to maids who prefer to take their free time in this manner.

Evenings, weekends, bank holidays

The normally accepted working periods are 9.00 a.m. to 5.00 a.m. Monday to Friday, and those outside these are often called 'unsocial hours'. However, in many industries including hotels, hospitals and other residential establishments, housekeeping services are required outside the normal working periods.

Evening work
In hospitals, residential homes and clinics the evening work may consist of straightening beds, tidying the day room and lounge, serving hot drinks and washing up afterwards, laying up breakfast trays. In hotels, evening work may be required for cloakroom service, turning down beds and tidying bathrooms, room service, and baby sitting if required.

In some small and traditional English hotels, housekeeping staff may be required to work a split day. This is not very satisfactory if the morning duty starts early and the evening one ends late. The difference between the starting hour in the morning and the finishing hour in the evening is known as 'spreadover'. For example, if the morning shift starts at 7.00 a.m. and the evening one at 10.00 p.m. there is a 14-hour spreadover. If spreadover exists the employer must pay the appropriate rate.

Weekend work
In most residential establishments work has to continue on Saturday and Sunday. Weekend working hours are frequently considered as unsocial hours, but they need not be for some people. Part-time staff may only be available for work at weekends: students, parents who will have their partners available at weekends to care for children, or people who have other weekday work and require to earn extra at the weekends.

It is advisable not to rely entirely on part-time staff at weekends, but to have one or two regular staff doing a weekend duty to give continuity. Weekend rotas can be drawn up so that regular staff work every other weekend or one in three or four, depending upon the number of staff available.

Holidays and bank holidays
Holiday rotas should be arranged several months in advance of the relief staff being booked. Special holiday charts can be purchased, but they can be drawn up to suit the special needs of the establishment. It is helpful if holiday dates can be discussed and arranged to the convenience of the staff and the department. Having two experienced members in one department away at the same time should be avoided if possible.

Holiday staff can be recruited from college

catering departments or from school leavers seeking work experience. It is helpful to have the relief staff coming in at weekends to work with the regular member, to see what has to be done. In some establishments one department may be off peak during the holiday season, so staff from that department may be transferred to another. For example, the banqueting department may not be working at full capacity during the summer. Sometimes part-time staff will work another one or two hours, and take on the work of the member on holiday.

Bank holidays should be recorded for each member of staff – whether they have been taken, paid for in lieu, or other days taken off in lieu. This information should be recorded on the employee's personal hours worked record sheet.

Training

Although many companies realize the benefits of training, one often hears the cry 'We don't have time for training' or 'As soon as we have trained them, they leave and we have to start all over again'. Some of the benefits of training are

1 New employees learn jobs and become effective quickly.
2 The work performance of existing employees is improved.
3 Productivity is improved and mistakes (sometimes expensive) are avoided.
4 Management time can be used for planning and development if staff do not have to be closely supervised.
5 Labour turnover is reduced and staff morale improved because of better job satisfaction.
6 Health and safety is better ensured.
7 Staff can be more flexible if trained in different areas.
8 Better quality staff are attracted when a company has a good reputation for training.
9 A good reputation for quality and standards attracts business.

Levels of training

Figure 52 shows the three main levels of training

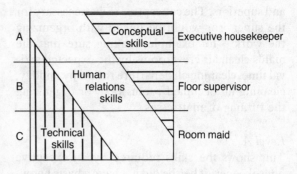

Figure 52 *Levels of training*

which are necessary in the housekeeping department of a large hotel.

Level C

This indicates the basic training level – that of the room maid or a cleaner. It can be seen that the majority of training required will be in the area of technical skills – the actual working skills, such as making beds and cleaning floors. The amount of human relations skills required is the same throughout all levels. This includes both verbal and non-verbal communication. Human relations skills are necessary for the maid to communicate with superiors, guests and other employees. On the right hand side of Figure 52, it can be seen that the maid requires a small amount of training in conceptual skills. This refers to those skills which are connected with planning, forecasting and organizing. Although a maid's job is primarily of a practical nature, if he/she is not organized in cleaning procedures, the work would take longer to accomplish.

Level B

This shows the training level appertaining to a supervisor. A supervisor's job should be split equally between technical skills, human relations skills and conceptual skills. It is essential that he/she has a sound technical knowledge, in order to train the maids and to maintain standards of work. Human relations skills are necessary for communication with guests, subordinates, peers and superiors. The conceptual skills necessary for the supervisor would be linked with organizing the work – for example, making sure that the maids clean air crew rooms by the expected arrival time, cleaning all departure rooms by midday, cleaning all occupied rooms first, or organizing the turning of mattresses.

Level A

This shows the skills required by an executive housekeeper. If he/she did not have a basic knowledge of the skills involved within his/her department, then he/she would be unable to maintain standards. Human relations skills are also essential, but the majority of skills required by any manager, are the skills of being able to conceptualize ideas, and to be able to plan, forecast, organize and control.

What is training?

Training is 'The development of human ability and behaviour in order to achieve individual growth'. Training may be applied to *Specific skills* (such as those required by a maid or cleaner) or *open-ended skills* (management or supervisory skills).

Before embarking on any form or training, the trainer must assess the costs of training; the benefits of training; and the most effective way of training.

The costs include the following

1   Learning costs
   (a)   Payment to employees when they are learning their jobs and when they are attending training sessions.
   (b)   Materials wasted in training.
   (c)   Sales lost by incorrect decisions.
   (d)   Reduced productivity in on the job training.
2   Training costs
   (a)   Part of manager's salary – time spent coaching staff.
   (b)   Training manager's/supervisor's salary.
   (c)   Capital outlay and running costs of training room/centre.

   (d)   Training aids – over head projector, projector, screen, films, books, other visual aids, fees to visiting speakers, visits, cost of external courses.

The training budget is often used for these items. There may also be the cost of the risk that when an employee is trained, he/she may leave and join another company.

The benefits of training have been outlined on page 255. These have to be assessed in relation to each situation.

Successful training

The establishment and the management must be committed to training. There should also be training policies laid down and money made available for training. The people doing the training, and the employees being trained must be equally committed.

Training structure

Part of the success of training is having a systematic training structure or cycle, as shown in Figure 53.

Identifying training needs (Stage 1)

If people are training for no specific purpose then the exercise is futile. In a housekeeping department there are many ways of trying to identify training needs. Any one of the following examples may indicate a training need:

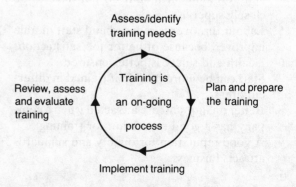

Figure 53   *A systematic training cycle*

Accidents
Guest complaints
New equipment
Low productivity
Low morale
Redeployment
Breakages
Changing laws and policies
Bad communication
Absenteeism
Promotion from within

It also helps to break down the need area into the training skills categories suggested on page 255. Having decided on the type of skill deficiency, it is then far easier to move on to the second stage of the training cycle.

Planning and preparing the training (Stage 2)
Most of the skills required by the maid are technical ones. The best way of training for technical skills is 'on the job' training, sometimes referred to as 'skills training'. Skills training is performed on a 'one to one' basis – the trainer explaining the skills individually to the trainee.

For human relations and conceptual skills, there are several ways of performing a training session:

Lecture
Discussion
Debate
Case study
Project
Lesson
Talk
Exercise
Films/slides
Role play
Group dynamics
Closed circuit TV

Many of these types of training are more suitable for supervisors and management than maids or cleaners. Before deciding on the appropriate method of training, it is advisable to ask seven questions.

1 *Who* will perform the training session?
2 *Which* people will attend the training session?
3 *Why* will they attend?
4 *What* subject will the training session cover?
5 *Where* will the session be given?
6 *When* will it be given and for what length of time?
7 *How* will the training be delivered (what method)?

Implementing the training (Stage 3)
People learn by receiving information via their senses, in approximately the following proportions.

Seeing	75%
Hearing	13%
Feeling	6%
Smelling	3%
Tasting	3%
	100%

The old Chinese proverb is relevant to training:

'I hear   – I forget
I see   – I remember
I do   – I understand'

All training sessions should have three parts: introduction, content and closure.

A mnemonic used for the *introduction* of a session is

I *Interest*. The first three minutes is an essential period in any session to catch the trainee's attention.
N *Need*. Explain the relevance of this training session.
T *Title*. Give the title of the session, so that the trainee knows what he or she is about to learn.
R *Range*. The topic that will be covered this session and what it will be followed by.
O *Objective*. What the trainee will be able to do by the end of this training session.

The following guidelines relate to the *content of* the session.

1   Clarity of communication – explanations and instructions must be clearly understood.
2   Material should be relevant.
3   Knowledge – new knowledge should be related to previous knowledge.
4   Pacing – movement from one part of the lesson to the next should be in a step by step method at a suitable speed.
5   Visual aids.
6   Teaching methods should be suitable to the trainees and to the topic.
7   Student involvement participation.
8   Question technique – suitable use of questions.
9   Relationship with students.
10 Length – people lose concentration after about 20 minutes so topics should be changed after 20 minutes.

Towards the end of the session the *closure* or summing up should include:

1   Repetition of the major points covered – this reinforces the learning process.
2   Any questions.
3   Preparation of the trainee for the next step of the training.
4   A practice session or exercises – giving a deadline.

Evaluating training (Stage 4)
The purpose of evaluating the training is

1   To assess the performance of the trainer, so that improvements may be made.
2   To provide the trainees with feedback, to motivate them to continue with their good performance or encourage them to do better. Always encourage strengths and help people to become aware of their weaknesses in order that they may overcome them.
3   To assess whether the training has been worthwhile. Have the objectives been achieved? Have the needs been fulfilled?
4   To assess what improvements can be made to provide better training on the next cycle.

Evaluation should not simply take place at the end of a cycle, but should continue throughout it.

Hotel and Catering Industrial Training Board (HCITB)
The HCITB was set up in 1966 but at the time of writing is under review by the Government. The HCITB is responsible for seeing that the quality and quantity of training is adequate to meet the needs of the hotel and catering industry in Britain. Its main duties are

1   To ensure that sufficient training is provided.
2   To publish recommendations on the nature, content and length of training for occupations in the hotel and catering industry and for further education establishments.
3   To produce training material and aids such as booklets, slides, films etc. in order that establishments may get more involved in training, but also to help the Board itself be more self-sufficient and less reliant on the government.

Under the 1964 and 1982 Industrial Training Acts, hotel and catering employers are required to:

1   Keep records of all training done.
2   Produce those records for examination by a member of the HCITB.
3   Complete returns of training information.

This is to enable statistics on training to be kept, and to help the HCITB forecast training needs for the future. The statistics are required for levies and grants. The HCITB currently has the power of imposing a levy on employers in the industry at a rate equal to 1 per cent of the annual payroll. 0.1 per cent of this levy is kept by the Board to cover administration costs and the remaining 0.9 per cent is subject to exemption. In 1983 companies with a payroll of less than £110,000 p.a. were excluded from the levy, but this situation may alter in the future. Section 14 of the Industrial Training Act 1982 allows that 'where an industrial training board is satisfied that a company is doing adequate training, then exemption applies'. This means that the company could receive up to 90 per cent payroll levy back. The employer also has the right to appeal to an Industrial Tribunal against the training levy.

Training grants are currently available from the HCITB for the following (but could be subject to change)

1 Craft training, e.g. City and Guilds of London Institute Examinations.
2 BTEC certificate courses.
3 Approved training projects.
4 Training hygiene instructors.
5 Training sales trainers.
6 Research and development.
7 Training craft trainees (those registered before March 1983).

Further reading

Beach, D., *Personnel* (Collier-Macmillan 1980).
Boella, M., *Personnel Management in the Hotel and Catering Industry*, 3rd Ed. (Hutchinson 1983).
Kenny, J., Donnelly, E., and Reid, A., *Manpower, Training and Development* (IPM 1981).
Torrington, D., and Chapman J., *Personnel Management* (Prentice-Hall 1979).

Useful addresses

The Hotel and Catering Industry Training Board,
PO Box 18,
Ramsey House,
Central Square,
Wembley, Middlesex HA9 7AP
Tel: 01-902 8865

National Educational Media, Inc.,
21601 Devonshire Street,
Chatsworth,
California 91311,
USA

NEM Films available in the UK from:
Training Films International Ltd,
St. Mary's Street,
Whitchurch,
Shropshire
Tel: Whitchurch (0948) 3341

Video Arts Ltd,
Dumbarton House,
68 Oxford Street,
London W1N 9LA
Tel: 01-637 7288

The Lady,
39–40 Bedford Street,
London WC2E 9ER

Consumers' Association,
14 Buckingham Street,
London WC2N 6DS

21 Health and safety

The Health and Safety at Work Act 1974

Prior to 1974, The Offices, Shops and Railways Premises Act had little power to ensure safety in hotel and catering establishments. However, the Health and Safety at Work Act 1974 has made everybody responsible for safety in all establishments, although it excludes domestic situations. The aims of the act are:

1   To secure the health, safety and welfare of persons at work.
2   To protect persons other than those persons at work (e.g. guests or contractors).
3   To control storage and use of explosive or highly flammable or dangerous substances (for example methylated spirits or book matches).
4   To control the emission into the atmosphere of noxious or offensive substances from premises of any class (this refers primarily to other industries than hotels).

The Act specifies that it is the duty and responsibility of both employer and employee to conduct undertakings in such a way as is reasonably practicable to prevent the risk of health and safety. The term 'reasonably practicable' is used a great deal throughout the Act and means that if the risk to health and safety is greater than the cost involved, action must be taken. If on the other hand it can be proven that the cost far outweighs any risks to health and safety, then probably no action would be taken. The employer must create an awareness of the importance of achieving a high standard of health and safety. Management has the responsibility of seeing that:

1   All preventative measures are taken and the building and the equipment is made as safe as possible.
2   Danger areas are adequately lit.
3   Worn or inadequately maintained equipment is repaired or replaced.
4   When selecting equipment and tools, adequate safeguards are built in.
5   Training/instruction is given to staff for the correct use and maintenance of equipment, and that guards, where necessary, are provided and remain in use.
6   Protective clothing and guards are provided for the operators of the equipment.
7   Training is given in safe work procedures.
8   Worn floors, carpets and unstable furniture are replaced or repaired.
9   Immediate action is taken to investigate any reported safety hazard.
10 The accident Books are available and kept up to date.

The Health and Safety at Work Act states that 'new staff must have such information, instruction, training and supervision as is necessary for their health and safety'. This should include the following.

Induction/orientation

Although there is no legal obligation to give induction training to new staff, it is certainly a very good way to deliver information and instructions with regard to health and safety (see Chapter 20).

Skills training

Efficient training will cover health and safety aspects (see Chapter 20).

Fire training

A fire certificate will lay down training requirements necessary for staff, especially new employees, including fire training given during the induction period. Day staff require two fire training sessions per year and night staff four. Fire training should include fire drill, evacuation procedure and use of equipment. A fire training log book must be kept up to date as it may be inspected by the local fire officer, the local authority and the HCITB.

First aid

The First Aid Regulations 1981 specify that there must be at least 1 qualified first aider for every 150 staff. There must also be a correct size of first aid box, which should be filled with the stipulated first aid dressings, as laid down in the regulations. All staff should know: who the first aider/s are; where the first aid equipment is kept; and the first aid procedure, including how to call an ambulance. The St John Ambulance and British Red Cross Society run expert courses in first aid.

Health and safety policy

Each establishment must have an adequate health and safety policy statement of which the employees should also be made aware. It must include details of training, correct use of equipment and materials, safe methods of working, personal safety (including protective clothing), accident procedure and infection control (in hospitals).

Accident prevention

Industrial accidents are usually caused by one of the following:

1 Improper methods of work.
2 Improper conditions or circumstances.
3 Attitudes.

Accidents caused by improper methods of work could be prevented by adequate training and supervision and well thought out method of work. Accidents caused by improper conditions or circumstances could be prevented by adequate reporting systems for faulty equipment, necessary repairs and maintenance, and health and safety hazards. Reporting systems are useless unless acted upon. Accidents caused through peoples' attitudes are a little more difficult to overcome. Staff selection could play a major role in employing the most suitable staff in the first place, but efficient training programmes and supervision and management are essential. Above all, staff must realize their own responsibilities as far as the Health and Safety at Work Act is concerned.

1 All staff must take reasonable care of the health and safety of themselves and others who may be affected by their actions at work.
2 Staff should co-operate with their employer and other persons giving a duty request.
3 Protective clothing provided by the employer must be worn and guards should not be removed from equipment.
4 Training should be followed.

In general accidents are caused by

1 Failure in supervision.
2 Lack of or inadequate instruction and training.
3 Faulty design of machinery and equipment.
4 Incorrect use of equipment.
5 Irresponsible behaviour.
6 Failure to follow laid down procedure.
7 Failure to notice and report potential dangers.
8 Maliciousness and vandalism.
9 Breakdown of equipment through lack of maintenance.
10 Distressed staff being allowed to use potentially dangerous equipment.
11 Excessive noise.
12 Not using the correct tool for the job.
13 Running.
14 Not replacing tools and utensils in the correct position.

Accidents and illness

If there is not a resident nurse in the establishment, the housekeeper will be required to attend to accidents, injuries, illness and death. He/she should have a knowledge of first aid and procedures for dealing with injuries and illnesses. Discretion, tact and calm authority is essential and staff must be told the necessity of not panicking and spreading alarm and the news of what has happened to the guests and other members of the staff. Never apply more than the basic first aid unless trained. If an accident or illness appears to be serious, go to the scene of the incident, taking a first aid box (or sending someone to collect it) and send for a doctor or ambulance. Do not leave the patient alone. In a public area ask the other occupants to move to another area to avoid embarrassment to them and the patient. Screen the patient with upturned tables/chairs or screen if available, with room for the access of ambulance men. Do not move the patient except where there is risk of continued danger. If the patient thinks he/she can move, warn him/her not to so if it causes pain as further damage can be done.

In cases of a fit or convulsion move the patient from a confined area, as the involuntary thrashing of body and limbs can cause physical harm. If possible help the patient to adopt a prone position, head on one side, in case there is vomiting. Unless there is limb or back injury, bend the leg to relax the stomach muscles.

Reception and the manager should be informed. Relatives should be informed if the patient might be expected home. If the patient is admitted to hospital, it is kinder if relatives are informed personally.

Fill in the accident book immediately the patient has been taken care of. Never give alcohol to the patient, nor indulge yourself until the patient and records have been dealt with.

To call in emergency services

1 Take a deep breath, and pause a second or two to make sure that you have all the relevant information to give to the service.
2 Dial 999.
3 State service required, or give nature of emergency.
4 Give Name of speaker and status.
       Address at which there is the emergency.

Name and address of patient (if known).
Nature of casualty.
Approximate age and stature of patient.
Diagnosis (if possible).

5 In a large establishment, state which access will be the most convenient for the ambulance.

If a hotel customer is ill in bed, the housekeeper will be called to attend the invalid. He/she should enter the room cheerfully, without showing any anxiety.

Ask the patient if he/she is receiving medication of any sort or if this is a condition with which they are familiar. If it does not appear to be a serious illness, make the patient comfortable and arrange for meals to be sent to the room. If the patient appears to require a doctor, call the doctor, giving details that you have ascertained.

Inform reception that there is a sick person and the room may be required for longer than the booking. Tell them that the doctor will be coming so that the housekeeper can be informed immediately.

Infectious illnesses
In cases of suspected infectious illness, limit those attending the patient to one or two people only. This applies to heavy colds, sore throats and sickness and diarrhoea. Since sickness and diarrhoea can be brought about by food poisoning, it is important to ask the patient at what time he/she last ate before the symptoms appeared. Get details of:

1 What was eaten.
2 Where it was eaten.
3 At what time as exactly as possible.
4 Whether any companions ate the same food at the same time.

If the food has been eaten on the premises:

1 Alert the kitchen.
2 Have the remainder of the suspect food isolated, and discontinue serving it.
3 Keep the food ready for inspection by the health inspector.

Death

If death is even only suspected, call the doctor immediately – a person appearing dead may not be but in a deep coma. If death has been pronounced, telephone the police who will inform or attempt to inform the next-of-kin. They and the doctor will deal with the necessary things like calling an undertaker.

Inform only the most involved and responsible members of staff. The police and doctor and undertakers will co-operate with the requirements necessary for the discreet removal of the body of the deceased. Collect the belongings of the person, make an inventory with copy and have them packed ready for collection by the relatives. An outstanding bill, including any extra expenses involved should not be overlooked, and it should be dealt with by the deceased's solicitors.

Notifiable accidents and injuries

Under the notification of Accidents and Dangerous Occurrences Regulations, 1980, employers must notify the enforcing authority of

1 Any accident causing death or major injury to an employee.
2 Any accident which occurs on the premises which are under your control, causing death or major injury to a self-employed person or to a member of the public.
3 Any notifiable dangerous occurrence affecting the work or equipment either of your firm, or self-employed persons working on the premises which are under your control even if no-one is injured.

'Major injury' is defined as follows

1 Fracture of the skull, spine or pelvis.
2 Fracture of any bone in the arm, other than a bone in the wrist or hand, or in the leg, other than a bone in the ankle or foot.
3 Amputation of a hand or foot.
4 The loss of sight of an eye.
5 Any other injury which results in the person injured being admitted into hospital as an in-patient for more than 24 hours, unless that person is detained only for observation.

If you do not know to whom to report, tell the nearest office of the Health and Safety Executive. They will pass on your report.

Enter details of the accident/dangerous occurrence in your record book. Form F2509 may be used for this purpose. Within seven days send a written report, on Form F2508, to your enforcing authority. Other injuries to employees are also notifiable if they result in more than three days' absence from work, but all you need to do is

1 Enter details of the accident in the accident record book (or other record system). Form F2509 may be used for this purpose.
2 Complete Form Bl 76 (relating to a claim for industrial injury benefit) when asked to do so by your local DHSS office.

For the purpose of insurance and possible legal action being taken the following notes of serious accidents should be made

1 Names of those involved and their occupation.
2 Place and time of accident.
3 Nature of injury.
4 First aid (whether given and by whom).
5 Doctor called.
6 Hospital attended (if any).
7 Statements from witnesses of the accident.
8 Whether or not the people involved where authorized to be in that area.
9 How long had the employee been doing the job or using the equipment.
10 Whether the employee had been given training for the job and/or in the use of the equipment/machine.
11 Whether the accident occurred during normal working hours.
12 The condition of the machine/equipment being used, and when it was last serviced.
13 What might have been done to prevent the accident, and what could be done to prevent a reoccurrence.

The health and safety committee

All establishments should have a safety

committee. If the staff are unionized, the union will back this function. If the establishment is not unionized, a safety committee can be organized by having safety representatives from the various departments. The committee should be comprised of members of staff with just one or two members of management.

The functions of the safety committee and representatives include

1 Ensuring that adequate safety rules are displayed.
2 Putting forward new designs for pieces of equipment etc.
3 Putting forward new ideas in relation to health and safety matters.
4 Examining the accident book or accident reports, to identify how the accident happened and what steps can be taken to avoid a similar occurrence.
5 Carrying out hazard spotting exercises and making trouble reports to the maintenance department in order that potential dangers may be put right.
6 Observing any slackness in use of safety measures.
7 Advising on training.
8 Promoting the awareness of the importance of health and safety to all employees.

Fire

According to the Fire Precautions Act, 1971, all premises possessing sleeping accommodation for more than six people, whether they be staff or guests; possessing sleeping accommodation for staff or guests in buildings with a second or more floors, or possessing sleeping accommodation for staff or guests below the ground floor of the building, are included in the first order issued under the Act, which came into effect in 1972. All these premises must now be covered by a fire certificate under the Offices, Shops and Railway Premises Act, 1963 or the Factories Act, 1961. Where sleeping accommodation is not provided, a fire certificate must be provided where more than twenty people are employed or more than ten are employed above ground level.

Fire certificates

A fire certificate is only given when the authority considers that the fire fighting equipment, fire exits and fire warning systems are adequate. All fire certificates must be kept on the premises. The occupier must notify the authority before carrying out any material alterations or extensions to the property. Where the authorities consider it necessary, they may insist that old certificates are amended or that new ones be issued. The penalties for operating without a fire certificate where one is required are a fine of up to £400, or two years' imprisonment, or both. Fire drills should be regularly practised. Power supplies should be carefully and regularly checked.

The fire certificate states in detail what is required for each establishment, and the conditions must be strictly adhered to. It is issued after the fire officer has inspected the building and made recommendations, and the recommendations have been met. These will include

1 Fire warning systems.
2 Methods and means of escape: adequate staircases and all escape routes from upper floors.
3 Separation of risk areas from escape routes.
4 Secondary and emergency lighting to illuminate routes.
5 Use of fire resistant paints for specific areas.
6 Extinguishers: types suitable for specific areas and siting.
7 Use of reinforced glass.
8 Fire drill and instruction to staff on fire prevention and what to do in the event of fire.
9 Types of doors and self-closing appliances.
10 Posting of 'What to do in the event of fire' notices.
11 How exit doors are to be opened in emergency.

After issuing the fire certificate, the fire officer makes periodic checks to see that the conditions are being carried out.

Fire precautions

Where there is no engineering or technical department, the housekeeper may advise on fire precautions. A chief engineer will normally consult with her/him on such matters.

Fire detectors
Apart from being installed in the recommended places, such as corridors and service areas, the housekeeper may suggest additional detectors to be fitted as safety measures.

Fire alarms
Especially in the case of old peoples' homes, the housekeeper may be asked for advice on the positioning of some alarms. A policy must also be decided upon for such residents as those who are deaf, blind or disabled.

Keys in boxes
Where these are accepted by the local fire authority they should be checked on the daily round to see that none have been tampered with or removed.

Fire extinguishers
These should be checked each day to see they are in the correct place, not changed or so placed that when a door is opened the aparatus is not apparant. When siting fire extinguishers, the housekeeper may be able to point out inconvenient situations where the staff work. A wall mounted appliance may be too heavy to be lifted from a bracket. Appliances placed too near doors and on the side on to which the door opens make them too handy for use as door stops.

Fire prevention
Apart from the fire certificate requirements, attention should be paid to the following

1 Regular cleaning of chimneys, ventilating ducts, extractor fans and flues.
2 Use of flame retardant materials for furnishings, furniture, wall coverings and decorating materials.
3 Ashtrays designed so that a smouldering cigarette will not fall out. They should be made of metal (as should waste bins), glass, china or earthenware.

4 No smoking signs that can be understood by non-English speakers at appropriate points.
5 Keeping curtains and other combustible material away from candles or high wattage bulbs. Glass can concentrate the sun's rays, so combustible material should be kept away from a window which allows in constant sunshine.
6 Candles should be placed in non-flammable holders and never in arrangements of dried flowers or fabric.
7 Sockets should not be overloaded with adaptors. Electrical cables should be inspected regularly for any fraying.
8 Stable and adequate fireguards in front of gas, electric and open fires.
9 Televisions switched off at the socket at night and in vacant rooms.
10 Paints and thinners should not be stored in lofts or boiler houses.
11 Thatched roofs are highly flammable, and the lofts should be inspected regularly to ensure that combustible material is not being stored there.
12 Convector heaters should never be covered, and a prominent sign should ensure that users are aware of this.
13 Smoking in bed should be discouraged with prominent notices.

Automatic fire detection
A fire detector sends signals to the central panel, to the alarm and in some systems directly to the fire station. If the fire station is not alerted by the system, then a telephone should be adjacent to the panel so that it can be phoned quickly. There are three types of detector: smoke (and combustion gases), radiation and heat.

Extinguishers
The principles underlying all appliances are

1 To prevent the flames being supplied with oxygen.
2 To remove the heat or fuel.
3 To reduce the flammability of adjacent material.

Water is the most obvious extinguisher of flames, but should never be used on electrical or fat fires. Water is a good conductor of electricity, and would add to the danger if used on a fire from electric appliances or cables. Water would also spread fat, thus spreading the fire. Therefore there are special extinguishers for use in certain areas.

Fire blankets are stored in a drum, and can be pulled out by tugging a loop or ring. They are *placed*, not thrown, over flames, or used to wrap up an individual whose clothing is burning.

Sand or soil can be used to extinguish or contain small fires, or to mop up spillages of flammable liquids. In an emergency a soda syphon can be used to put out a small fire, when paper in an ashtray or waste paper basket ignites.

Extinguishers are coded by colour to indicate the contents and the type of fire for which they are intended.

Red   Water type suitable for wood, paper, textiles, or any other material which burns with an ash. They can be used to soak adjacent materials which might be in danger of catching fire while the main fire is being dealt with.

Green   Vapourizing liquid extinguishers, suitable for liquid (oil or fat) and electrical equipment fires.

Blue   Dry powder type, suitable for liquid and electrical fires.

Cream   Foam-filled suitable for fires which are contained e.g., a large fish-fryer.

Black   Carbon dioxide-filled, suitable for electrical and liquid fires.

The size of the appliance varies according to the contents and the risk they are designed to cover. Water appliances are generally sited on the line of exit adjacent to the fire alarm-activating points, and they are the most common type to give general cover.

In areas of specific risk the appropriate type should be sited. For example kitchens should have a dry powder or carbon dioxide type. They should not be placed too near the risk source, but near the line of exit. An appliance placed next to a fish-fryer could not be reached should the fryer catch fire.

Hoses are installed in some buildings. They have the advantage of an unlimited supply of water, are easy to handle, but they can do much damage. Hoses should be tested from time to time.

Emergency lighting

Emergency lighting in public buildings is designed to come on whenever there is a failure in the normal current supplying normal lighting (see Chapter 18). Emergency lighting luminaires are coded

1   *NM (non-maintained)* which are illuminated only when the mains power fails.
2   *M (maintained)* which are illuminated at all material times and automatically switch over to a battery supply when the mains supply fails.
3   *S (sustained)* which have two or more lamps: (a) mains powered lamps which extinguish when mains power fails, and (b) battery powered lamps which illuminate automatically when the mains power fails.

In the event of fire

Each establishment will have its own policy and instructions with regard to fire and bomb scare procedures. In the case of evacuation, the housekeeper will normally be expected to take the staff duty rota in order that all housekeeping staff on duty may be accounted for at the assembly point.

In a hotel, the reception staff are normally responsible for guest lists, but in other accommodation establishments, this may be the job of the housekeeper. It is of utmost importance that any list be accurate so that all human beings present in the building can be accounted for.

After a fire, leave the scene and look after people. The fire service will look after the scene of the fire and they need to be left unhampered to do any salvage work and to assess from the debris the cause of the fire. The housekeeper will usually be called in to inspect the damage, but should not touch anything until the assessor arrives. An inventory of the contents of the building should be kept in a safe place away from the building. Occupants of the building will submit to the management their own losses.

Insurance

Premiums are paid to ensure that what has been destroyed, lost or damaged can be replaced. After a fire, insurance companies call in independent assessors to assess the extent of the damage and the value of what has been lost and its replacement. Smoke and fumes contaminate, so a room which may have been untouched by actual fire, may have contaminated clothes, food, furniture, furnishings and wall coverings.

Useful addresses

The British Institute of Management,
Management House,
Parker Street,
London WC2B 5PT

The Fire Protection Association,
Aldermary House,
Queen Street,
London EC4N 1TJ

The HCITB,
PO Box 18,
Wembley,
Middlesex HA9 7AP

Useful films

Anatomy of Fire, *Plastics in Fire*, *Fire in Store*, available from
Central Film Library,
Chalfont Grove,
Gerrards Cross,
Bucks.

22 Security

When people are staying away from home, one of the most important assets that an accommodation establishment can offer is security, which to the guest means peace of mind.

Keys

Whether keys are of the traditional or electronic type, staff must realize their responsibility in handling the keys which open guest rooms, store rooms and offices.

Grand master/emergency master key

This key should open *all* doors in the building whether or not they be double locked. In a hotel this key is usually held only by the general manager, duty manager or front office manager. Ideally there should only be one grand master key in order to maximize security.

The main purposes of a grand master key are

1 Use in case of fire.
2 To double lock a guest room from the outside if
   (a) The guest has requested the room to be locked in this manner.
   (b) The guest has not paid his bill or is suspected of being a 'walk out' (someone who has walked out without paying).
   (c) The guest has reached the daily limit of expenditure and is required by reception to settle his or her account.
3 If someone has locked themselves out or lost another key to any door within the establishment.

Master key

A master key may be held by all department heads who have any connection with the guest rooms. The executive housekeeper, the chief engineer, the front office manager and the chief security officer may hold a key of this type, but the more master keys there are, the less security there is. A master key will open all guest room doors unless they are double locked. There is usually a separate master key for office doors. The master key is used only for the purpose of work – to allow those people who work within the Rooms Division to do their work more effectively. In some smaller establishments even the maids have master keys.

Sub-master/floor master keys

A floor master key opens all the guest room doors on one particular floor. In a smaller establishment, the term sub-master key would be used, as this key would probably open all doors in a particular part of the building, for example, a particular wing. The floor master key is held by anyone who has to work in the particular area which is covered by the key. The room maid and floor housekeeper will carry this type of key, as will perhaps, a room service waiter or mini-bar attendant in a large hotel.

Section key

A section key will only open a certain number of rooms, for example, the fifteen rooms which make up a particular maid's section. Section keys are only usually found in larger establishments where a high occupancy rate is constant. If the occupancy rate is variable the maid will have to carry several section keys around with her in order that she may complete her quota of rooms.

The advantage of having section keys is a much

tighter control on security. If a theft occurs, it is much easier to identify who was responsible for the key in that particular section.

Electronic keys

At the time of writing, electronic keys are only found in large, luxury, modern hotels, simply because of the extremely high investment cost involved. Several companies are now making this type of key, which resemble bank cards and are used in a similar way. The guest is issued with the key by the hotel reception. Behind the desk there is a computer console which randomly codes and issues the key card. The receptionist who issues the guest key is also controlled; he/she must use an authorization key in order to operate the computer and the number on the authorization key is recorded so that the person who issued each key can be traced.

The guest room door is fitted with a battery operated lock which will accept the key card. When the guest checks out, he/she takes the key – a souvenir and often a form of advertising. The next guest who arrives will be issued with a new key with a different code. The door lock will then only accept the new code. With the traditional key system there is the constant worry of keys being lost or stolen but with an electronic system, if the guest loses a key, a new one may be issued with a completely different code, thus making the previous key useless. Some systems hold up to 4 billion codes at random with no starting point for the key codes; these are the most secure on the market.

As with the traditional system, section keys, master keys, and grand master keys can also be produced and codes may be easily changed should any one of the keys be lost or stolen. The batteries in the door lock usually last for a period of about two years and then can easily be changed. If there is an electricity power cut manual programmers are used to open guest room doors.

Control of keys

If a conventional key is lost or stolen, the door lock should immediately be changed if satisfac-

tory security is to be maintained. This situation is however both time consuming and costly. To overcome such problems there are locks available which have interchangeable cores.

Housekeeping keys should either be kept secured to the person by means of a chain, leather belt or an expandable key ring and when not in use, they should be locked away in a key cabinet. Housekeepers are noted for carrying around bunches of keys. This is because there are many cupboards and store rooms besides many items actually in guest areas which have keys in order to prevent petty pilferage. Very often the following articles are all kept locked: soap dispensers, toilet roll holders, towel dispensers, sanitary towel dispensers, tissue holders and other guest service vending machines.

When staff come on duty, they should always sign for their keys. Similarly, when they go off duty, they should sign the keys back in. This will help to ensure that all the keys can be accounted for.

Crime prevention

Key control, as described above, is the first step towards preventing theft. Training and induction for staff is also important. Staff should be clearly told of their responsibility towards both guest and hotel property, and of regulations concerned with suspected theft, and the consequences of any transgression. Staff should be trained

1 Never to open doors for guests who have 'lost their key'. They should politely tell the guest to go to reception for a replacement.
2 Never to unlock doors for contractors or other employees. They should go through the proper channels.
3 To apply for a package pass if they have been given a gift by a guest, or if they are authorized to take uncollected lost property or discarded hotel property home.
4 To keep their keys on their person – never to leave them on top of a trolley or in the lock.
5 Place the trolley in front of the door of the room in which he/she is working to prevent

other people entering a room which is being cleaned.

6   To keep an eye out for suspicious-looking guests. The following might be regarded as suspicious and should be reported
   (a)   The guest with little or no luggage – he/she might be a 'walk-out'.
   (b)   Guests who sleep out of their rooms.
   (c)   Guests who double lock their doors or display a 'Do not disturb' notice for a long period. They may have walked out, or may be ill or even dead.
   (d)   Guests who are drunk or rowdy.
   (e)   Suspected prostitutes.

Staff should be provided with a locker for bags and coats. They should never be allowed to take bags to their place of work. A safe should be available for use of guests and staff, and notices should advertise it. Peep holes and security chains on guest room doors are another useful measure. Cloakrooms may be a target for thieves, especially if a large function is taking place. It should be secure and staffed by trustworthy personnel.

Petty pilfering

Petty pilfering is one of the most common problems within the hotel and catering industry. Many establishments do not worry too much about petty pilfering and write off the costs. Guests can be equally guilty of petty pilfering.

It is the housekeepers' responsibility to take precautions to guard against petty pilferage and theft. In profit-making establishments, it is the responsibility of the housekeeper to advise on guest supplies and give-aways and to control them. Sometimes it is better to buy cheap ashtrays with the hotel logo on. When such cheap items may be stolen with a possible advertising advantage.

Theft

The maid is always the first person to be suspected of theft if something goes missing from a guest room. If a housekeeper is to maintain staff morale and self-respect he/she should always

back up staff. However, any member of staff who has access to guest rooms has to be investigated if there is a suspected theft and it is always a good idea to keep a confidential record in case a future pattern emerges.

Large properties will have their own security staff who handle such problems as thefts. Some establishments have very sophisticated security equipment such as close circuit television, which, although very expensive to install, acts as a very good deterrent. Smaller establishments delegate the responsibility of security to a member of the management team and of course in some cases it is necessary to call in the police, especially if it is at the wish of a guest or member of staff. If a problem can be solved without calling in the police so much the better.

The utmost diplomacy must be used when handling thefts and investigations must be handled fairly and thoroughly. Some establishments make use of a special form where all the relevant information can be entered, whether the problem is to be dealt with privately or by the police.

Lost property

Any accommodation establishment must have a policy on lost property which is also in line with the law. In the rest of Europe, items of lost property must usually be kept for the period of one year, whereas in England, ordinary items should be kept for a period of three months and more valuable items for six months. The housekeeper is usually in charge of lost property and all items wherever they may be found should be handed in as soon as possible. A guest may often be reunited with his belongings, if staff are alert, before he has even left the building.

Housekeeping staff especially should be trained to hand in items of lost property as soon as possible, rather than leaving them on their trolleys where they may be stolen.

If the item is of extreme importance, e.g. a wallet or passport, and contains the name and address of the owner, then he/she should be contacted and the item returned after identification has been proved satisfactory. It is not normal practice for guests to be contacted to tell them that the establishment believes that they have left items behind after their stay. Postage and telephone calls are very expensive. All lost property items should, however be entered into a log book. Such a book will also record the cost of postage and packing and any other expenditure relating to the return of the item.

Depending on company policy, at the end of the holding period one of the following procedures may take place

1 Return to finder.
2 Items sold and monies used for staff benefit, e.g. Christmas Party or present.
3 Items given to a worthy cause.

If staff benefit from handing in lost property items they are more likely to be motivated to do so.

If the owner cannot collect the item in person the collector should have some form of identity and a letter of authorization. Items of extreme value should be handed to the police for safe keeping.

Lost property items should be stored in clearly marked sealed packages such as envelopes or plastic laundry bags. The decision on whether to keep a lost property item or not, should lie with the housekeeper and not with the finder.

Insurance

Theft represents another situation where the hotelier has to protect the property of guests as well as his own. Theft by staff should be covered under a separate policy. It is important that adequate safety precautions and security checks be made to deter thefts, otherwise claims may become invalid. A straightforward theft policy is not always adequate.

Liability insurance

Protection of guests' property is often better covered under liability insurance. A hotelier's liability to a guest can arise in a variety of ways – dangerous premises, incompetent staff and impure food. In addition, the Employer's Liability (Compulsory Insurance) Act, 1969 requires employers to take out an approved insurance policy to cover all possible claims by employees in connection with injuries. Failure to do so is a criminal offence. Normally, liability policies do not cover liabilities entered into under hire, leasing and franchise contracts. It is possible to take out a policy to cover plate glass and hoteliers are well advised to insure against such things as the loss of licence and loss of revenue resulting from seasonal bad weather, fire or storm damage.

Whenever an accident occurs, it is important that no comment should be made that will commit the management/owners' insurance company until an investigation has been made.

The Act limits the sum to which the host may be responsible, and the guests should be encouraged to hand over for safe keeping, in a safe, article of value in excess of a certain sum. Many hotels now have safes installed in the rooms for the use of the guests. An observant housekeeper may notice items of exceptional value in a guest's room and suggest that they be handed over to the management, for safe keeping.

Further reading

Field, D., *Hotel and Catering Law*, 4th edition (Sweet and Maxwell 1982).

Useful addresses

Information available from the Chief Fire Officer of local fire service station.

23 Economic control

Financial control is important in both public and private sector enterprises. The public enterprise, such as a hospital, may not be required to make a profit, but it has to operate within a strict budget and must provide the best possible service for the money. A commercial enterprise, such as a hotel, exists in order to make profits for the owners, shareholders or financing company.

Profits

Gross profit is the difference between the purchase price of the goods plus wages and the revenue received from selling the goods. Net profit is obtained by deducting overheads from gross profit. Overheads will include many items for which the housekeeping department is responsible, for example, laundry and cleaning, furniture and fittings, linen. If the housekeeper can keep all these expenses as low as possible, net profit will be increased.

Budgets

A budget is an annual estimate of expenditure for the department.

Capital budget
This budget makes provision for all items of capital expenditure. It takes into account all items which are guaranteed to have a life span of a number of years. It is very important to keep records of purchase and repairs as a form of control. A decision may have to be taken at some stage, as to whether it is more beneficial to have a piece of equipment repaired or to simply buy a new one. The type of item which are provided for in the capital budget are as follows:

1 Large equipment and machinery, e.g. trolleys, shampoo machines.
2 Fixtures and fittings.
3 Furniture and fittings in bedrooms or public areas, e.g. beds and bedding, carpets, soft furnishings, pictures, lamps.
4 Linen and towels.
5 Uniforms.
6 Special projects, e.g. a new conference room.
7 Miscellaneous. It is quite normal to have a certain amount of money allocated under such a heading in order to make provision for emergencies, problems which could not have been foreseen, alterations required by law and so on.

Operating budget
An operating budget makes provision for all those items which are needed for day to day operation of the department. Domestic departments in hospitals are usually far more strict in adhering to operating budgets than other accommodation establishments. In many cases, the housekeeper in an hotel would not be expected to produce an operating budget. Examples of items which should be provided for in this budget are as follows

1 Cleaning agents.
2 Small items of cleaning equipment such as rubber gloves, door stops, buckets, dusters, cloths.
3 Staff and guest supplies, e.g. soap, tissues, toilet paper.
4 Contract services.

It is very easy to make false economies in this particular area. A cheaper brand of cleaning agents will not necessarily have the quality of the more expensive pack so it may be necessary to use much more of the cheaper brand, thus increasing expenditure in the long run.

Repair and maintenance budget

In many establishments, this budget is prepared by the chief engineer or the maintenance manager but there will be liaison with the housekeeper. It makes provision for all repairs and replacements in the building. The type of input that the housekeeper may be expected to contribute would include

1. Maintenance or service contracts on pieces of housekeeping machinery, e.g. vacuum cleaners.
2. Purchase of spare parts for equipment which is repaired in-house.
3. Floor and wall coverings which need to be repaired due to wear and tear or replaced due to damage.
4. Repairs and maintenance to fixtures, fittings and furniture.

Payroll budget

The housekeeping payroll budget may be as much as 75 per cent of operating costs, leaving only 25 per cent to provide for cleaning agents and equipment. In some cases, the housekeeping payroll is as high as 90 per cent of operating costs.

Preparation of the budget

A budget should not be prepared at the last minute. Ideally, the housekeeper should have a list placed in a convenient spot in the office and makes notes throughout the year of improvements he/she would like to make. Standard forms are usually issued to each department head for completion and a yearly deadline date is set. Discussions should have previously taken place between the general manager and other department heads in order that they are aware of future company objectives which may be reflected in the budgets.

Past records and previous budgets may be used as a basis for the new budget, taking into account an inflation percentage. The housekeeper must also consider any changes in company purchasing policy. He/she should also be aware of new technology and better products which have appeared. Market research may be carried out to find the best products at the best price. Often a large company will have their own means of doing such research, but for the small business it is a good idea to read trade magazines and publications such as *Which?*

When the budget forms have been completed and competitive prices obtained, the forms are usually forwarded to the financial comptroller in order that the costings may be evaluated against the forecasted profit of the establishment. Discussions then take place with the general manager and the head office. This is usually the time when economies are made and the housekeeper has to state his/her case regarding the necessity of specific budget items. It is common practice to overestimate budget requirements in order that when any cutbacks are made, the department head still ends up with suficient funds to meet his/her needs. This practice does of course put into question the validity of the whole budget exercise.

Once the budget has been agreed, the housekeeper may then proceed to make purchases. Some people prefer to do their buying immediately, so taking advantage of lower prices and ensuring that all necessary items are bought, in the hope that there may be a little money left over for extras or re-allocation of funds at the end of the year.

Other department heads tend to spend money gradually over the year so that expenditure is equally distributed throughout the year. In the case of the operating budget the latter practice is usually essential.

Under- or overspending on the budget may have serious consequences for the department head responsible. When a budget is underspent ideally the monies saved should be allocated to a contingency fund for future projects or emergencies, rather than being spent on unnecessary items.

When a budget is overspent, the situation is usually more serious. The housekeeper will have to submit a report accounting for the reasons why the budget is overspent. In some establishments, this matter is regarded as a very serious offence and will not be tolerated. Overspending may be carried forward to next year's budget, so that less money is available next year. On the other hand, the establishment may realize that insufficient money has been allocated and the housekeeper may have extra funds next year. Overspending may even be a recognized practice.

Purchasing procedures

Purchasing procedures will vary according to the size and type of establishment. Capital expenditure items are normally bought from trade suppliers, but items such as cleaning agents may be bought in various ways. It is not uncommon for very small units to purchase their cleaning agents, toilet rolls etc. from the local 'Cash and Carry'. The establishment usually has a van and shopping is usually done on a weekly basis. Items are purchased in sufficiently large quantities to take advantage of semi-bulk purchase, but small enough amounts to cope with carriage, storage, cash flow and usage problems.

Medium-sized units usually take advantage of local suppliers, who make deliveries either on a weekly or monthly basis. Reasonably large quantities of trade products may be bought in this way and the suppliers usually have quite a large range of products to meet the needs of local hoteliers and other establishments.

It must be remembered, however, that both of these methods of purchase are using middle men who also have to make a living. They usually add on a percentage to the basic cost of the product in order to cover their expenses and make their profit. Although trade products could perhaps be bought cheaper direct from the factory, the accommodation manager must consider the following points

1　Convenience of delivery and regular ordering from a local supplier who normally allows discounts if certain quantities are bought.

2　Some produces refuse to sell direct to users because of administration and customer relations problems. They prefer to sell direct to wholesalers who are better equipped to handle regular supplies, give advice and provide storage.

3　Insufficient need or inadequate storage for bulk purchase.

Many local suppliers have agreements with local authorities such as the health service and educational establishments. This means that an accommodation manager can take advantage of discounted prices but he/she has limited choice. In some instances it may be possible for him/her to prove the value of a superior product.

In a large establishment, items may be bought either by the individual establishment or through a centralized purchasing office. Large hotels usually have a purchasing manager who is responsible for buying everything from meat to toilet soap.

Storekeeping and stock control

Without good storekeeping and stock control, monetary control within the department will suffer. It is good management practice to delegate the responsibility of stock control to a certain degree, making supervisors responsible for his/her own supplies.

Where stores are ordered on a systematic basis, requisitioning is usually carried out once a week or once a month. Large accommodation units have general stores, separate from other stores, where housekeeping supplies are kept. With the use of computers, stock control and storekeeping has become far less of a chore but of course not every establishment has this facility. All items held in the general store are catalogued – either on a manual or computerized system. The supervisor, when checking declining stock levels completes the stock requisition form and hands it in to the housekeeper's office.

It is a good idea to indicate the price per article in order to emphasize the need for cost control. On receipt of the stock requisition forms from supervisors, the housekeeper then may prepare a general stores order, while at the same time controlling the amount of supplies requested. When stores are delivered to the department, they should be carefully counted and checked before being distributed to the service areas, or wherever individual stores are located.

Variance analysis

It is good practice to maintain a monthly consumption sheet to record and control the amount of supplies used by the department each month. This may then be compared with a computer print-out or statistics received from the finance department showing the amount of expenditure to date in relation to the budget.

By comparing a series of monthly consumption sheets it is relatively easy to analyse the reason for fluctuation in consumption. Once irregularities have been identified, it is a management responsibility to take a suitable course of action. There are many possible reasons for an increase in usage.

Hoarded stock in the supervisor's store cupboards will distort the amount of expenditure over the month although it is storage not usage. If hoarding takes place to a great extent, it could lead to cash flow problems or wastage, as some products have a short shelf life.

High occupancy levels are a legitimate reason for higher consumption. Pilferage on the other hand must be dealt with. Wastage may occur for several reasons. Staff sometimes have no idea of costs involved and have access to plenty of supplies. There may be no proper issue and control system or staff may not have been trained to use the correct amount of supplies. Bad buying might also lead to greater usage – a cheaper brand may not last as long.

There are, similarly, many reasons for a decrease in usage. Low occupancy levels, a change to a better quality product or improved work methods may be legitimate reasons for less usage. However, declining usage may indicate problems, such as work not being carried out adequately or frequently enough. It may also indicate a reduction in supplies to staff because of bad storekeeping, leading to the staff running out of cleaning materials etc.

Reduction of costs

The following check list summarizes some practical methods of reducing housekeeping costs

Areas where efficiency may be increased	Methods of saving
Purchasing	Bulk purchase
	Multi-purpose cleaning agents
	Market research
	Purchase of labour saving devices
	Negotiation of discounts or contract prices
	Establish a purchasing policy which provides for the needs of the unit
	Product analysis and performance testing
Stock control	Good storekeeping
	Good security systems
	Fire precautions and insurance policies
	Consumption analysis
Staff	Selective interviews
	Induction and training
	Efficient rotas and use of staff
	Work study and productivity controls
	Reduce manning levels
	Labour saving equipment
	Contract services
Extravagance	Save it campaign
	Use of computers
	Avoid wastage
	Staff training and communication
	Selling off old stock

Areas where efficiency may be increased	*Methods of saving*
	Cannibalization (using old pieces of equipment to repair others)
	Assess customer and staff needs
	Study financial reports and statistics
	Obtain regular price quotations and prepare comparison studies
	Staff/user suggestion schemes
	Recycling
	Awards and bonus schemes
Housekeeping work load	Use modern equipment
	Use up to date working methods and materials
	Easy to clean surfaces and fabrics
	Reduce or mechanize guest services and supplies
	Fewer giveaways

Utilization of space

Property is usually the most expensive capital asset of an establishment, so every inch must be used to its full potential. Space usage surveys should be carried out occasionally, to make sure that each room, cupboard or store is being used to the best advantage. The purpose of the study is to take a close look at facilities, in a way that is often forgotten during the day-to-day running of the operation. The following are a few examples of suggested changes that might result from a space usage survey

1 Lounge areas. These are often simply a resting place, but they can be turned into a selling space if afternoon tea, coffee and snacks are served in them.
2 Shop space can be rented out in foyers or lobbies.
3 Corridors may be better used if an art exhibition is put up. It not only brightens up the area, but it may attract custom.
4 Old stable blocks, or other wasted space may be converted to staff or guest accommodation, or storage space.
5 A cellar could be turned into an income unit such as a wine bar or discotheque.

When considering any measures of this sort, take into account the cost of conversion, the numbers of likely users or customers, the staffing implications and whether the rest of the operation can cope with any inflex of new custom.

Space-saving equipment

When selecting any equipment, bear in mind that space-saving alternatives, such as the following, might be available

1 Foldaway beds.
2 Vanitory units disguised by a folding door panel – these allow the room to be used for several purposes.
3 Revolving surface writing boards for conferences. If they can be disguised completely, the room can be used for other purposes such as banquets or dances.
4 Tables that pull down from the wall.
5 Portable dance floors which can be packed into small squares.
6 Mobile folding stages.
7 Foldaway tables for room service or banquets.

Index